E N S I N O

I|U

EDIÇÃO
Imprensa da Universidade de Coimbra
Email: imprensa@uc.pt
URL: http//www.uc.pt/imprensa_uc
Vendas online: http://livrariadaimprensa.uc.pt

COORDENAÇÃO EDITORIAL
Imprensa da Universidade de Coimbra

CONCEÇÃO GRÁFICA
Imprensa da Universidade de Coimbra

INFOGRAFIA
Mickael Silva

EXECUÇÃO GRÁFICA
KDP

ISBN
978-989-26-2463-1

ISBN DIGITAL
978-989-26-2464-8

DOI
https://doi.org/10.14195/978-989-26-2464-8

© JUNHO 2023, IMPRENSA DA UNIVERSIDADE DE COIMBRA

EUROPEAN

PUBLIC SECTOR ACCOUNTING

2ª EDIÇÃO

PETER C. LORSON
SUSANA JORGE
ELLEN HAUSTEIN
(EDS.)

I|U

CONTENTS

Abbreviations 13
List of figures 17
List of tables 19
Foreword 23
Introduction 25

Chapter 1. Approaches to public sector accounting
and reporting in Europe 33
    1. Introduction and background 34
    2. Scope of reporting units 37
    3. Sources of PSA information 40
    4. Accounting systems and techniques 47
    5. Geographic focus 50
    6. PSA standards in the EU 51
    7. Reporting units 53
    8. Conclusion 54

Chapter 2. Specificities of Public Sector Accounting:
Insights for governmental accounting from history and theory 57
    1. Introduction 58
    2. Origins of public sector accounting:
        examples and insights from history 59
    3. Specificities of public sector accounting:
        examples and insights from theory 71
    4. Concluding remarks 87

Chapter 3. Budgets and budgetary accounting 95

1. Introduction 95
2. Budgetary accounting in the family of PSA systems 96
   - Link between budgeting and accounting 97
3. The functions and principles of budgets 97
   - Accountability and transparency principles 99
   - Other budget principles 99
4. Traditional annual budgets and modern variants 101
   - Budget appropriations 102
   - Accrual budgeting 106
   - Performance-based budgeting 112
   - Other planning and reporting modes 114
5. Budget-linked budgetary accounting 116
   - Parallel accounting systems 116
6. Conclusion 118

Chapter 4. Theoretical approaches to financial accounting purposes and principles 123

1. Introduction 123
2. Accounting theories 124
   - Proprietary theory 125
   - Entity theory 125
   - Fund theory 126
   - Cameral accounting theory 127
   - Bookkeeping models 128
3. Accounting conventions and principles 129
   - Accounting entity 130
   - Money measurement 131
   - Going concern 131
   - Cost concept 132
   - Realisation concept 133

Accruals principle 134
4. Conceptual frameworks 138
　　Users of general purpose financial statements 138
　　Primary users in the public sector... 139
　　Valuation and measurement of financial statement
　　　　elements Historical costs and current costs........................ 140
　　The Governmental Accounting Standards Board (GASB)
　　　　divides valuation into four approaches 140
　　Initial and subsequent measurement 141
　　a) Initial amounts 141
　　b) Remeasured amounts 141
　　Balancing competing objectives of financial reporting.............. 142
　　Theoretical approaches to PSA frameworks 145
5. Conclusion 147

Chapter 5. Different Perspectives in Public Sector
Accounting Harmonisation: IFRS, IPSAS and GFS 151
　　1. Introduction 152
　　2. Harmonisation of the private sector accounting system 153
　　3. Harmonisation of the public sector accounting system 161
　　4. Harmonisation of Government Finance Statistics...................... 165
　　5. The link between accruals accounting/IPSAS and statistics 170
　　6. Conclusion 172

Chapter 6. IPSAS: History, spread and use.................................. 177
　　1. Introduction 178
　　2. Transnational regulation 180
　　2. Stages of the IPSASB evolution.. 181
　　3. Advancing our understanding of the spread of IPSAS 188
　　4. Challenges in IPSAS adoption 198
　　5. Conclusion 203

Chapter 7. The IPSASB's conceptual framework and
views on selected national frameworks 209

    1. Introduction 210

    2. The role of the CF *versus* the public sector accounting standards 214

    3. The IPSASB's CF 216

    4. Comparative analysis of different CFs 236

    5. Developments in the IPSASB's CF – work in progress 243

    6. Conclusion 246

Chapter 8. Reporting components and reliability issues 251

    1. Introduction 252

    2. The context of GPFR 255

    3. GPFR components; comparative analysis 266

        Statement of financial performance 273

        Statement of changes in Net Assets 277

        Cash Flow Statement 278

    4. GPFR reliability issues: the importance of auditing 289

    5. Conclusion 293

Chapter 9. Overview of IPSAS on public sector specific topics 297

    1. Introduction and background 298

    2. Selected Public Sector Specific IPSASs 300

    3. Accounting for property, plant and equipment 302

    4. Accounting for revenue from non-exchange transactions 316

    5. Accounting for non-exchange expenses 320

    6. Accounting for service concession arrangements: Grantor 326

    7. Conclusion 331

Chapter 10. IPSAS: case study 335

    1. Introduction 336

    2. Description of the case study 337

3. Selected transactions of property, plant and equipment 340
      Transaction 1: Purchase of assets 340
      Transaction 2: Self construction of a road 342
      Transaction 3: Subsequent measurement of the library building 344
      Transaction 4: Subsequent measurement of library's lot of land 346
      Transaction 5: Subsequent measurement of the road
         and its provisions for DRR costs 348
      Transactions 6-8: Impairment of non-cash generating assets 350
      Transaction 6: Depreciated replacement cost approach 351
      Transaction 7: Restoration cost approach 352
      Transaction 8: Service units approach 353
   4. Selected transactions of non-exchange transactions 355
      Transaction 9: Taxation of citizens 355
      Transaction 10: Donation of an asset with obligation 356
   5. Selected transaction of non-exchange expenses 358
      Transaction 11: Expenses for municipal education 358
      Transaction 12: Payments for making available sport infrastructure. 359
      Transaction 13: Cash transfer for social housing 360
      Transaction 14: Grant for a culture association 361
      Transaction 15: Disability pensions 362
   6. Selected transactions of service concession arrangements 363
      Transaction 16: Construction and fixed-payment
         operation of a tunnel by an operator 363
      Transaction 17: Construction and operation of a tunnel by an
         operator with the right to earn revenue from third-party users ... 366
   7. Conclusion 369

Chapter 11. Consolidated financial statements 375
   1. Introduction: The group as an accounting phenomenon 376
   2. The objectives of consolidated financial reporting 379
   3. The group as a fictional entity and the area of consolidation 382
   4. Consolidation methods and theories of consolidated accounts 392

5. Procedures for full consolidation 398
6. Organizational challenges 405
7. Conclusion 408

Chapter 12. Consolidation methods 415
1. Introduction 416
2. Definitions and background 417
3. Overview about relevant IPSAS 421
4. Process of consolidated financial reporting 423
5. Full consolidation (initial and subsequent consolidations) 433
6. Equity method (initial and subsequent consolidations) 455
7. Conclusion 460

Chapter 13. The accounting harmonization challenge in the European Union and the EPSAS 463
1. Introduction to the EU harmonization challenge and EPSAS ... 464
2. The process 466
3. Challenging issues 497
4. Conclusions 499

Chapter 14. Alternative reporting and non-financial accounting formats 505
1. Introduction 506
2. The role of alternative and non-financial reporting 507
3. The main formats of alternative and non-financial reporting 511
4. Evaluation of alternative and non-financial reporting formats 527
5. Conclusion 531

Conclusion 535

Additional material 539
1. Questions 539

Chapter 1	539
Chapter 2	540
Chapter 3	542
Chapter 4	543
Case study question	545
Assignments	548
Appendix to case study questions	551
T-accounts	553
Chapter 5	554
Chapter 6	555
Chapter 7	556
Chapter 8	558
Chapter 9	559
Chapter 10	561
Chapter 11	562
Chapter 12	564
Chapter 13	566
Chapter 14	568
Solutions	571
Glossary and keyword index	575
Authors' biographies	591

ABBREVIATIONS

ACCA	Association of Chartered Certified Accountants
ACE	Accountancy Europe
AE	Associated entity
APSAS	Armenian Public Sector Accounting Standards
AR	Accounting Rules
ASOBAT	A Statement of Basic Accounting Theory
BCE	Before the Current Era
BoJ	Bank of Japan
BPM	Balance of Payments and International Investment Position Manual
C / CF	Cash flow
CCGFS	Central government financial statement
CDSB	Climate Disclosure Standards Board
CE	Current Era
CE	Controlled entity
CF	Conceptual Framework
CF-LSU	Conceptual Framework-Limited Scope Update
CFR	Consolidated financial reporting
CFS	Consolidated financial statements
CGov	Central Government
CIPFA	Chartered Institute of Public Finance and Accountancy
CNOCP	Conseil de normalisation des comptes publics
COVID-19	Coronavirus Disease 2019
DRR	Dismantling, removing and restoring
EC	European Commission
ECB	European Central Bank
ECIIA	European Confederation of Institutes of Internal Auditing
ED	Exposure Draft
EDP	Excessive Deficit Procedure

EE	Emerging Economies
EFRAG	European Financial Reporting Advisory Group
EGPA	European Group for Public Administration
EPSAS	European Public Sector Accounting Standards
ESA	European System of Accounts
ESAP	European Single Information Access Point
ESG	Environmental, Social, and Governance
ESRS	European Sustainability Reporting Standards
EU	European Union
EY	Ernst &Young
FAO	Food and Agriculture Organisation
FASAB	Federal Accounting Standards Advisory Board
FASB	Financial Accounting Standards Board
FED	US Federal Reserve
FEE	Fédération des Experts Comptables Européens
FP	Financial performance
FreM	The Government Financial Reporting Manual
FS	Financial statements
FTI	First-time implementation
FVA	Fair value accounting
FVLCTS	Fair value less costs to sell
GAAP	Generally accepted accounting principles
GAAS	Governmental Accrual Accounting Standards
GASB	Governmental Accounting Standards Board
GDP	Gross domestic product
GFS	Government Finance Statistics
GFSM	Government Finance Statistics Manual
GGS	General government sector
GPFR	General purpose financial reporting
GPFRs	General purpose financial reports
GPFS	General purpose financial statement
GRI	Global Reporting Initiative
HGrG	Haushaltsgrundsätzegesetz (German Act on budgetary principles)
i	Interest rate
IAS	International Accounting Standards
IASB	International Accounting Standards Board
IASC	International Accounting Standards Committee

IFAC	International Federation of Accountants
IFRIC	IFRS Interpretations Committee
IFRS	International Financial Reporting Standards
IFRS-SDS	IFRS-Sustainability Disclosure Standards
IG	Implementation Guidance
IIRC	International Integrated Reporting Council
IMF	International Monetary Fund
IOSCO	International Organization of Securities Commission
IPSAS	International Public Sector Accounting Standards
IPSASB	International Public Sector Accounting Standards Board
IR	Integrated Reporting
ISAR	International Standards of Accounting and Reporting
ISSB	International Sustainability Standards Board
IT	Information Technology
k	kilo (i.e. 1.000)
KPI	Key Performance Indicator
LGoV	Local government
LIC	Low-income countries
MGDD	Manual on Government Deficit and Debt
MS	Member States
NATO	North Atlantic Treaty Organization
NCI	Non-controlling interests
NPFM	New public financial management
NPG	New public governance
NPM	New public management
NZ	New Zealand
OBB	Output- and outcome-based budgets
OECD	Organisation for Economic Cooperation and Development
ONS	Office for National Statistics
PAFA	Pan African Federation of Accountants
PAFR	Popular Annual Financial Reports
PBB	Performance-based budgets
PPBS	Planning – Programming – Budgeting System
PPE	Property, plant, and equipment
PPP	Public Private Partnership
PSA	Public sector accounting
PSC	Public Sector Committee

PULSAR	Public Sector Accounting and Reporting Programme
PwC	PricewaterhouseCoopers
R&LGov	Regional and local government
ROSC	Reports on the Observance of Standards and Codes
RPG	Recommended Practice Guideline
SAI	Supreme Audit Institutions
SASB	Sustainability Accounting Standards Board
SDG	Sustainable Development Goals
SEC	Securities and Exchange Commission
SFS	Separate financial statements
SGP	Stability and Growth Pact
SIC	Standing Interpretations Committee
SNA	System of National Accounts
SNC-AP	Sistema de Normalização Contabilística para as Administrações Públicas
SOE	State-Owned Enterprises
TF	Task Force
TFEU	Treaty on the Functioning of the European Union
UK	United Kingdom
UN	United Nations
UNAIDS	United Nations Programme on HIV/AIDS
UNCTAD	United Nations Conference on Trade and Development
UNO	United Nations Organisation
US	United States
USA	United States of America
VIU	Value in use
WFP	World Food Programme
WG	Working Group
WGA	Whole of government accounts
WGFR	Whole of government financial reporting
XBRL	Extensible Business Reporting Language

LIST OF FIGURES

Figure 1.1: Scope of reporting depending on information needs of users of financial statements and reports 45

Figure 2.1: Specificities of financial economy of government: sources and uses of resources 73

Figure 2.2: Central Government Debt Outstanding and Total Assets of Central Banks since 2007. Sources: OECD (2021), Figure 1.9 (left panel); Banque de France (2021), Chart1 (right panel), reprinted with permission 85

Figure 2.3: Sovereign Debt Amount and Share held by Domestic Central Banks over time Source: Data retrieved from International Monetary Fund - IMF, Sovereign Debt Investor Base for Advanced Economies, 29 April 2022, designed by Arslanalp & Tsuda (2014) 86

Figure 3.1: A full accrual-based budget with separate partial budget plans 110

Figure 3.2: Government planning and reporting system 115

Figure 5.1: Governance framework of the IFRS Foundation and related institutions (Source: IFRS Foundation, 2018a) 156

Figure 5.2: EU endorsement mechanism (Based on Oversberg (2007), p. 1599f.; Pellens et al. (2017), p. 83) 158

Figure 5.3: Main components of the public sector Source: GFSM 2014 166

Figure 7.1: Differences between accountability and decision usefulness Source: Laughlin (2008, p.249) 218

Figure 7.2: Qualitative characteristics – balance and constraints Source: IPSASB (2014, CF 3.32-3.42) 227

Figure 7.3: Measurement bases. Source: IPSASB (2014, CF 7) 235

Figure 7.4: The Measurement Hierarchy proposed by ED76 245

Figure 8.1: Transparency, accountability and financial information
Source: Lourenço et al. (2013). 253

Figure 8.2: Stakeholders (deemed users)
of public sector entities' financial reporting 256

Figure 8.3: The scope of financial reporting in the public sector 262

Figure 9.1: Hierarchy of IPSAS Pronouncements 300

Figure 9.2: Revaluation model:
Accounting treatment of revaluation surpluses / deficits 313

Figure 9.3: Flowchart of accounting
for non-exchange transactions (IPSAS 23.29) 318

Figure 11.1: Scope of consolidation – between hierarchy and market 384

Figure 11.2: Macroeconomic public sector reporting entity
(Source: Brusca and Montesinos, 2009) 388

Figure 11.3: Financial reporting entity
(Source: Brusca & Montesinos, 2009) 390

Figure 12.1: Indicators to distinguish between
amalgamations and acquisitions (IPSAS 40) 420

Figure 12.2: Process of full consolidation
(Source: Lorson, Poller and Haustein, 2019) 432

Figure 13.1: The process in the EPSAS project 468

Figure 13.2: Elements of the Draft EPSAS Conceptual Framework 484

Figure 13.3: Proposed EPSAS governance structure
in the Public Consultation 485

Figure 14.1: Example of expenditures included in a popular report ... 514

Figure 14.2: UN-SDGs 518

Figure 14.3: European Commissions SDGs priorities 520

Figure 14.4: German SDG indicator set for
Federal Government and Länder (excerpt) 521

Figure 14.5: Integrated thinking, integrated reporting and SDGs.
Source: Adams (2017), p.14 527

Figure 14.6: Proposed information transfer to addressees/users
(e.g. citizens) 529

Table 14.2: Comparison of selected alternative
and non-financial reporting formats 530

LIST OF TABLES

Table 1.1: Principles of double entry bookkeeping 48

Table 1.2: Roadmap of topics presented in this book 54

Table 2.1: The cameral account structure 70

Table 2.2: Comparative analysis of notions of commercial revenues to the business entity, and operating inflows to the governmental entity 74

Table 2.3: Variety of business accounting models (adapted from Biondi 2012, Table 1, p. 605) 81

Table 3.1: Wholly transferable appropriations - example 103

Table 3.2: Gross versus net budgeting – an example 104

Table 3.3: A cash-based budget – an example 105

Table 3.4: Commitment-based budget – an example 105

Table 3.5: An accrual-based budget – an example of budgeted depreciation costs 111

Table 3.6: Example of a performance budget (Finnish municipality of Lempäälä: Annual budget 2022, Old peoples' care service section of the annual budget). 113

Table 3.7: Linkages between budget types, budget appropriations and accounting 119

Table 4.1: Summary of Section 3 137

Table 4.2: Examples of valuation alternatives: 1 million € investment for a day care facility and 1 million € investment for production equipment, useful life for both is (for reasons of simplicity) 10 years. 143

Table 4.3: Comparison of the static and dynamic views 145

Table 4.4: Summary 147

Table 5.1: GFS versus IPSAS Source: Adapted from Caruana et al. (2019) 168

Table 6.1: Overview on the individual IPSAS 188

Table 6.2: Selected Studies that examine the spread of IPSAS [2010-2021] 191

Table 7.1: Users of GPFRs. Source: IPSASB (2014, CF 2) 220

Table 7.2: Comparative-international analysis of different CFs 240

Table 8.1: Statement of financial position according to IPSAS 1 270

Table 8.2: Statement of financial performance (by nature) according to IPSAS 1 274

Table 8.3: Statement of financial performance (by function) 275
according to IPSAS 1 275

Table 8.4: Cash Flow Statement according to IPSAS 2 (direct method) 283

Table 8.5: GPFR main components (annual accounts) – comparative-international analysis 286

Table 9.1: Cost versus Revaluation Model 309

Table 9.2: Boundaries of different types of non-exchange expenses (IPSASB's ED 72) 321

Table 9.3: Examples for service concession arrangements (IPSAS 32 IE) 327

Table 10.1: Inventory list to compile the opening balance sheet 338

Table 10.2: Opening balance sheet 20X1 339

Table 10.3: Details for Transaction 1 340

Table 10.4: Transaction 1: Acquisition cost of lot of land 341

Table 10.5: Transaction 1: Acquisition cost of library building 342

Table 10.6: Details for Transaction 2 343

Table 10.7: Transaction 2: Acquisition cost of road 343

Table 10.8: Transaction 3: Subsequent measurement for Transaction 1 346

Table 10.9: Details for Transaction 4: Fair values of the lot of land 347

Table 10.10: Transaction 4: Revaluation of lot of land 348

Table 10.11: Transaction 5: Subsequent measurement of the provision 349

Table 10.12: Details for Transactions 6-8 351

Table 10.13: Transaction 6: Depreciated replacement cost approach... 352
Table 10.14: Transaction 7: Restoration cost approach 353
Table 10.15: Transaction 8: Service units approach 354
Table 10.17: Closing balance sheet 20X1 (simplified)......................... 370
Table 10.18: Statement of Financial Performance 20X1 371
Table 10.19: Statement of Cash Flows 20X1... 372
Table 11.1. Impact of different consolidation methods....................... 395
Table 11.2: Remeasurement alternatives
for the purposes of consolidation 400
Table 11.3: Status quo of consolidated accounting in selected
European countries (Adapted from: Brusca et al. (2015))................... 409
Table 12.1: Overview of IPSASs relating to consolidation 422
Table 12.2: Overview of IPSAS prescriptions concerning
consolidation area and methods 427
Table 12.3: Balance sheets II for Eucity and CE
at initial consolidation date 437
Table 12.4: Example 1: Determination of the aggregated
balance sheet as at 1st Jan 20X1.. 439
Table 12.5: Example 1: Consolidation table as at 1st Jan 20X1 440
Table 12.6: Balance sheets II for Eucity and CE
at subsequent consolidation date... 441
Table 12.7: Example 2: Determination of the aggregated
balance sheet as at 31st Dec 20X1 443
Table 12.8: Example 2: Consolidation table as at 31st Dec 20X1 444
Table 12.9: Example 3: Consolidation table as at 1st Jan 20X1 447
Table 12.10: Example 4: Consolidation table as at 31st Dec 20X1 449
Table 12.11: Adjustment of the investment's book value
according to the equity method.. 458
Table 13.1: EPSAS Issue papers 489
Table 13.2: Table of Contents of an Issue Paper.................................. 490
Table 13.3: EPSAS Screening reports published 492
Table 13.4: EPSAS Screening reports
under preparation (October 2022).. 493

Table 13.5: Procedure followed in the
Screening report IPSAS 2 – Cash flow statements 494

Table 13.6: Conclusions in the Screening report IPSAS 2 –
Cash flow statements 495

Table 14.1: Summary of expected impact of alternative
and non-financial reporting (Source: Own elaboration) 528

Table 14.2: Comparison of selected alternative
and non-financial reporting formats 530

FOREWORD

This second edition of the book on European Public Sector Accounting was written around 4 years after the first edition, against the backdrop of a span of developments in European politics, the Covid-19 pandemic, and the ongoing war in Ukraine. The crises also led to the fact that the 2019-2024 European Commission did not take any decision regarding a potential implementation of European Public Sector Accounting Standards (EPSAS), but it was further postponed to the next election period. In addition, the landscape of public sector accounting and reporting increasingly widened towards non-financial and alternative reporting formats, particularly as a response to demands of the capital markets and due to the global climate change and the need to better address a concept of sustainability that goes beyond financial sustainability. Meanwhile, the International Public Sector Accounting Standards Board (IPSASB) released two new standards, namely IPSAS 43 on *Leases* and IPSAS 44 on *Non-current Assets Held for Sale and Discontinued Operations*, placed several amendments to existing standards, and started projects with regards to for example measurement, revenue, transfer expenses, heritage, infrastructure assets and natural resources. A remarkable consultation of the IPSASB referred to the questions whether there is demand from stakeholders for sustainability reporting guidance and the extent to which the IPSASB should be involved in supporting the process, the priority areas for guidance, and how this might be approached.[1]

---

[1] https://www.ipsasb.org/focus-areas/sustainability-reporting

We tried to capture these developments by amendments and extensions of this second edition of the book. To only name the most prominent changes, a new Chapter 14 has been added, which addresses alternative and non-financial reporting formats. Moreover, the previous Chapters 2 and 3 on public sector accounting history and differences between the public and the private sector have been merged by also drawing more on theory for explaining public sector accounting representations. Also, changes in IPSAS were incorporated by updating Chapter 7 on the IPSASB's conceptual framework and the IPSAS specific Chapters 9 and 10 by now applying IPSAS 42 on *Social Benefits*. Finally, to reflect the developments in the European Union, Chapter 13 on EPSAS has been updated, too.

All these changes also go along with changes in several authors of the chapters, since the former DiEPSAm project that included the first edition was completed. Without receiving any external funding for this second edition, we are very grateful and proud to have met so much support by new authors for 11 out of 14 chapters, so that we are again able to publish this book in open access at no cost. Thus, the textbook second edition does not fit to the videos and other material of the DiEPSAm online course at the platform Offene Universität Rostock as those remain unchanged and linked to the first edition of the book.

The book editors

INTRODUCTION

Peter C. Lorson, Ellen Haustein
both University of Rostock, Germany
peter.lorson@uni-rostock.de
https://orcid.org/0000-0002-2699-5451
ellen.haustein@uni-rostock.de
https://orcid.org/0000-0002-1218-1043

Susana Jorge
University of Coimbra, Portugal
susjor@uc.pt
https://orcid.org/0000-0003-4850-2387

Public sector accounting (PSA) and reporting is a theme of high relevance for both academia and practitioners in the European Union (EU). The reasons do not only lie in the considerable national reforms of PSA during the last decades,[2] but can be traced back to a project run by the European Commission (EC) aiming to harmonize the heterogeneous accounting systems of its member states by the adoption of European Public Sector Accounting Standards (EPSAS), initiated in 2013 and still to be developed.

The EPSAS project arose primarily as a response to the financial and economic crises beginning in 2008 and the reliability issues that became apparent, especially with the public debt and deficit data delivered to the EC by some EU member states, as data from PSA is the input for governmental financial statistics in the National Accounts. The EU plans

---

[2] See, for example, Manning and Lau (2016) pp. 39 ff.

to develop EPSAS with International Public Sector Accounting Standards (IPSAS) as a reference, and until 2020 provided financial support to public sector entities as well as jurisdictions that opted for a voluntary use of IPSAS. Initially, the period of 2020-2025 was defined as a transition to EPSAS by the EC, leading to a homogeneous EU-landscape of PSA and reporting. However, this would have implied that the EPSAS development and implementation project would have been completed and a legal basis for the adoption in the EU member states would have been found, which did not happen so far. Since the first edition of this book, a screening of all IPSAS standards has been started to assess their fit to the EPSAS Conceptual Framework draft (for 24 IPSAS this is completed already and for 12 IPSAS the process is ongoing (as of April 2023)). Most of the 24 already screened double-entry IPSAS did not pose any major conceptual problems and were assessed as compliant with the EPSAS Conceptual Framework draft. Still, some IPSAS may require additional guidance on specific accounting issues or to eliminate choices in order to ensure consistent application in the EU context (e.g., IPSAS 5, 17, 19, 23 and 41). Also, the screening reports showed that discretionary decisions and estimates are somewhat unavoidable and occasionally may have an impact on comparability.[3] An impact assessment is ongoing but further decisions are pending.[4] Against the backdrop of the Covid-19 pandemic and the war going on in Ukraine, the decision about EPSAS was postponed to the next EC which is to be elected in 2024 for the 2025-2029 election period.

As PSA in Europe is currently still very heterogeneous,[5] professionals and academics in Europe face tremendous challenges. In particular, there will be a large need for university graduates that are knowledge-

---

[3] See EC (2020) and the related screening reports.
[4] See EC (2019), p.6 and also the Conclusion of this book.
[5] See Brusca et al. (2015) and, Vašiček and Roje (2019) and Polzer et al. (2022) for such an overview of PSA in single European countries.

able in PSA and that are aware of the differing PSA standards and PSA systems across Europe. The first edition of this book contributed to this kind of capacity building, and was one intellectual output of an EU funded Erasmus+ project ("Developing and implementing European Public Sector Accounting modules" (DiEPSAm)), which aimed to develop teaching materials concentrated on existing methods and systems of PSA in Europe. The objectives of the DiEPSAm project were to support the development of academic modules for Bachelor's or Master's degree programmes by offering online lectures, slides, additional materials and this complementing textbook.

The DiEPSAm project was a cooperation between the Johannes Kepler University Linz (Austria), the Tampere University (Finland), the University of Rostock (Germany), the University of Coimbra (Portugal) and the University of Leicester (United Kingdom; UK). These partner countries (Austria, Finland, Germany, Portugal, and the UK) represent diverse national PSA traditions, thereby enriching the textbook by diverse views (at times contradicting) and leading to the discussion of alternative approaches. They are also the focus of some comparative studies across the book; this second edition is now further enriched by additional country perspectives, for example Italy.

Accordingly, it must be underlined that this book is not about EPSAS, but tackles PSA in Europe. Thus, the aim is to provide different views not taking position of one or the other approach to PSA. Still, of course, each of the chapters represents not necessarily the view of all authors of the book. On the contrary, the DiEPSAm project and the textbook concept were driven by the idea to present an overarching European perspective and to integrate different views,[6] which continued in this second edition.

---

[6] The lecture materials which correspond to the first edition of the book are accessible at no cost (open access) here: https://www.uni-rostock.de/weiterbildung/offene-uni-rostock/onlinekurse/european-public-sector-accounting/

In each chapter, additional readings are offered and topics for discussion are presented, in order to critically reflect on the themes presented. These topics might also serve for essays or seminal papers. At the end of the book, assessment questions (both multiple-choice and open questions) are listed, per chapter, so that the reader can assess the knowledge gained. The solutions for the multiple-choice questions are also provided, whereas the open questions can be derived from the text or additional readings. The main part of the book is structured as follows.

Chapter 1, authored by *Ellen Haustein* and *Peter Lorson*, provides an **introduction to PSA** and offers a map through the book by explaining important terms with respect to European PSA and by highlighting which concepts this book will focus on. In **Chapter 2**, *Yuri Biondi* addresses the long and varied history of PSA, sketches the **key developments, and explains the specificities of public sector accounting**. He draws on the financial economy of the government to show why there are differences in the accounting representation between public sector entities and those in the private sector.

Despite the focus of the EPSAS project on financial reporting, budgeting and budgetary accounting and reporting take a centre stage in PSA. **Chapter 3**, authored by *Lasse Oulasvirta*, is thus devoted to explaining approaches to **budgeting**, also addressing the roles and functions of the budget as well as budget planning and budget-linked accounting. A more theoretical lens on PSA is applied also by *Lasse Oulasvirta* in **Chapter 4** while describing **theoretical accounting foundations and principles for PSA,** which may influence and interact with financial accounting standards and practices.

Accounting harmonization in PSA bears several challenges because there may be frictions between the accounting standards of the private sector and of the public sector, on the one hand, and the statistical data requirements on the other hand. This topic is addressed by *Giovanna Dabbicco* in **Chapter 5**. She takes a closer look at **PSA harmonisation between IFRS, Government Finance Statistics (GFS) and IPSAS**.

Due to their high relevance and international dissemination, IPSAS plays an important role in this book, which is also reflected in the Chapters 6 to 12. *Caroline Aggestam Pontoppidan* starts these chapters by addressing **IPSAS** in **Chapter 6**, introducing their **history, spread and use**. *Susana Jorge* and *Josette Caruana* continue in **Chapter 7** to explain conceptual frameworks (CFs) in PSA, particularly addressing the IPSASB's CF. The chapter also offers brief views on selected national CFs from a group of European countries. **Chapter 8**, also authored by *Susana Jorge* and *Josette Caruana*, is devoted to **reporting components**, namely the financial statements, primarily building on IPSAS 1 and 2, also briefly addressing **reliability issues**, tackling transparency and auditing. In order to provide an **overview of IPSAS on public sector specific topics**, *Ellen Haustein, Peter Lorson, Johan Christiaens* and *Christophe Vanhee* draw on selected IPSASs in their **Chapter 9** and present an **IPSAS case study** in **Chapter 10**. The general accounting treatment of property, plant and equipment (IPSAS 17, 21 and 26), revenue from non-exchange transactions (IPSAS 23) and service concessions from the perspective of the grantor (IPSAS 32) are explained in Chapter 9. It was now expanded by accouting for social benefits according to IPSAS 42. The same IPSASs are then applied in Chapter 10 to present an IPSAS case study by developing accounting records and illustrating the consequences on the financial statements.

Up to Chapter 10, primarily individual financial statements are addressed, which are financial statements for a single public sector entity only. However, when public sector entities run different (public sector) entities to provide public services, individual financial statements fail to provide a true and fair view of the whole economic entity because of the financial interactions between these separate entities. Thus, some public sector entities are required to prepare

consolidated financial statements that combine all entities under control of a public entity. This topic is addressed by *Ellen Haustein, Peter Lorson* and *Eugenio Anessi Pessina* in **Chapter 11**, where they explain the basic ideas and theories of consolidation and how to aggregate the transactions of the parent (i.e. controlling) entity and its controlled entities by using consolidation techniques. The topic is continued by the same three authors in **Chapter 12**, addressing **consolidation methods and reporting** with a stronger focus on applying IPSAS.

In **Chapter 13**, *Francesca Manes Rossi, Isabel Brusca* and *Sandra Cohen* look at the EPSAS project again and describe **PSA future challenges** by giving an **EPSAS outlook**.

In **Chapter 14**, a new topic was added to this second edition of the textbook, since **alternative reporting and non-financial accounting formats** are increasingly important in public sector accounting and reporting. *Francesca Manes Rossi, Isabel Brusca Sandra Cohen* and *Peter Lorson* discuss widespread formats, including popular reporting, sustainability reporting, the most recent Sustainable Development Goals (SDGs) reporting and integrated reporting, which are finally compared in a synopsis.

This second edition of the book received no more financial support by an external funding body. We would therefore like to express our huge gratitude to all remaining and new authors that contributed with their time and knowledge to this open access publication without any additional funding. A big **THANK YOU** goes to *Caroline Aggestam Pontoppidan, Eugenio Anessi Pessina, Yuri Biondi, Isabel Brusca, Josette Caruana, Sandra Cohen, Johan Christiaens, Giovanna Dabbicco, Francesca Manes Rossi, Lasse Oulasvirta,* and *Christophe Vanhee*. Moreover, renowned experts offered their support in reviewing selected chapters of this textbook for which they also deserve highest recognition: *Marco Bisogno* (University of Salerno, Italy), *Eugenio Caperchione* (University of Modena and Reggio Emilia, Italy), *Jens*

Heiling (EY Stuttgart, Germany), *Christoph Reichard* (University of Potsdam, Germany) and *Mariafrancesca Sicilia* (University of Bergamo, Italy). Likewise, we would like to thank *Coimbra University Press* for helping us again to publish the second edition of this book. Last but not least, the project team was supported by *Silke Große, Alicia Schlünß, Moritz Muhtz* and *Theodora van der Beek* at University of Rostock. Thank you to all!

Any mistakes and misunderstandings in the book, as expected, clearly remain within the chapter author(s) responsibility. Usual disclaimer applies.

Bibliographic references

BOVAIRD, Tony and LOEFFLER, Elke (Eds.) (2016) – Public Management and Governance, London and New York: Routledge, ISBN: 978415501859, 3rd ed.

BRUSCA, Isabel; CAPERCHIONE, Eugenio; COHEN, Sandra and MANES-ROSSI, Francesca (Eds.) (2015) – Public Sector Accounting and Auditing in Europe – the Challenge of Harmonization; Basingstoke: Palgrave Macmillan, ISBN: 9781137461339.

EC (2019) – Reporting on the progress as regards the European Public Sector Accounting Standards (EPSAS), Brussels, 5.6.2019, SWD(2019) 204 final.

EC (2020) – Introduction and Overview to EPSAS Screening Reports, Consultation prior to the EPSAS Working Group meeting to be held in autumn 2020, EPSAS WG 19/09rev Luxembourg, 19 June 2020.

POLZER, Tobias, GROSSI, Giuseppe and REICHARD Christoph (2022) – Implementation of the international public sector accounting standards in Europe. Variations on a global theme, Accounting Forum, 46:1, 57-82.

VAŠIČEK, Vesna and ROJE, Gorana (Eds.) (2019) – Public Sector Accounting, Auditing and Control in South Eastern Europe; Basingstoke: Palgrave Macmillan, ISBN: 9783030033538.

Chapter 1
Approaches to Public Sector Accounting and Reporting in Europe

Ellen Haustein, Peter C. Lorson
both University of Rostock, Germany
ellen.haustein@uni-rostock.de
https://orcid.org/0000-0002-1218-1043
peter.lorson@uni-rostock.de
https://orcid.org/0000-0002-2699-5451

Summary

This chapter aims to provide both a context and a foundation for the book. Thereby it introduces important terms used throughout the book and differentiation of contents. By deriving a roadmap, it serves as a guidance through the different chapters and points out connections between chapters and the overall structure of the textbook.

After finishing this chapter, readers will know about the relevance of public sector accounting as a field of study, the current public sector accounting developments in the EU, the reasons for differences in public sector accounting between countries and the key terms used in public sector accounting.

Keywords

Public sector reporting, accounting concepts, harmonization, EPSAS

https://doi.org/10.14195/978-989-26-2464-8_1

1. Introduction and background

Public sector accounting (PSA) and reporting internationally have undergone severe reforms during the last decades.[1] Within these reforms there has been the change from cash to accrual accounting.[2] However, the extent of reforms and thereby also the implementation of accounting systems and norms, differs considerably between governments on an international scale. This is a problem particularly striking for the European Union (EU), as the European Commission (EC) needs to rely on statistical data about e.g. financial debt of its member states (MS). For these statistics, the reference is the European System of National and Regional Accounts (ESA), which is accrual-based and uses double entry bookkeeping data. However, the accounting systems in the MS range from pure cash-based systems, combinations of cash- and accrual-based accounting, modified accrual accounting to accrual accounting.[3] In addition, the accounting systems even differ between the different levels of government within one country. Thus, there is a risk of inconsistent data being reported to the EC.

There are various reasons for the differences in PSA and reporting norms across countries.[4] Firstly, countries differ in their legal and juridical system. This refers for example to the extent of power that central governments have. In some countries, like Germany, the central government is not legally entitled to enforce accounting reforms at the municipal level, but only the state governments, in which the municipalities are located. As such, the central government alone would not be able to enforce harmonized accounting

---
[1] See e.g. Manning and Lau (2016), pp. 39 ff., in: Bovaird and Loeffler (2016).

[2] For example, in Europe, see Brusca et al. (2015), p. P. Xiii.

[3] See EY (2012) and Brusca et al. (2015) for an overview.

[4] See for the following eight reasons: Jorge et al. (2011) with reference to Brusca Alijarde and Condor (2002), Brusca Alijarde and Benito López (2002).

norms even in its own country. Secondly, the organization of the public sector differs. Some countries have a centralised state (such as France) and others run a federal system (such as Germany). Depending on the country, federal states can have an own right to determine their accounting system. Differences in the accounting traditions may thirdly lead to differences in specific objectives of governmental financial reporting. Whereas in the Continental European countries accountability is the utmost objective, in Anglo-Saxon countries typically decision usefulness takes a centre stage. Differences in these objectives determine different accounting norms. Depending on divergent views about the principal users of financial reporting as a fourth point, the reporting contents can be different. One example is the difference between standards of the Governmental Accounting Standards Board (GASB, i.e. the accounting norms for US local government) and the International Public Sector Accounting Standards (IPSAS) Board. Whereas the citizenry is seen as the main user in the GASB Framework (there is not only focus on financial terms, but also on contents about economy, efficiency and effectiveness), IPSAS focus on service recipients and resource providers, hence suggesting a more general, financial perspective.

Fifth, the type and extent of financial resources suppliers may influence the type of information and reporting needed in order to assess financial wellbeing and the ability to repay debt. Important external financiers such as the World Bank or the International Monetary Fund (IMF) do indeed influence the accounting norms that their governmental borrowers use. As sixth and seventh reasons, national institutions can play a role in differences. Stimuli towards or resistance against reforms of governmental accounting may come from regulatory bodies such as financial regulation authorities or competition authorities or professionals such as accounting profession bodies. A final main reason are differences in the political and administrative environment. Whereas European Continental countries have a strong culture of administration and the Rechtsstaat, a so called rule of law, Anglo Saxon countries rely on common law. This leads to differences in the number of individual circumstances that have to be addressed by accounting norms and standards.

In order to reduce differences in PSA and reporting, the EC strives for harmonization of the heterogeneous accounting systems of its MS by the adoption of European Public Sector Accounting Standards (EPSAS). The EPSAS project arose as a response to the financial and economic crises beginning in 2008 and the reliability problems that became apparent with the public debt data (and other fiscal data to monitor fiscal discipline) delivered to the EC by some EU MS. Thus, in 2011, the EC passed a set of measures to reform the Stability and Growth Pact and to provide greater macroeconomic surveillance. Inter alia, Directive 2011/85/ EU was released claiming for more homogeneity of the budgeting rules among the MS and requiring the EC to assess whether the IPSAS would be suitable for adoption in all MS. After this review the EC came to the conclusion that "IPSAS standards represent an indisputable reference for potential EU harmonised public sector accounts"[5], but need some adjustments so that these "would be suitable as a reference framework for the future development of a set of European Public Sector Accounting Standards".[6]

As a consequence, the EC instructed its statistical office Eurostat to undertake such an assessment of IPSAS. Thus, the Eurostat EPSAS Task Force has been founded in 2012 and is still in place. Initially, the period of 2020-2025 was indicated by the EU as a transition to EPSAS, leading to a homogeneous EU-landscape of PSA and reporting. However, this would have implied that the EPSAS implementation project is completed and a legal basis for the adoption in the EU

---

[5] EC (2013), p. 7.

[6] EC (2013), p. 8.

MS has been found, which is (as of April 2023) not yet the case. To date, the results of an ongoing impact assessment[7] are awaited to discuss different scenarios of the bindingness of the EPSAS pronouncements, especially the Conceptual Framework and standards.

As of April 2023, due to the recent crises such as the COVID-19 pandemic and the war in the Ukraine, the decision about the implementation of EPSAS is postponed to the next EC after the European elections in 2024. More details on the EPSAS background and development are provided in the Chapters 5 discussing the challenge for harmonization and 13 providing an EPSAS status quo and outlook.

The remainder of this chapter will derive a map through the book by explaining important terms with respect to European PSA and by highlighting on which concepts this book will focus on. Section 2 starts with identifying the reporting units, whereas Section 3 discusses sources of PSA. The different types of accounting are addressed in Section 4. On which geographic focus this book will draw, is explained in Section 5 with more specific explanations of PSA standards in the EU in Section 6. Finally, different reporting units are explained (Section 7) and a conclusion with a roadmap is provided (Section 8).

2. Scope of reporting units

In order to narrow down the content of this book, the public sector needs to be differentiated from the private sector. This chapter draws on the differentiation of ESA, i.e. the statistical system of the EU. According to its internationally recognized definition, the public sector consists of all institutional units resident in one economy that are controlled by the government. The private sector

---

[7] See EC (2019), p. 6.

consists of all other resident units (ESA 1.35). Therefore, the concept of control is the first criterion to distinguish the public sector. Control is defined as the ability to determine the general policy or programme of an institutional unit (ESA 1.36).[8]

Second, a differentiation between market and non-market activities is considered to distinguish between public sector entities belonging to the general government sector and the corporations sector. A market activity has the following conditions, which do not have to be met perfectly (ESA 1.37):

(1) Sellers act to maximise their profits in the long term, by selling goods and services freely on the market;
(2) Buyers act to maximise their utility given their limited resources;
(3) Effective markets exist, where sellers and buyers have access to, and information on, the market.

Thus, the public sector consists of the general government and public corporations, both being controlled by the government. Public sector corporations are distinguished between non-financial and financial corporations with e.g. the central bank belonging to the latter type. However, only general government units are in the focus of this chapter. Government units are legal entities established by a political process, which have legislative, judicial or executive authority over other institutional units within a given area. Their principal function is to provide goods and services to the community and to households on a non-market basis and to redistribute income and wealth (ESA 20.06). The general government is classified further, into four levels of entities.

---

[8] Further details in relation to the definition of control can be found in the ESA guidelines and in this book in Chapter 11, p. 383 ff.

The **central government** subsector includes all administrative departments of the state and other central agencies whose competence normally extends over the whole economic territory, except for the administration of social security funds (ESA 2.114). On a lower level, the **state government** subsector consists of those types of public administration which are separate institutional units exercising some of the functions of government (e.g. education, road infrastructure), except for the administration of social security funds, at a level below that of central government and above that of the governmental institutional units existing at local level (ESA 2.115). As a third subsector, the **local government** includes those types of public administration whose competence extends to only a local part of the economic territory, apart from local agencies of social security funds (ESA 2.116). Finally, the **social security funds** subsector includes central, state and local institutional units whose principal activity is to provide social benefits and in which, by law or by regulation, certain groups of the population are obliged to participate in the scheme or to pay contributions; and for which general government is responsible for the management of the institution in respect of the settlement or approval of the contributions and benefits independently from its role as supervisory body or employer (ESA 2.116).

This book focuses on public entities of central, regional or state and local government. In the following and throughout the book, these are referred to as **public sector entities**.[9] These have specific characteristics that distinguishes them from private sector entities. On the one hand, public sector entities have sovereignty that is depending on the structure of government, are ultimately controlled by politicians who hold power and responsibility in the

---

[9] Although, at times, strictly speaking, one would need to refer to government entities.

legislative and executive systems. On the other hand, public sector entities seek to produce public goods and services, which can also lie in the redistribution of income or the regulation of industries. In order to raise financial resources, public sector entities hold the power to tax. As public goods and services are often delivered for free, governments entities do not strive for profits but for recovery of their costs.[10] These differences, which are also explained in more details in Chapter 2, also lead to adjustments compared to private sector reporting as e.g. the aim of the units differ and there are potentially different stakeholders.[11] Also different sources of PSA information have been developed, which are explained in the next section.

3. Sources of PSA information

PSA information can be derived from different sources. A selected list of accounting sources is shortly introduced in the following:

Budgeting, (2) Budgetary accounting and reporting, (3) Financial reporting, (4) Management accounting, (5) Sustainability and Integrated reporting and (6) Government financial statistics.

Budgeting: Government sector entities are organizations ultimately controlled by politicians. A major responsibility of politicians refers to their authority to establish a budget. The budget is an estimation of expenditures/expenses to provide public goods and services, to suppress public needs, as well as the estimated revenue to cover those expenditures/ expenses. Usually, the budget is established for one to two years. However, besides being merely a plan, the budget also serves as an authorization

---

[10] Jones and Pendlebury (2010), pp. 2 f.

[11] See e.g. Pallot (1991).

by the deliberative body (such as elected politicians) to the executive body, for any expenditure which is later on undertaken by the public entity's administration. Therefore, the budget is formalized by law. It is therefore also made publically accessible, so that citizens in general can inform themselves about how resources are spent and which public services are planned to be delivered. However, mainly, the budget is used by managers of the administration, the politicians and legislative overseers. Especially due to its legal bindingness, the budget is central in PSA and reporting.

Therefore, budgeting and budgetary accounting will be discussed in more detail in Chapter 3 of this book.

Budgetary accounting and reporting: After the budget has been approved, in the respective budgetary year the actual payments and receipts (and/or expenditures and revenues) are documented, i.e. accounted for, and compared with the previously agreed (bi-/) annual budget. The budgetary reports provide information about the extent to which the budget has been realized, therefore the information is made publicly available. The statements such as budget out-turn reports (comparing budgets planned and spent), financial balance sheets and explanations of significant variances, are used by public managers, politicians, legislative overseers and also citizens. Budgetary reports are produced at least annually, however mostly also supplemented by quarterly or monthly reports.

Financial accounting and reporting: Besides a comparison of planned versus actual budgetary figures at the reporting date, public sector entities can also prepare an overview of the resources, i.e. assets and sources of finance (liabilities & net assets), as well as an overview of the resource consumption and creation, i.e. expenses & revenues; cash in- & outflows, during the reporting period. The documents thereby produced on an annual basis are called financial statements which are composed by, e.g., a balance sheet (disclosing assets and liabilities), income statement (comparing revenues and expenses) and cash flow statement (showing cash inflows and outflows from three activities (operations, investing, financing – see also Chapter 8). As such, compared to the budget and budgetary reports, financial reporting information can deliver further relevant accounting information such as reliable accounting measures in the form of net costs for services provided, assets and liabilities.[12] Conceptually, by deducting assets from liabilities the net assets are derived, which differ to some extent from the concept of equity that is known in the private sector. Still, the fundamentals of accounting are the same in both sectors,[13] if based on accrual accounting and double entry bookkeeping. Nonetheless, as Lüder (2011) asserts, financial accounting, reporting and auditing "is not mainstream and only a few scholars are working in this field" in most countries.[14] Due to this reason, and particularly because the main reforms of PSA and reporting internationally, in the last years, has centred on financial accounting and reporting,[15] and also the EPSAS project only covers this source of accounting information, the focus of most chapters in this book is on financial accounting and reporting.

Management accounting: In the public sector management accounting and control is traditionally structured around budgeting,[16] however its functions go beyond pure budgeting because the information delivered is more detailed and user-oriented. Management accounting refers to the calculation of the resource consumption

---

[12] Jones and Pendlebury (2010), p. 115.

[13] Jones and Pendlebury (2010), p. 30.

[14] Lüder (2011), p. 5, in: Jones (2011).

[15] In particular, also because budgeting has a strong legal basis in each country and thus international accounting standard setting bodies focused on financial accounting and reporting (Jones and Pendlebury, 2010, p. 85).

[16] Jones and Pendlebury (2010), p. 85.

(costs) of organizational units or product/service units for control or pricing purposes. Statements produced on a monthly or quarterly basis are, e.g., costing systems or cost allocation sheets which refer to single product or service units or organisational units, but can also cover the entire organisation. In contrast to budgetary or financial reporting, management accounting is basically for internal users such as public managers, administration, politicians, and legislative overseers. A further difference to financial reporting is that management accounting information may, besides past information, also contain future information, e.g., in the form of cost forecasts or replacement costs. Furthermore, management accounting can focus on financial and non-financial performance (of public or political policies and programmes), thus be named performance accounting.

Sustainability and Integrated Reporting:[17] Both of these approaches of reporting are alternative approaches compared to traditional financial reporting as these cover also non-financial information. Both, Sustainability Reporting and Integrated Reporting address organizational stakeholders and contain past, but also future-orientated information in the form of strategy reporting. Both approaches not only concentrate on the reporting entity itself, but also cover how the entity interacts with its environment, society and governance. Therefore, Sustainability Reporting aims at delivering an overview of an economic, environmental and social performance of an organization, whereas Integrated Reporting can be seen as a wider approach to report on organizational public value creation during a reporting period. Integrated Reporting is about representing clearly and concisely how a public entity creates and sustains public value (e.g. public welfare), taking into account economic, social and environmental factors (IIRC, 2013) by reporting financial

---

[17] Performance reporting, another source of PSA information is not introduced here.

and non-financial information in an interconnected way. Reasons for Integrated Reporting and how it can be prepared in the public sector are addressed by, e.g., Cohen and Karatzimas (2015), Oprisor et al. (2016) and Katsikas et al. (2017). With respect to the extent of reporting, Sustainability and Integrated Reporting go beyond what is covered by General Purpose Financial Statements, a term that is introduced below. An overview on alternatives of financial and non-financial reporting in the public sector is provided in the new Chapter 14 of this book.

Government Financial Statistics: In contrast to the reporting approaches introduced above, Government Financial Statistics (GFS) do not only focus on single entities, but cover a total economy (e.g., region, country or group of countries) and report on all of its sectors (i.e. households, corporations and governmental entities). The aim of GFS is to deliver a systematic and detailed description of a total economy, its components and its relations with other total economies, building on an (internationally compatible) accounting framework. For the EU, the ESA 2010 is relevant, whereas on an international level, the System of National Accounts of the United Nations (SNA 2008) is used. Differences between ESA and SNA lie especially in their presentation. Accounting measures of GFS are, e.g., the net worth of a total economy (stocks of assets deducted of liabilities), its Gross Domestic Product (i.e. the sum of value added (gross)) and the value added of an industry (sum of incomes generated in an industry). Conceptually in the ESA, the demand for any product or product group has to equal its supply from within or outside the economy. Primary users of GFS information are politicians, statisticians, managers, oversight bodies (such as the EC) and the main statements produced are institutional sector accounts using an input-output framework. In the EU, GFS requirements have also driven the call for harmonizing PSA across the member states (as the latter provides input for the former) and thus the EPSAS project. GFS will be explained in more details in Chapter 5.

With respect to sources of PSA information, not only the different approaches to accounting play a role, but also the scope of reporting. In this notion, the terms General Purpose Financial Statements (**GPFSs**) and General Purpose Financial Reports (**GPFRs**) have been coined, which play a key role and therefore are explained in the following and depicted in Figure 1.1[18].

Information useful as input to assessment of accountability and for resource allocation and other decisions				
All Financial Reporting				Other information – economic statistical, demographic and other data
General Purpose Financial Reports (incl. annual financial reports and other reports)		Special Purpose (and other) Financial Reports outside scope of IPSASB e.g. donor and other special purpose and compliance reports, and finance statistics and other financial reports and forecasts outside GPFRs		
General Purpose Financial Statements (incl. notes)	Additional information – may include non-financial prospective financial, compliance and additional explanatory material			

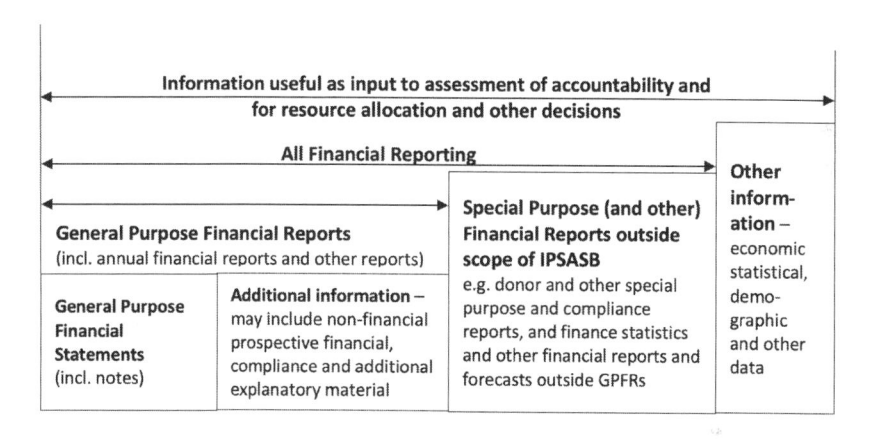

Figure 1.1: Scope of reporting depending on information needs of users of financial statements and reports

In the preface of the IPSASs, GPFRs are defined as "financial reports intended to meet the information needs of users who are unable to require the preparation of financial reports tailored to meet their specific information needs."[19] In a consultation paper for the Conceptual Framework in 2008, the IPSASB aimed to distinguish GPFRs from GPFSs and other reporting concepts. Typically, GPFSs contain financial information about financial position, financial

---

[18] IPSASB (2008), 1.14 Figure 1.

[19] Preface 9, IPSASB (2018), p. 14.

performance and cash flows[20] and are often accompanied by narrative information in the notes. GPFRs go beyond GPFSs and include additions such as non-financial prospective information, compliance information and additional explanatory material.

Thus, GPFRs encompass the annual financial reports and other reports. For example, the IPSAS pronouncements also entail non-binding Recommended Practice Guidelines (RPGs) with voluntary additional non-financial (e.g. service performance) information.

Despite of financial reports that are not tailored to meet specific information needs, also Special Purpose Financial Reports and other reports can be prepared, for those users that have the authority to demand specific reports for their information needs. Such reports could be e.g. donor reports, compliance reports, finance statistics and other financial reports and forecasts outside GPFRs. Special Purpose Financial Reports are outside the scope of IPSAS (see Chapter 8). Together, GPFRs and Special Purpose Financial Reports form the concept of 'all financial reporting'. Also the IPSASB (2008, 1.15) states, GPFRs "may not provide all the information users need for accountability, decision-making or other purposes". Thus, in an extension of all financial reporting, the entirety of information that is "useful as input to assessment of accountability and for resource allocation and other decisions", as well as other information such as economic statistical, demographic and other data, can be included into the reports.

In the meantime, both the IFRS Foundation and the IPSASB acknowledge that the significance of their standards on GPFSs and GPFRs has decreased from the users' decision usefulness perspective by actively addressing this shortcoming through expanding their authoritative activities into the area of non-financial sustainability information.

---

[20] IPSASB (2018), CF 2.17.

In the following, this book will focus on GPFRs and primarily will introduce financial accounting and reporting, as well as budgeting and budgetary reporting to some extent.

4. Accounting systems and techniques

As already indicated in Section 3 and when addressing the reforms in PSA, there are different systems of accounting in place, which will be introduced in this section and more thoroughly are explained in particular in Chapter 4. Thereby, a distinction is made between single entry and double entry bookkeeping as well as cash accounting and accrual accounting systems.

With respect to transaction recording techniques, one can distinguish between single entry and double entry bookkeeping. In general, bookkeeping is defined as recording of financial impacts of economic transactions or events of an organization. Using the **single entry bookkeeping technique**, each transaction is only recorded once. Mostly, the transactions recorded are based on the inflows and outflows of cash. Advantages of single entry bookkeeping relate essentially to the simplicity of the system, which however comes with the disadvantages of risking lack of comprehensiveness and coherence.

In contrast, by using **double entry bookkeeping**, for each transaction there are at least two related recordings, balancing between each other. This leads to the advantage that an income statement and a balance sheet can be derived from the accounting data as assets and liabilities are recorded. However, the system is much more complex and requires extended knowledge for its use.[21] The relevance of double entry bookkeeping for PSA has

---

[21] Van Helden and Hodges (2015), p. 57.

been much debated in literature[22] and its history will be explained in Chapter 2. A basic principle of double entry bookkeeping is that for each transaction at least a debit entry on one account and a credit entry on another account is to be recorded. The system is closed so that all accounts must balance. Over an accounting period, the monetary value of debit entries must equal the monetary value of credit entries. Table 1.1 provides an overview of the changes of debit and credit entries depending on the types of accounts.

Groups of accounts	Debit entries (D)	Credit entries (Cr)
Assets accounts	Increase ↑	Decrease ↓
Liability accounts	Decrease ↓	Increase ↑
Capital or equity (net assets) accounts	Decrease ↓	Increase ↑
Revenues accounts	Decrease ↓	Increase ↑
Expenses accounts	Increase ↑	Decrease ↓

Table 1.1: Principles of double entry bookkeeping

Regarding the timing of the recognition of revenues and expenses, in general, cash accounting and accrual accounting are distinguished. For **cash accounting**, revenues and expenses are only recognized when the receipt/payment occurs. Thus, in its pure form, cash accounting does not allow for the recording of assets and liabilities. As such, the system has been criticized for not being transparent with respect to financial implications of economic events (e.g. receivables). In contrast, when using **accrual accounting**, revenues are recognized in the period earned and expenses in the period in which these are incurred, regardless when they are received/paid.

Often, single entry bookkeeping is combined with cash accounting systems and, particularly in the public sector, used for budgeting and

---

[22] See e.g. Soll (2014).

budgetary accounting.[23] In the public sector of German-speaking countries, a system called cameral accounting that also uses the combination of single entry bookkeeping with cash accounting has evolved and is partially also still in place (e.g. at central level). Cameral accounting will be addressed in more details in Chapters 2 and 4.

To illustrate the differences between cash and accrual accounting, the following example can be used: On 15.11.20X0 a public entity delivers services, worth 10,000 EUR. At the same date, the service recipient receives a bill but does only pay in cash in the next year, on 01.02.20X1. In a cash- based system, revenues will only be accounted for together with the cash when the payment is received, so on 01.02.20X1. Thus, revenues are not shown in the year X0, in which the service was delivered. In contrast, when using an accrual-based system, revenues are already recorded on 15.11.20X0 together with accounts receivable. Thus, the revenues fall in the year 20X0. After the payment, cash is accounted for and the accounts receivable are cleared (without affecting the statement of financial performance). As such, both systems lead to a different timing of revenue and expense recognition and reporting. This is particularly the case for the purchase of non-current assets and their depreciation which is only recorded in an accrual-based system.

Besides a strict distinction between cash and accrual accounting, also modified regimes are in place in many countries, which are further distinguished between the public and private sector. Thus, according to the extent of use of accrual accounting, Lande (2011) distinguishes four types of accounting systems.[24] In a **modified cash accounting system**, only monetary (e.g. cash-based) assets and liabilities are accounted for. Thus, the list of assets only contains cash and cash equivalents and loans and investments of the year. This

---

[23] Bergmann (2009), p. 66.
[24] See Lande (2011), p. 17 for details.

system is currently prevalent in the Netherlands and at the central state level of Germany. A **modified accrual accounting system** is more developed, because assets also cover receivables, and liabilities also encompass payables. Thus, financial assets and financial liabilities are accounted for. **Accrual accounting at the public sector level** means that most assets and liabilities are accounted for as this is the case in the public sector of Austria, Finland, Sweden, the UK and for the EC. In general, in the EU, **full accrual accounting** is used for the private sector and aimed for in the public sector by running the EPSAS project. This means that reporting units have to account for all their assets, including intangible assets, and all liabilities, including provisions. However, exemptions from full accrual accounting may exist, e.g. for smaller reporting units, or building on their legal form, as in the case in Germany.

Throughout this book, both main bookkeeping techniques and both accounting regulation regimes will be addressed, despite a focus on double entry bookkeeping and accrual accounting.

5. Geographic focus

With respect to the geographic focus drawn in this book, the authors decided for the first edition to concentrate on the countries of the partners of the former DiEPSAm project and, to a wider extent, also on the EU due to its underlying EPSAS project. The strategic partners of the DiEPSAm project represent diverse national PSA traditions and can therefore contribute with contradictory and alternative approaches to create an enriched European society. Thus, in the book a transnational and comparative approach is sought for. Subsequently, at least the public sector financial accounting and reporting systems in the following countries are introduced: Austria, Finland, Germany, Portugal and the United Kingdom (UK). It needs to be stressed that the brief descriptions only cover financial but not budgetary accounting. Also, it needs to be distinguished between the government levels: Finland, Portugal and the UK have two government levels (central and local), whereas in Austria and Germany there are three levels of government (central, state and local).[25]

In Finland, Portugal and the UK, both at the central and local government level, accrual accounting systems are in place. In Austria and Germany, the systems are heterogeneous at the different levels of government. In a top-down approach of the three levels of government in Austria, in 2013 only the central government fully switched to accrual accounting. At the regional and local government levels diverse systems were in place. The transition procedure to accrual accounting was completed at the regional level in 2019 and at the local government level in 2020. In Germany, the most diverse systems are currently in use. In general, there is an option to choose between modified cash and accrual accounting at central and state level. However, currently the central government uses modified cash as well as twelve of the sixteen federal states, so only four federal states decided to use accrual accounting. Instead, at the local level, most federal states (twelve) enforced accrual accounting for the municipalities comprised within them.

As such, where applicable, the book will at least draw on comparative studies between Austria, Finland, Germany, Portugal and the UK and also will shed light on the EPSAS project in the EU.

6. PSA standards in the EU

As outlined in the introduction, currently the EC, authorizing via the Eurostat, aims to harmonize PSA in Europe. Thereby, EPSAS are

---

[25] See Brusca et al. (2015) for detailed descriptions of the accounting systems.

to be developed that might use the IPSAS as a basis of reference. However, potentially, with respect to the accounting norms to be used for the EU MS, there are different options to consider.

On the one hand, there are the internationally accepted accounting standards produced by private standard setting bodies. However, on the other hand, private standard setting bodies do not have the power to enforce their norms into any national accounting system. Therefore, these accounting standards can either be used voluntarily by reporting units, or mandatorily by endorsement in each country individually. For the private sector, the International Financial Reporting Standards (IFRS) released by the IASB are widely used for (consolidated) group accounts of capital market-oriented corporations as (controlling) parent. IFRS are used as a basis of reference for the IPSAS released by the IPSASB, being adjusted to the public sector context.

Despite a voluntary use or adoption of international accounting standards, of course also national or local standards can be in place that have to be mandatorily used by resident reporting units. For private sector entities, in many countries there are national commercial codes. These often also serve as a basis of reference for PSA norms. As such, some countries have their own accounting regimes for the public sector or they adjust IFRS or IPSAS to be used in the public sector. Examples of the countries involved in the former DiEPSAm project are: Finland and Germany that adjusted their national commercial code for the public sector; Portugal and Austria that use modified IPSAS; and the UK that primarily adapted IFRS directly. Therefore, the question remains – which set of norms has superior suitability for serving as an EPSAS basis.

This book aims to shed light on different accounting standards such as IPSAS, potential EPSAS, but also national systems in the partner countries, to provide comparative transnational insights.

7. Reporting units

With respect to financial accounting and reporting, also the reporting unit needs to be considered, i.e. the boundaries according to which one entity is distinguished, and the extent of reporting economic transactions. Typically, **financial statements** and consolidated financial statements are distinguished.[26] Accordingly, financial statements concern the individual public entity only. If a public entity holds interests in subsidiaries, these are shown as a financial asset. However, if a public entity has close and strong economic relationships with other entities, financial statements do not clearly depict the financial performance and financial situation of that public entity, if e.g. liabilities have been outsourced together with an asset. Therefore, in contrast to financial statements, **consolidated financial statements** (for the group) combine all entities under control of a public entity. By applying consolidation methods, holdings, liabilities and groups transactions are combined within one statement. Consolidated financial statements are the content of Chapter 11, whereas consolidation methods and reporting will be addressed in Chapter 12.

More recent concepts, such as **whole of government accounting**, follow the statistical treatment by creating an economic entity that entails all public sector entities in one country. As such, the financial statements cover all government entities at all levels of government and all entities that are controlled by the government (see Section 2 of this chapter for a definition). Therefore, the approach is much broader than consolidated financial statements. Countries using this approach are New Zealand and the UK.[27] Whole of government accounting will be addressed in Chapter 11 in more details.

---

[26] Bergmann (2009), pp. 161 ff.
[27] Bergmann (2009), pp. 157 ff.

8. Conclusion

This chapter aimed to present key terms of PSA and reporting and in doing so, also to narrow down the content of the book. As PSA in Europe is currently still very heterogeneous, professionals and academics in Europe face tremendous challenges.[28] In particular, there will be a large need for university graduates and practitioners that are knowledgeable in PSA and that are aware of the differing PSA systems across Europe. In order to account for this development, this book concentrates on PSA in Europe. The key terms used and the linked concepts are presented in Table 1.2 below. The topics that this book addresses in the following chapters are faded out in grey.

Scope	Public sector					Private sector	
	General government		Public corporations				
Sources of PSA information	Budgeting	Budgetary accounting and reporting	Financial accounting and reporting	Management accounting	Sustainability and Integrated Reporting	Government Financial Statistics	
Types of accounting	Bookkeeping technique			Timing of recognition			
	Single entry	Double entry		Cash accounting		Accrual accounting	
Geographic focus	Inter national	Europe	EU	Selected EU countries			
				Austria	Finland	Germany	Portugal	UK
Accounting standards	International standards		EU Standards EPSAS		National standards		
	IFRS	IPSAS	IFRS-based	IPSAS-based	Own regime		IFRS-based
Reporting unit	Single entity financial statements			Consolidated financial statements			

Table 1.2: Roadmap of topics presented in this book

---

[28] Adam et al. (2019).

Bibliographic references

ADAM, Berit; BRUSCA, Isabel; CAPERCHIONE, Eugenio; HEILING, Jens; JORGE, Susana and MANES ROSSI, Francesca (2019) – "Are higher education institutions in Europe preparing students for IPSAS?", International Journal of Public Sector Management, 33(2/3), pp. 363-378. https://doi.org/10.1108/IJPSM-12-2018-0270

BERGMANN, Andreas (2009) – Public Sector Financial Management, Harlow et al.: Prentice Hall, ISBN: 9780273713548.

BOVAIRD, Tony and LOEFFLER, Elke (2016) – Public Management and Governance, London and New York: Routledge, ISBN: 978-415-50185-9, 3rd ed.

BRUSCA, Isabel; CAPERCHIONE, Eugenio; COHEN, Sandra and MANES-ROSSI, Francesca (eds.) (2015) – Public Sector Accounting and Auditing in Europe – the Challenge of Harmonization, Basingstoke: Palgrave Macmillan, ISBN: 9781137461339.

BUDDING, Tjerk; GROSSI, Giuseppe and TAGESSON, Torbjorn (2015) – Public Sector Accounting, London: Routledge, ISBN: 9780415683159.

COHEN, Sandra and KARATZIMAS, Sotirios (2015) – Tracing the future of reporting in the public sector: introducing integrated popular reporting, International Journal of Public Sector Management, 28(6), pp.449-460.

EC (2013) – Report from the Commission to the Council and the European Parliament: Towards implementing harmonised public sector accounting standards in Member States, The suitability of IPSAS for the Member States, Brussels, 6.3.2013, COM(2013) 114 final.

EC (2019) – Reporting on the progress as regards the European Public Sector Accounting Standards (EPSAS), Brussels, 5.6.2019, SWD(2019) 204 final.

EC (2022) – EPSAS Expert Group and subgroups, https://ec.europa.eu/eurostat/web/epsas/expert-groups .

ESA (2010) – European system of accounts, Luxembourg: Publications Office of the European Union, ISBN: 9789279312427.

E&Y (2012) – Overview and comparison of public accounting and auditing practices in the 27 EU Member States, Prepared for Eurostat, Final Report.

IIRC (2013) – The International <IR> Framework, The International Integrated Reporting Council, London.

IPSASB (2008) – Consultation paper for the Conceptual Framework.

IPSASB (2018) – Handbook of International Public Sector Accounting Pronouncements, New York: IFAC, ISBN: 9781608153626, 2018 Edition, Vol. 1.

JONES, Rowan and PENDLEBURY, Maurice (2010) – Public Sector Accounting, New York: Pearson Education, ISBN: 9780273720362, 6th ed.

JONES, Rowan (ed.) (2011) – Public Sector Accounting, Vol. IV: Comparative International, Los Angeles et al.: Sage, ISBN: 9780857225197.

JORGE, Susana; CAPERCHIONE, Eugenio and JONES, Rowan (2011) – Comparative International Governmental Accounting Research (CIGAR): Bridging Researching and Networking, in JONES, Rowan (ed.) Public Sector Accounting, Vol. IV: Comparative International, Los Angeles et al.: Sage, ISBN: 9780857225197, pp. ix-xxiv.

KATSIKAS, Epameinondas; MANES-ROSSI, Francesca and ORELLI, Rebecca L. (2017) – Towards Integrated Reporting Accounting Change in the Public Sector, Cham: Springer, ISBN: 9783319472355.

LANDE, Evelyne (2011) – Accrual Accounting in the Public Sector, in: JONES, Rowan (ed.): Public Sector Accounting, Vol. IV: Comparative International, Los Angeles et al.: Sage, ISBN: 9780857225197, pp. 15-28.

OPRISOR, Tudor; TIRON-TUDOR, Adriana and NISTOR, Cristina Silvia (2016) – The integrated reporting system: a new accountability enhancement tool for public sector entities, 14(139), Audit Financiar, pp. 749-762.

SOLL, Jacob (2014) – The Reckoning: Financial Accountability and the Rise and Fall of Nations, Philadelphia: Basic Books, ISBN: 9780465031528.

VAN HELDEN, Jan and HODGES, Ron (2015) – Public Sector Accounting for Non-Specialists, London et al.: Palgrave Macmillan, ISBN: 9781137376985.

WEYLAND, Bernadette and NOWAK, Karsten (2016) – EPSAS Update, in: Der Konzern, 12/2016, pp. 558-569.

Additional readings

BERGMANN, Andreas (2009) – Public Sector Financial Management, Harlow et al.: Prentice Hall, ISBN: 978-0-273-71354-8.

BRUSCA, Isabel; CAPERCHIONE, Eugenio; COHEN, Sandra and MANES-ROSSI, Francesca (eds.) (2015) – Public Sector Accounting and Auditing in Europe – the Challenge of Harmonization, Basingstoke: Palgrave Macmillan, ISBN: 978-1-137-46133-9.

Discussion topics

- Reasons for harmonization in public sector accounting and reporting
- Cash accounting and accrual accounting: What suits the public sector better?
- Accounting regimes for the public sector: Internationally accepted standards vs. local norms
- The concept of decision-usefulness: A critical discussion

Chapter 2
Specificities of Public Sector Accounting: Insights for Governmental Accounting from History and Theory

Yuri Biondi
National Centre for National Research (CNRS), France
yuri.biondi@gmail.com
https://orcid.org/0000-0002-5545-5550

Summary

Accounting has as long a history as writing. The purposes of accountability and control appear to be constitutive of institutional economic organisation of governments across epochs. Models and examples of public sector accounting (here governmental accounting) can be found in ancient civilisations and the Middle Age. Modern public sector accounting systems have co-evolved with the constitution and evolution of modern states. In this context, public sector accounting design relates to the specificities of modern public administration, featured by management of taxation and public finances, as well as accountability toward sovereigns and parliaments.

This chapter aims to denote these specificities through their historical emergence and main features. The modern government consummates resources acquired through taxation and borrowing, so as to redistribute them at the macroeconomic level. In turn, citizens contribute with resources to be redistributed by paying taxation and subscribing governmental debt issuance and refinancing (including for monetary base management). Moreover, the government takes non-debt commitments to assure social protection on behalf of its constituencies. This specific financial-economic working by the government differs from that by the business entity, requiring a specific accounting representation. From this perspective, recent reforms driven by new public management (NPM) and new public governance (NPG) – aiming to align public sector and business sector accounting systems - constitute yet another unfolded evolution whose implications shall be assessed over time and in context.

Keywords

financial sustainability of government; public sector specificity; accountability; public sector accounting history; public sector accounting theory

1. Introduction

This chapter aims to provide some insights from history and theory for accounting for the public (governmental) sector in view to better understand the specificities of public sector accounting (here governmental accounting), their origins and reasons.[1]

Section 2 provides some illustrative examples from history of governmental accounting. Models and examples can be found in ancient civilisations, including ancient Greece, the Roman Empire, and the Islamic states. For sure, the emergence of modern public sector accounting goes along with the constitution and the evolution of the

---

[1] From an historical viewpoint, the notions of 'public sector' and 'governmental sector' may be changing. Consequently, this chapter employs the two as somewhat equivalent.

modern state from the feudal state. The modern public administration is then featured by the connection between state sovereignty, fiscal power, and public borrowing.

Section 3 investigates these features which differentiate public sector accounting from business sector accounting. Specificities include: absence of commercial revenues; public debt and monetary base management; public debt management for redistribution purpose; and assurance of social protection (social benefits) through non-debt commitments. In this context, budgets constitute an essential instrument of public sector accounting, assuring both internal control and accountability to citizens and their representatives. A cash basis of accounting is consistent with this budgeting procedure (see Section 3.3 below and Chapter 3).

From this perspective, recent reforms driven by new public management (NPM) and new public governance (NPG) – aiming to align public sector and business sector accounting systems - constitute yet another unfolded evolution whose implications shall be assessed over time and in context.

2. Origins of public sector accounting: examples and insights from history

Accounting has as long a history as writing. The purposes of accountability and control appear to be constitutive of institutional economic organisation of governments across epochs. Book-keeping implies defining and tracing operations, which can be either material (good or services; in-kind) or financial (in cash and credit), while making accountable the people in charge of those operations. According to Dubet and Legay (2010), the core of public sector accounting through modern history has been the fight against misappropriation, fraud and embezzlement; prevention of financial distress; and budgeting including prospective budgeting.

Models and examples of non-business accounting can be found in ancient civilisations and during the Middle Age, especially monasteries and feudal tax management systems. But modern public sector accounting systems have been developed along with the constitution and evolution of modern states. On the one hand, modern states manage an increasingly centralised web of activities, contrary to feudal states which were more decentralised; moreover, modern state treasuries take over management of public finances, including taxation and public debt management. On the other hand, state sovereignty is based upon controlling territories and the subjects who live there. Accounting systems contribute to both financial management and sovereign control by these public administrations. At the same time, the stakeholders – including the subjects themselves - demand the sovereign to be accountable, as for it levies taxes, makes expenditures and asks for credit. Therefore, modern states do, or at least are asked to, enact sovereign authority under the law. Supreme Audit Courts or Offices have been therefore established to supervise public finances on behalf of Parliaments and the citizenship.

This Section provides some illustrative examples from history of governmental accounting through epochs. The rest of the section is organised as follows. Section 2.1 provides examples from ancient civilisations, including ancient Greece and the Roman Empire. Section 2.2 focuses on the Middle Age in Europe and the feudal state. Section 2.3 denotes the development of the modern state in Europe, featuring the connection between state sovereignty, fiscal power, and public borrowing.

2.1 Ancient civilisations

This chapter cannot provide a comprehensive, comparative or retrospective account of public sector accounting across epochs.

For sure, the purposes of accountability and control appear to be constitutive of institutional economic organisation of governments, but local variants are critical for a proper understanding, as for accounting is embedded in socio-economic and institutional contexts which vary through time and space.[2]

As a technique, public sector accounting (also accounting or governmental accounting thereafter) comprises and performs various techniques concerned with recording of transactions and operations, assuring their classification and traceability. This recording generally involves numerical systems pointing to the material (in kind) or financial (in cash and credit) dimensions of those operations. These recordings and related numbers make accountable the persons in charge of those operations. As a design, accounting relates then to numeracy and eventually mathematics, as well as to socio-economic organisation of an economy and a polity. Managers, gatekeepers, supervisors and stakeholders are all involved in its various historical settings. As a rule, accounting definitely governs the working of public administrations, assuring managerial, control and accountability purposes.

The oldest known system of public sector accounting was developed in central China, in the city of Xian, during the Southern Song Dynasty around 7000 BCE. It served as a budgeting system to control expenditure by the court according to budgeted revenues.[3]

In Mesopotamia, city states developed public sector accounting systems around 5000 BCE. The financial officials used clay tablets with pictographic characters to record financial transactions. According to Carmona and Ezzamel, "far from being a rudimentary,

---

[2] Besson (1901); Legay (2010); Baxter (1957); Binney and Edward (1958); Schneider (1952); Buchholz (1992); Waquet (1990); Zannini (1994), Margairaz (1991); Bezes et al. (2013).

[3] Chatfield and Vangermeersch (1996).

accounting practices in both ancient civilisations [such as Egypt and Mesopotamia] displayed remarkable levels of detail."[4]

In Egypt, various civilisations developed over a long period from 3000 to 300 BCE. According to Carmona and Ezzamel (2007, 189), "the royal palace and the temples constituted two influential institutions in the economy of ancient Egypt." State administration was a pillar of ancient Egypt's development. It maintained a sophisticated system of taxation and redistribution in kind. "Once tax was assessed and collected, it was transported to the state granaries, and this process was organised and documented carefully by the scribes".[5]

In ancient India, according to Sihag (2004), during the 4th century BCE, Kautilya developed bookkeeping rules to record and classify operations, emphasized the critical role of independent periodic audits, and proposed the establishment of two distinct offices - the Treasurer and Comptroller-Auditor -, in view to improve control and foster accountability, thus reducing the scope for conflict and fraud.

In ancient Athens (Greece), public administration was disclosing financial statements to the people. The Senate employed provisional budgeting to plan and gather resources required to fund public works or wars. State inflows came mainly from the public domain (land, roads, bridges, mines, theatres, temples) but also confiscations and levies. According to Aristotle (Politics, Book V chapter VIII, p. 186), public disclosure was a critical mean to avoid fraud:

> *To prevent the exchequer from being defrauded, let all public money be delivered out openly in the face of the whole city and let copies of the accounts be deposited in the different wards, tribes and divisions.*

---

[4] Carmona and Ezzamel (2007, 196).

[5] Carmona and Ezzamel, (2007, 192).

In the ancient Roman Republic[6], administration of public finances was under supervision by the Senate, whose acts were publicly disclosed, kept under custody by the Ceres Temple, and held under the responsibility of elected magistrates (the Ediles). According to LaGroue (2014), the roman civilisation employed accounting instruments in a cogent manner, including inventory lists, inflow-outflow statements in both cash and kind, and a single-entry system that monetized the value of goods. These instruments were employed for management, control and making public servants accountable toward the public and the judge:

> *the one cultural area where their accounting material prominently featured was in the legal setting. Accounting ledgers and data were critical records which were clearly relied upon. Accounting was needed in banking and wills, and its perceived value alone could prove the innocence or guilt of an individual. These uses underscore the functionality of Romans' accounting documents in their society.*[7]

According to Zaid (2004), innovations overcoming the Roman epoch emerged in early Islamic accounting practices during the mid-7th through 10th centuries. Once the Quran and Sharia law became the basis for all Muslim states, it became necessary to keep track of the Zakat, a religious levy for all Muslims which is applied to returns on wealth exceeding certain thresholds. Furthermore, Zaid states that "the Quran requires the writing and recording of debts and business transactions in accordance with the"[8, 9] *Surah Al-Baqarah Ayat* (Qu'ran, 2:282). In this context, Islamic public

---

[6] Humbert (1886).

[7] LaGroue, (2014, p. VIII).

[8] Zaid (2004, 154)

[9] Cooper et al. (2004, 154).

administrations employed budgeting and auditing for control and accountability purposes. Both public sector and business sector accounting systems were developed, surely influencing the European developments which followed.

2.2 Middle Age in Europe

After the disappearance of the Western Roman Empire, the great Carolingian institutions such as the kingdom and the monasteries kept levying feudal dues, which appear to be somehow evolving from the Roman tax system and through the progressive adoption of Roman law across medieval Europe from the end of the eleventh century. According to Beguin and Genet (2017):

> *like the Roman taxes, these feudal dues based on both men and land were regular and largely foreseeable; they were linked to the exercise of the* dominium, *which can be understood as public authority exercised collectively by the* domini *class which seized control at the time of the collapse of the Carolingian Empire, and imposed the dues on their dependants.*

Middle age political authorities - such as the commune or the prince - only had access to fiscal resources of feudal origin (for instance, customs, tolls, tonlieux [stallholder taxes], and market taxes; but also granting monopolistic privileges; performing expropriations through the ancient power of purveyance; and selling public functions and nobility titles), levied through an elaborated system of privileges and obligations between the lords and the vassals. In case of urgent need, those authorities may have recourse to arbitrary measures, which were often regarded as abusive and susceptible of provoking grievances and rebellions. The superposition of powers –

by the church, the emperor, and the lords - over the same territory was a common and viable practice under feudalism.

Generally speaking, levy gathering was at that time delegated to local stewards, while specific levies were often devoted to particular activities and requested on a regular or an occasional basis. For instance, from the 12th century, the local sheriffs of each county of England were audited by the great nobles sitting in the Exchequer.[10] The Exchequer met twice a year, at Easter and Michaelmas (29 September). This court of law could discharge the sheriff (with the Latin words "*et quietus est*") or rule an amount that was owed to be paid by the sheriff into the lord's treasury. These procedures originated in France and were brought to England with the Norman invasion of 1066. They ensured the accountability of county sheriffs to the lords for their revenue collection and local expenses. They were based upon a charge-discharge system whose objective was to calculate and record the sums owed to the lord by the sheriff of each county. According to Cooper, Funnell and Lee[11], the sheriff as

> "*the steward was charged with the sums for which he was responsible (opening balance, plus receipts), and discharged of his legitimate payments; the end balance showed what he must handover to his lord.*"

2.3 The modern state in Europe

Throughout the second millennium, economic development revitalized cities, regions and trade, leading to the monetization of the economy. According to Bonney and Ormrod (1999), it was clearly

---

[10] Cooper et al. (2012).
[11] Cooper et al. (2012, 198).

during the fourteenth century that western monarchies began to cross the frontier between the feudal state and the fiscal state, a frontier that the Italian cities had already crossed in the previous century; at the same time, those cities also developed modern accounting and financial techniques for the private sector, including the double book-keeping system lately summarised by Luca Pacioli in his famous treaty. According to Beguin and Genet (2017):

> *This [Italian] society of bankers and merchants also had the financial techniques: all or nearly all the technologies of taxation and credit originated in Italy, including public debt consolidation and the creation of government [securities], as well as theoretical debate on questions such as whether the interest charged on these [securities] counted as usury. They had all the technologies, but state-building had not occurred, or only on a small scale. The Italians continued to play a leading role in the development of the European states, their tax systems and their finances.*

One of the crucial factors in the emergence of the modern tax systems which feature the modern state has been war – including the Crusades[12] – and related borrowing. The funding of wars triggered taxation beyond the customary and regular levies of the Middle Age, enacting the taxing power of the sovereign. Yet, this power encountered limits and depended on the political consensus to be obtained and maintained: when it went out of line, war financing caused financial distress and political outturns.

This connection between state authority, the organisation of state fiscal capacity, and the management of state borrowing emerged progressively and became the backbone of the modern state by the

---

[12] Russell (1975).

end of the eighteenth century, when tax and debt became structural elements of the finances of all western European countries.

By then, modern monarchies followed the early examples by the cities in Italy and northern Europe to develop both borrowing arrangements with bankers and issuance of public debt securities.[13] Secondary exchanges for governmental securities developed since those securities became transferable, paving the way to the emergence of private investors and financial market-makers in public debt. Central banking was progressively established to organise public debt management and currency issuance at the junction with private banking. According to Bordo[14]:

> *The story of central banking goes back at least to the seventeenth century, to the founding of the first institution recognized as a central bank, the Swedish Riksbank. Established in 1668 as a joint stock bank, it was chartered to lend the government funds and to act as a clearing house for commerce. A few decades later (1694), the most famous central bank of the era, the Bank of England, was founded also as a joint stock company to purchase government debt. Other central banks were set up later in Europe for similar purposes, though some were established to deal with monetary disarray. For example, the Banque de France was established by Napoleon in 1800 to stabilize the currency after the hyperinflation of paper money during the French Revolution, as well as to aid in government finance. Early central banks issued private notes which served as currency, and they often had a monopoly over such note issue.*
>
> *While these early central banks helped fund the government's debt, they were also private entities that engaged in banking activities. Because they held the deposits of other banks, they came*

---

[13] North and Weingast (1989; Beguin and Genet (2017).
[14] Bordo (2007, 1).

> to serve as banks for bankers, facilitating transactions between banks or providing other banking services. They became the repository for most banks in the banking system because of their large reserves and extensive networks of correspondent banks. These factors allowed them to become the lender of last resort in the face of a financial crisis. In other words, they became willing to provide emergency cash to their correspondents in times of financial distress.

According to Teichova and Matis (2003), under the influence of the Enlightenment, the English and French courts acted as a centralising force, while the unification of administration promoted a sense of political unity among the royal subjects. Accordingly, the modern state connects with the materialisation of a novel 'public sphere' in Europe against the background of the disintegration of the feudal system, including the repudiation of the Church's and the Empire's claims to universality, and the rise of civil (bourgeois) society. By centralising and unifying administrative processes, introducing compulsory mass education and military service, and forging a common economic area, modern monarchies asserted the idea of state sovereignty over particularistic forces arising out of regionalism and the persistence of traditional social orders.

However, modern monarchies – such as Prussia, France, England, and Spain - were by no means the only agencies in developing the modern state. Political institutions were evolving with the very notion of representative government emerging often out of political unrest, featuring Parliaments with a central role alongside the sovereigns and a judiciary independent of the sovereigns as well. In this context, the French Revolution of 1789 further paved the way to the constitution and dissemination of the modern state and representative government throughout Europe, providing the political and ideal foundations of centralised public administration by law[15]. In particular, the French 'Declaration des Droits de l'Homme et du Citoyen' (Declaration of Human and Civic Rights of 26 August 1789) proclaimed the people's sovereignty over public finances[16]:

> *Article 13*
> *For the maintenance of the public force, and for administrative expenses, a general tax is indispensable; it must be equally distributed among all citizens, in proportion to their ability to pay.*
> *Article 14*
> *All citizens have the right to ascertain, by themselves, or through their representatives, the need for a public tax, to consent to it freely, to watch over its use, and to determine its proportion, basis, collection and duration.*
> *Article 15*
> *Society has the right to ask a public official for an accounting of his administration.*

Accordingly, public budgets were to be submitted to the approval by the French Parliament, which had to consent to pay taxes and approve expenditures on behalf of the people. Since the beginning of the nineteenth century, a Supreme Court of Audit was also established to audit public accounts and supervise public financial management on behalf of both the government and the Parliament.

Moreover, the public sector accounting system was further developed by cameral accounting, that is, an accounting system featuring a financial basis of accounting and capable to trace and control financial flows and stocks through time and circumstances. This system has been evolving and implemented since the beginning of the 14th century in German speaking countries (Germany, Austria, Switzerland) and has

---

[15] Besson (1901, p. 262 ff.).
[16] Normanton (1966).

influenced accounting in Nordic countries, the Netherlands, Belgium, Hungary and Italy.[17] Cameral accounting was also employed in Russia from the early 18th century until the 20th century.[18]

The cameral accounting structure is symmetric for revenues and expenditures (Table 2.1). It provides a consistent design to organise and implement a cash basis of accounting, featuring its importance for public sector accounting.

	Revenues (financial inflows), or Expenditures (financial outflows) Over a time period between *t-1* and *t*			
	Balances of residual dues brought-forward (B/F)	Current dues (CD)	Actuals (A)	Balances of residual dues carried-forward (C/F)
Transactions/ operations by type and class	= Initial Balance $B/F = C/F_{t-1}$	= Increases over period *t*	= Decreases over period *t*	= Ending Balance $C/F_t = B/F + CD_t - A_t$
Totals				

B/F: balances unsettled (unpaid and/or not-received) in the previous period and brought-forward from the previous accounting period
CD: payment (or receipt) instructions made in the current period
A: payments/expenditures (or receipts/revenues) liquidated in the current period
C/F: balances unsettled in the current period and carried-forward to the next accounting period

Table 2.1: The cameral account structure[19]

Monsen[20] claims that

> *cameral bookkeeping method for centuries has been used in the public sector, as opposed to the commercial bookkeeping method.*

---

[17] Monsen (2002); Filios (1983); Forrester (1990); Coronella (2007); Canziani and Camodeca (2010).

[18] Nazarov and Sidorova (2016); Platonova (2017).

[19] Adapted from Monsen (2002), Table 1, p. 50.

[20] Monsen (2002), 45.

Cameral book-keeping is based upon single entries which are recorded either on the revenues (financial inflows) or the expenditures (financial outflows) side of the cameral accounts. It can be consistently connected with the budget through current dues and actuals, which are both recorded on a cash basis of accounting. To be sure, current dues and actuals constitute the financial flows which feature the dynamic of cameral accounts. They comprise both cash (actuals) and cash equivalents (dues), assuring a comprehensive representation of treasury management. Moreover, transactions and operations can be disentangled and classified between operational, financing and investment flows, expanding financial management and control through comprehensive cash flow statements.

In sum, the modern state is featured by its territorial sovereignty which justifies its taxing power and monetary management by the law, on which depends its public borrowing that gathers resources for public administration deployment. The next section shall investigate these specificities from a theoretical perspective.

3. Specificities of public sector accounting: examples and insights from theory

Public sector accounting design relates to the specificities of modern public administration, featured by management of taxation and public finances, as well as accountability toward governments, parliaments and the citizenship.

The modern government consummates resources acquired through taxation and borrowing, so as to redistribute them at the macroeconomic level. In turn, citizens contribute with resources to be redistributed by paying taxation and subscribing governmental debt issuance and refinancing (including for monetary base management). Moreover, the government takes non-debt commitments on behalf of its constituencies.

This specific financial-economic working by the government differs from that by the business entity, requiring a specific accounting representation. Specificities include: absence of commercial revenues; public debt and monetary base management; public debt management for redistribution purpose; and assurance of social protection (social benefits) through non-debt commitments.

From this perspective, recent reforms driven by new public management (NPM) and new public governance (NPG) – aiming to align public sector and business sector accounting systems - constitute yet another unfolded evolution whose implications shall be assessed over time and in context (see Section 3.4 below).

The rest of this section is organised as follows. Section 3.1 denotes the specific financial economy of governments. Section 3.2 highlights the accounting representation which is consistent with these specificities. In particular, Section 3.3 discusses the relationship between the cash basis and the accrual basis of public sector accounting. Section 3.4 addresses the NPM and NPG ideology which argues for aligning public sector and business sector accounting systems.

3.1 The specific financial economy of the government

Business entities seek to recover accrued costs or invested values through commercial revenue generation. This revenue is supposed to be spent, reinvested or distributed to stakeholders, including shareholding investors. Consequently, the business sector accounting system aims to represent this business economic process of profit-seeking and commercial revenue generation.

Contrary to the business entity, the public sector entity is not supposed to generate positive financial values (or profits) from its ongoing activities. Tax-payers expect the direct satisfaction of public needs (individual or collective) through non-lucrative activities based on social redistribution of resources. This satisfaction is the ultimate result or performance, and it is fundamentally disconnected from generation of "surplus". Therefore, the overarching purpose of public sector accounting system shifts from generation of net values (or net profits) to financing and covering of costs absorbed.[21]

In this context, financial sustainability of central government depends on (Figure 2.1): (i) the taxing power; (ii) public debt management and its issuance and refinancing mechanisms; and (iii) collective commitments such as pay-as-you-go pension obligations.

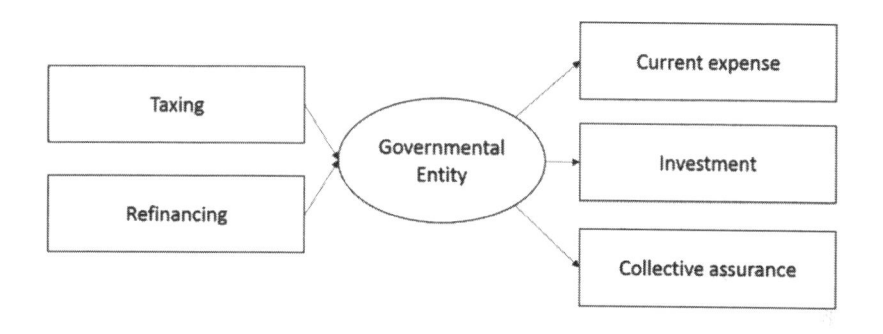

Figure 2.1: Specificities of financial economy of government: sources and uses of resources[22]

Public sector specificities include[23]: absence of commercial revenues (Section 3.1.1); public debt and monetary base management (Section 3.1.2); public debt management for redistribution purpose (Section 3.1.3); and assurance of social protection (social benefits) (Section 3.1.4).

---

[21] Biondi (2012).

[22] Reprinted from Biondi and Boisseau-Sierra, (2017a), Figure 1.

[23] Biondi (2012) and (2016); Biondi and Boisseau-Sierra (2017a).

3.1.1 Absence of commercial revenues

Concerning the business entity, recovering inflows are commercial revenues related to the prices of goods and services exchanged in business transactions. On the contrary, typical operating inflows to the governmental entity such as taxation are generated by non-commercial transactions which do not involve prices and an equivalent exchange of products and services against those prices (Table 2.2, left column).

Commercial Revenues to the business entity	Operating inflows (contributions) to the governmental entity
(a) Involve the transfer of a good or service in exchange for a transfer of cash;	(a) These operating inflows are a transfer that is not measured at the equivalent price of a commercial transaction;
(b) Imply a profit motive, i.e., the seeking of a satisfactory (reasonable) business income (the basis for recovering);	(b) The non-business activity does not have – by definition – profit (lucrative) motive;
(c) Incorporate in pricing a judgment about the utility of the purchased item (based on the voluntary nature of the exchange under competitive conditions);	(c) This transfer does not imply any evaluation, even crude, of the utility of the generating activity;
(d) Are determined by prices which reflect the client's willingness to pay; no business firm refuses to be paid more for the same service, does it?	(d) This transfer is not based on the willingness to pay of the beneficiaries, but on their capacity to pay;
(e) Complete the financial relationship between the client and the business entity. Nothing further is charged to the client, who in turn does not have any control or influence over the utilization of the revenues realized by the transaction.	(e) This transfer does not conclude the financial relationship between the beneficiaries and the entity, since they are still subject to the future implications of the relationship (for instance, the tax levy by the state).

Table 2.2: Comparative analysis of notions of commercial revenues to the business entity, and operating inflows to the governmental entity[24]

---

[24] Adapted from Biondi, (2016), Table 1, p. 209.

Commercial revenues are the backbone of the financial economy of the business firm. Consequently, the business accounting system requires them to recover outflows (either values, cash or economic outflows, see section 3.3 below). However, in the normal functioning of the public sector entity, no such things as commercial revenues exist. Not only taxes and transfers, but also the direct operating inflows (contributions) generated by public sector entities providing services for a consideration do not usually involve prices fixed in commercial transactions (Table 2.2, right column). According to the US Governmental Accounting Standards Board[25]:

> *Businesses receive revenues from a voluntary exchange between a willing buyer and seller, governments obtain resources primarily from the involuntary payment of taxes. Taxes paid by an individual taxpayer often bear little direct relationship to the services received by that taxpayer.*

3.1.2 Public debt and monetary base management

Central government is deemed to be financially sustainable when it can pursue its ongoing public benefit missions while fulfilling its financial obligations when they are due in time and amount.[26]

This financial capacity depends not only on tax revenues but also on public debt management.[27] In this context, governmental debt capacity consists in placing sovereign debt – for sake of debt issuance and refinancing – with: (i) governmental entities; (ii) resident and

---

[25] GASB (2006), 'Why Are Separate Accounting and Financial Reporting Standards Essential for Governments?', p. 1.

[26] Biondi (2018).

[27] Biondi (2016).

foreign debt-holding investors; (iii) monetary financial institutions (banks); and (iv) central banking. The latter two placements relate to the monetary base management (so-called monetization). Financial markets may facilitate some of these transactions on sovereign debt.

Therefore, fiscal policies, welfare policies and public debt management are linked, while governmental debt capacity constitutes an integral part of its financial sustainability.

3.1.3 Public debt management for redistribution purpose

Governmental borrowing is systematically employed to both "wake-up" sleeping cash hoardings, and to manage the monetary base. On the one hand, governmental borrowing generates additional spending by mobilizing cash holdings held by households and other final investors. On the other hand, placement of governmental debt in portfolios managed by financial institutions relates to monetary base creation and administration. Last but not least, when central banks issue currency and grant loans to financial institutions, government debt may be (and generally is) bought or collateralized. This joint process makes governmental debt an essentially monetary phenomenon.[28]

This process is made possible by continued refinancing of governmental debt at every capital installments. When one cohort of debt securities becomes due, a new debt issuance is performed to replace the expiring one. In this way, the governmental entity can sustain a virtually permanent negative balance (deficit spending), as long as lenders go on subscribing its refinancing issuances over time and circumstances. Public deficit spending is then functionally connected with public debt refinancing.[29]

---

[28] Biondi (2018).

[29] Biondi (2016 and (2018).

From the viewpoint of individual holders, governmental debt is to be remunerated by interest charges and repaid by capital installments at its nominal value. However, at the aggregate level, governmental borrowing enables transferring these borrowed funds in view to redistribute them across citizens. As Macaulay[30] explained,

> *here it is sufficient to say that the prophets of evil were under a [...] delusion. They erroneously imagined that there was an exact analogy between the case of an individual who is in debt to another individual and the case of a society which is in debt to a part of itself; and this analogy led them into endless mistakes about the effect of the system of funding.*

These 'prophets' – in Macaulay's words - neglect the dynamic and collective dimensions of public debt management, misunderstanding the economic effects of its financial process of borrowing. On the one hand, governmental debt relates to the use of borrowing to fulfil public benefit missions with an overall redistributive purpose (welfare policies). On the other hand, it relates to the monetary base management (monetary policies).

Governmental borrowing does not, of course, create legal-tender money and still less does it create real goods and services. It is employed to fund transfers and non-market provision of goods and services. It does, therefore, something – it is perhaps easier to see this in the case of expansion of monetary base to finance public expenditure – which, in its economic effects, may lead to the creation of real goods and services that could not have been created without this practice. Social welfare improvement is therefore not synonymous of absolute or relative reduction of governmental debt (Biondi 2016).

---

[30] Macaulay (1848, p. 400).

3.1.4 Assurance of social protection (social benefits)

A further specificity relates to the connection of public debt management to general interest missions performed by governments to assure collective obligations and guarantees over time and circumstances. On the one hand, the refinancing mechanism (see Section 3.1.3 above) enables issuing fresh debt to roll over debt obligations that become due, instead of repaying them from tax revenues. On the other hand, collective assurances may eventually become future payments in due course, but governmental entities are not yet liable for them today.

Pension commitments provide an illustrative example of these collective assurances. For instance, 'pay-as-you-go' pension schemes refer to a system of paying pensions when due; consequently, these schemes are generally unfunded and do not involve refinancing needs on their financial position until pension payments become due. Moreover, a decrease on interest rates facilitates their financial sustainability, contrary to funded defined contribution pension schemes.[31]

The same analysis applies to collective guarantees and contingencies that may presently exist as potential (but not yet actual) governmental obligations. Pension and other collective commitments are assured by governments as general interest missions, in view to achieve intergenerational solidarity and redistribution purposes (welfare policies).

3.2 Features of public sector accounting representation

According to the GASB's White Paper:[32]

Governments are fundamentally different from for-profit business enterprises in several important ways. They have different

---

[31] Biondi and Boisseau-Sierra (2017b) and (2018).

[32] GASB (2006), 'executive summary', p. 1.

purposes, processes of generating revenues, stakeholders, budgetary obligations, and propensity for longevity.

Consequently, "the purpose of government is to enhance or maintain the well-being of citizens by providing public services in accordance with public policy goals"[33]. So-called revenues are operating inflows which are not generated by commercial transactions, contrary to the business entity (see Table 2.2 and Section 3.1.1 above), while public spending has to be made accountable to citizens and their representatives by law. Therefore, "governmental budgets can be the primary method by which citizens and their elected representatives hold the government's management financially accountable"[34].

In this context, the government consummates resources acquired through taxation and borrowing, so as to redistribute them at the macroeconomic level. In turn, citizens contribute with resources to be redistributed by paying taxation and subscribing governmental debt issuance and refinancing (including for monetary base management). Moreover, the government takes non-debt commitments on behalf of its constituencies.

This specific financial economy of governments makes them different from business entities and requires a specific accounting representation. According to Chan[35]:

> *Government accounting and financial reporting aims to protect and manage public money and discharge accountability. These purposes, and the nature of public goods and tax financing, give rise to differences with commercial accounting.*

---

[33] GASB (2006), 'Major Environmental Differences between Government and Businesses', p. 6.

[34] GASB (2006), Major Environmental Differences between Government and Businesses, p. 9.

[35] (2003), abstract.

To be sure, this specific economic process has never prevented modern states to be funded and refinanced for centuries by final investors active on Securities Exchanges (see Section 2.3). Investment practice has been accepting for long that structural debt is issued and refinanced over time to cover governmental expenditure, including for but not limited to investment purpose.

From this perspective, the accounting system is expected to represent the governmental entity as a going concern. Public sector accounting system shall be carefully designed to cope with public sector specificities (see Section 3.1 above), including but not limited to absence of commercial revenues, public debt and monetary base management, public debt management for redistribution purpose, and assurance of social protection (social benefits). Both the cash basis and the accrual basis of accounting should be adapted to properly represent these specificities.

3.3 Cash basis and accrual basis of accounting

The dialogue between public sector and business accounting systems is not new. From an historical perspective, public administrations have been generally reluctant to adopt merchant book-keeping for functional, ideal and political reasons.[36]

From a theoretical perspective, a convergence with the business sector would be "straightforward" only if a unique business accounting model existed. However, as a matter of fact, at least three main accounting models have been proposed for the business enterprise:[37]

---

[36] Lemarchand (2010); Monsen (2002).

[37] This approach disentangling static (current value) and dynamic (historical cost) accounting draws upon the original work by E. Schmalenbach, E. Walb and other accounting thinkers especially from Germany, Italy and US throughout the first half of the XX century; see Biondi and Zambon (2012) for an historical overview of national traditions.

- A static model (patrimonial, wealth-basis), focusing on the net worth of the enterprise and its valuation at a specific moment in time;
- A financial model (cash flow-basis), focusing on the financial inflows and outflows of the enterprise; it represents the resources available, at a particular time, to meet the needs or purposes of the enterprise;
- A dynamic model (economic flow-basis), focusing on the economic inflows and outflows of the enterprise; it represents the resources absorbed by the activities of the enterprise during a particular period.

These views imply very different configurations for the business accounting system (Table 2.3).

	Static model	**Financial model**	**Dynamic model**
Orientation	*Wealth*	*Cash Flows*	*Income*
Focus	*Net worth*	*Resources available*	*Resources mobilized (and utilized)*
Basis of reference	*Properties and claims*	*Cash outflows and inflows*	*Matching of costs and revenues*
Timing	*Moment in time; changes between moments*	*Time period*	*Time period*
Recovery of ...	**Values conferred**	**Cash outflows**	**Costs absorbed**

Table 2.3: Variety of business accounting models
(adapted from Biondi 2012, Table 1, p. 605)

In particular, these models imply a very different notion of **recovery**:

- The **static model** (patrimonial) asks: did the entity recover the *values* invested in the enterprise by its owners?
- The **financial model** (cash flow) asks: did the entity recover the *financial outflows* incurred by the enterprise during a period of time?
- The **dynamic model** (economic) asks: did the entity recover the *costs* absorbed by the enterprise during a period of time?

The static model is consistent with a current value basis of accounting, a balance sheet approach and a stock method of accounting. The latter constitute the background of international accounting standards (both IAS/IFRS and IPSAS). The financial model is consistent with a cash basis of accounting and a cameral accounting approach (see section 2.3 above) which featured the public sector accounting system through history in several European countries. The dynamic model is consistent with a cost basis of accounting, an income statement approach and a flow method of accounting. The latter used to be the backbone of business sector generally accepted accounting principles in the 20th century.[38] In fact, this dynamic model may be made compatible with the financial model.[39]

Because of a variety of accounting models for business, the so-called 'accrual basis' of accounting cannot be applied straightforwardly to the public administration. No such a thing as one accrual basis of accounting exists. Public sector specificities require a careful adaptation of the accrual basis of accounting. A public

---

[38] Biondi (2011); Biondi and Zambon (2012).
[39] Biondi and Oulasvirta (2022).

sector accounting model has to be developed to cope with public sector specificities. In this context, instead of replacing cash basis of accounting, an accrual basis of accounting may be adapted to become complementary to, and compatible with budgeting by combining a flow method of accounting with an historical cost accounting approach.[40]

In particular, financial sustainability for central government is framed and shaped by the specific use of governmental debt for non-market, redistributive purpose.[41] Accordingly, under an accrual basis of financial accounting, accrued deficit or surplus (resulting from a balance between expenses and contributions attached to the same period, and its accumulation over time) acquires a distinctive meaning that is different from accrued business income: be it positive or negative, this matching balance shows ongoing capacity of contributions (mainly taxation, in case of governments) to cover incurred expenses.[42]

This interpretation points to a featuring difference with the business enterprise. In the business context, enterprises seek for profits. Consequently, accrued business income provides a key indicator of financial performance, since the latter depends on the capacity of the business to transform incurred expenses in commercial revenues through time. In the public sector context, financial performance depends on the capacity of the entity to cover incurred expenses through time, while the overall performance relates to the satisfaction of general interest needs through non-lucrative activities which are paid by those expenses.

Generally speaking, concerning the public sector, accrual-based (accumulated) balance is materially negative and has

---

[40] Biondi (2012); Biondi and Oulasvirta (2022). See also Chapters 3 and 4.
[41] Biondi (2016).
[42] Biondi (2012).

increased over time for central governments all around the world. This fact has surely been the case throughout the twentieth century, showing that modern states employ debt issuance (and refinancing) to cover for operational expenses (see also Figures 2.2 and 2.3). Accordingly, governmental borrowing performs a specific economic function as a macroeconomic redistributive policy: in a nutshell, governments employ debt to redistribute incomes and fortunes across stakeholders over space and time.[43]

3.4 New Public Management (NPM) and New Public Governance (NPG)

Recent reforms driven by NPM and NPG ideology aim to align public sector and business sector accounting systems.[44] These reforms constitute yet another unfolded evolution whose implications have to be assessed over time and in context. Generally speaking, they claim for privatisations and outsourcing of public service including through private-public partnerships (whenever possible), deregulation, downsizing of public administration including tenured public servants, private auditing on public sector entities, and an overall favour for the business sector and the private financial sector. These reforms were accompanied by a preferred reference to international standards in many fields including accounting regulation – the case of the International Public Sector Accounting Standards (IPSAS) being emblematic here -, along with fostering emission of sovereign debt on international financial markets, denominated in either local or foreign currencies.

---

[43] Biondi (2016).

[44] Hood (1991); Osborne (201); Biondi (2012) providing further references.

Figure 1.9. Outstanding central government marketable debt in OECD countries, 2007-2021, nominal and as a percentage of GDP

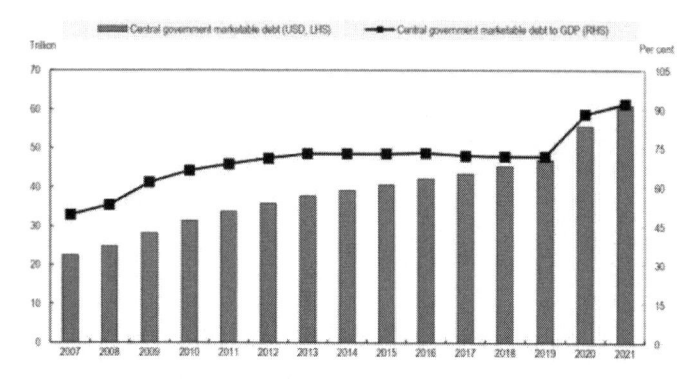

Source: 2020 Survey on Central Government Marketable Debt and Borrowing; OECD Economic Outlook (December 2020); IMF World Economic Outlook Database (October 2020); Refinitiv, national authorities' websites and OECD calculations.

Chart1: Balance sheets of the Eurosystem, the FED and the BoJ (in amounts and as a % of GDP)

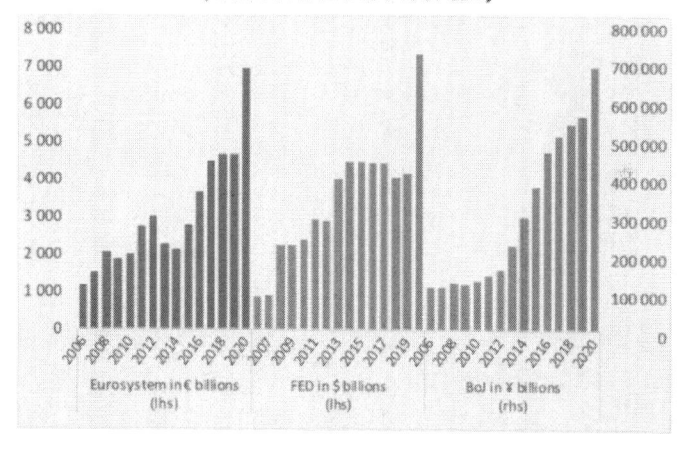

Figure 2.2: Central Government Debt Outstanding and Total Assets of Central Banks since 2007
Sources: OECD (2021), Figure 1.9 (left panel); Banque de France (2021), Chart1 (right panel), reprinted with permission[45]

---

[45] Balance sheets of the European Central Bank and related network (Eurosystem), the US Federal Reserve (FED) and the Bank of Japan - BoJ (in amounts). Data retrieved from: ECB, FED, BoJ. Amount in billions of euros (G€), dollars (G$), and yen (G¥).

85

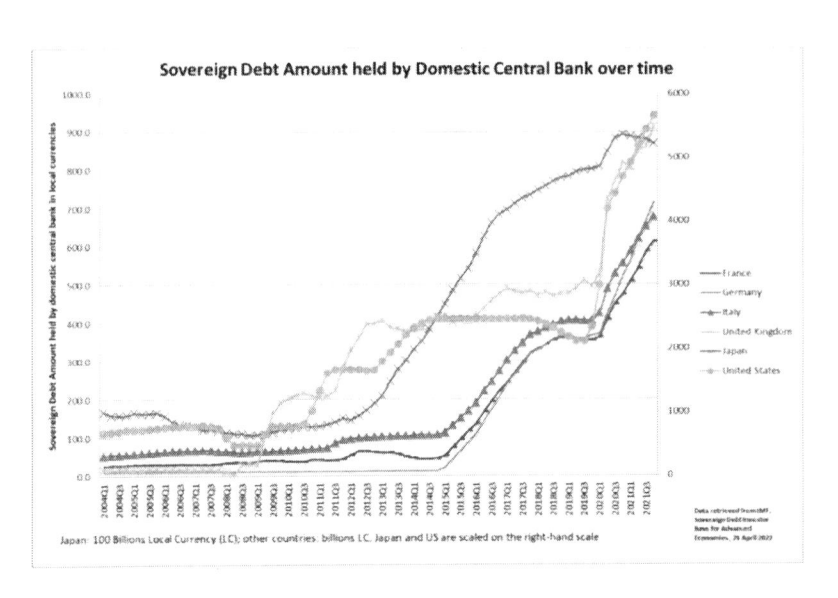

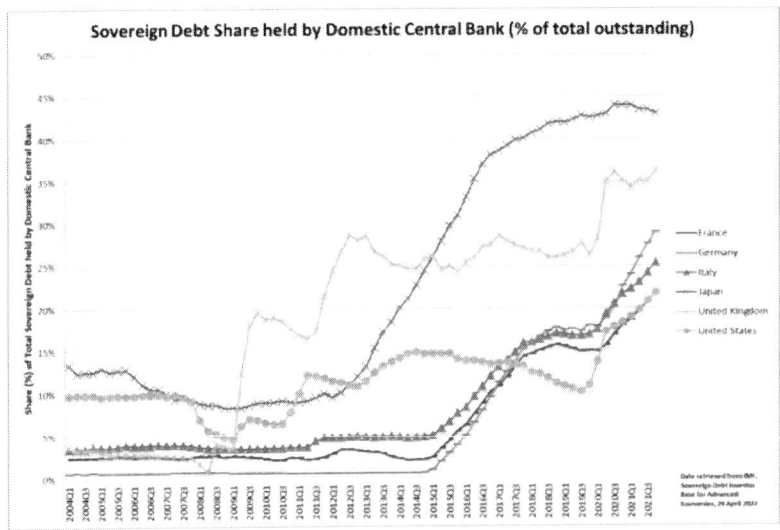

Figure 2.3: Sovereign Debt Amount and Share held by Domestic Central Banks over time
Source: Data retrieved from International Monetary Fund - IMF, Sovereign Debt Investor Base for Advanced Economies, 29 April 2022, designed by Arslanalp & Tsuda (2014) [46]

---

[46] Database weblink: https://www.imf.org/~/media/Websites/IMF/imported-datasets/external/pubs/ft/wp/2012/Data/_wp12284.ashx

So far, these reforms did not challenge the specificities of governments as denoted above. Quite the contrary, these specificities have been magnified by the response to the financial crisis of 2007-8, the pandemic management of 2020-22, the war in Ukraine since 2022 and the related energy crisis in Europe and abroad. Central banking, public debt issuances and governmental guarantees stand at the core of the public policy response to all these crises (Figures 2.2 and 2.3). Moreover, central banking has been further involved in supporting climate change policy, including in the European Union (ECB 2022). To be sure, new public management and new public governance reforms have been affecting the ways public money is managed, gathered and allocated, reshaping the redistributive effects of public policies across stakeholders.

4. Concluding remarks

Public sector (governmental) accounting has been co-evolving with public finances and the financial organisation of the state through history and contexts. This chapter has briefly summarised its historical evolution through examples from ancient civilisations, the feudal state and the modern state, which is featured by the connection between state authority, the organisation of state fiscal capacity, and the management of state borrowing. This financial organisation emerged progressively and became the backbone of the modern state by the end of the eighteenth century, when tax and debt became structural elements of public finances of all Western European countries.

Under this financial organisation, some specificities feature the financial economy of public administration: absence of commercial revenues; public debt and monetary base management; public debt management for redistribution purpose; and assurance of social protection (social benefits) through non-debt commitments.

Public sector accounting has to properly represent these specificities while assuring the purposes of accountability and control which appear to be constitutive of institutional framework of governments. Its core through modern history have been the fight against misappropriation, fraud and embezzlement; prevention of financial distress; and budgeting including prospective budgeting.

By referring and adopting accounting models and practices from the business sector in the wake of the NPM and NPG ideas, public sector accounting may mislead public sector management away from its general interest missions, transforming public sector activities in for-profit ventures which would neglect their role in achieving intergenerational solidarity and redistribution purposes (social welfare).

Bibliographic references

This chapter benefited from previous work by Wynne (2018a and 2018b). Previous versions of this research work were read as keynote speech at the EGPA Permanent Study Group XII "Public Sector Financial Management" Spring Workshop, Rostock, on 3-4 May 2018, and as virtual research seminar at the University of Tampere, on 15 December 2021.

References

ARISTOTLE (1888) – Politics. English translation: A Treatise on Government, translated from the Greek by William Ellis, London: Routledge.

ARSLANALP, Serkan and TSUDA, Takahiro (2014) – Tracking Global Demand for Advanced Economy Sovereign Debt, IMF Economic Review, Volume 62, Number 3, Washington DC.

BANQUE DE FRANCE (2021) – Understanding the expansion of central banks' balance sheets, authored by Emmanuel Cerclé, Hervé Le Bihan and Michaël Monot, Eco

Notepad Post n°209, Paris. URL: https://blocnotesdeleco.banque-france.fr/en/blog-entry/understanding-expansion-central-banks-balance-sheets

BAXTER, Stephen B. (1957) – The Development of the Treasury, 1660-1702, London, Cambridge, Mass.: Harvard University Press.

BÉGUIN, Katia and Jean-Philippe GENET (2017) – Taxation and the Rise of the State: Introductory Remarks. Béguin, Katia, and Anne L. Murphy (eds.) State Cash Resources and State Building in Europe 13th-18th century. Paris: Institut de la gestion publique et du développement économique, 2017. URL: <http://books.openedition.org/igpde/3809>.

BESSON, Emmanuel (1901) – Le contrôle des budgets en France et à l'étranger : étude historique et critique sur le contrôle financier des principaux États depuis les temps les plus reculés jusqu'à nos jours (2e édition). Paris : A. Chevalier-Marescq. URL : https://gallica.bnf.fr/ark:/12148/bpt6k5549250p

BEZES, Phillippe, DESCAMPS, Florence, KOTT, Sébastien and TALLINEAU, Lucile (2013) eds. – L'invention de la gestion des finances publiques. Du contrôle de la dépense à la gestion des services publics (1914-1967). Paris: Institut de la gestion publique et du développement économique. doi:10.4000/books.igpde.2886

BINNEY, John Edward Douglas (1958) – British Public Finance and Administration 1774-1792, Oxford, Clarendon Press.

BIONDI, Yuri (2011). – The Pure Logic of Accounting: A Critique of the Fair Value Revolution. Accounting, Economics, and Law, 1(1). https://doi.org/10.2202/2152-2820.1018

BIONDI, Yuri (2012) – Should Business and Non-Business Accounting be Different? A Comparative Perspective Applied to the French Central Government Accounting Standards, Vol. 35: International Journal of Public Administration, pp. 603-619. DOI: https://doi.org/10.1080/01900692.2012.661186

BIONDI, Yuri (2016) – Accounting representations of public debt and deficits in European central government accounts: An exploration of anomalies and contradictions. Accounting Forum, DOI: http://dx.doi.org/10.1016/j.accfor.2016.05.003

BIONDI, Yuri (2016) – Debt Capacity and Financial Sustainability in Central Government. Entry in: Global Encyclopedia of Public Administration, Public Policy, and Governance. Edited by Ali Farazmand, November. DOI: http://link.springer.com/referenceworkentry/10.1007/978-3-319-31816-5_2269-1

BIONDI, Yuri (2018) – The Financial Sustainability Conundrum in Central Government. Accounting, Economics, and Law: A Convivium. DOI: http://dx.doi.org/10.1515/ael-2018-0003

BIONDI, Yuri and BOISSEAU-SIERRA, Marion (2017a) – Financial Sustainability and Public Debt Management in Central Government. Chapter in: M. P. R. Bolívar ed. Financial Sustainability in Public Administrations, Basingstoke (UK): Palgrave Macmillan Pub. URL: http://dx.doi.org/10.1007/978-3-319-57962-7_7

BIONDI, Yuri and BOISSEAU-SIERRA, Marion (2017b) – Pension Obligations in the European Union: A Case Study for Accounting Policy. Accounting, Economics, and Law: A Convivium, 7(3), 20170027. https://doi.org/10.1515/ael-2017-0027

BIONDI, Yuri and BOISSEAU-SIERRA, Marion (2018) – Pension Management between Financial Market Development and Intergenerational Solidarity: A Socio-Economic

Analysis and a Comprehensive Model. Socio-Economic Review, Volume 16, Issue 4, October, Pages 791–822, https://doi.org/10.1093/ser/mwx015

BIONDI, Yuri and OULASVIRTA, Lasse (2022) – Accounting for public sector assets: Comparing historical cost and current value models, chapter in: Josette Caruana, Marco Bisogno, Mariafrancesca Sicilia eds. Measurement of Assets and Liabilities in Public Sector Financial Reporting: theoretical basis and empirical evidence, Emerald Publishing, forthcoming.

BIONDI, Yuri and ZAMBON, Stefano (2012) eds. – Accounting and Business Economics: Insights from National Traditions, New York: Routledge. DOI: https://doi.org/10.4324/9780203094723

BONNEY, Richard and ORMROD, William Mark (1999) – Introduction, chapter in: W. M. Ormrod and R. Bonney (eds.), Crises, revolutions and self-sustained growth. Essays in European fiscal history, 1130–1830, Stamford: Shaun Tyas, pp. 1-21.

BORDO, Michel D. (2007) – A Brief History of Central Banks, Federal Reserve Bank of Cleveland, December, Cleveland/OH.

BUCHHOLZ, Werner (1992) – Öffentliche Finanzen und Finanzverwaltung im entwickelten frühmodernen Staat : Landesherr und Landstände in Schwedisch-Pommern, 1720-1806, Cologne, Böhlau.

CANZIANI, Arnaldo and CAMODECA, Renato (2010) – Il Bilancio dello Stato nel Pensiero degli Aziendalisti Italiani, Universita degli Studi di Brescia, Dipartimento di Economia Aziendale, paper n. 100, Febbraio.

CARMONA, Salvador and EZZAMEL, Mahmoud (2007) – "Accounting and accountability in ancient civilizations: Mesopotamia and ancient Egypt", Accounting, Auditing & Accountability Journal, Vol. 20 No. 2, pp. 177-209

CHAN, James L. (2003) – Government Accounting: An Assessment of Theory, Purposes and Standards, Public Money & Management, 23:1, 13-20, DOI: 10.1111/1467-9302.00336

CHATFIELD, Michael and VANGERMEERSCH, Richard (1996) eds. – The History of Accounting: An International Encylopedia, Oxon: Routledge.

FUNNELL, Warwick; COOPER, Kathie; LEE, Janet (2012) – Public sector accounting and accountability in Australia. (2 ed.). Sydney, Australia: UNSW Press.

CORONELLA, Stefano (2007) – Lo sviluppo della contabilità di Stato nel XIX secolo: il contributo dei 'precursori' dell'Economia aziendale, Rivista Italiana di Ragioneria e di Economia Aziendale, 107, 7-8.

DECLARATION OF HUMAN AND CIVIC RIGHTS of 26 August 1789, official translation provided by the Conseil Constitutionnel). URL: https://www.conseil-constitutionnel.fr/sites/default/files/as/root/bank_mm/anglais/cst2.pdf

DUBET, Anne and LEGAY, Marie-Laure Avant-Propos, in : LEGAY Marie-Laure (dir.), – Dictionnaire historique de la comptabilité publique (1500-1850), Rennes : PUR, 2010.

ECB – European Central Bank (2022) – Climate Change and the ECB, institutional webpage, Frankfurt an Main. URL: https://www.ecb.europa.eu/ecb/climate/html/index.en.html

FILIOS, Vassilios (1983) – The Cameralistic Method of Accounting – A Historical Note, Autumn, 10(3): Journal of Business Finance & Accounting, pp. 443-450.

FORRESTER, David A. R. (1990) – Rational Administration, Finance and Control Accounting: The Experience of Cameralism, 1(4): Critical Perspectives on Accounting, pp. 285-317.

GASB – Governmental Accounting Standards Board (2006) – Why Governmental Accounting and Financial Reporting Is – and Should Be – Different, White Paper, Norwalk, CT: GASB.

HOOD, Christopher (1991) – A Public Management for all Seasons?", Public Administration. 69 (1): 3–19. DOI:10.1111/j.1467-9299.1991.tb00779.x

HUMBERT, Gustave (1886) – Essai sur les finances et la comptabilité publique chez les Romains, 2 Volumes, Paris : Ernest Thorin Editeur.

LAGROUE, Lance Elliot (2014) – Accounting and Auditing in Roman Society, PhD Dissertation, University of North Carolina At Chapel Hill.

LEGAY, Marie-Laure (2010) ed. – Dictionnaire historique de la comptabilité publique (1500-1850), Rennes: PUR.

LEMARCHAND, Yannick (2010) – «Parties doubles », entry in : Legay M.-L. (dir.), Dictionnaire historique de la comptabilité publique (1500-1850), Rennes: PUR, 2010.

MACAULAY, Thomas Babington (1848) – The History of England from the Accession of James II, Vol. IV, Philadelphia: Porter & Coates [1848/1887].

MARGAIRAZ, Michel (1991) – L'État, les finances et l'économie. Histoire d'une conversion 1932-1952. Vincennes: Institut de la gestion publique et du développement économique, 1991. URL: http://books.openedition.org/igpde/2276

MONSEN, Norvald (2002) – The Case for Cameral Accounting. Financial Accountability & Management, 18: 39-72.

NAZAROV, Dmitry and SIDOROVA, Marina (2016) – Russian Public Sector Accounting: The Case of Experimental Estate Konskaya Volya (1893-1905). 10.2991/icaat-16.2016.36

NORMANTON, E. Leslie (1966) – The Accountability and Audit of Governments: a comparative study, Manchester: Manchester University Press and New York: Frederick A. Praeger.

NORTH, Douglass C. and WEINGAST, Barry R. (1989) – Constitutions and commitment: the evolution of institutions governing public choice in seventeenth-century England. The Journal of Economic History, 49 (4), 803-832.

OECD (2021) – OECD Sovereign Borrowing Outlook 2021, OECD Publishing, Paris. DOI: https://doi.org/10.1787/48828791-en

OSBORNE, Stephen P. (2010) ed. – The New Public Governance? Emerging perspectives on the theory and practice of public governance. London and New York: Routledge.

PLATONOVA, Natalia V. (2017) – Accounting and the Reforms of Government in Eighteenth-Century Russia, Jahrbücher für Geschichte Osteuropas , 2017,65(2), pp. 200-238. URL: https://www.jstor.org/stable/26381419

QU'RAN, Surah Baqarah Ayat, URL: https://myislam.org/surah-baqarah/ayat-282/

RUSSELL, Frederick H. (1975) – The just war in the Middle Ages, Cambridge, Cambridge University Press.

SCHNEIDER, Franz (1952) – Geschichte der formellen Staatswirtschaft von Brandenburg-Preussen, Berlin, Duncker & Humblot.

TEICHOVA, Alice and MATIS, Herbert (2003) eds. – Nation, State and the Economy in History. Cambridge: Cambridge University Press. DOI: 10.1017/CBO9780511497575

WAQUET, Jean-Claude (1990) – Le Grand-duché de Toscane sous les derniers Médicis, Ecole française de Rome.

WYNNE, Andy (2018a) – History of public sector accounting and alternatives, chapter 2 in Peter C. LORSON, Susana JORGE, Ellen HAUSTEIN (eds.), European Public Sector Accounting, Coimbra: Coimbra University Press. DOI: 10.14195/978-989-26-1861-6_2

WYNNE, Andy (2018b) – Difference between private and public sector accounting, chapter 3 in Peter C. LORSON, Susana JORGE, Ellen HAUSTEIN (eds.), European Public Sector Accounting, Coimbra: Coimbra University Press. DOI: 10.14195/978-989-26-1861-6_3

ZAID, Omar Abdullah (2004) – Accounting Systems and Recording Procedures in the Early Islamic State. The Accounting Historians Journal, vol. 31, no. 2, 2004, pp. 149–70. JSTOR: http://www.jstor.org/stable/40698304

ZANNINI, Andrea (1994) – Il Sistema di revisione contabile della Serenissima. Istituzioni, personale, procedure (secc. XVI-XVIII), Venise, Albrizzi editore.

Additional readings

BIONDI, Yuri (2012) – Should Business and Non-Business Accounting be Different? A Comparative Perspective Applied to the French Central Government Accounting Standards, Vol. 35: International Journal of Public Administration, pp. 603-619. DOI: https://doi.org/10.1080/01900692.2012.661186

BIONDI, Yuri (2016) – Accounting representations of public debt and deficits in European central government accounts: An exploration of anomalies and contradictions. Accounting Forum, DOI: http://dx.doi.org/10.1016/j.accfor.2016.05.003

BIONDI, Yuri (2018) – The Financial Sustainability Conundrum in Central Government. Accounting, Economics, and Law: A Convivium. DOI: http://dx.doi.org/10.1515/ael-2018-0003

BIONDI, Yuri and BOISSEAU-SIERRA, Marion (2017) – Financial Sustainability and Public Debt Management in Central Government. Chapter in: M. P. R. Bolívar ed. Financial Sustainability in Public Administrations, Basingstoke (UK): Palgrave Macmillan Pub. URL: http://dx.doi.org/10.1007/978-3-319-57962-7_7

WYNNE, Andy (2018a) – History of public sector accounting and alternatives, chapter 2 in Peter C. LORSON, Susana JORGE, Ellen HAUSTEIN (eds.), European Public Sector Accounting, Coimbra: Coimbra University Press. DOI: 10.14195/978-989-26-1861-6_2

WYNNE, Andy (2018b) – Difference between private and public sector accounting, chapter 3 in Peter C. LORSON, Susana JORGE, Ellen HAUSTEIN (eds.), European Public Sector Accounting, Coimbra: Coimbra University Press. DOI: 10.14195/978-989-26-1861-6_3

Discussion topics

- Implications of public sector accounting history for current public sector accounting
- Applicability of private sector accounting standards to the public sector
- The role of public debt management and its implications for public sector accounting

CHAPTER 3
BUDGETS AND BUDGETARY ACCOUNTING

Lasse Oulasvirta
Tampere University, Finland
lasse.oulasvirta@tuni.fi
https://orcid.org/0000-0003-4195-1331

Summary

This chapter describes various approaches to budgeting, which is the traditional essence of public sector accounting. This includes budget planning and budget-linked accounting. The roles and functions of budgets are presented as well as the ideas and practices of both traditional budgets and modern variants such as output- and performance-based budgets.

Keywords

Budget planning, budgetary accounting, budget models, types of appropriations

1. Introduction

In the public sector, the traditional core area of financial decision-making and management is related to budgeting and budget implementation. Elected representative bodies are the ultimate decision-makers in a democracy. One elementary part of this role is the budget power of the representative body.

The duty to be publicly accountable is more significant in government than in business financial reporting. As a consequence of the accountability of public administration to citizens and to their representative bodies (parliaments, councils, etc.), the principles of publicity and transparency are important in budgetary and financial reporting. This includes the lawful and regular behaviour of budget entities, compliance with the approved budget and striving to provide as much value as possible with the entrusted collective resources. Instead of the narrower profitability assessment in the private sector, in the public sector, the many-sided performance and value- for-money assessments are crucial.

Public sector budget structures and accounting conventions have been shaped by national practices. It is just lately that harmonisation pressures have emerged. Public sector accounting (PSA) is nowadays shaped more than ever before by international accounting standards, in addition to domestically developed accounting conventions. However, this international standardisation is more targeted to general-purpose financial statements than to budgets, and even this phenomenon is at an early stage in many countries.

In this Chapter 3 we first explain in Section 2 the budgetary accounting as one part of PSA. Section 3 is devoted to functions and principles of budgets such as the publicity and transparency principle. This is followed with a description of traditional annual budgets and modern variants such as performance-based budgets, and budget appropriations in Section 4 and budget-linked budgetary accounting in Section 5. The last section gives a conclusion.

2. Budgetary accounting in the family of PSA systems

The **budgetary accounting** approach emerges from the agreed budget in the public sector. Bookkeeping must follow the logic and structure of the budget regarding the allocation of income and expenditure to the correct budget codes. If the budget is cash-based, then the follow-up bookkeeping must also be cash-based. If the budget is accrual-based, then the follow-up bookkeeping must also be accrual-based.

Cash-based budgeting and accounting can achieve money control purposes in the public sector. Accrual budgeting means spending measured on a cost basis rather than on a cash basis.[1] Accrual budgeting and accrual accounting also serve the need for management information with their steering and control functions.

Link between budgeting and accounting

The chart of accounts for budgetary accounting is derived from the budget structure. Budget entities may establish more detailed accounts as subaccounts to those accounts derived from the budget for management accounting and intra-organisational steering and control purposes.

If budgetary accounting and financial accounting are on the same basis, these two accounting systems can be merged into one serving both budget reporting and financial statement reporting purposes. For instance, if the budget is on an accrual basis, the entries made during the year into the ledger make up a double-entry system that generates both the budget outturn reports (budget statements) and accrual based financial statements.

3. The functions and principles of budgets

Budgets in the public sector have several purposes. Annual legal budgets are normally supplemented with medium- to long-term

---

[1] Schick (2007), p. 118.

strategic multi-year plans. These are typically less legally binding, but more proactive and forward-thinking than annual budgets. They contain policy decisions regarding financing priorities, service provision priorities, etc.

Annual budget plans involve short-term planning by nature: they are financing and resource allocation tools for public sector entities. Available financing and resources are allocated to each department, unit and activity inside the organisation. Budgets contain not only allowed amounts of expenditure, but often also the amount and maybe also the quality standards of the services that are to be provided.

Annual budgets have a financial control function because the approved budget is used as a control tool during the budget year. Appropriations are authorisations to use money according to budget rules, and unauthorised use of resources should be prevented with budget control. Control should guarantee the compliance of activities and spending using the budget, budget laws, regulations and rules. In addition, counterproductive and wasteful use may be prevented with proper budget control. Auditors have the responsibility to report on any essential breaches that they may identify.

The reporting function is fulfilled by publishing budget plans, but also ex-post budget reports (budget outturn statements). Reporting may include both interim reports and final reports. Actual figures are compared to both the first approved and the final adjusted budget figures. Published final budget statements should be audited by professional and independent auditors.

Budgets are also a means of empowerment and delegation inside each public sector organisation. Along with the allocation of resources, the budget also aligns with the division of tasks to responsible budget entities inside the organisation. Furthermore, it is a communication device inside the organisation, and the budget and budget processes deliver information through the organisation. Budgeting also has behavioural aspects and effects on the budget entity's performance.

It serves at best as a motivation tool for personnel: for instance, it may reward good performance. It has an impact on budget entity managers' and all employees' motivation and behaviour.[2]

Accountability and transparency principles

International Public Sector Accounting Standard (IPSAS) 24 does not require budgets to be published. From the democracy, accountability and transparency point of view, it is self-evident that public sector budgets should be published. Published budgets, budget out-turn reports and the associated audit reports are key elements of public sector accountability.

Budgets, budget out-turn statements and audit reports of budget compliance and performance should be easily accessible to any addressee via up-to-date kept web pages. A very important factor here is that governments have established professional and independent public audit institutions.

In addition, one method of enhanced budget accountability and responsiveness to people living in the jurisdiction is to create public involvement in budgetary process through participatory budgeting practices.[3]

Other budget principles

In addition to publicity and transparency, some other important budget principles are explained below.[4]

---

[2] Coombs and Jenkins (2002), pp. 83-86; Bergmann (2009), pp. 44-48; Prowle (2010), pp. 189-191.

[3] Yilmaz and Beris 2008, pp. 16-41.

[4] Jones (1996), pp. 56-59; Coombs and Jenkins (2002); PSC (2004); Prowle (2010).

Budget preparers have the responsibility to anticipate and estimate all expenditure and revenue for the budget period. The completeness principle in budgeting means that all expenditures and revenues (gross) should be included and not be offset or netted off against each other.

Extra budgetary funds not included in the approved budget should be avoided. Furthermore, use of "off-budget" fiscal mechanisms should be very constrained. We may refer here to the OECD (Organisation for Economic Cooperation and Development) recommendation (2015):

> "Governments should include and explain public programs that are funded through non-traditional means – e.g. PPPs – in the context of the budget documentation, even where (for accounting reasons) they may not directly affect the public finances within the time frame of the budget document."[5]

PPP refers to Public-Private Partnership. This is a cooperative arrangement between at least one public and private sector actor typically of a long-term nature.[6] These PPP arrangements should be transparently explained in reporting.

The prudence principle in budget planning means deliberate avoidance of exaggerating revenues or understating expenses. However, this may be a disputed principle if its practice goes against the principle of unbiased information, which requires that preparers must not adjust figures to achieve certain predetermined results. The reasonable balance principle means that budgets should not lead to unsustainable indebtedness. We may also talk about a formal

---

[5] OECD (2015).

[6] Jones (1996), pp. 56-59; Coombs and Jenkins (2002); PSC (2004); Khan (2013); Prowle (2010); IPSAS 24.

budget financial balance rule that means that all budget expenditure must have corresponding budget financing. Public sector entities must plan budgets so that expenditures can be paid from incomes, loan income included. If their own revenues are not enough, public sector entities must borrow money (or use donations) to meet their obligations.

4. Traditional annual budgets and modern variants

Traditionally, local government budgets were split into recurrent budgets and capital budgets. In central government, it has been more usual to have only one comprehensive budget without splitting it.

Capital budgets include investments that the government is planning
– their timescale is often more than one year (for instance, infrastructure projects such as constructing highways, railways, tunnels, airports, harbours, universities, hospitals and so on).

Modern budgeting has been developed from detailed and strictly limited use of money to lump-sum budgets, one-line item allocations and the delegation of budgetary power to separate budget entities. This leaves more flexibility for the managers of budget entities to manage their entities
– when connected to performance-related rewards, this should lead to appropriate and productive behaviour in the budget entities.

Furthermore, one-line item budgets have often been connected to activity performance goals. This means that the counterpart to the added decision-making powers regarding budget entities operations is the added responsibility to produce outputs of defined quality and with desirable impacts on society.

Strategy-linked budgets are drawn up so that the annual budget functions as a tool to implement longer-term strategic goals. A new budget strand is the phenomenon-based budgeting, in which the budget decision-makers allocate earmarked resources, for instance, to carbon neutrality actions mitigating climate change, or to actions enhancing gender equality or the position of children in the budget allocation.

Budget appropriations

Decision rules connected to the budget are important. One vital aspect is how the budget money usage is authorised. An appropriation is an authorisation granted by a legislative body to allocate funds for purposes specified by the legislature or similar authority (IPSAS 24.7, definitions).

The timing basis of appropriations can be divided to three classes:

1) cash-based appropriations;
2) commitment-based appropriations; and
3) accrual-based appropriations.

Furthermore, another trait, the particularity of appropriations, is connected to how detailed or less detailed the appropriations are. Budget appropriations may be strictly detailed line item appropriations or, at the other end of the continuum, one-line (lump-sum) general appropriations.

Virement rules are a process of controlling the transfer of funds from one budget head to another. Virement rules may be stricter or more flexible from the point of view of the budget entities.

In addition, budget appropriations may be either fixed (restricted to the current year) or transferable (some ability to carry-forward part of the funds to the next year). The possibility to transfer usage of unspent appropriations to the next year is one factor that demotivates waste of public money before the end of the budget year.

Budget year: Appropriation transactions	X €	X+1 €
Appropriation – transferable	1,000	0
Spent part of the appropriation	700	
Unspent and transferred part	300	
Spending of the transferred part		300
Note: A two-year transferable appropriation for the whole expenditure is included in the budget for Year X (usable during X or X+1 years). €300 is not included in the budget for Year X+1, but is transferred from the appropriation for Year X.		

Table 3.1: Wholly transferable appropriations - example

If the government is using the carry-forward option, this prohibits waste in the end of the budget year. However, it may lead to excessive liquidity because all appropriations must have full cover on the financing side (the formal balancing requirement).

Another at least equally important factor is the choice between gross and net appropriations. Traditionally, public sector entities have had gross budgets. Nowadays, it is quite common for budget entities to have net appropriations. Net appropriations have both a spending portion and a revenue portion. They encourage budget entities to be active and creative in generating their own additional revenues.[7]

If net budgeted revenues are more than estimated in the budget, the entity may by its own decision increase its expenditure, as long as it does not exceed the net appropriation. In our example in Table 3.2, the net expenditure is fixed at 600 €.

Not all government revenues are suitable for net budgeting: tax incomes should not be earmarked for the tax agency's own

---

[7] Khan (2013), pp. 342-345, Brusca et al. (2015), OECD (2017), p. 19.

spending, neither should fines be earmarked for a police station's own spending.

Net budgeting is an incentive to innovate on the revenue side because revenues earned can be kept inside the budget entity for incurred expenditures as long as the net sum approved in the budget is not exceeded. There is also a risk to the net budget entity that the revenues fall below the estimate used in the approved budget. In that case, the budget entity will be required to reduce its expenditures to achieve the agreed level of net expenditure.

A) Gross budget entity	Budget €	Actual €
Expenditure	1,000	1,000
Income	400	500
B) Net budget entity	**Budget**	**Actual**
Expenditure	1,000	1,100
Income	400	500
Difference/ Net expenditure (=net appropriation)	600	600

Table 3.2: Gross versus net budgeting – an example

Innovativeness and improvements on the revenue side may thus be encouraged in budget entities when additional revenues earned are not lost to the Treasury or central financing office.

Traditionally public sector budgets have been prepared on a cash or modified cash basis. For these bases, the focus is on the money transfers and money control. Table 3.3 gives an example of a cash-based budget. The approved budgets allow cash outlays of 600 € during the first budget year and 400 € during the next budget year.

	Budget			
Cash basis	Budget year	X	X+1	Total
	Cash-based expenditure	600	400	1,000
	Actual payments	600	400	1,000
	Difference	0	0	0

Table 3.3: A cash-based budget – an example

There is a misunderstanding that governments have been using only a pure cash basis, while many governments have in reality been using not a pure but a modified cash basis. The short-term commitment basis in budgeting is an example of a modified cash basis. In this case, if goods or services are planned to be received in budget Year X, they may be paid in the first few months in Year X+1 and still belong to the budget Year X expenditure.

Budget planning should also take into consideration contracts, including goods or services that are received in later budget years that result in equivalent longer-term payment commitment. These payments should be included in the approved budgets for later years unless the government is using transferable appropriations that extend the usage of such appropriations beyond the current budget year.

	Budget year	X €	X+1 €	Total €
Commitment basis	Appropriation	700	300	1,000
	Account entries	700	300	1,000
	Spending margin	0	0	0
Note	Accounting for budget follow-up: 600 € was paid during Year X, and the budget entity has an obligation to pay a vendor 100 €. Accounts payable, credited with 100 € (expenses 700 €, bank account 600 € and accounts payables 100 €).			

Table 3.4: Commitment-based budget – an example

Accrual budgeting

What is accrual budgeting? According to Khan's definition:

> "Accrual budgeting means application of the accrual concept to the preparation and presentation of the budget. It entails planning that includes revenues and expenses in the budget of the year in which the underlying economic events are expected to occur, not necessarily in the year in which the related cash is expected to be received or paid."[8]

Accrual budgeting requires the application of generally accepted accounting principles in the preparation of the budget. However, accrual is not an overriding concept in accrual budgeting. According to Khan, for instance, estimating budgeted tax revenue on a long-term accrual basis (predicting future accruing tax incomes caused by taxable realised events in the budget year) could be subject to strong uncertainty (for instance, because of delayed taxation decisions, uncollectable taxes, etc.). Therefore, the estimate may be considered unreliable. In such a case, the accrual-based estimate may have to be changed to a measure that is closer to a cash-based estimate.

The reliability concept may override the accrual concept in PSA and budgeting. The accrual budget may also recognise cash implications of budgetary decisions. For instance, in Britain departments have both an accrual based appropriation and a cash limit. The accrual budget structure implies the use of both prospective accrual operating statements and cash flow statements. The accrual budget may also contain a prospective balance sheet with projected assets, liabilities and net equity .

---
[8] Khan (2013), p. 340.

In practice, accrual budgeting does not entail a systematic use of accrual appropriations in OECD countries. Many countries use a mix of accrual and cash appropriations. Examples of items that may not be included in budgetary appropriations include the following:

- Provisions;
- Depreciations, inventory value changes;
- Losses arising from changes in market values of assets and liabilities.

Examples of budgetary appropriations/revenue estimates kept on a cash basis in (modified) accrual budgets include:

- Repayment of debts – cash basis;
- Tax revenues – cash basis.

Capital expenditures may require both accrual- and cash-based approval and legal control. Furthermore, accrual budgets may be combined with commitment appropriations – a government can have an accrual budget but exercise legislative control at the commitment stage. Usually, in practice, governments exercise controls over both cash items and accrual items.[9]

Proponents of accrual budgeting argue that it provides incentives to better manage capital assets, especially the acquisition, disposal and maintenance of fixed assets.

Planning and recording only cash movements may give too late information about the impacts of policy decisions. Accrual budgeting facilitates the better planning of investments and maintenance and also provides incentives for public sector or-

---

[9] Khan (2013), pp. 342-345; Brusca et al. (2015); OECD (2017), p. 19.

ganisations to dispose of assets that are unnecessary. It provides (and compels the planning of) more fiscal indicators than cash budgeting.[10]

However, presenting accrual budget information in a user-friendly manner is challenging. Scope for manipulation and creative accounting is increased because adjustments in discount rates, changing ways of capitalising expenses and revaluing assets and so on can be manipulated. Personnel, Information and Communication Technology capacity requirements may hinder accrual budgeting – it requires skilled staff and sophisticated information technology facilities.

New public financial management (NPFM) generally favours and promotes accrual-based budgeting. However, in practice, modified accrual- based budgeting is more realistic and popular than full accrual-based budgets. One reason for this is that full accrual-based budgeting requires high maturity in a country's accounting resources, information systems and accounting skills. In many countries, not all the preconditions of fully-fledged accrual basis are available in practice.

According to Schick, accrual budgeting is not ready for widespread application as a budget decision rule because of its complexity. However, for most countries it suffices rather as an analytical tool than a decision rule in budgeting. Without appropriate discretion, managers are likely to regard accruals as technical entries that have no bearing on the resources available for expenditures.[11]

A full accrual-based government budget structure is illustrated in Figure 3.1 below. After the budget year, the annual actual figures are reported in budget statements. Budget statements con-

---

[10] Based on Khan (2013), pp. 349-358.

[11] Schick (2007), pp. 131, 137-138.

tain comparisons between the approved budget plans and actual realised budget figures.

This figure shows some important influences from one part of a budget plan to another using the arrows. For instance, if the public sector entity invests in fixed assets (investment budget), this has ramifications for the operational recurrent budget because the asset in use typically creates depreciation expenses. It also has ramifications for the planned balance sheet and naturally for the cash flows during the budget period.

The annual margin before depreciations is the starting item in the cash flow budget. The net cash flow after operations and investments is an important balance ratio: if it is negative, it typically means that the local government must raise new debts. Net borrowing is shown in the funding cash flow section. After several adjustments that eliminate all non-cash items from the figures, the cash flow budget ends up showing the change in the liquid assets of the local government. If the local government has a buffer in its cash reserves, it may use also liquid assets to finance net investments.

A surplus or deficit in the income statement budget will show the anticipated influence on the net assets. Typically, a local government should aim to have an annual margin that covers its depreciations. If the result after depreciation is positive, the local government may earmark provisions for needed new investments or alternatively let the surplus accrue to the balance sheet. However, local governments should not accrue surpluses continuously because this would be a sign of collecting too much tax from local tax-payers.

Example of a full accrual-based local government budget structure

Recurrent budget impacts: maintenance costs, depreciations, etc.

- **Recurrent budget**
  - Operational units – expenses and revenues, depreciations, surplus/deficit of the unit, service performance goals (output and outcome)

- **Investment budget** Renovations and extensions of production machinery, property selling, external grants (net investments)

Sum of expenses and revenues, depreciations

Sum of investment expenditure, sum of received investment grants and sum of property selling income

- ■ Income statement budget
- ■ Balance of the recurrent activities
  - ❏ Annual (contribution) margin
  - ❏ Result after depreciations
  - ❏ Surplus/deficit

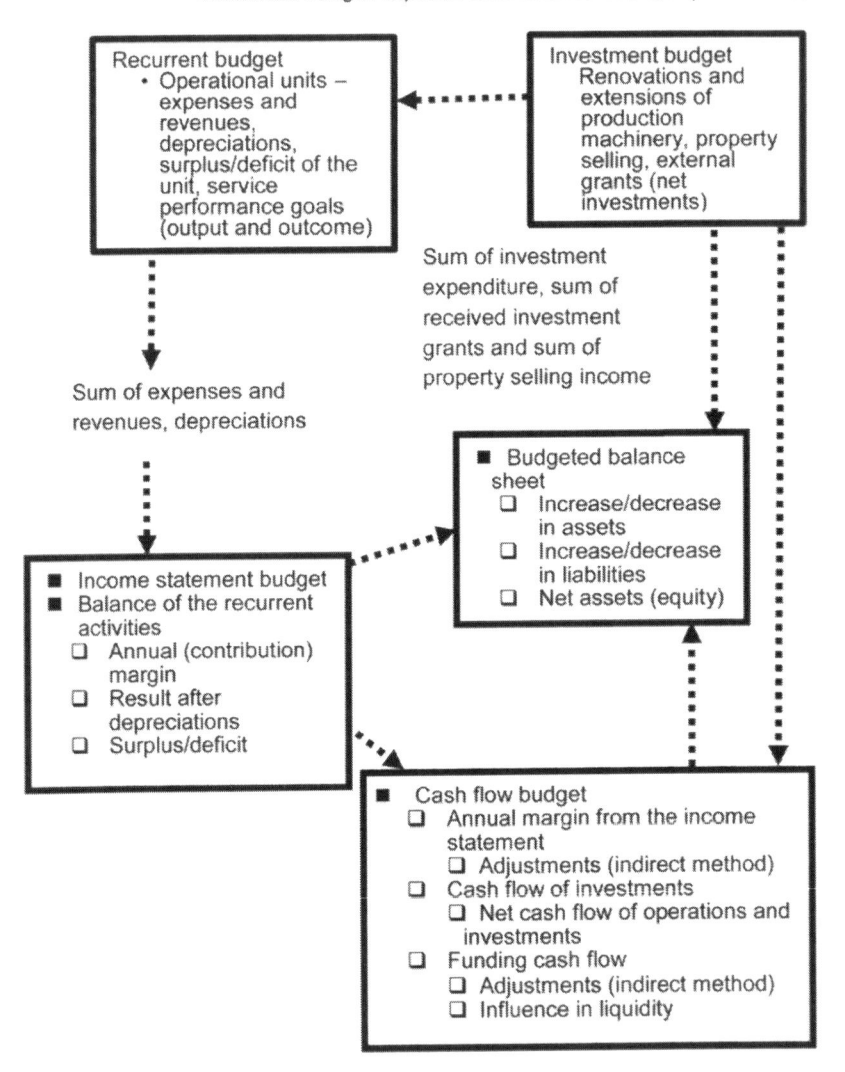

- ■ Budgeted balance sheet
  - ❏ Increase/decrease in assets
  - ❏ Increase/decrease in liabilities
  - ❏ Net assets (equity)

- ■ Cash flow budget
  - ❏ Annual margin from the income statement
    - ❏ Adjustments (indirect method)
  - ❏ Cash flow of investments
    - ❏ Net cash flow of operations and investments
  - ❏ Funding cash flow
    - ❏ Adjustments (indirect method)
    - ❏ Influence in liquidity

Figure 3.1: A full accrual-based budget with separate partial budget plans

In a fully-fledged accrual budget, the depreciation costs of fixed assets are included as appropriations. In addition, changes in the inventory and other accruals must be recognised in the budget according to the rules of business accounting.

Table 3.5 gives, for the reason of simplicity, an example of only depreciation costs in an accrual-based budget. Usually, depreciation costs are not an appropriation, but rather an informative element in the budget. However, it affects the accrual financial performance and the balance sheet. Budgets that are on a cash basis or commitment basis do not have depreciation costs in the budget, or such allocation items as changes of inventory during the accounting period.

	Budget items / Budget year	X €	X+1 €	Total €
Accrual basis	Operation (recurrent) budget and income statement budget			
Item example:	Depreciation costs	0	50	50
Note	The investment is planned in the investment budget. Straight-line depreciations 100 per year, the construction is taken into use 1.7.X+1 (so only half a year of depreciation in this year).			

Table 3.5: An accrual-based budget – an example of budgeted depreciation costs

The allocation of expenditures, expenses, incomes and revenues to the budget should be defined clearly. Appropriate financial management must have a systematic and consistent manner for how to budget; it cannot be done in an undefined way. Legally binding appropriations must be clearly defined so that they can be distinguished from other non-binding budget information. Budget decision-makers have the right to know and understand how the budget information and authorisations have been allocated to the annual budgets.

Performance-based budgeting

The so-called Planning – Programming – Budgeting System (PPBS) was invented in the 1960s based on the ideal rational planning and decision- making model that flows from overall goals to programmes and annual budgets all in perfect congruence with each other. This is a model that is closely related to the idea of strategy-linked budgeting.

Later the emphasis was laid on budgeting for results and for outcomes or performance-based budgeting. Input-based budgets have been transformed more or less into output- and outcome-based budgets (OBB) or performance-based budgets (PBB).

Activity goals 2022 Strategic	Means of implementation	Indicators
Promote care and welfare of the elderly Preventive treatment of the elderly A customer control system based on multi-agency service plans for those customers in need of personalized services.	Group-based services for old people increased, service group sizes decreased, recreational services increased in cooperation with non-profit organizations and volunteer operators.	Customers and customer visits in close daytime services have increased at least with 20 % compared to the level of 2020. Weekly cultural and physical exercised offered included in close daytime services for old people. A Service Barometer of customers satisfaction is collected and published at regular intervals.
Digitization of service supply	Digitalized service supply targeted to home care, sheltered nursing homes, family carers and rehabilitation service groups.	Customers of Remote Service of VideoVisit-increase during the year with 60 % compared to the year 2020. Usage of Remote Service will enlarge to customers using both home care and rehabilitation services, at least 10 customers participate yearly to remote rehabilitation.
Involvement of old people	Involvement of old people with the personal budget system.	The customers of the personal budget system (Hebu) during the first year of installment 2022 are at least three. Hebu-customers get multi-agency service, and their customer satisfaction is 4 in the measuring scale from 1 to 5.

Old people care 2022 (statistical data)	Number
Home care customers	175
Home care visits	77,340
Customers of support services (meal service, etc.)	260
Caring for close relatives, number of persons in dependent care	70
Residents in sheltered housing (outsourcing service)	90
Old people's home, bed days in long-term care	24,820

Table 3.6: Example of a performance budget (Finnish municipality of Lempäälä: Annual budget 2022, Old peoples' care service section of the annual budget).

The real-life example in Table 3.6 is from Finland. In Finland, output targets included in the approved budget are binding. Appropriations must be dimensioned in the original budget so that the output targets can be achieved. If it seems during the budget year that they cannot be achieved, either the goals, the appropriations or both must be changed by council decisions so that they are again compatible (the output targets must be achieved with the funding) in the final and executed budget.[12]

Generally, it is more difficult to calculate from qualitative outcome goals to costs than from quantitative output (product) goals to costs. Cost-effectiveness is in principle the ultimate key ratio in public sector activities, meaning that the budget money should be allocated and used in the best possible manner in providing outputs with desirable outcomes related to citizen needs and agreed activity goals. Economy alone is not a comprehensive yardstick, because it measures costs related to output – for instance, economy as euros/patient care operation – but not

---

[12] In Finland, output goals decided in the council are as binding budget rules as financial budget rules. Section 110 § (4) of the Local Government Act of 2015: "The budget shall include the appropriations and revenue estimates required to fulfil the duties and meet the operating targets, and an indication of how the financing requirement will be covered. The appropriations and the revenue estimates may be stated in gross or net terms. Budgets and financial plans shall have a section covering operational finances and an income statement, and a section on investment and financing."

effectiveness as euros/cured patient (outcome). In practice, it is many times easier to measure and report the cost per output figures than cost-effectiveness figures containing quality and impact assessments.

Budget reforms often go hand-in-hand with lump-sum budgeting, which means that budget authorisations do not go to detailed single line items, but rather contain total revenues, total expenses and investments, or even only a total result figure. Budget entity managers have greater freedom, as long as they do not exceed the gross amounts and reach their performance targets.

These reform features mean that budget entity managers should have more flexibility and power to operate, for instance, regarding personnel policies, recruiting, outsourcing, etc. On the other hand, responsibilities regarding activity performance have increased in terms of output and outcomes with budget resources.

Budget reforms in the above-described style may have not only efficiency ramifications, but also problematic democracy and personal effects, often linked to reducing the powers of trade unions and general public sector staff. So such reforms may not increase the democratic culture of public sector entities, especially when they are linked to senior managers being paid what can be seen as grossly inflated salaries.

In addition, if the government entity managers lack operational decision-making power and the entity lacks reliable and sufficient data on outputs and outcomes, performance-based budgeting is not in practice a realistic budget model.[13]

Other planning and reporting modes

If governments only prepared annual budgets, the planning horizon would be incomplete. That is why governments also make and

---

[13] Schick (2007).

publish separate strategic plans, multi-year budgets, medium-term spending frameworks and long-term fiscal sustainability reports. It is important to align operative budget plans with government strategic plans However, when a government has or is planning to have a wide array of plans and reports, it is often in practice so that they turn out to be more or less disconnected from one another, giving rise to confusion and reform fatigue.[14] The idea of purposive strategy-linked budgeting tries to reduce this risk.

From the point of view of the budget decision-maker, it would be ideal for them to be supplied not only with consistent information on yearly costs but also the total life-cycle costs of long-term liabilities caused by contracts, commitments and investments to which the government is planning to bind itself. If this information is not directly in the budget figures, it could be in budget overview text or in budget supplements. Furthermore, life-cycle calculations of significant investments or complicated PPP arrangements may be included and transparently explained in other plans and documents. In this case, the budget documents should make reference to these other sources of information.

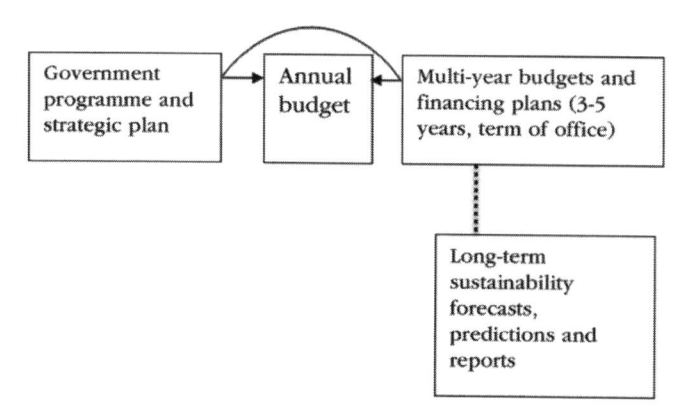

Figure 3.2: Government planning and reporting system

---

[14] Schick (2007), p. 121.

5. Budget-linked budgetary accounting

As already mentioned, the link between budgeting and accounting forms the basic feature of governmental accounting. Allocation of expenses, revenues and capital expenditures into the budget may follow a cash basis, modified cash basis, commitments basis or accrual basis. Because budget accounting (budget bookkeeping) is budget-linked, the recognition principles of budgetary accounting must correspond to the allocation principles of the associated budgets. This should help to secure proper control during budget execution.

Financial management and budget surveillance require an account classification for budgetary accounting to be created. The chart of budgetary accounts should be derived from the legally binding budget. The main budgetary accounts may be further divided into subaccounts according into different management and reporting needs inside the organisation.

Parallel accounting systems

Some countries have established accrual-based financial accounting besides the traditional budgetary accounting that has remained mainly on a modified cash basis. Recording financial information in both financial accounts and budgetary accounts may happen simultaneously inside one combined information system. Information technologies with sophisticated software allow the integration of these two subsystems. Alternatively, budget entities may carry out reconciliations between the accrual financial accounting and budgetary accounting systems.[15]

---

[15] Brusca et al. (2015).

Below is what the IPSAS 24 requires:

> "47. The actual amounts presented on a comparable basis to the budget in accordance with paragraph 31 shall, where the financial statements and the budget are not prepared on a comparable basis, be reconciled to the following actual amounts presented in the financial statements, identifying separately any basis, timing and entity differences:
>
> (a) If the accrual basis is adopted for the budget, total revenues, total expenses and net cash flows from operating activities, investing activities and financing activities; or
>
> (b) If a basis other than the accrual basis is adopted for the budget, net cash flows from operating activities, investing activities and financing activities.
>
> The reconciliation shall be disclosed on the face of the statement of comparison of budget and actual amounts or in the notes to the financial statements."[16]

A reconciliation between the budgetary results and the financial statements is provided, for instance, in the OECD financial statements.[17] The financial statements of the OECD are prepared on an accrual basis following the IPSAS. The OECD budget is prepared on a commitment basis for expenditures and an accrual basis for revenues. The most significant of the IPSAS adjustments relates to changes in employee- defined benefit liabilities. Another important difference lies in the treatment of investments.

---

[16] IPSAS 24 Presentation of budget information in financial statements: Reconciliation of Actual Amounts on a Comparable Basis and Actual Amounts in the Financial Statements, paragraph 47.

[17] The Financial Statements of the Organisation for Economic Co-operation and Development as at 31 December 2020.

6. Conclusion

In the public sector, approved and authoritative budgets are the core area of PSA and accountability. The budget-based approach emerges from the authoritative budget and its execution, management and control.

The budget needs budgetary-linked accounting. This accounting must follow the logic of the budget, especially regarding the allocation of incomes and expenditures to the budget (budget codes). If the budget is cash-based, the associated bookkeeping must also be cash-based. If the budget is accrual-based, the bookkeeping must also be accrual-based.

At the same time, it must be understood that general accrual-based financial accounting and reporting may or may not be merged with the budgetary accounting and reporting. If they are not merged, a government will have to maintain a dual accounting system for different purposes with different reporting modes. In some countries, governments may account for and publish only budget-based statements.

It is crucial to note that public sector performance is only partly captured with financial figures and financial performance. That is why non-financial activity performance, accounting of outputs and outcomes are important for public accountability. These matters are planned and reported using performance-based budget systems.

With New Public Financial Management, a movement towards accrual-based budgets and performance-based budget has evolved. However, they face many practical obstacles that hinder their proper functioning and hence their ability to reach their ultimate goals of better information used in decision-making and better performance than before. Performance-based budgeting is easy to explain but difficult to implement on a strict basis (as a budget decision rule). Accrual-based budgeting is difficult to explain and even more difficult to implement.

Performance-based budgeting and accrual budgeting are very demanding regarding data quality and reliability. Their success is also dependent on politicians' and managers' willingness and ability to use the additional information provided by the budgeting and accounting systems.

The Table 3.7 summarizes the linkages between budget types, budget appropriations and accounting.

Budget type dimensions	Budget appropriations	Type of budget-linked accounting
Timing basis		
Cash-based	Cash-based	Cash accounting
Commitment-based	Short-term accrual-based	Weak modified accrual accounting
Accrual-based	Modified accrual-based	Modified accrual accounting
Fixing of budget items (input-output dimension)		
Strategy-based	Appropriations must be itemized to means in a way that the strategic goals can be achieved with the budget.	Chart of accounts and cost centers organized in a way that enable appropriate follow-up.
Phenomenon-based (subcategory of a strategy-based budget)	Appropriations must be itemized across sectors to meet the claims, for instance of combating climate change and proceeding to carbon neutrality.	Chart of accounts and cost centers organized in a way that enable appropriate follow-up.
Performance-based (output-based)	Appropriations must be dimensioned in the budget so that the output targets can be achieved.	Chart of accounts and cost centers organized in a way that enable appropriate follow-up.
Resource-based (input-based)	Appropriations are fixed to expenditure categories (factors of production)	Chart of accounts organized according to expenditure (revenue) categories

Table 3.7: Linkages between budget types, budget appropriations and accounting.

Lastly, we want to stress that it is necessary for governments to have reliable auditing institutions. Here we may refer to Schick's conclusions:

"For performance budgeting and accrual budgeting to take root, it is essential that governments have formal procedures for reviewing reported results, including accepted standards for measuring outputs and outcomes and for reporting costs and liabilities."[18]

Bibliographic references

ANTHONY, Robert (1965) – Planning and Control Systems: A Framework for Analysis. Harvard Business Press, Boston, ISBN: 9780875840475.

BRUSCA, Isabel; CAPERCHIONE, Eugenio; COHEN, Sandra and MANES-ROSSI, Francesca (Eds) (2015) – Public sector accounting and auditing in Europe, The Challenge of Harmonization, Houndmills: Palgrave and Macmillan, ISBN: 9781137461346.

BUDDING, Tjerk; GROSSI, Giuseppe and TAGESSON, Torbjorn (2015) – Public Sector Accounting, New York: Routledge, ISBN: 9780415683159.

CANCIANO, Marco; CURRISTINE, Teresa / LAZARE, Michel (Eds.) (2013) – Public Financial Management and Its Emerging Architecture, Washington: International Monetary Fund, ISBN: 9781475531091, pp. 339-359.

COOMBS, Hugh Malcolm and JENKINS, David Ellis (2002) – Public Sector Financial Management, Padstow: Pat Bond, ISBN: 9781861526755, 3rd ed.

GASB (1987) – Objectives of Financial Reporting, Concepts Statement No. 1 of the Governmental Accounting Standard Board, No. 037, May 1987.

HODGE, Graeme A. and GREVE, Carsten (2007) – Public–Private Partnerships: An International Performance Review, Public Administration Review, 67(3), pp. 545-558.

IPSASB: IPSAS 24 standard (2006) – Presentation of budget information in financial statements: IFAC, Handbook of International public sector accounting pronouncements.

JONES, Bernard (1996) – Financial Management in the Public Sector, Maidenhead: McGraw-Hill, ISBN: 0077078888.

JONES, Rowan and PENDLEBURY, Maurice (2010) – Public Sector Accounting, Harlow et al.: Pearson Education, ISBN: 9780273720362, 6th ed.

KHAN, Abdul (2013) – Accrual Budgeting: Opportunities and Challenges, in: CANCIANO, Marco; CURRISTINE, Teresa and LAZARE, Michel (Eds.): Public Financial Management and Its Emerging Architecture, Washington: International Monetary Fund, ISBN: 9781475531091, pp. 339-359.

MONSEN, Norvald (2002) – The Case for Cameral Accounting, in: Financial Accountability & Management, 18(1), pp. 39-72.

MUNICIPALITY OF LEMPÄÄLÄ (2022) – Budget plan 2022 and economy plan 2022-2024.

---

[18] Schick (2007), p. 120.

OECD (2020) – The Financial Statements of the Organisation for Economic Co-operation and Development as at 31 December 2020.

OECD (2015) – Recommendation of the Council on Budgetary Governance.

PALLOT, June (1992) – Elements of a Theoretical Framework for Public Sector Accounting, in: Accounting, Auditing & Accountability Journal, 5(1), pp. 38-59.

PROWLE, Malcolm (2010) – Managing and Reforming Modern Public Services: The Financial Management Dimension, Harlow: Pearson Education Ltd, ISBN: 9780273722816.

SCHICK, Allen (2007) – Performance budgeting and Accrual Budgeting: Decision rules or Analytic Tools?, in: OECD Journal on Budgeting, Vol. 7, No. 2, 2007: OECD, pp. 109-138.

YLMAZ, Serdar and BERIS, Yakup (2008) - Good Governance and the Emergence of a New Accountability Agenda, in: Gábor Péteri (Ed.): Finding the Money, Public Accountability and Service Efficiency through Fiscal Transparency, Budapest: Open Society Institute, ISBN: 978 963 9719 09 5, pp. 16-41.

Additional readings

BRUSCA, Isabel; CAPERCHIONE, Eugenio; COHEN, Sandra and MANES-ROSSI, Francesca (Eds.) (2015) – Public sector accounting and auditing in Europe, The Challenge of Harmonization, Houndmills: Palgrave and Macmillan, ISBN: 978-1-137-46134-6.

BUDDING, Tjerk; GROSSI, Giuseppe and TAGESSON, Torbjörn (2015) – Public Sector Accounting, New York: Routledge, ISBN: 9780415683159.

JONES, Rowan and PENDLEBURY, Maurice (2010) – Public Sector Accounting, Harlow et al.: Pearson Education, ISBN: 978-0273720362, 6th ed..

SCHICK, Allen (2007) – Performance budgeting and Accrual Budgeting: Decision rules or Analytic Tools?, in: OECD Journal on Budgeting, 7(2), pp. 109-138.

Discussion topics

– What would you prefer as the best choice on the continuum from cash basis to accruals basis in public sector budgeting and why?

– Find some examples of different budget types from the web pages of local government budgets or state/central government budgets in your country or internationally and discuss how informative they are.

Chapter 4
Theoretical Approaches to Financial Accounting Purposes and Principles

Lasse Oulasvirta
Tampere University, Finland
lasse.oulasvirta@tuni.fi
https://orcid.org/0000-0003-4195-1331

Summary

The theories of accounting are described first, followed by the conventions and principles of accounting and their interpretation in the public sector. Public sector Conceptual Frameworks for financial accounting are outlined especially from the point of view of the primary users' needs, valuation and measurement principles. Different and competing theoretical approaches to public sector accounting frameworks are also explained.

Keywords

Financial accounting, accrual, cash and modified basis of accounting, accounting theories, conventions and principles, conceptual framework

1. Introduction

The aim of this chapter is to describe basic accounting theories, concepts and principles for public sector accounting (PSA). Theoretical accounting foundations and principles influence and interact with financial accounting standards and practices. The European Public Sector Accounting Standards (EPSAS) are still under preparation and are open to development. Therefore, it is important to relate this development to the basic theories, concepts and principles of financial accounting.

2. Accounting theories

What do we mean by accounting theory? According to the definition by Hendriksen (1982, p.1), accounting theory may be defined as logical reasoning in the form of a set of broad principles that provide a general frame of reference by which accounting practice can be evaluated and guide the development of new practices and procedures.

Accounting theory may also be used to explain existing practices to obtain a better understanding of them. But the most important goal of accounting theory should be to provide a coherent set of logical principles that form the general frame of reference for the evaluation and development of sound accounting practices.[1]

Below, we briefly explain the following common accounting theories:

- Proprietary theory;
- Entity theory;
- Funds theory;
- Cameral theory.

In the private sector, entity and proprietary theories have been popular as frames for accounting approaches. In contrast, the cameral and funds theories have been targeted mainly at the public sector.[2]

---

[1] Glautier and Underdown (1994), p. 23.
[2] Monsen (2002).

Proprietary theory

The proprietary theory of accounting emphasises that financial accounting must be structured in a way that satisfies the owner's interests. All accounting principles and concepts are defined from the owner's point of view.

The owner's purpose is assumed to be to increase his or her wealth. Revenue is defined as an increase in proprietorship wealth, and an expense is defined as a decrease in proprietorship wealth. The two key accounting equations are:

> Equity (wealth of owner) = Assets − Liabilities
> Result = Distribution of profit to owners + Earnings retained in the firm.

According to the private sector international standard-setter International Accounting Standards Board (IASB) and its draft conceptual framework:

> "The objective of general purpose financial reporting is to provide financial information about the reporting entity that is useful to existing and potential investors, lenders and other creditors in making decisions about providing resources to the entity. Those decisions involve buying, selling or holding equity and debt instruments, and providing or settling loans and other forms of credit."[3]

Entity theory

The entity theory was developed by the critics of the proprietary view of accounting. Although this theory was developed for corporate

---

[3] IASB (2015), paragraph 1.2.

accounting, supporters of entity theory believe that it can be applied to proprietorships, partnerships and even non-profit organisations. The crucial question is whether accounts and transactions should be classified and analysed from the point of view of the operating entity unit or from the point of view of the proprietorship or other single interests.[4]

In this entity approach, an enterprise is understood as an entity separate from its owners. Principally, both equity and debts are seen as the financial capital of the entity. Share capital belongs to the entity. The two key accounting equations for entity theory are:

- Assets = Financial capital (all assets must be financed whether from own(er) capital or debt capital);
- Result = Distribution of profit to owners + retained earnings + share of lenders (debt interest).

Fund theory

Under fund accounting, funds have restrictions on the use of resources from the accounting entities. On the one hand, special funds can be established to account for revenues earmarked, for instance, for schools, museums or parks. A capital project fund is, on the other hand, established to account for funds to be used only for capital facilities, debt service funds etc.[5] Fund theory is mainly used in the public or not-for-profit sectors.

In this approach, the focus is on restrictions and the service potential of assets, not on their income earning capacity. Assets are acquired in order to contribute to increased service production by the fund.

---

[4] Monsen (2017), pp. 23-24.
[5] Monsen (2017), pp. 60-62.

Assets are not acquired in order to earn profit; any profit (or surplus) is not seen as belonging to the proprietor (proprietary theory) or to the organisation itself (entity theory) but is retained to further the objectives of the fund. In principle, this approach suits budget-linked governmental accounting. Here, budgetary decisions represent the authority to use and receive money and also to provide restrictions on the use of disposal of assets. Even though fund theory of accounting was originally developed for the business sector, it has not gained a stronghold there. Later was further developed and applied mainly in the governmental sector in the Anglo-Saxon countries.[6]

Funds accounting is also used in the US. Local governments and states have several separate public funds for different purposes. In funds accounting, financial statements present a short-term (annual) view of governmental fund activities.

Cameral accounting theory

This theory was developed for use in the public sector. It has a money and budget control purpose. Budget control in public sector entities ensures that public (tax) revenues are managed (money management) according to the politically adopted budget (budgetary control). Cameral accounting was developed originally as single-entry bookkeeping.[7]

In cameral accounting, no cash can be received or paid by an organisational unit without receiving a previous or simultaneous payment instruction from another higher organisational unit having this competence (payment control). Cameral accounting is explained further in Chapter 2 of this book.

---

[6] Monsen (2017), p. 77.
[7] Monsen (2002, 2011, 2014).

Bookkeeping models

As introduced in Chapter 1, the two basic alternatives in current bookkeeping are single-entry or double-entry bookkeeping.

Cash-based single-entry bookkeeping involves recognising money outflows and inflows in the cash/bank account. Within modern commercial accounting, the principle of single-entry bookkeeping has been replaced by that of double-entry bookkeeping. The money (cash) focus has been replaced with a financial performance (profit accruals) focus. We can call this commercial double-entry bookkeeping for profit accounting purposes.[8]

Cameral single-entry bookkeeping does not have the purpose of profit accounting, but fulfils the purpose of money accounting and budget control. In the government sector, both cameral accounting and fund accounting have a strong link with the budget. It is important to realise that both are not only based on actual cash receipts and payments. The money accrual principle includes, in addition to realised cash movements, payments that become due later in the short term.

The double-entry bookkeeping was developed to measure commercial profit. Each entry has two aspects, the debit and the credit.

Cash-based accounting is comparatively simple and objective, and suites in the public sector to fulfil the needs of money-usage control. Accrual-based commercial bookkeeping is more complicated, but offers information on service costs (depreciation costs included), assets and liabilities to assist resource management. On the other hand, accrual-based commercial bookkeeping may lead in the public sector to decisions on accounting treatment being made on doubtful grounds and to loss of control.[9]

---

[8] Monsen (2011).
[9] Wynne (2007).

3. Accounting conventions and principles

Several accounting principles and conventions have been developed in the accounting literature. A possible systematisation of these can be arranged according to a three-level structure:

- pervasive principles (conventions);
- broad operating principles;
- detailed principles.

Theoretically, the principles of each level should interrelate with the principles at the other two levels. However, many accounting practices have not been based on higher principles, but have simply evolved from experience.[10]

If accounting rules are *principles-based*, they do not have to be very detailed (as with accounting law in the European Union, IFRS and IPSAS). If accounting standards are *rules-based*, standards are written in a very detailed manner to encompass a wide variety of practical situations (as with the US approach to accounting standard setting). We will now explain briefly some important concepts and principles.

Accounting principles/concepts	
1. Accounting entity	6. Consistency
2. Money measurement	7. Prudence
3. Going concern	8. Accruals principle
4. Cost concept	9. Matching
5. Realization principle	10. Periodicity

---

[10] McCullers and Schroeder (1982), p. 27.

Accounting entity

The purpose of the **entity** concept is to make a clear distinction between the economic affairs of the accounting entity and other entities.

The difficulty comes in defining what constitutes the government accounting entity and what off-budget entities should be consolidated into it. Several criteria could be used:

- government ownership and control of the entity;
- the entity's dependence on government transfers;
- the legal form of the entity.

General government as a whole is **divided into several levels of government** (central/federal, regional/state and local/municipal).

Furthermore, central, regional, and local governments may consist of sub-organisations, and there are many and varied criteria which determine which of these sub-organisations form accounting sub-entities that maintain their own separate accounting books. This may not be determined simply by legal ownership.

Defining the **demarcation lines between accounting entities** and the extent to which the consolidation should be done determines the sphere of annual financial reporting. Questions related to consolidation are handled in the Chapters 11 and 12 of this book. Consolidation is an approach that originated from the private sector and has only really been applied in the public sector over the last 20 years or so. The accounts of several subsidiary entities are combined to produce the accounts of one larger combined (economic or service-providing) entity.

Money measurement

The business accounting convention is to measure all transactions with (constant) monetary units.

The main difference in the public sector regarding this convention is that many transactions are non-exchange transactions. These include non-exchange inflows such as tax revenues or non-exchange expenses such as grants and social benefits. Furthermore, many assets including human resources and heritage assets, both cultural and natural, are difficult to value in money terms. Groundless monetisation of heritage assets in financial statements may cause misapprehensions and biased judgments.[11]

In the public sector, expenses are usually not related to future revenues. Usefulness (consumers' utility) of free and tax-financed services cannot be measured directly with prices. Hence, non-financial and efficiency reporting[12] of the services provided by a public sector entity is at least as important (in terms of public accountability) as traditional financial reporting.

In some cases, even if money measurement is possible, for instance, information on military assets, may be sensitive and may not be willingly disclosed publicly.

Going concern

The **going concern** principle is based on the assumption that the business is a continuing one, at least in the near future not on the verge of cessation and bankruptcy. Many assets in a business entity derive their value from their employment in the profit-creation process

---

[11] Carnegie et al. 2022.

[12] Chapter 14 of this book explains different non-financial reporting formats.

and are therefore generally carried at amortised cost. Should the firm cease to operate, the value which could be obtained from these assets on a (maybe forced) sale basis would be an appropriate measurement basis and probably be much less than their accounting or book value. Independent countries normally have a good foundation for continuity, so the going concern as a postulate is generally correct in the public sector. Governments have sovereign power, tax financing and statutory functions that do not abruptly cease in a bankruptcy-like situation. However, they may in practice fall into a financial crisis and lose their loan payment capacity. Furthermore, a hostile neighbouring country may try to occupy an independent country and remove its legitimate government.

On the other hand, many kinds of accounting entities inside the government, agencies and so on can cease to exist on the basis of administrative or political decisions. In this case, the going concern principle is not guaranteed.

However, and this is important, although public entities may sometimes be dissolved, the rights and obligations entrusted in them by the sovereign power are not cancelled as a result, unlike business entities for which the amounts due on liquidation are limited to existing net assets.[13] So the debts of a cancelled subnational government would become those of the national government. In addition, public sector entities are rarely abolished purely for financial reasons. This issue was discussed more in Chapter 2.

Cost concept

In PSA, cost measurement has been based typically on **historical costs** rather than on **current costs**. Historical cost is based on reference to the cost of acquisition or construction of assets.

---

[13] CNOCP (2014), paragraph 34.

While the historical cost concept may raise many problems for the business accountant, it raises far fewer such problems for the public sector accountant. In the public sector, accounting for historic or actual costs is more important than indicating what profits may have been earned.

The historical costs of acquisition or production of assets do not take into consideration changes in the purchasing power of money. Some assets face abnormal inflation and rising prices, which means, among other things, that depreciation calculated from historical asset values will not finance replacement costs. The historical cost approach is not always followed consistently, because in some cases revaluations are accepted in the public accounting tradition, for instance, regarding real estate, if the reassessed value is considered reasonably permanent.

Realisation concept

The **realisation** concept refers to the point in time at which the accounting entity realises an asset through sale or other way of disposal. The realisation price compared to the book value reflects the profit earned or loss incurred by this disposal. The realisation principle has been criticised, and commercial accounting standards accept revaluations and holding gains or holding losses that are included in the profit of the period.

In the public sector, holding gains and holding losses are less useful concepts, because assets are kept for service and goods provision for citizens, and it may be more meaningful to account for only realised transactions that have money and budget effects. The accountability purpose of PSA requires reliable information on past performance, based on realized transactions rather than speculative or subjective information.

Consistency is important for making relevant comparisons between accounting periods. If there is no continuity of accounting methods and rules, using the information becomes difficult.

Comparability between accounting entities and consistency in accounting methods over time increase the value of accounting information. According to this principle, it is advantageous if accounting standards do not change continuously, causing the need for constant and costly training and changes in accounting technology.

Prudence is a general guiding principle for financial statements. Prudence means, among other things, that all costs must be recognised fully and that only realised profits are recognised in the income statement. Provisions providing for future costs are shown both in the income statement (expenses) and in the balance sheet (liabilities). Prudence in the public sector means care in estimating budget incomes so that they are not exaggerated and care in estimating **all** budget expenditures so that they are not underestimated.

Accruals principle

The accrual concept is described in Chapters 1 and 2. In commercial accounting, accruals are required to match income and expenditure in the calculation of profit. This is the normal basis of the preparation of accounts for commercial undertakings.[14] Furthermore, the accrual basis of financial accounting serves the information needs of cost and management accounting.

According to Chan,[15] accruals can be practised in the public sector with different strengths. Furthermore, it must be understood that implementing accrual accounting is not only a technical accounting

---

[14] Brockington (1993), p. 6.
[15] Chan (2003), p. 17.

exercise. To work well, a cultural change is needed, which should be linked to broader public management reforms in governments that may not be used to the accrual mindset. According to Hepworth (2017), if financial accrual accounting is not used for managerial purposes, its advantages get lost at the entity level. Merely making information available achieves nothing unless someone uses that information. Again, according to Hepworth, technical training for preparers of financial statements and potential users is not enough. Managers must have an interest in using accrual information and must have managerial discretion powers that motivate them to use the accrual information for making better decisions. Politicians must be willing to support accrual reform.[16]

Furthermore, the capacity of citizens and parliamentarians to assess general purpose financial reports independently is limited. From the citizens' and politicians' point of view, financial statements derived from on a less complicated modified cash basis may be preferable to those prepared on a more complicated and stronger accrual basis.

Matching is a fundamental accounting principle in the private sector, which means that when computing profit, all costs are matched against the revenues to which they relate. Many practical difficulties arise to hinder perfect matching. Depreciation is one of the most important means of allocating costs of assets to accounting periods. This means allocating asset costs to those accounting periods in which the asset is used.

Theoretically, matching in the public sector does not fit non-exchange transactions. These form the major part of governmental transactions. In non-exchange transactions (for instance, transfers to enterprises and households or tax revenues) one cannot find a direct causal relationship between expenditures and tax revenues.

---

[16] Hepworth (2017).

When services are delivered free of charge to inhabitants, direct matching of expenditures and revenues is not possible. However, the public sector income statement refers to revenues earned and expenses incurred during the accounting period and shows a balance or lack of balance between them. In the public sector, non-exchange transactions are common, which makes matching, in the private sector sense, impossible (for instance, general taxes are not earmarked for specific expenditures). When direct reverse matching is not possible accountants have to recourse to matching expenditures and incomes to the proper time period.[17]

Costs of production factors can be matched with the usage (consumption) of those same production factors. For instance, if a total investment cost of 8 million € of a school building is spread over its useful life of 40 years, this means a 200,000 € depreciation expense per year using the straight-line method of write-offs.

Depreciation can be interpreted in the public sector *as a means* for distributing the investment expenditure over the whole use-period of the investment, so that only the costs of goods and services used in providing services during the year should be included in the financial performance statement. However, this depends on whether the performance or efficiency of the government is to be indicated by such statements, or merely how the money was used.

Periodicity means that the life of an accounting entity must be divided into constant periods **for reporting purposes.** Matching makes it possible to match revenues and expenses for the accounting period. However, in PSA, profitability is not the aim of matching. The income received in a year must simply be matched with the expenditure in the same year.

---

[17] Biondi & Oulasvirta (2023).

Conventions/ principles	Public sector Applications	Explanations
1. Accounting entity	Demarcation lines between the whole government and other sectors (consolidation principles)	Demarcation lines outside and inside the multi-level public sector (division into sub-entities doing separate book closures).
2. Money measurement	Not entirely valid	Often one-sided actions, non-exchange transactions.
3. Going concern	Partly valid	Abrupt dismantling possible at the agency/organisational level.
4. Cost concept	Historical cost	Less use of changing current values compared to the private sector.
5. Realisation concept	Emphasised in the public sector	Revaluations and holding gains and holding losses less useful compared to the private sector.
6. Accruals concept	Money accruals, nowadays also modified profit accruals	In the not-for profit sector, modified cash basis common, accruals pushed less far than in the private sector.
7. Matching concept	Valid but not usually in the same way as in business accounting	Direct matching of incurred expenses to earned revenues not possible in non-exchange transactions. Time period matching of expenses and revenues is frequently valid in tax-financed public sector entities.
8. Periodicity	Valid as such	Technically the entity's lifetime must be divided into accounting periods.
9. Consistency	Valid as such	Constant changes of rules problematic, especially in poor jurisdictions with low accounting resources.
10. Prudence principle	Emphasised	Favoured in the public sector, based on strict end-of-year cut-off rules.

Table 4.1: Summary of Section 3

4. Conceptual frameworks

This section discusses theoretical approaches that may lie behind accounting standards and their conceptual frameworks.

Users of general purpose financial statements

Accounting approaches and conceptual frameworks usually start with the objectives and purposes of accounting and financial statements. The information needs of users of financial information should have a crucial impact upon the conceptual framework of accounting. Two main concepts in conceptual frameworks are accountability and decision usefulness, demonstrating the usefulness of financial information. Information should serve the control purpose of making an assessment of the behaviour of the accountable administration that used the collective resources. Furthermore, information should be appropriate for making decisions regarding the future usage of collective resources in the best possible way.

Accountability is related to the past, with the control of the managerial actions (agents) taken in the past on behalf of the principals. Information for this purpose serves the principal's decisions regarding the agents; for instance, discharge of liability, need to change the manager, ways to develop steering and incentive systems, etc.

Decision usefulness is related to the future and the usefulness of information in forecasting the economic viability of the entity, whether it is a going concern or not, capacity to cope with obligations, medium- and long-term sustainability, etc.

The most common international framework for financial statement presentation is the conceptual framework of the IASB, which issues International Accounting Standards (IAS) and International Financial Reporting Standards (IFRS). The IASB emphasises shareholders and creditors as primary users, and hence their needs regarding financial reporting information.

The conceptual framework of the IASB assumes that financial accounting information that satisfies the needs of shareholders and creditors also satisfies the information needs of other users of the financial statements. According to IASB, the objective of general purpose financial reporting is to provide financial information about the reporting entity that is useful to existing and potential investors, lenders and other creditors in making decisions about providing resources to the entity. Those decisions involve buying, selling or holding equity and debt instruments, and providing or settling loans and other forms of credit.[18]

Primary users in the public sector

The interpretations of accountability and decision usefulness are different in the public sector because of different user needs. The primary users are the citizens. The **primary users** of state and local governmental financial reports are those to whom government is primarily accountable, the citizenry and the legislative and oversight bodies that directly represent the citizens.

Elected politicians have a responsibility to steer public financial matters and have an accountability relationship towards their electorate, citizens. In these roles, they must be able to read, understand and interpret accounting information in their constituencies. Hence, the main objective of GPFS is to fulfil the information needs of the citizenry and the legislature representing citizens.[19]

---

[18] IASB (2015).

[19] Mann et al. (2019), Oulasvirta (2021).

Valuation and measurement of financial statement elements
Historical costs and current costs

There are two main alternatives regarding the valuation method in financial accounting. The first is the historical cost method of valuation. This refers to the amount of money for which an asset was originally acquired or produced.

The other main alternative is the current cost method of valuation. This uses current values, not historical values from the original transactions and events. As the basis of valuation of an asset, it uses the amount which it would currently cost to obtain. This may be interpreted as the cost of replacement or the opportunity cost of the asset.[20]

The opportunity cost is the cost of an action in terms of the value of the best alternative opportunity thereby forgone,[21] for instance, the value of the opportunity forgone by using a certain asset in service provision instead of selling it.

The Governmental Accounting Standards Board (GASB) divides valuation into four approaches[22]

1. **Historical cost** is the price paid to acquire an asset or the amount received pursuant to the incurrence of a liability in an actual exchange transaction.
2. **Fair value** is the price that would be received from selling an asset or paid to transfer a liability in an orderly

---

[20] Brockington (1993), p. 66.
[21] Brockington (1993), p. 161.
[22] Concepts Statement No. 6 Measurement of Elements of Financial Statements (2014).

transaction between market participants at the measurement date.
3. **Replacement cost** is the price that would be paid to acquire an asset with equivalent service potential in an orderly market transaction at the measurement date.
4. **Settlement amount** is the amount at which an asset could be realised or a liability could be liquidated with the counterparty, other than in an active market.

The settlement amount can be used in either an initial measurement approach or in a remeasure approach

Initial and subsequent measurement

    a) Initial amounts

Initial measurement reflects the value at the transaction date (when the asset was acquired/produced or liability incurred).
In the assessment of whether current-year revenues cover the cost of the government's services, the most relevant cost associated with these assets is the cost that has been incurred by the government – the cost based on the initial amount.

    b) Remeasured amounts

Subsequent measurement reflects the conditions in effect at the financial statement date. Re-measurement changes the amount reported for an asset or liability from an initial amount or previous remeasured amount to an amount indicative of the value at the financial statement date, providing information to assess the financial position, including the service potential of assets and the ability to meet obligations when due. When remeasured amounts are used in a statement of financial position, those assets and liabilities may have more meaning because they reflect a value as of a common date.[23] However, this is because private sector financial statements are indicative of future profitability, which is not the case in the public sector.

Balancing competing objectives of financial reporting

According to the GASB, the statement of financial position and the resource flows statement are both important, yet because a single measurement approach is required to be selected for a particular transaction, the choice may indicate which financial statement is more important in that circumstance.

According to the GASB, "initial amounts generally have less relevance than remeasured amounts when evaluating the statement of financial position to assess the level of services that can be provided by a government. However, initial amounts generally have more relevance than remeasured amounts when evaluating the cost of services information that is presented in a resource flows statement."[24]

---

[23] GASB (2014).
[24] GASB (2014), p. 20.

Date of acquisition 1.1.XX Beginning of usage 1.1.XX Straight-line depreciation	Historical cost – remeasured value at 1.1.XX+5	Replacement cost – remeasured value at 1.1.XX+5	Realisable value Potential sale of asset at market value at 1.1.XX+5	Net present value of future income at 1.1.XX+5
Not-for-profit entity Initial asset acquisition cost 1,000,000 € (municipal day care facility)	500,000 € (1,000,000 less depreciation for half its estimated life)	600,000 €	400,000 € (No active markets, estimation of a settlement amount)	The asset generates no or insignificant cash flows. However, the asset's ability to provide future services may have a greater value than the sale of the asset now.
For-profit entity Initial asset acquisition cost 1,000,000 € (production equipment)	500,000 € (1,000,000 – depreciation for half its estimated life)	700,000 €	700,000 € Market price in active markets	1,200,000 € Estimation of discounted present value of future cash inflows (from year X+5 to the end of the useful life of the asset)

Table 4.2: Examples of valuation alternatives: 1 million € investment for a day care facility and 1 million € investment for production equipment, useful life for both is (for reasons of simplicity) 10 years.

Historical costs often are reliable and verifiable. Furthermore, this approach facilitates a comparison of actual financial results and the approved budget prepared on a historical cost basis. This is essential in the public sector where officials are accountable for the amounts that are spent compared to the agreed budget.

According to Glautier and Underdown, current value accounting consists of three forms[25]: Replacement cost accounting (entry price), realisable value accounting (exit price), and net present value of future income generated from the asset.

---

[25] Glautier and Underdown (1994), p. 346.

Current replacement costs are relevant to assessments of the current cost of services and operational capacity, but are not relevant for assessing financial capacity.

Realisable value is relevant when assets are used to provide services measured at market value. However, relevance decreases or vanishes if services are provided in non-exchange transactions or on subsidised terms. It is relevant for assessing financial capacity because it gives information on the amounts that would be received on the sale of an asset. Observe here that the net selling price, which is entity-specific and includes the entity's costs of sale, differs from the market value concept.[26]

Net present value relates to the concept of value in use (the asset's remaining service potential or ability to generate economic benefits). In the public sector context, it is generally inappropriate because most assets are not generating economic benefits measured in cash. In addition, the calculation of value in use can be very complex.

Public sector-specific non-exchange transactions require their own recognition criteria: a) non-exchange revenues, taxes, and b) and non- exchange expense transactions, such as grants, social benefits and other contribution transfers. These are often recognised either based on the pure cash movements they cause or based also on their short-term obligations causing due payments in near future.

The GASB requires **(only) government investments** to be measured at fair value. An *investment* is defined as a security or other asset that (a) a government holds primarily for the purpose of income or profit and (b) has a present service capacity based solely on its ability to generate cash or to be sold to generate cash.

---

[26] Glautier and Underdown (1994), p. 346.

A fair value measurement of a liability would assume that the liability would be transferred to the market participant and not settled with the counterparty.[27]

Theoretical approaches to PSA frameworks

Broadly, we can discern two different accounting methods as reference frames that have an impact upon the determination of elements of financial statements, recognition and measurement criteria. These are the revenue-expense-led approach and the asset and liability-led approaches. The former represents a dynamic view and the latter a static view. These views may have an influence on the contents of conceptual frameworks (adapted from Biondi 2012 and 2013):

Accounting views	Static	Dynamic
Method	Stock method of accounting (assets-liabilities approach)	Flow method of accounting (revenues-expenses approach)
Measurement	Fair value	Historical cost
Focus	Net worth of the entity at a specific moment in time	Resource outflows and inflows Resources mobilised and utilised by the activities (matching)

Table 4.3: Comparison of the static and dynamic views

The **revenue-expense-led approach** is based on the dynamic view and the flow method of accounting. The matching of periodic expenses and revenues to the income statement is emphasized. Furthermore, the realisation principle is applied, that is why it is transaction-based and uses historical costs rather than fair value

---

[27] GASB (2015). Observe also that IPSASB has issued 2021 an Exposure Draft (ED) 77, Measurement, it will be explained in the book later in another chapter.

measurements. Realisation occurs mainly when flows are generated through transactions which have occurred with independent third parties. The historical cost accounting approach is based upon these transactions of the accounting entity with independent third parties. According to Biondi accounting is not made dynamic by taking into account the current value of an imagined future (as the static model would do), but by referring to the accrual of actual expenditures related to the ongoing productive process of the accounting entity over time and circumstances.[28]

The **asset and liability-led approach** focuses on the balance sheet. Neutrality rather than prudence is emphasised. Furthermore, because fair values and market values are used, holding gains and losses are recognised. In order to create a consistent and coherent framework, there are arguments for not mixing the two different approaches. When we take into consideration specific public sector characteristics, arguments favour the revenue-expense-led approach. However, many consider this to be a controversial statement and, at the same time, may stress that public sector entities should follow as much as possible the private sector approach, which has been developing in the direction of the asset and liability-led approach with a focus on the balance sheet.

Some argue that the revenue-expense–led approach is a better choice for the public sector than the asset and liability-led approach. According to Biondi, a dynamic entity view is preferable to a static proprietary view in the public sector.[29]

These different approaches create discussion, for instance, about the recognition and valuation of fixed assets in governments. One argument for the revenue-expense model is that public sector assets are often maintained only to provide social benefits. In business

---

[28] Biondi (2012), p. 606.
[29] Biondi (2012), p. 611.

accounting, all assets are kept for reasons of economic benefit and one can argue that therefore recognising and valuing fixed assets in the public sector should not be copied from the IFRS. In the public sector, most of the property and equipment is not intended to yield economic benefits, especially regarding heritage assets, of which the economic objectives are very limited.

Accounting views	Private sector Applications	Public sector applications
Primary users of GPFRs Especially GPFSs	Owners, investors and creditors	Citizens and their representatives (parliaments and other representative bodies) Resource providers and service recipients – as secondary users
Purpose and objectives	Decision usefulness regarding buying/selling/ holding equity and debt instruments, lending decisions	Discharge of liability for accountability purposes, also prospective financial and non-financial information for prospective decision-making purposes
Statement emphasised	Balance sheet	Income statement
	Net worth of entity	Balance of budget
Accounting method	Stock method of accounting	Dynamic method of accounting
Measurement	Current value	Historical cost

Table 4.4: Summary

5. Conclusion

In this chapter, we have described the normative approach containing several principles and conventions of accounting developed for the for-profit sector. Then we analysed how we may interpret these conventions and principles in the context of tax-financed public sector organisations. We also analysed how the accounting theories and principles are reflected in the possible conceptual frameworks of public sector financial accounting. The analysis shows that principles and concepts in conceptual frameworks for the public sector cannot be directly taken from the corresponding private sector principles and concepts.

Bibliographic references

BARTON, Allan (2005) – Professional Accounting Standards and the Public Sector – A Mismatch, Accounting System, Abacus, 41(2), pp. 138-158.

BIONDI, Yuri (2012) – Should Business and Non-Business Accounting Be Different? A Comparative Perspective Applied to the New French Governmental Accounting Standards, International Journal of Public Administration, 35(9), pp. 603-619.

BIONDI, Yuri and OULASVIRTA, Lasse (2023) - Accounting for public sector assets: Comparing historical cost and current value models. In: CARUANA, Josette; BISOGNO, Marco; SICILIA, Mariafrancesca (eds.) Measurement in Public Sector Financial Reporting: Theoretical Basis and Empirical Evidence, Emerald Publishing.

BIONDI, Yuri (2013) – Accounting and Business Economics: Understanding the Past to 0(ed.): Accounting and Business Economics, Insights from National Traditions, New York: Routledge, ISBN: 9780415887021, pp. 485-493.

BUDDING, Tjerk; GROSSI, Giuseppe and TAGESSON, Torbjörn (2015) – Public Sector Accounting, New York: Routledge, ISBN: 9780415683159.

BRUSCA, Isabel; CAPERCHIONE, Eugenio; COHEN, Sandra and MANES-ROSSI, Francesca (Eds) (2015) – Public sector accounting and auditing in Europe, The Challenge of Harmonization, Houndmills: Palgrave and Macmillan, ISBN: 9781137461346.

CARNEGIE, Garry., FERRI, Paolo, PARKER, Lee, SIDAWAY, Shannon and TSAHURIDU, Eva. (2022). Accounting as Technical, Social and Moral Practice: The Monetary Valuation of Public Cultural, Heritage and Scientific Collections in Financial Reports. Australian Accounting Review (2022), 0 (0), pp. 1–13.

CHAN, James L. (2003) – Government Accounting: An Assessment of Theory, Purposes and Standards, Public Money & Management, 23(1), pp. 13-20.

EC (2013) – Report from the Commission to the Council and the European Parliament: Towards implementing harmonised public sector accounting standards in Member States, The suitability of IPSAS for the Member States, Brussels, 6.3.2013, COM(2013) 114 final.

CNOCP (2016) – Conceptual Framework for Public Accounts, Prepared on an Accruals Basis, Opinion N° 02.2016: Conseil de normalisation des comptes publics.

GASB (2014) – Concepts Statement No. 6 on concepts to Measurement of Elements of Financial Statements.

GASB (2015) – Statement No. 72 of the Governmental Accounting Standards Board, Fair Value Measurement and Application.

GLAUTIER, Michel William Edgard and UNDERDOWN, Brian (1994) – Accounting Theory and Practice, London: Pitman Publishing, ISBN: 0273604724, 5th ed.

IASB (2015) – Conceptual Framework for Financial Reporting, London, ED/2015/3: International Accounting Standards Board, IFRS, ISBN: 781909704817.

HENDRIKSEN, Eldon (1984) – Accounting Theory (Fourth Edition). Howewood, Illinois: Irwin, ISBN0-256-02588-6.

HEPWORTH, Noel (2017) – Is implementing the IPSASs an appropriate reform?, 37(2): Public Money & Management, pp. 141-148.

IPSASB: IPSAS 24 standard (2006) – Presentation of budget information in financial statements: Handbook of International public sector accounting pronouncements: IFAC.

IPSASB (2014) – The Conceptual Framework for General Purpose Financial Reporting by Public Sector: Entities International Public Sector Accounting Standards Board (IPSASB) of IFAC.

JONES, Rowan and PENDLEBURY, Maurice (2010) – Public Sector Accounting, London: Pearson Education, ISBN: 9780273720362, 6th ed.

MANN, Bianca, LORSON, Peter C., OULASVIRTA, Lasse and HAUSTEIN, Ellen (2019): The Quest for a Primary EPSAS Purpose – Insights from Literature and Conceptual Frameworks. Accounting in Europe, 2019, Vol. 16, No. 2, 195–218.

MONSEN, Norvald (2002) – The Case for Cameral Accounting, in: Financial Accountability & Management, 18(1), pp. 39-72.

MONSEN, Norvald (2011) – Commercial accounting, fund accounting and cameral accounting: Introduction and comparison with a view to use in the governmental sector, Bergen: NHH Norwegian School of Economics, Department of Accounting, Auditing and Law.

MONSEN, Norvald (2014) – Governmental accounting: Comparing commercial, fund and cameral accounting, Bergen: NHH Norwegian School of Economics, Department of Accounting, Auditing and Law.

MONSEN, Norvald (2017) – Commercial accounting, fund accounting and cameral accounting: Introduction and comparison with a view to use in the governmental sector, Bergen:

NHH Norwegian School of Economics, Department of Accounting, Auditing and Law, 6th ed.

OULASVIRTA, Lasse (2021) - A consistent bottom-up approach for deriving a conceptual framework for public sector financial accounting, Public Money & Management, Published online: 17 Feb 2021. https://doi.org/10.1080/09540962.2021.1881235.

PALLOT, June (1992) – Elements of a Theoretical Framework for Public Sector Accounting, in: Accounting, Auditing & Accountability Journal, 5(1), pp. 38-59.

RUTHERFORD, Brian A. (2000) – An Introduction to Modern Financial Reporting theory, London: Paul Chapman Publishing Ltd., ISBN: 9780761966074.

WYNNE, Andy (2007): Is the move to accrual-based accounting real priority for public sector accounting? Public Fund Digest, Vol. VI, No. 1, 2007, pp. 25-38.

Additional readings

BARTON, Allan (2005) – Professional Accounting Standards and the Public Sector – A Mismatch, Accounting System, Abacus, 41(2), pp. 138-158.

BIONDI, Yuri (2012) – Should Business and Non-Business Accounting Be Different? A Comparative Perspective Applied to the New French Governmental Accounting Standards, International Journal of Public Administration, 35(9), pp. 603-619.

CHAN, James L. (2003) – Government Accounting: An Assessment of Theory, Purposes and Standards, Public Money & Management, 23(1), pp. 13-20.

MONSEN, Norvald (2011) – Commercial accounting, fund accounting and cameral accounting: Introduction and comparison with a view to use in the governmental sector, Bergen: NHH Norwegian School of Economics, Department of Accounting, Auditing and Law.

PALLOT, June (1992) – Elements of a Theoretical Framework for Public Sector Accounting, in: Accounting, Auditing & Accountability Journal, 5(1), pp. 38-59.

Discussion topic

– What is your judgement on the two different approaches presented here: the revenue-expense-led approach (income statement emphasised) vs. the asset and liability-led approach (balance sheet emphasised), and their suitability for government accounting?

CHAPTER 5
DIFFERENT PERSPECTIVES IN PUBLIC SECTOR ACCOUNTING HARMONISATION: IFRS, IPSAS AND GFS

Giovanna Dabbicco
ISTAT National Accounts Directorate, Italy
dabbicco@istat.it
https://orcid.org/0000-0002-3056-5112

Summary

In order to compare financial information across companies, organisations, and public sector entities, accounting standards and accounting practices have to be harmonised. For this purpose, first, the International Financial Reporting Standards (IFRS) have been developed for the preparation of general purpose financial statements (GPFS) of profit-oriented entities. Some governments also have based their national public sector accounting standards on IFRS. Furthermore, public sector accounting could be harmonised at the global level by adopting the International Public Sector Accounting Standards (IPSAS). Finally, Government Finance Statistics (GFS) provide a set of macroeconomic statistics on financial operations, financial and liquidity positions, especially of the general government sector, and support fiscal analysis. This chapter describes these different perspectives and refers to challenges associated with accounting harmonisation.

Keywords

Public sector accounting, accounting harmonisation, IFRS, IPSAS, GFS.

1. Introduction

In general, accounting harmonisation is associated with greater international comparability of financial information. However, different historical developments in accounting systems in countries, on the basis of the different styles of management and culture, may hamper such harmonisation.[1] When accounting practices are harmonised, there are multiple potential benefits across the private and public sectors. For example, multinational companies are able to prepare and consolidate financial statements without considering different national accounting practices, and the financial situations of governments can be compared. Next to transparency and usability, accounting harmonisation is advantageous for the use of decision-making instruments, such as investment appraisal or performance management, due to ease of use and comparability. Advantages may be also observed in efficiencies for professional training, using a harmonised conceptual framework and standards.

Having these benefits of accounting harmonisation in mind, this chapter aims to describe different perspectives of accounting harmonisation and related challenges. International accounting harmonisation is realised by applying international accounting

---

[1] Dabbicco and Mattei (2021).

standards and regulations, such as the **International Financial Reporting Standards** (IFRS), and the **International Public Sector Accounting Standards** (IPSAS). **Government Finance Statistics** (GFS) facilitate macro measurement, allowing the monitoring and assessment of the impact of a government's economic policies and other activities, on the economy, and to assess the financial soundness of the general government and public sectors in ways commonly applied to other sectors of the economy.

In particular, this chapter has the following objectives:

- Describing different perspectives of accounting harmonisation (namely related to IFRS, IPSAS and GFS) and linking them to their significance in PSA.
- Discussing reasons why accounting harmonisation is important.
- Outlining challenges associated with PSA harmonisation.

The chapter is structured as follows: **Section 2** illustrates harmonisation efforts of the private sector accounting system and describes the IFRS in more detail. **Section 3** gives an overview of harmonisation in PSA, refers to the IPSAS and briefly introduces the EPSAS project (Chapter 13 covers this in more detail). **Section 4** concentrates on GFS, explaining the purposes of GFS and the differences between GFS and IPSAS. **Section 5** concludes by summarising the different perspectives on PSA harmonisation.

2. Harmonisation of the private sector accounting system

The emergence of IFRS began with the establishment of the International Accounting Standards Committee (IASC) in 1973. At that time, there were major differences in national accounting laws and standards between the founding member states of the IASC (Australia, Canada, France, Germany, Japan, Mexico, the Netherlands, the United Kingdom and Ireland, and the United States of America), so that financial information was not fully comparable for international investors and other user groups. Therefore, the IASC Agreement and Constitution aimed to develop and publish basic accounting standards and to promote their worldwide acceptance.[2] Even though the IASC (which later became the International Accounting Standards Board (IASB) in 2001) was restructured several times and confronted with conflicting national interests throughout its history, its original mission of advancing private sector accounting harmonisation remains unchanged. The current IFRS Foundation Constitution specifies the objectives of developing a single set of principle-based, high-quality, understandable, enforceable and globally accepted financial reporting standards, and to promote the worldwide use and rigorous application of those standards.[3]

The IASC published International Accounting Standards (IAS; which were later complemented by International Financial Reporting Standards (IFRS)), interpretations and a conceptual framework.

An important step with regards to the support for IFRS was the agreement reached with the International Organization of Securities Commission (IOSCO):

> *In 1995, an agreement was reached between the IASC (the predecessor of the IASB) and the International Organization of Securities Commission (IOSCO) whereby IASC agreed to develop a core set of accounting standards, and IOSCO in turn agreed to recommend that these standards be allowed for use in global capital*

---

[2] Camfferman and Zeff (2015), pp. 8-9.
[3] IFRS Foundation (2018a), para 2.

markets. This agreement confirms that one of the primary reasons for international harmonisation was to facilitate the operations of worldwide capital markets.[4]

IAS/IFRS are designed for the preparation of GPFS of profit-oriented entities (namely entities engaged in commercial, industrial, financial and similar activities). To this goal, IFRS set out the main requirements with regard to recognition, measurement, presentation and related disclosures dealing with specific transactions and events relevant for private sector entities' GPFS. The overall objective of IFRS is to provide financial information about the reporting entity that is useful for the economic decision making, primarily for investors and creditors. To achieve this objective, the fair presentation principle from the preparers' point of view and true and fair view from the auditors' point of view, require that the financial statements shall present fairly the financial position, financial performance and cash flows of the reporting entity.[5] The Board presumes that full compliance with IFRS will usually result in a fair presentation.

The term IFRS has to be interpreted broadly and is used to indicate the whole body of literature published by the IASB, including:

- Still effective **IAS**;
- The **Conceptual Framework** (CF) for Financial Reporting, which describes the objectives and general principles for the preparation of GPFS.

---

[4] Caruana (2018).

[5] Caruana (2018); IFRS Foundation (2018b). In recent times, the scope of work has been enlarged to non-financial (sustainability) issues. On 3 November 2021, the IFRS Foundation Trustees announced the creation of a new standard-setting board—the International Sustainability Standards Board (ISSB)—to help meet this demand. This brother board of the IASB shall develop IFRS-Sustainability Disclosure Standards (IFRS-SDS) (IFRS Foundation (2018b).

- Interpretations by the interpretation committee[6], which give authoritative guidance on reporting issues that would otherwise likely lead to divergent practices or unacceptable treatments for a large number of addressees[7] and which must be approved by the IASB.

In fulfilling its objective of creating a single set of globally accepted financial reporting standards, the IFRS Foundation identified the need to develop a governance **framework** that ensures transparency in developing and maintaining accounting regulations as well as establishing structures for effective communication and involvement of its constituency. Therefore, the IFRS Foundation Constitution[8] sets out a governance framework of different institutions involved in developing and maintaining IFRS (see Figure 5.1).

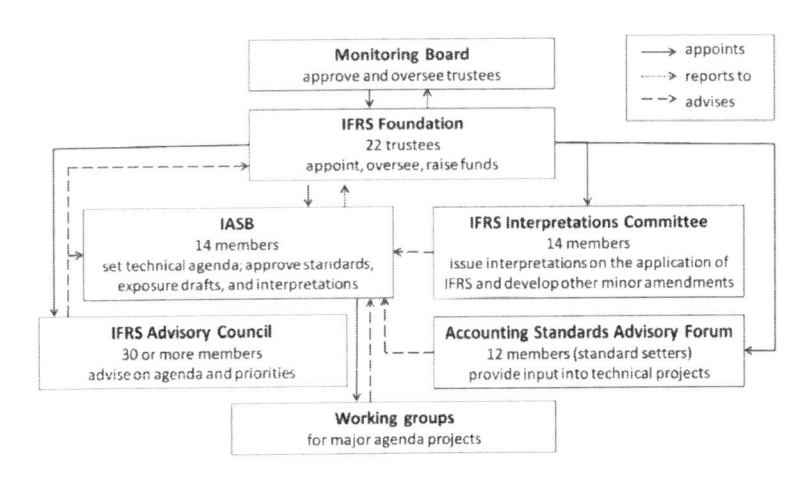

Figure 5.1: Governance framework of the IFRS Foundation and related institutions (Source: IFRS Foundation, 2018a)

---

[6] The Committee's name has changed over time: the IFRS Interpretations Committee (IFRIC) and its predecessor the Standing Interpretations Committee (SIC).

[7] In some point in time, the IFRIC refused to care about early retirement programs because they were deemed to be a local (German) issue, only.

[8] IFRS Foundation (2018a).

As the IASB is an international sector standard-setter, it has no legal authority to prescribe the mandatory use of IFRS in any jurisdiction. Therefore, countries that want to adopt IFRS have to implement an **endorsement mechanism** that mandates or allows the use of IFRS. Throughout the history of the IASB, different countries made different commitments regarding international financial reporting, from a full adoption of IFRS as issued by the Board, to adopting a modified version of IFRS, or developing national accounting standards that are substantially converged with IFRS.[9] As of April 2018, 144 out of 166 profiled jurisdictions worldwide allowed the use of IFRS for at least a subset of their domestic listed companies[10]. However, there is still a lack of acceptance in important jurisdictions.

In 2002, the EU required IFRS for the preparation of consolidated financial statements of listed companies within all member states, starting from 2005. The **EU endorsement mechanism** starts with the publication of a new IFRS/IFRIC (or amendment) by the IASB. The new standard is then assessed by technical experts within the European Financial Reporting Advisory Group (EFRAG). EFRAG is a private association that is tasked with providing advice to the European Commission (EC) on whether a new IFRS/IFRIC should be endorsed.[11] (see Figure 5.2)

Although by applying these endorsement procedures the EU can adopt a modified version of IFRS, in practice, these modifications

---

[9] For an overview of different endorsement mechanisms in different jurisdictions refer to Pacter (2017).

[10] IFRS Foundation 2018b

[11] EFRAG has to consider the three main endorsement criteria: Does the new standard fulfil the "true and fair view" principle? Is the standard conducive to the European public good? Does the standard meet the four qualitative criteria of understandability, relevance, reliability and comparability? Recently, the scope of work of EFRAG enlarged to drafting European Sustainability Reporting Standards (ESRS). 12 draft ESRS have been submitted to the EC on the mid-November 2022 (EFRAG, 2022).

will be limited to rare cases, as otherwise IFRS as adopted by the EU would not be comparable to full IFRS.[12]

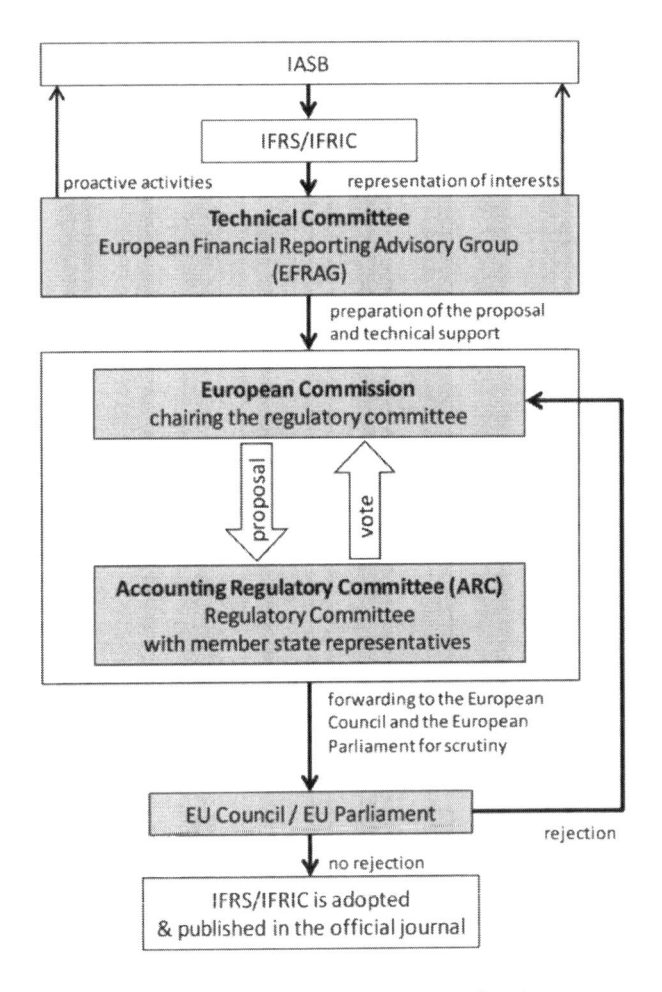

Figure 5.2: EU endorsement mechanism
(Based on Oversberg (2007), p. 1599f.; Pellens et al. (2017), p. 83)

---

[12] During the financial crisis, the EC made use of this option, which was followed by amendments to IAS 39 and IFRS 7, allowing the reclassification of some financial assets. The amendments were issued on 13 October 2008 without due process and became retrospectively effective by 1 July 2008; as a consequence, both IAS 39 and IFRS 7 were eventually accepted by the EU in 2010 ..https://www.ifrs.org/projects/completed-projects/2008/reclassification-of-financial-assets-amendments--to-ias-39-and-ifrs-7/.

The influence of the "Big 4" consulting firms, the move from national standards toward harmonisation and comparability, and the power struggles in the evolution of standard setting at a supranational level are all issues to which accounting literature for the private sector has devoted a significant degree of attention.[13]

In this context, even though IFRS can be seen as an important and successful tool for achieving the objective of private sector accounting harmonisation, there are still several challenges to be dealt with (not without difficulties) in the future:

- Several requirements in the standards are not in line with aspects of the CF and with other standards, leading to **inconsistencies in financial reporting**. For example, alignment of the accounting for Financial Instruments with characteristics of Equity with the accounting for other obligations that are conditional on events or choices that are beyond the entity's control; guidance to improve an entity's disclosures about its exploration and evaluation expenditure and activities under IFRS 6; and the prudence principle as an implicit notion of the faithful representation principle conflicting with impairment provisions in different standards.[14]
- Complexity and extensive disclosure requirements make financial reports based on IFRS **more error prone** as compared to national accounting guidelines.
- IFRS often include estimates based on the judgement of financial statement preparers. Accountants' professional judgment appears an important and controversial topic seen as

---

[13] For example, Durocher et al. (2007); Jorissen et al. (2012); Pelger (2016); Richardson and Eberlain (2010).

[14] Lorson and Haustein (2019).

leading to considerable **management discretion** and reduces the reliability of financial reports, for example requiring fair value approaches[15]. The level of subjectivity linked to other various issues, such as depreciation, provisions and impairment policies, usually associated with companies' earnings management, is also controversial. However, this a general issue, which can be referred to accrual-based accounting systems and not (only) to IFRS.

- IFRS still **lack global acceptance**. IFRS are still not fully applied in some notable economies (such as Japan and the United States), or not adopted at all. Furthermore, several countries only apply modified versions of IFRS, which decrease international comparability and, therefore, limit the objective of international accounting harmonisation.
- Major problems are observed in the implementation and compliance of application, which limit in practise IFRS adoption. IFRS implementation requires to set the institutional environment to ensure the standards would not conflict or overlap with other existing national laws and standards, as well as to define the role and responsibilities of the bodies regulating the standards. Implementation also requires considering the constraints on capacity building, to staff and for funding the regulatory bodies. IT infrastructure development, including the difficulties in implementing digital systems and capturing necessary data for disclosure, are only a few examples of challenges in implementation. Implementation of IFRS also requires amendments to audit arrangements, and to specifically consider how to deal with complexities for small and medium-sized enterprises and microenterprises.

---

[15] Heidhues and Patel (2011).

3. Harmonisation of the public sector accounting system

IPSAS is a prominent means for international harmonisation in public sector accounting. IPSAS are designed for public sector entities (for example, central governments, municipalities and other local authorities, hospitals, universities, schools, etc.) whose main objectives are to provide goods and services for collective benefit and to redistribute income and wealth, but also applicable for international organisations (e.g. NATO). These public sector entities are primarily financed by taxation, not profit.

The public sector is reforming its accounting system due to several reasons. The first aim is to provide a fair view and control of public finances. This is related to assessing the full costs of government operations. A new accounting style is associated with enhanced transparency and accountability, strategic resource management, and improved awareness and management of costs. The New Public Management trend at a global level extended the adoption of private sector practices in the public sector, explaining current reform processes in line with the overall objective of financial reporting by public sector to provide information about the entity that is useful for both accountability and decision-making purposes.[16]

In general, public management could be modernised by introducing a performance culture. Beside the importance of accounting for performance, financial crises and high levels of public debt underline the importance of harmonised accounting standards to provide timely and reliable financial and fiscal data and enable complete and comparable financial reporting, facilitating monitoring. Financial reporting harmonisation may provide for improved conditions to obtain financing and good practice for the preparation of GFS.

---

[16] IPSASB Conceptual Framework, para. 2.1.

The progressive adoption of **accrual-based accounting standards** should provide an improved "true and fair view" of government finances at country level and a public sector accounting harmonisation will improve comparability (both at national and international levels). Accrual-based accounting means that transactions are budgeted or recognised in the financial reports at the time at which the underlying economic event occurs, regardless of when the related cash is received or paid. Assets and liabilities are then budgeted and/or reported in a balance sheet.

According to surveys published in 2017/2018, 73 % of OECD countries (national government; central level) and 35% of European countries currently use accrual-based accounting for annual public sector financial reports.[17] The accounting basis for annual financial reports, however, differs from the preparation basis for budgets of national governments.[18] These great differences in accounting bases for annual financial reports and preparation bases for budgets are linked to the status of accrual reforms.[19] Furthermore, there are large differences concerning the type of standards used.

The 2021 report of the IFAC/CIPFA shows updated progress in implementing accrual-based reporting. According to this report, at global level, 49 jurisdictions reported on accrual in 2020, and 28 (57%) are using IPSAS – directly or indirectly or as a reference point. The report forecasts positions for European countries reflecting current reform programs, irrespective of a decision on the EPSAS project. The number of countries reporting on accrual is forecast to be 29 in 2025, compared with 19 in 2020.[20] **Chapter 7** of this book refers to IPSAS, and their use in more detail.

---

[17] OECD/IFAC (2017) p. 13; IFAC/CIPFA (2018), p. 2; IFAC/CIPFA (2021).
[18] Van Helden and Reichard (2016; 2018).
[19] OECD/IFAC (2017) p.24, p. 27, p. 30.
[20] IFAC/CIPFA (2021).

As in the private sector, there are **numerous challenges of implementing public sector accounting reforms towards accruals, harmonisation and IPSAS**:[21]

- Stakeholder consensus and political support;
- Adapting existing laws and regulations and developing legislation on public sector accounting, considering the time needed for regulatory reforms;
- Adapting the IT systems to the new requirements;
- Identification and valuation of assets and liabilities as part of the opening balance sheet;
- Developing guidance and training; consider the profession qualified for public sector financial accounting and PSA education at higher education level;
- Defining the public sector reporting entities in the national context, alongside the scope for preparing consolidated financial statements;
- Preparing financial statements in a timely manner;
- Preparing for audit requirements and addressing audit qualifications;
- Estimating, monitoring and controlling the costs of the reform;
- Applying principles consistently so that the accounting outcome is the same for comparable transactions.

The different focus of public *versus* private sector indeed matters in the context where accrual accounting and IPSAS should be implemented. The organizational and legislative level, stakeholder consensus and political support, the wider/narrower support of private consultants; the availability of information and professionally

---

[21] See for example Brusca and Martinez (2016); PWC (2014).

qualified accountants; and the costs and the type of transactions to be covered, are thus important aspects to consider.[22]

Notwithstanding, the development of IPSAS acknowledges the differences but pursues an alignment between IPSAS and IFRS as a guiding principle, wherever a public sector specific issue is not identified. This is particularly relevant when implementation should be applied to mixed private sector and public sector groups.

In this vein, it may also be observed that development of accounting reforms adopted in some countries involved a so-called 'neutral approach'. For example, New Zealand and Australia harmonised their reporting systems on the basis of a 'neutral' standards approach for both private and public sector, unless a different treatment was specifically required. However, this policy was reversed by New Zealand in 2011, when a differentiated standard approach for profit and non-profit (so called 'public benefit entities') was adopted and a new conceptual framework was adopted starting from 2012. The current standards for non-profit entities in New Zealand are based on IPSAS[23].

Next to harmonising public sector accounting by IPSAS, there are recent public sector reform efforts especially in Europe. The European Commission is working on a project whereby EU member states would use a common set of accrual-based standards, namely the **European Public Sector Accounting Standards (EPSAS).** These would be inspired by IPSAS but more in line with EU needs. Similar to IPSAS, it is expected that EPSAS would strengthen the harmonisation of accounting standards and stimulate transparent, credible and comparable financial statements between and within EU Member States. This will support policy-making, accountability and public budgets management at the macro level and at the entity level.[24] This scenario

---

[22] Gomes et al. (2022) ; Redmayne (2021).

[23] Dabbicco (2016).

[24] PWC (2014), pp. 4 ff.

was an important stimulus for accounting research, notably the study of the current situation of EU government accounting, which is highly heterogeneous,[25] although an increasing number of countries has adopted accrual accounting and IPSAS since the start of the project. Eurostat is taking forward the EPSAS project work through an EU network of experts representing all levels of government, as well as other key EU and international stakeholders, and is providing technical support and some co-financing to member states' government accounting reforms. **Chapter 13** outlines in more detail the European efforts for PSA, describes EPSAS and also refers to the challenges and risks of EPSAS implementation.

4. Harmonisation of Government Finance Statistics

European **Government Finance Statistics** (GFS) are produced in accordance with the European System of Accounts 2010 (ESA 2010) – the European version of the world-wide System of National Accounts (SNA), supplemented by further interpretation and guidance documentation from Eurostat. This ensures that GFS are based on common concepts, definitions, classifications and accounting rules, in order to arrive at a consistent, reliable and comparable quantitative description of government finances. In this respect, GFS are already highly harmonised in Europe.

GFS are part of national accounts describing macroeconomic changes in various ways, for instance through main aggregates including GDP, institutional sectors, supply, use and input-output tables, and deficit and debt of the general government.

The SNA is the core statistical system and serves as an "umbrella" framework by providing definitions and concepts for all other

---

[25] Brusca et al. (2018).

macroeconomic statistics. GFS and SNA are largely consistent. Since 1970, the Government Finance Statistics Manual has provided guidance to compile GFS. It was lastly updated in 2014 (GFSM 2014) to up-dated SNA 2008 and two specialised systems, namely, the Balance of Payments and International Investment Position Manual (BPM6) and the Monetary and Financial Statistics Manual (MFSM). The ESA is based on the SNA. Contrary to the SNA, the ESA is an EU Regulation, which comprises a methodology and a compulsory transmission programme of data by member states.

The "Manual on Government Deficit and Debt" (MGDD) provides guidance at European level regarding GFS, complementing ESA 2010 to better understand the methodology applied to government finance data, notably in the context of the Excessive Deficit Procedure (EDP).[26]

The sectorisation of the general government sector of the public sector may be illustrated as in Figure 5.3.

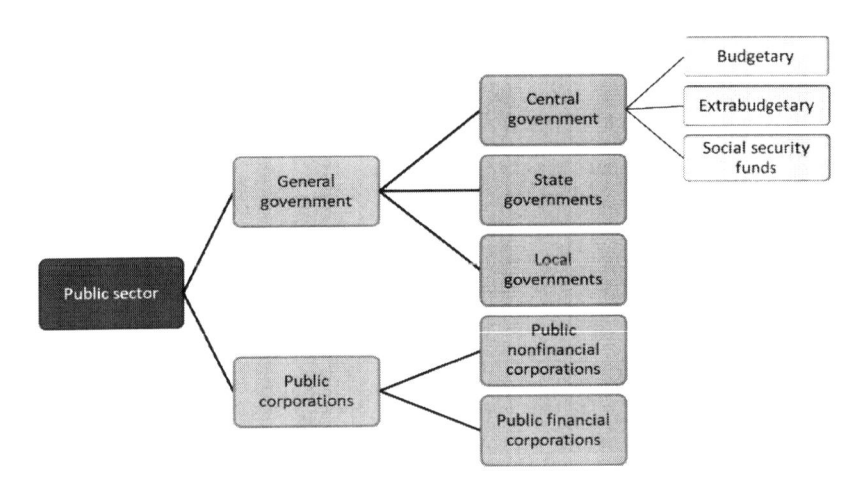

Figure 5.3: Main components of the public sector
Source: GFSM 2014

---

[26] Council Regulation (EC) No 479/2009, as amended by Council Regulation (EU) No 679/2010 and Commission Regulation (EU) No 220/2014. For more detail on EDP reporting see https://ec.europa.eu/eurostat/web/government-finance-statistics/excessive-deficit-procedure

The **General Government Sector** (GGS) comprises non-market producers creating output for individual and collective consumption. They are financed by compulsory payments from units belonging to other sectors. The sector's main functions consist of satisfying collective needs (e.g., defence) and household's needs (e.g., state health care). In order to finance these needs, it redirects money, goods and services among units (e.g., redistribution of national income). The GGS can be divided into:

- Central government: responsibilities cover the whole economic territory of a country;
- State government: separate institutional units responsible for exercising various government functions;
- Local government: provision of services to local residents;
- Social security funds: Includes all social security units, regardless of the level of government (if not included in Central Government).

Table 5.1 summarises the **differences between GFS and IPSAS**. The statistical reporting unit is an institutional unit, defined as an entity that is *capable of owning goods and assets, of incurring liabilities and of engaging in economic activities and transactions with other units in their own right.*[27] Although the reporting entity is an institutional unit, the focus of GFS is on a group of entities, such as the GGS or a subsector. At the level of consolidated financial statements, the reporting entity represents an economic entity, defined as a group of entities that includes one or more controlled entities and may be extended to the Whole of Government.[28]

---

[27] ESA (2010); EC (2013) para 1.57 p. 12.

[28] Caruana et al. (2019), p. 153. See Chapter 11 of this book for further information on Whole of Government Reporting.

Issue	IPSAS	GFS
PERSPECTIVE	Micro	Macro
REPORTING BOUNDARY	Reporting entity ranges from an individual entity to the public sector as a whole	Institutional Unit / Institutional sectors GGS /public sector
INCOME PERSPECTIVE	Comprehensive	Other economic flows separated from revenues and expenses
USERS	Governments, international organisations, taxpayers, members of the legislature, creditors, suppliers, *media*, employees and the general public	European Community institutions, governments, analysts and decision-makers of fiscal policies and other social and economic agents
USERS' NEEDS	Information about the financial position, financial performance and cash flows of an entity, useful for decision making and evaluating about the allocation of resources	Aggregated data for economic analysis, decision making and policy making
GOALS	Management Analysis Financial reporting	Economic analysis Fiscal policies-related decision making
OBJECTIVES	Accountability Decision making	Analysis and evaluation Providing information for preparing, implementing and monitoring the economic policies of the European Monetary Union
RECOGNITION	Financial accounting accrual basis	Full accrual basis for all transactions (monetary and non-monetary), except for taxes and social contributions
MEASUREMENT	Historical cost – purchase price or production cost Market prices exceptionally admitted	Market prices as main reference

Table 5.1: GFS versus IPSAS
Source: Adapted from Caruana et al. (2019)

Harmonising GFS also involves numerous **challenges** that restrain from comparing data across countries in an economic and monetary union, such as the EU.[29] In Europe, the mission of the Eurostat is to contribute to methodological developments in public finance leading to more harmonised public finance statistics. In this respect, additional guidelines may be provided for regional arrangements such as "rulings" or "fiscal policy rules" on specific transactions, aggregates, or balancing items (e.g., MGDD of the EU). Existing guidelines on concepts and definitions may be clarified in order to provide the appropriate treatment of statistical issues raised in the EU regarding government finance statistics and to help to better understand the methodology applied to government finance data for the EDP.

Statistics also frequently face challenges to delineate units for sector classification and in many cases borderline cases need to be addressed to ensure full comparability across the EU. Furthermore, it should be transparent which units are included and which are not part of GFS. Accordingly, European GFS requires the publication of the list of the entities included in the GGS of each member state. It also recommends – on a voluntary basis – to publish a list for Public Corporations. This helps in understanding the delineation of the public sector and of the GGS as part of it.

Moreover, GFS harmonisation is challenged by recording economic events across countries. Whereas some countries apply the cash basis of accounting, others adopt the accrual basis of accounting. Although there is a trend towards accrual accounting,[30] there are various mixed accounting systems. This implies that, the starting point to calculate the government deficit is different, requiring different adjustments. Finally, the measurement of gross and net debt has to be comparable across all countries of an economic and

---

[29] IMF (2014), p. 339.

[30] IFAC/CIPFA (2018, 2021).

monetary union, so that national definitions have to be adapted to international agreed definitions of debt[31].

5. The link between accruals accounting/IPSAS and statistics

Besides the IPASB's policy of alignment between private (IFRS) and Public sector (IPSAS), harmonisation in PSA also requires the consideration of the relationships and linkage between the different reporting systems and the main issues that can be addressed for an increased harmonization between them. As mentioned earlier in this chapter, macroeconomic statistics under ESA 2010 are based on the accounts of single entities and governments as basic data sources. The ESA 2010 contains recording rules which cover the whole economy, but also contains specific rules for recording government entities and certain transactions. The same ESA transaction categories are used in the compilation of GFS.

GFS and public sector accounts share some common terminology, such as 'assets and liabilities', and 'expense and revenue'. However, the definition may be different, as well as recognition and measurement criteria. For EU fiscal surveillance purposes, a set of reconciliation tables with data from underlying public sector accounts is provided in the biannual notification of EDP statistics, alongside related questionnaire tables and several supplementary tables.

Technically speaking, **a micro-macro linkage of underlying public sector accounts under the ESA is used to compile consistent and comparable statistics**. Transparent linking is obviously crucial for GFS quality as well as their comparability, but this is only possible with a consistent set of concepts. Standardised and aligned chart of accounts are needed where public sector accounts and financial reports show a lack of uniformity of the structures,

---

[31] See: Public Sector Debt Statistics : Guide for compilers and users 2011 (PSDSG-2011)

definitions and principles (for example, cash *versus* accrual basis) in public sector entities' accounts. Statisticians use data sources from these not harmonised public sector accounting systems and make appropriate adjustments to reach harmonised statistical measures. The reconciliation of inconsistencies in the information from primary accounting data is developed through linkage tables and charts of accounts, and bridge tables for the different classifications used (i.e. financial and non-financial transactions versus current and non-current transactions, type of activities, boundary of reporting entity).[32]

But the two sets of reporting, from accounting and statistics, remain different as shown in Table 5.1. In addition, the reconciliation of GFS to public sector accounting is challenged by non-harmonised public sector accounting sources (i.e., the lack of a consistent system).

The EPSAS project on harmonisation of accrual-based public sector accounting standards for all EU member states at all levels of government, proposes a new approach for the link between public sector accounting and statistics, using accrual-based IPSAS as the starting point for development and with consideration of public sector specificities, as well as IFRS, ESA and other relevant standards, such as national GAAP, in compiling public sector accounts.

Major issues being considered in EPSAS development have included:

- the definition of the public sector "reporting entity";
- the definition of the reporting boundary;
- the recognition criteria, and the various implementations of accrual accounting in the public sector;
- the notion of control, as a delineation criterion for the public *versus* private boundary and consolidation; and
- valuation differences with different criteria of measurement underpinning the systems.

---

[32] Dabbicco (2018).

Using harmonised accrual-based EPSAS in public sector accounting in the EU would improve the transparency of government finances and allow improvements in the reliability of GFS.

6. Conclusion

The increasing use of IFRS illustrates efforts toward standardisation of accounting over the last two decades. The extent to which this development results in harmonisation and improved comparability of financial statements across firms will depend on the actual implementation of the standards .and on the various factors of applicability in jurisdictions and entities

With this backdrop, investors and capital markets have demanded supplementary standardised non-financial (sustainability) information, in order to base their decisions on a holistic picture of companies.[33] This is a 'new frontier' of harmonisation of standards.

The public sector is following the reform path of the private sector in implementing accrual accounting practices into public sector accounting regimes. At the global level, harmonisation of public sector accounting should be realised by adopting the IPSAS, a well-developed set of accounting standards for use by public sector entities. Despite a number of drawbacks and deficiencies, IPSAS and IFRS are important references for reforming public sector accounting system in countries.

Standardisation and harmonisation are important steps for accounting comparability. Harmonisation can be pursued in different ways, covering both vertical and horizontal aspects. In this vein, it may be in the same sector or in different sector. (i.e. private and

---

[33] Also refer to Chapter 14 in this book.

public).[34] Harmonisation efforts should consider the diversity of situations at entity level, and find a good balance between the benefits of comparability and the costs of a 'one size fits all' approach (for example with respect to small and medium sized entities).

In Europe, the EPSAS are currently being developed in order to harmonise public sector accounting in EU member states and create a uniform accrual-based accounting system for use by all public entities in the EU. However, the EPSAS project focuses on financial reporting and – following IPSAS – does not take a position on the accounting basis for budgeting, which may result in the coexistence in some member states of two different accounting systems for budgeting and financial reporting.

Harmonisation between the public sector accounting and GFS is increasingly seen as an important step towards the harmonisation of public sector accounting approaches across EU countries, but the analysis above has highlighted their differences, besides their linkages and areas of convergence. IPSAS and EPSAS developments have taken into consideration that conceptual differences between public sector accounting and national accounts are likely to remain, and that this should be reconciled when translating the data between the two reporting systems.[35]

Bibliographic references

This chapter benefited from work in the previous edition, and preserved the connection with it. Different perspectives in public sector accounting harmonisation: IFRS, GFS and IPSAS by Lisa SCHMIDTHUBER, Dennis HILGERS, Hannes HOFBAUER (2019).

---

[34] Caruana (2018), ESA (2010); EC (2013) para 1.57 p. 12.
[35] Caruana et al. (2019).

BRUSCA, Isabel; CAPERCHIONE, Eugenio; COHEN, Sandra and MANES-ROSSI, Francesca (2018) – IPSAS, EPSAS and other challenges in European public sector accounting and auditing. In The Palgrave Handbook of Public Administration and Management in Europe (pp. 165-185). Palgrave Macmillan, London.

CAMFFERMAN, Kees and ZEFF, Stephen A. (2015) – Aiming for Global Accounting Standards, The International Accounting Standards Board, 2001-2011, Oxford 2015.

CARUANA, Josette (2018) – Harmonisation. In: Farazmand, A. (eds) Global Encyclopedia of Public Administration, Public Policy, and Governance. Springer, Cham. https://doi.org/10.1007/978-3-319-20928-9_2281

CARUANA, Josette; DABBICCO, Giovanna; JORGE, Susana and JESUS, Maria Antónia (2019) – The Development of EPSAS: Contributions from the Literature, Accounting in Europe, 16:2, 146-176, DOI: 10.1080/17449480.2019.1624924

DABBICCO, Giovanna (2016) – A comparison of Government Accounting and Government Finance Statistics. Ph.D. thesis in Economics of public sector entities, University of Naples "Parthenope", Italy.

DABBICCO, Giovanna (2018) A comparison of debt measures in fiscal statistics and public sector financial statements, Public Money & Management, 38:7, 511-518, DOI: 10.1080/09540962.2018.1527543

DABBICCO, Giovanna and MATTEI, Giorgia (2021) – The reconciliation of budgeting with financial reporting: A comparative study of Italy and the UK, Public Money & Management, 41:2, 127-137, DOI: 10.1080/09540962.2019.1708059

DUROCHER, Sylvain; FORTIN, Anne and CÔTÉ, Louise (2007) – Users' participation in the accounting standard-setting process: a theory-building study, Accounting, Organizations and Society, Vol. 32 Nos 1–2,pp. 33-63

EFRAG (2022) – presentation by Saskia Slomp at High-level panel: Recent developments in financial and sustainability reporting requirements and related standard-setting developments and their implications for practical implementation, ISAR 39th SESSION, 1-3 November 2022, Geneve.

EUROPEAN COMMISSION (2013) – European System of Accounts (ESA 2010).

HEIDHUES, Eva and PATEL, Chris (2011) – IFRS and exercise of accountants' professional judgments: Insights and concerns from a German perspective. Working Paper, Macquarie University.

IFAC/CIPFA (2018) – International Public Sector Financial Accountability Index: Status Report. Retrieved from hiips://www.ifac.org/system/files/publications/files/IFAC-CIPFAPublic-Sector-Index-2018-Status.pdf. (22nd January 2019).

IFAC/CIPFA (2021) – International Public Sector Financial Accountability Index: Status Report. Retrieved from retrieved from https://www.ifac.org/publications/international-public-sector-financial-accountability-index-2021-status-report (11 November 2022)

IFRS FOUNDATION (2018a) – Constitution, London.

IFRS FOUNDATION (2018b) – Use of IFRS Standards around the world, London.

INTERNATIONAL MONETARY FUND (2014) – Government finance statistics manual 2014.

International Monetary Fund (2011) Public Sector Debt Statistics, Guide for Compilers and Users: Guide for Compilers and Users https://doi.org/10.5089/9781616351564.069

GOMES, Patrícia; BRUSCA, Isabel; FERNANDES, Maria J. and VILHENA, Estela (2022) – The IPSAS implementation and the use and usefulness of accounting information: a comparative analysis in the Iberian Peninsula, Journal of Public Budgeting, Accounting & Financial Management, Vol. ahead-of-print No. ahead-of-print. https://doi.org/10.1108/JPBAFM-12-2021-0169

JORISSEN, Ann; LYBAERT, Nadine; ORENS, Raf and VAN DER TAS, Leo (2012) – Formal participation in the IASB's due process of standard-setting: a multi-issue/multi-period analysis, European Accounting Review, Vol. 21 No. 4, pp. 693-729.

LORSON, Peter and HAUSTEIN, Ellen (2019) – Debate: On the role of prudence in public sector accounting, in: Public Money & Management, Vol. 39, Issue 6/2019, pp. 389–390, https://doi.org/10.1080/09540962.2019.1583907

OECD/IFAC (2017) – Accrual Practices and Reform Experiences in OECD Countries, OECD, Publishing, Paris. hiip://dx.doi.org/10.1787/9789264270572-en

OVERSBERG, Thomas (2007) – Übernahme der IFRS in Europa: Der Endorsement-ProzessStatus quo und Aussicht. Der Betrieb, Heft 30, 1597-1602.

PACTER, Paul (2017) – Pocket Guide to IFRS Standards: the global financial reporting language, London 2017.

PELGER, Christoph (2016) – Practices of standard-setting an analysis of the IASB's and FASB's process of identifying the objective of financial reporting, Accounting, Organizations and Society, Vol. 50, pp. 51-73.

PELLENS, Bernhard; FÜLBIER, Rolf Uwe; GASSEN, Joachim and SELLHORN, Thomas (2017) – Internationale Rechnungslegung, 10th ed., Stuttgart 2017.

PWC (2014) – Collection of information related to the potential impact, including costs, of implementing accrual accounting in the public sector and technical analysis of the suitability of individual IPSAS standards. hiips://ec.europa.eu/eurostat/ documents/1015035/4261806/EPSAS-study-final-PwC-report.pdf

RICHARDSON, Alan J. and EBERLEIN, Burkard(2011) – Legitimating transnational standard-setting: the case of the international accounting standards board, Journal of Business Ethics, Vol. 98 No. 2, pp. 217-245.

REDMAYNE, Nives Botica; LASWAD, Fawzi and EHALAIYE, Dimu (2021) – Evidence on the costs of changes in financial reporting frameworks in the public sector, Public Money & Management, 41:5, 368-375, DOI: 10.1080/09540962.2019.1679482

SCHMIDTHUBER, Lisa; HILGERS, Dennis and HOFBAUER, Hannes (2019) – Different perspectives in public sector accounting harmonization: IFRS, GFS and IPSAS, in: Lorson, Peter/Jorge, Susana/Haustein, Ellen (2019, eds.): European Public Sector Accounting, Coimbra University Press.

VAN HELDEN, Jan and REICHARD, Christoph (2016) – Why cash-based budgeting still prevails in an era of accrual-based reporting in the public sector. Accounting Finance & supraGovernance Review, 23(1-2), 43-65.

VAN HELDEN, Jan and REICHARD, Christoph (2018) – Cash or accruals for budgeting? Why some governments in Europe changed their budgeting mode and others not. OECD Journal on Budgeting, 18(1), 91-113.

Additional readings

BRUSCA, Isabel and MARTÍNEZ, Juan Carlos (2016) – Adopting International Public Sector Accounting Standards: a challenge for modernizing and harmonizing public sector accounting. *International Review of Administrative Sciences*, 82(4), 724-744.

MANES ROSSI, Francesca; CAPERCHIONE, Eugenio; COHEN, Sandra, and BRUSCA, Isabel (2016) – Harmonizing public sector accounting in Europe: thinking out of the box. *Public Money & Management*, 36(3), 189-196.

Discussion topics

- Why is public sector accounting harmonisation important?
- Discuss how the member states of the European Union can achieve accounting harmonisation.
- Discuss the conceptual differences between IFRS and IPSAS.
- Discuss the relationship between accrual accounting and GFS.

CHAPTER 6
IPSAS: HISTORY, SPREAD AND USE

Caroline A. Pontoppidan
Copenhagen Business School, Denmark; University of Kristianstad, Sweden
cap.acc@cbs.dk
https://orcid.org/0000-0002-9979-6023

Summary

International Public Sector Standards (IPSAS) have been in existence for more than two decades now.[1] Developed by the International Public Sector Accounting Standards Board (IPSASB), the IPSAS are designed for application by national, regional and local governments, as well as related national and transnational public sector organisations. Convergence of accounting practices and systems across borders advances a largely homogenous basis for financial reporting in the public sector. Thus, IPSAS serve as a mechanism that supports convergence and harmonization of public sector accounting and financial reporting across borders. Recent data show that close to 70 jurisdictions have partially adopted IPSAS,[2] but adoption approaches differ between jurisdictions. This chapter provides some examples of countries that adopt accrual based IPSAS through this path. The adoption of IPSAS

---

[1] The first IPSAS were published in May 2000.
[2] IFAC (2021).

has been progressing globally; this chapter provides a high-level overview of such progress. Despite progress, challenges have persisted over time, in particular with regard to advancement in the competences of accountants in the public sector and the implementation of a sound institutional structure to support IPSAS-based reporting.

Keywords

IPSASB, IPSAS, international public sector accounting, accounting harmonisation.

1. Introduction

The International Public Sector Accounting Standards (IPSAS) contain a set of accrual-based accounting standards as well as an IPSAS for cash basis financial reporting in the public sector.[3] A general aim of IPSAS is to provide a uniform global basis for the preparation of annual financial statements in the public sector.[4] IPSAS are predominantly based on the International Financial Reporting Standards (IFRS), with areas of divergence to ensure a fit in the public sector context. IPSAS are increasingly recognized as an international benchmark for accrual-based public sector financial reporting. Governments across the world face the decision of whether to fully adopt IPSAS, partially adopt IPSAS (that is, only some standards), adapt certain standards or not implement IPSAS at all.

Implementing IPSAS often brings wide-spanning change in accounting and financial reporting practices for governments and other

---

[3] Cash Basis IPSAS, Financial Reporting under the Cash Basis of Accounting.

[4] Schmidthuber et al. (2022) provide an up to date literature review on research studies that pertain to IPSAS.

public sector entities. The scope of the changes required varies from jurisdiction to jurisdiction. In general, the closer a jurisdiction is to cash accounting the more comprehensive changes are required to move to accrual based IPSAS. Some countries choose to start with IPSAS cash basis and then incrementally move to accrual based IPSAS. This chapter provides some examples of countries that adopt accrual based IPSAS through this path.

Adopting IPSAS is however not limited to technical accounting changes. It typically includes a wide range of challenges relating to: accounting systems; adopting new infrastructure for technology to support accrual-based accounting and reporting; the continuous education and re-education of professional accountants in the public sector.[5] A recent literature review study focused on classifying the IPSAS literature that has engaged with the following questions; which factors have influenced the adoption of IPSAS, to what extent has accrual accounting based on IPSASs already been implemented and what are the outcomes of adopting IPSAS?[6]

The adoption of IPSAS has been progressing globally; this chapter provides a high-level overview of such progress. Despite progress, challenges have persisted over time, in particular with regard to advancement in the competences of accountants in the public sector and the implementation of a sound institutional structure to support IPSAS-based reporting.

Therefore, this chapter focuses on IPSAS and has the followings aims:

- Providing a summary of the evolution of the IPSAS and the role of the IPSAS Board (IPSASB) in the development of IPSAS and other public sector accounting pronouncements.

---

[5] For further reading on the matter see the recent study by Tawiah (2022).
[6] See Schmidthuber et al. (2022).

- Providing an overview of the IPSAS and which countries and organisations have adopted IPSAS till date.
- Explaining benefits and challenges associated with the transnational spread and use of IPSAS.

2. Transnational regulation

Due to the work of the IPSASB, public sector financial reporting is becoming increasingly transnationally comparable. The role of standards at the transnational level is often described as having the aim of creating coherence and social order across nation states[7]. Research in the area of standards and standardization at the transnational level seeks to better understand how such standards fruitfully span national boundaries over time.[8]

The term transnational suggests that nation specific boundaries are softened. In our contemporary world, it becomes increasingly difficult to separate what takes place within national boundaries and what takes place across and beyond nations. Studies propose that the subtle opposition between 'globalization' and 'nation states' frequently surfaces in debates that regard harmonization and convergence of practices. This is also the case in the area of transnational convergence of public sector accounting practices.[9]. Transnational governance proposes that national autonomy cannot be taken for granted. Scholars in the field of transnational governance explain that governance activities are embedded in particular geopolitical structures and thus embrace multiple and interacting institutional webs.[10]

---

[7] Brunsson and Jacobsson (2000).

[8] Botzem and Dobusch (2012).

[9] This paragraph draws on the writings of Eberlein & Newman (2008) who engage in research on international governance.

[10] Eberlein and Newman (2008).

During the last few decades there has been a formidable explosion of standards for the regulation of transnational corporate affairs;[11] IPSAS appear in this trend of the transnational governance of public affairs. IPSAS can be construed as technologies of transnational governance.[12] The public sector is characterized by the need for ensuring accountability[13], which in turn is often described as a complex, elusive and multifaceted character, which goes beyond the financial and stewardship dimensions.[14] IPSAS are believed to improve accountability as a central purpose of public sector financial reporting.[15]

There is no standardized way of adopting and implementing IPSAS to be found worldwide.[16] This means that the scope of IPSAS implementation varies tremendously. This alludes to scholarly work that echoes that "standards are contested and volatile, and only become authoritative rules under certain conditions that need further specification".[17] The need for legitimacy and strategies of legitimation are also central themes that underpin accounting reforms in the public sector and thus also the advancement of IPSAS.[18]

3. Stages of the IPSASB evolution

Prior to engaging with the global adoption patterns of IPSAS, this chapter will take brief consideration of the key stages of the

---

[11] See Brunsson and Jacobsson (2000).
[12] Garsten and Jacobsson (2011).
[13] See chapters 5 and 7 of this book for a definition of accountability.
[14] Almquist et al. (2013).
[15] IPSASB (2014) Conceptual Framework.
[16] See ACCA (2017).
[17] Botzem and Dobusch (2012), p. 738.
[18] Ansari and Euske (1987).

work of the IPSASB.[19] The section is divided into three subsections that take us from the initial activities that lead to the establishment of a Public Sector Committee (PSC), under IFAC, to our contemporary umbrella of accrual based IPSAS published by the IPSASB. Note that there are further readings into the history of IPSAS and the IPSASB [20].

Phase I. Planting the seeds for transnational regulation in public sector accounting

Deliberations on the global harmonization of accounting and financial reporting in the private sector was initiated in the late 1960s and early 1970s. Advancements in the public sector followed, but approximately two decades later than that of the private sector.[21] At the time, the early deliberations on need to undertake harmonization in the area of public sector accounting led to the establishment of a Public Sector Committee (PSC) under the auspices of the International Federation of Accountants (IFAC)[22].

More explicitly, the PSC was established in 1986, to address public sector accounting matters through research and publications. At the root of this development was an increasing problematization of the fact that little financial data existed for public sector entities and governmental organizations. Better fi-

---

[19] See also https://www.ifac.org/knowledge-gateway/supporting-international-standards/discussion/twenty-years-international-public-sector-standard-setting.

[20] See for example Jensen (2018).

[21] See Andernack and Aggestam-Pontoppidan (2016) and Rocher (2010).

[22] In addition to the early versions of IPSAS, the PSC published Study 14, Transition to the Accrual Basis of Accounting: Guidance for Public Sector Entities, Study 11, Governmental Financial Reporting: Accounting Issues and Practices, and Financial Reporting under the Cash Basis of Accounting (Jensen, 2018).

nancial accountability within the public sector became a driver in this process.

Phase II. The rise of the IPSASB

The world witnessed financial restraints on public expenditure during the 1990s. This resulted in increased accountability requirements for limited resources and continuous efforts to improve the efficiency and effectiveness of public services. This movement was instituted based on the principles of New Public Management (NPM). Accounting practices became an integral part of the NPM movement from the 1990s onwards. In line with the NPM movement, the starting point for the work of the PSC on accounting standards was a consideration of where existing private sector accounting could be applied within the public sector. Subsequently, in 1996, the PSC started its standards development program and moved beyond its early work on providing guidance in various forms to work towards international standard-setting in accounting for the public sector.

The first set of IPSAS were largely based on International Accounting Standards (IASs) and incorporated the accrual method of accounting. In 2003, IFAC commissioned a review of the PSC by an externally chaired review panel. The review became known as the 'Likierman Review'. The final findings of the 'Likierman Review' pointed towards a number of reasons for justifying the establishment of an independent accounting standard-setter in the public sector, and thus reforming the role of the PSC. Subsequent to these finding, as part of a general reorganization of the International Federation of Accountants, the Public Sector Committee was superseded by the IPSAS Board (IPSASB) in 2004. At this point the IPSASB started to more explicitly address issues specific to the public sector and these started to be considered in the standard-making processes.

Phase III. IPSASB in contemporary transnational society

During the last decades the adoption of IPSAS has expanded across the world. Likewise, the number of standards released by the IPSASB grew over the years (see Table 6.1). An important development for the IPSASB was that in 2015, the European Union announced plans for the establishment and adoption of European Public Sector Accounting Standards (EPSAS) based on IPSAS.[23] A few of the more recent advancements include the release of an updated IPSAS-IFRS alignment dashboard as of June 2019. This dashboard indicates the extent of alignment between individual IPSAS and the corresponding IFRS. The current IPSASB work programme (2022) comprises key projects on the following key topics: presentation of financial statements; differential reporting; and a global consultation on advancing public sector sustainability reporting. In addition, the Board has launched a centrally located digital gateway to the international standards, to guide the accountancy profession on IPSAS.

In alignment with the rapid movement in developing private sector sustainability reporting the IPSASB released a consultation paper on advancing public sector sustainability reporting. This development came subsequent to the World Bank's January 31, 2022 report, 'Sovereign Climate and Nature Reporting'. The World Bank report addresses five key questions regarding sovereign climate and nature reporting: (a) why is a sovereign reporting framework needed? (b) what is required to develop a reporting framework for sovereigns? (c) how is materiality important in driving a reporting framework for sovereigns? (d) what is the potential for unintended consequences? and (e) what are the recommended next steps to develop and implement a reporting framework for sovereigns?

---

[23] Pontoppidan and Brusca (2016).

Following the release of the IPSASB consultation on sustainability reporting, the Board also released a consultation paper on natural resources, in 2022, which is its first step in developing guidance on the recognition, measurement, presentation and disclosure of natural resources in the public sector. One key question is whether a natural resource can be recognized as an asset in general purpose financial statements. The paper includes the following sections: discussion of the description of natural resources; discussion of accounting for activities related to each topic; application of asset recognition criteria; measurement considerations for each topic; and disclosure considerations. Sustainability reporting in the public sector is covered in an in-depth manner in Chapter 14 of this book.

IPSAS	Title of standard	Focus	Drawn from	Effective date[24]	Superseded by
1	Presentation of financial statements	General reporting	IAS 1	January 1, 2008	-
2	Cash flow statement	General reporting	IAS 7	July 1, 2001	-
3	Accounting policies, changes in accounting estimates and errors	General reporting	IAS 8	January 1, 2008	-
4	The effect of changes in foreign exchange rates	Accounting recognition and measurement	IAS 21	January 1, 2010	-
5	Borrowing costs	Specific balance sheet items	IAS 23	July 1, 2001	-
6	Consolidated and separate financial statements	General reporting	IAS 27	-	IPSAS 36 since January 1, 2017

[24] This is the date the standard as a whole became effective for annual financial statements covering periods beginning on or after this date. However, it is possible that the effective date of individual (amended) paragraphs differs from the general effective date. A list of them can be found in each standard (under the heading 'Effective date').

IPSAS	Title of standard	Focus	Drawn from	Effective date	Superseded by
7	Interest in associates	Specific balance sheet items	IAS 28	-	IPSAS 36 since January 1, 2017
8	Interests in joint ventures	General reporting	IAS 31	-	IPSAS 37 since January 1, 2017
9	Revenue from exchange transactions	Accounting recognition and measurement	IAS 18	July 1, 2002	-
10	Financial reporting in hyperinflationary economies	General reporting	IAS 29	July 1, 2002	-
11	Construction contracts	Specific balance sheet items	IAS 11	July 1, 2002	-
12	Inventories	Specific balance sheet items	IAS 2	January 1, 2008	-
13	Leases	Specific balance sheet items	IAS 17	-	IPSAS 43 from January 1, 2025 on
14	Events after the reporting date	General reporting	IAS 10	January 1, 2008	-
15	Financial instruments: disclosure and presentation	Specific balance sheet items	IAS 32	-	IPSASs 28-30 since January 1, 2013
16	Investment property	Specific balance sheet items	IAS 40	January 1, 2008	-
17	Property, Plant and Equipment	Specific balance sheet items	IAS 16	January 1, 2008	-
18	Segment reporting	General reporting	IAS 14	July 1, 2003	-
19	Provisions, contingent liabilities and contingent assets	Specific balance sheet items	IAS 37	January 1, 2004	-
20	Related party disclosures	General reporting	IAS 24	January 1, 2004	-

IPSAS	Title of standard	Focus	Drawn from	Effective date	Superseded by
21	Impairment of non-cash-generating assets	Specific balance sheet items	IAS 36	January 1, 2006	-
22	Disclosure of financial information about the general government sector	General reporting	-	January 1, 2008	-
23	Revenue from non-exchange transactions (taxes and transfers)	Accounting recognition and measurement	-	June 30, 2008	-
24	Presentation of budget information	General reporting	-	January 1, 2009	-
25	Employee benefits	Specific balance sheet items	IAS 19	-	IPSAS 39 since January 1, 2018
26	Impairment of cash-generating assets	Specific balance sheet items	IAS 36	April 1, 2019	-
27	Agriculture	Specific balance sheet items	IAS 41	April 1, 2011	-
28	Financial instruments: presentation	Specific balance sheet items	IAS 32, IFRIC 2	January 1, 2013	-
29	Financial instruments: recognition an measurement	Specific balance sheet items	IAS 39, IFRIC 9 & 16	January 1, 2013	-
30	Financial instruments: disclosures contents	Specific balance sheet items	IFRS 7	January 1, 2013	-
31	Intangible assets	Specific balance sheet items	IAS 38, SIC 29	April 1, 2011	-
32	Service concession arrangements: grantor	Specific balance sheet items	IFRIC 12 & SIC 29	January 1, 2014	-
33	First-time adoption of accrual basis IPSASs	General reporting	IFRS 1	January 1, 2017	-
34	Separate financial statements	General reporting	IAS 27	January 1, 2017	-
35	Consolidated financial statements	General reporting	IFRS 10	January 1, 2017	-

IPSAS	Title of standard	Focus	Drawn from	Effective date	Superseded by
36	Investments in associates and joint ventures	General reporting	IAS 28	January 1, 2017	-
37	Joint arrangements	General reporting	IFRS 11	January 1, 2017	-
38	Disclosure of interests in other entities	General reporting	IFRS 12	January 1, 2017	-
39	Employee Benefits	Specific balance sheet items	IAS 19	January 1, 2018	-
40	Public sector combinations	General reporting	-	January 1, 2019	-
41	Financial instruments	Specific balance sheet items	IFRS 9	January 1, 2023	-
42	Social benefits	Specific balance sheet items	-	January 1, 2023	-
43	Leases	Specific balance sheet items	IFRS 16	January 1, 2025	-
44	Non-current assets held for sale and discontinued operations	Specific balance sheet items	IFRS 5	January 1, 2025	-

Table 6.1: Overview on the individual IPSAS

4. Advancing our understanding of the spread of IPSAS

In public sector accounting research, the process through which IPSAS is adopted varies. In some countries elements of IPSAS are incorporated in local regulation[25]. It can entail the coexistence of different sets of standards, for example local regulation can embed IPSAS requirements. Over time, countries can see accounting requirements

---

[25] For further elaboration on this please see Brusca and Martínez (2016).

'converging' towards the same principles. The process of convergence can be carried out by a step-by-step implementation of changes of international standards into a local context. Convergence can take place between IPSAS and local accounting and financial reporting requirements within the public sector. Convergence can also take place within a country context, between various levels of governmental reporting (for example central government versus municipalities). An example is a recent study of IPSAS adoption in Brazil that concludes that it is not yet possible to state the level of convergence in the country.[26]

As a general principle, the World Bank encourages borrowers to prepare their public sector financial reports in accordance with IPSAS. More specifically, the World Bank promotes the adoption and implementation of accrual based IPSAS accounting standards through conditionality in loan agreements. The World Bank argues that the implementation of IPSAS facilitates the consolidation of whole of government financial statements[27]; valuation of loans at fair value; and accounting for complex debt creating arrangements.[28]

In order to be able to follow the progress of IPSAS adoption across nation states, the IFAC, in the *International Public Sector Financial Accountability Index: 2021 Status Report,* highlighted that the process towards providing high-quality public sector financial information begins with governments committing to the implementation of internationally recognized financial reporting standards. The data in the 2021 Status Report show that in the public sector, 40 of the 165 jurisdictions monitored under the index (24 per cent) have adopted IPSAS with no modifications. However, in many instances, adoption approaches differ between jurisdictions due to national political and economic positions that influence government decision-making. Many

---

[26] Lima and Lima (2019).

[27] See chapter 11 of this book for an explanation of whole of government accounting.

[28] See for example Polzer et al. (2020).

countries favour a gradual approach to accrual-based IPSAS and 53 jurisdictions (32 per cent) have adopted modified IPSAS to align with local contexts or national standards with reference to IPSAS.

The Association of Chartered Certified Accountants (ACCA) published a report in 2017 that studied IPSAS adoption across a range of developing countries, identifying commonalities and emerging issues. The study considers the adoption of IPSAS focusing on the following key matters: date of announcement and date of adoption; overview of progress to date; and success factors and challenges experienced. Table 6.2 provides an overview of recent academic studies that scrutinise the adoption of IPSAS across a range of countries.

Author	Research Question(s)	Theoretical stance(s)	Key findings
Adhikari et al., 2013	To investigate the role of external environmental factors in disseminating government accounting reform ideas in Nepal and Sri Lanka. Also, it seeks to unveil whether and to what extent these two countries have been successful in implementing these reform ideas.	Institutional theory	Public sector accounting reforms in Nepal and Sri Lanka have been much affected by overseas developments since the 1970s, reflecting the trends for New Public Management and New Public Financial Management.
Brusca & Martínez, 2016	To analyse the drivers and stimuli for countries to adopt IPSAS, as well as to identify the barriers that make the process challenging.	Contingency model	Both adopters and non-adopters value the benefits of IPSAS for achieving international comparability and for improving the quality of financial reporting systems.
Brusca et al., 2016	Examine the current state of play in the adoption and harmonisation of these rules internationally and in Latin America.	Institutional theory	The application of IPSAS is more rhetorical than practical. In these countries financial statements are not being used in decision-making process in government entities.

Polzer et al., 2022	What dominating trends can be identified in the literature on IPSAS adoption in emerging economies (EEs) and low-income countries (LICs) over time?	Diffusion theory	For various stages in the IPSAS implementation process, past studies have provided accounts on the idiosyncrasies of EEs and LICs. An explanation for the low number of studies that focused on the persuasion stage could be that the adoption is externally driven or supply-led innovation. In terms of outcomes or success of IPSAS adoption initiatives, the (limited) evidence was mixed. Some studies present positive accounts. However other studies showed issues of decoupling between adopted standards and their actual, indicating a lack of confirmation of the diffusion
Bekiaris & Paraponti, 2022	To provide an overview of the adoption status of IPSAS within OECD member states at the country level.	Conceptual	The results show a slow trend towards accounting harmonisation and an increasing influence of IPSAS. A total of 64% of the OECD member states present medium or high IPSAS adoption levels, with the majority (78%) having shifted to a higher level during the examination period. For the other 36%, IPSAS levels remain low.

Table 6.2: Selected Studies that examine the spread of IPSAS [2010-2021]

Below we will consider the spread of IPSAS in international organisations as well as across the different regions around the globe.

International Organisations

The OECD (Organisation for Economic Co-operation and Development) was an early adopter of IPSAS (issuing its first set of IPSAS-compliant financial statements in 2000) followed by NATO (North Atlantic Treaty Organization) in 2008. The year 2005 heralded a significant turning point, as the United Nations Organisation (UNO) as a standalone institution and the wider UN System of interlinked organisations (e.g., the World Food Programme (WFP)) decided to adopt IPSAS. The move to IPSAS was said to reflect the UN System's stated aim to "achieve consistent, high quality financial reporting across the System".[29] Subsequent to these developments, the UN General Assembly agreed to adopt IPSAS for the United Nations system, in 2006.[30] The Food and Agriculture Organisation (FAO) was the first organisation in the UN system to complete its IPSAS adoption.[31] Beneficial lessons learned were accumulated through the adoption of IPSAS in these international organisations.[32]

Regional adoption of IPSAS - An overview[33]

Africa

Africa has been at the forefront of IPSAS adoption, with several countries intending to formally adopt the standards as part of financial management reform programmes. Some of the incentives and programmes for IPSAS adoption in Africa have been funded by donors (such as IMF and World Bank)[34]. A PwC report of 2015 highlighted that 17 countries in Africa indicate their intention to move to

---

[29] Chow and Aggestam Pontoppidan (2019).

[30] Chow and Aggestam Pontoppidan (2019).

[31] Alesani et al. (2012).

[32] United Nations (2015); UNAIDS (2013).

[33] Data for this section on regional adoption is collected from a desk review of documents. In particular it relies on the ROSC reports of the World Bank as well as the 2018, 2019 and 2020 UNCTAD reports on International Accounting and Reporting Issues. The 2017 ACCA report is also used as a key source for this section.

[34] ACCA (2019); AL-Jawahry et al. (2022).

accrual accounting and thus converging with IPSAS. For example, in 2013, the Government of the United Republic of Tanzania adopted accrual-based IPSAS at all levels of government, with the National Board of Accountants and Auditors playing a key role in the IPSAS implementation process by participating in the National Steering Committee created by the Government to oversee implementation. The International Federation of Accountants, in *International Standards: 2022 Global Adoption Snapshot Report*, stated that the adoption of accrual-based standards would increase in Africa in 2020–2025.

Asia and the Pacific

Following the Asian crisis of the late 1990s, countries in South Asia embarked on financial management reforms in the private and public sectors. Some of countries that were most affected by the crisis were Indonesia, South Korea and Thailand, but other countries were also affected including Malaysia and the Philippines. Funding from donors such as the IMF and the World Bank required public finance management reforms, including the adoption of accrual accounting standards based on IPSAS. India, Pakistan, Nepal and Bangladesh adopted standards aligned to cash based IPSAS.

The IFAC, in *International Standards: 2021 Global Status Report*, stated that the adoption of accrual-based standards would increase in Asia in 2020–2025. The Asian Development Bank highlighted in 2020 that the enhancement of financial management capacity in Asia and the Pacific comprised a focus on IPSAS adoption, including in particular improving the quality of financial audits by private and public audit professionals; supporting the adoption of IPSAS; and developing the financial management and audit function capacity of staff in implementing agencies and supreme audit institutions in developing country members of the Asian Development Bank.[35]

---

[35] See https://www.adb.org/projects/52113-001/main.

Eastern Europe

In the Eastern European group, a number of countries have embarked on a journey towards adopting IPSAS. IPSAS implementation processes within the Eastern European group are not as widely published about, however a 2019 collection of country cases of south Eastern European countries is a valuable contribution to our understanding of the status of IPSAS in this part of the world[36].

In addition, country cases on IPSAS adoption processes can be located in a variety of policy reports. One example is that of Armenia, where the Government of Armenia decided to adopt accrual-based IPSAS[37]. The Ministry of Finance translated the IPSAS into Armenian in 2009 and then again in 2012. The 2012 version of IPSAS served as a reference for developing the Armenian Public Sector Accounting Standards (APSASs). According to the World Bank, APSASs are now being piloted in a number of government organizations and a Training-of-Trainers program is planned.[38] Another example is within the Russian Federation, which has finalised proposals to adopt national accounting rules based on IPSAS as it aims to improve the efficiency and effectiveness of government spending. The initiative, which is being run under the World Bank's Treasury Development Project, aims to improve the governance of Russia's public finances by presenting more complete, true and fair financial information[39]. It should be noted that Russia has applied accruals-based accounting for all public sector entities since 2006.[40]

---

[36] Vašiček and Roje, (2019).

[37] See https://cfrr.worldbank.org/publications/first-time-adoption-accrual-basis-ipsas.

[38] See https://www.ifac.org/about-ifac/membership/country/armenia.

[39] Legenkova (2016).

[40] See http://www.publicfinanceinternational.org/news/2013/02/russia-set-introduce-%E2%80%98ipsas-based%E2%80%99-accounting-standards

The Public Sector Accounting and Reporting Programme (PULSAR)[41] run through the World Bank is a regional and country-level programme targeting the Western Balkans and the European Union Eastern Partnership countries, to support the development of public sector accounting and financial reporting frameworks in line with international standards and good practices.[42] These countries are modernizing accounting and financial reporting in the public sector in the period up to 2025 and beyond.[43] A majority of jurisdictions have embarked on some form of public sector accounting reform towards accrual-based accounting and this has the potential to further strengthen current human capacity-building efforts and help coordinate joint reform efforts. Examples from European Union (EU) member states (MS), as well as states acceding to the EU (Albania, Montenegro, North Macedonia and Serbia) or aspiring to do so (Republic of Moldova and Ukraine) show that public sector accounting reforms mainly appear to be driven by external factors such as EU directives that require accrual-based accounting for fiscal reporting under the European System of National and Regional Accounts (2010) and the Eurostat initiative to develop and implement EPSAS.[44]

Western Europe

The European Commission (EC) has been working towards the establishment and implementation of uniform and comparable accruals-based accounting practices for all sectors of general

---

[41] See https://www.worldbank.org/en/region/eca/brief/pulsar.

[42] See https://cfrr.worldbank.org/programs/pulsar and https://www.worldbank.org/en/region/eca/brief/pulsar. *Note*: Current beneficiaries are Albania, Armenia, Azerbaijan, Belarus, Bosnia and Herzegovina, Croatia, Georgia, Kosovo, Montenegro, North Macedonia, the Republic of Moldova, Serbia and Ukraine.

[43] See https://cfrr.worldbank.org/publications/stocktaking-public-sector-accounting-and-reporting-environment-pulsar-beneficiary and https://cfrr.worldbank.org/index.php/node/4331.

[44] See https://cfrr.worldbank.org/publications/pulsar-drivers-public-sector-accounting-reforms.

government in EU member states (MS). To address this, Eurostat launched a public consultation on the suitability of IPSAS for EU MS in February 2012. This consultation on the suitability of IPSAS and harmonized accruals-based EU public sector accounting standards was considered an important component of building trust across the public sector. The overall conclusion from the public consultation was that EU MS did not think it is appropriate for the EU to adopt IPSAS, but instead should develop European Public Sector Accounting Standards (EPSAS).[45] Following the first consultation, and the subsequent decision to develop EPSAS, the EC held a second public consultation on EPSAS governance back in November 2013. This consultation revealed that the public sector accounting standards approach within the EU should be voluntary and progressive, focused on increased fiscal transparency in the short to medium term and comparability in the medium to long term.[46]

While no decisions have yet been taken at EU level regarding harmonised accounting standards, an EU-wide accounting framework could be implemented according to the following indicative timeframe: Phase 1: Increasing fiscal transparency in the EU MS in the short to medium term by promoting accruals accounting, e.g. IPSAS, in the period from 2016 to 2020, and in parallel developing the EPSAS framework (i.e. EPSAS governance, accounting principles and standards); Phase 2: Addressing comparability within and between the EU MS in the medium to longer term, by implementing EPSAS by 2025.[47]

---

[45] The EPSAS initiative of the EU is explained in Chapter 13.

[46] Bekiaris and Paraponti (2022).

[47] An OECD 2017 report on Accrual Practices and Reform Experiences in OECD Countries included a survey of financial reporting practices in selected OECD countries. The survey was carried out by the OECD in collaboration with IFAC and their 'Accountability Now Initiative' and was sent to Ministries of Finance and equivalent bodies of all 34 OECD countries. The survey's results show that most OECD countries have reformed and modernised their financial reporting practices over the last decades.

In 2020, the EC stated that "a future EPSAS standard setter will have to inform their work by drawing on different sources of information in order to form its conclusions. One of the potential main sources, beyond others such as cost-benefit considerations and inputs from stakeholder consultation exercises, would be the screening reports under preparation, which will provide technical input on the suitability of existing IPSAS standards" (p. 2). The purpose of these screening reports is to assess the consistency of individual IPSAS standards taking into account the draft EPSAS Conceptual Framework and the principle of European Public Good, and bringing this into the EPSAS standard setting process.

Finally, it is worthwhile highlighting that the EC commissioned PWC to write a report on *Government accounting, EPSAS and supporting the COVID-19 response* which was published in 2020. This report shows how the use of EPSAS in the EU would support greater transparency, greater democratic accountability as well as better public finance management, in relation to the government COVID-19 measures. The report argues for a number of explicit benefits of accrual based EPSAS. Examples include:

- Using a harmonised public sector accounting framework for cash transfers and other benefits to individuals and/or households to mitigate the effect of social risks (such as a risk of unemployment caused by COVID-19 lock-down measures) enables consistency in reporting by EU MS of large amounts of government expenditure.
- Accrual accounting requires a government to recognise the assets it has acquired on its balance sheet. Inventories such as protective equipment materials and medical devices are shown and their cost, or net realisable value if lower. Medical equipment that is used for the long term is also transparently displayed. [48]

---

[48] PWC (2020), p. 8-9.

Latin America and the Caribbean

Much of South America is moving towards adopting IPSAS, included as part of financial management reform programmes promoted and funded by donors. Chile, Colombia and Peru adopted IPSAS in 2018. South American countries have national governments, bodies and organizations that have adopted in part, or have plans to adopt IPSAS in the near future, namely Brazil, Costa Rica, Panama and Ecuador.[49]

Therefore, in Latin America, public sector accounting reforms are ongoing and IPSAS are becoming a reference in introducing accrual-based accounting. Brazil, Chile, Colombia and Costa Rica are advancing in IPSAS implementation, but at different speeds and levels of achievement. Ecuador, El Salvador, Guatemala, Panama and Paraguay have legally endorsed IPSAS and are working on implementation. The greatest advances are in the institutionalization of accounting offices, the professionalization of public technical experts in financial management and the improvement of information on public sector assets. This has helped in maintaining fiscal stability.[50]

5. Challenges in IPSAS adoption

Adopting IPSAS implies a major change for governments and public sector entities. These challenges have persisted in developed economies[51] and even more so in developing economies. Typically challenges entail various factors relating to the move from a cash-based to an accrual-based accounting system; adopting new infrastructure for technology to support accrual-based accounting and reporting;

---

[49] Brusca and Martínez (2016).

[50] Gómez-Villegas and Bergmann (2020).

[51] See for example; https://blog-pfm.imf.org/en/pfmblog/2021/08/german-state-of-hesse-tests-the-suitability-of-ipsas.

the continuous education of professional accountants in the public sector; ensuring that users of IPSAS-based financial information are trained to understand and use data for decision making; and embedding new institutional structures and functions to support IPSAS implementation[52].

The adoption of IPSAS has been progressing globally, yet some challenges have persisted, in particular with regard to advancement in the competency of accountants in the public sector and the implementation of a sound institutional structure to support IPSAS-based reporting. Such challenges can typically be framed through four pillars: (a) legal and regulatory, (b) institutional, (c) technical and (d) human capacity development-related challenges[53].

Legal and regulatory aspects

IPSAS implementation requires stakeholder and political support at the highest levels. In some cases, the need to import standards developed at the international level to replace existing national public sector accounting standards should be clearly presented and justified. The decision may require legislative or policy support.

It is necessary to assess the compatibility and compliance levels of current national legal and regulatory frameworks with international practices. The development and enactment of a primary law on public sector accounting is recommended. Delays in updating legal and regulatory frameworks could compromise the overall success of reforms.[54]

IPSAS implementation is frequently carried out through a phased approach, as opposed to a one-time approach that may often be

---

[52] For empirical data on IPSAS that is updated at regular intervals, please visit https://isar.unctad.org/annual-review/.

[53] See for example the annual International Accounting and Reporting reports issued by the UNCTAD-ISAR group; https://isar.unctad.org/annual-review/.

[54] World Bank tools, such as institutional and governance reviews, are examples of analytical reports that focus on the functioning of key public institutions; see https://openknowledge.worldbank.org/handle/10986/11334.

technically and financially challenging. In this section we thus briefly address a few country cases, drawn from the work of UNCTAD-ISAR, that describe countries that move from cash to accrual basis accounting using a phased approach.

A phased approach entails the adoption and implementation of cash-based IPSAS first; then a migration phase that might incorporate a modified cash-based IPSAS; and then, after a reasonable, defined period of time, the adoption and implementation of accrual-based IPSAS. Cash-based IPSAS do not indicate a clear correlation of expected results and resources employed, in contrast to accrual-based IPSAS. Countries use cash-based IPSAS in a variety of ways. Examples from selected countries with recent data available are as follows:[55]

Botswana. Financial Reporting Act, 2010, requires adherence to IPSAS and empowers the Accountancy Oversight Authority to enforce compliance with IPSAS. The Institute of Charted Accountants states that the Government has adopted modified cash-based standards using IPSAS as a reference and aims to transition to accrual-based IPSAS by 2023.

Cyprus. The Treasury, in cooperation with external advisers, prepared a comprehensive action plan for the transition of the public sector to accrual-based accounting, taking into account the views of and comments from all relevant ministries, the Audit Office and the Internal Audit Service. The Council of Ministers adopted the action plan in 2016 and authorized the Accountant General to take all actions necessary for its implementation in cooperation with all line ministries, departments and independent services.

---

[55] See https://www.ifac.org/about-ifac/membership/country/botswana; http://www.treasury.gov.cy/treasury/treasurynew.nsf/page74_en/page74_en?opendocument and https://www.ifac.org/about-ifac/membership/country/cyprus; https://www.ifac.org/about-ifac/membership/country/nepal; and https://openknowledge.worldbank.org/handle/10986/35096.

Nepal. Since 2009, the Accounting Standards Board has been developing public sector accounting standards based on cash-based IPSAS. The Institute of Chartered Accountants states that the Government plans to implement national public sector accounting standards in 16 ministries and has piloted their application in the Ministry of Physical Infrastructure and Transportation and the Ministry of Women, Children and Social Welfare.

Technical

Technical challenges are highlighted in a number of reports in regards to IPSAS adoption[56]. Technology currently in place in a country context will not necessarily support implementation. This would then entail investment in new technology to support IPSAS adoption. Reporting systems and infrastructure also needs to be revised as part of the transition process.

Institutional arrangements

The roles and responsibilities required in the successful implementation of IPSAS are usually assigned to multiple institutions in a country. The preparation of financial statements is the responsibility of the respective entities defined by the particular regulation, and audit work is conducted by an independent entity such as a Supreme audit institution or the office of the Auditor general, depending on the national regulatory tradition. The implementation of IPSAS may imply the application of globally recognized auditing standards. For example, a case study in the Philippines shows how the country introduced national auditing standards based on the international standards on auditing issued by the International Auditing and Assurance Standards Board, as part of the reform of public sector financial reporting. It is important to clarify who in the jurisdiction is responsible for setting

---

[56] ACCA (2019); OECD (2017).

public sector standards or approving or endorsing IPSAS as they are issued by the IPSASB. Coordination among the different institutions responsible for ensuring the sound management of public sector finance is also needed. For example, the Pan-African Federation of Accountants has published a guide for professional accountancy organizations that provides technical support to governments that have begun or are about to begin an IPSAS implementation process.[57]

Human capacity-building

Accounting education constitutes the fundamental basis of accounting practice; it is therefore constantly reviewed as a part of an effort to bridge the gaps between theoretical education and practical application.[58] Public sector accounting education plays an essential role in the proper functioning of government operations. The World Bank has noted that in promoting IPSAS, it is critical for national stakeholders, accountants, auditors, non-governmental organizations and the staff of parliamentary budget offices to have training opportunities to understand IPSAS in depth, including the benefits, and create drive for reform. It is critical to enable such stakeholders to have informed discussions about both how principles and standards should be applied and adapted in national systems and on assessing whether the application of the standards, once introduced, has been appropriately done.[59]

There is a chronic shortage of qualified accountants in the public sector.[60] To support governments and government entities wishing to report in accordance with accrual-based IPSAS, the IFAC has developed a train-the-trainer package of materials, designed to be

---

[57] See PAFA (2020).

[58] Karatzimas et al. (2022).

[59] See https://cfrr.worldbank.org/publications/pulsar-drivers-public-sector-accounting-reforms.

[60] Heiling, 2020.

delivered through a five-day course, providing an introduction to the current suite of IPSAS.[61]

The implementation of IPSAS is an interdisciplinary exercise. Comprehensive and accrual-based standards such as IPSAS require actuarial estimates for measurement purposes, for example in the context of pension benefits for employees in public sector institutions. Property, plant and equipment items might often require valuations by professionals to determine the carrying amounts for items to be entered in the accounting records of an entity. In many developing countries, such professionals are either few in number or lacking, and the need for capacity-building in these areas is critical.[62] Another area requiring strong institutional support is professional capacity development in accountancy and related disciplines such as actuarial science and valuations.

6. Conclusion

The adoption of IPSAS is still an ongoing venture. Transnational regulation, as seen through the case of IPSAS, is a mode of governance that structures and guides financial accounting and reporting activities and interactions beyond, across and within national territories. IPSAS are frequently embedded into national public sector standards and supported by other modes of local governance, a process that in itself may face difficulties. Adoption implies overcoming several obstacles, of which technical and human capacity-building are the most challenging ones. Therefore, despite many countries and jurisdictions already applying IPSAS, or planning to do so in the near future, practical implementation issues remain.

---

[61] See https://www.ifac.org/knowledge-gateway/supporting-international-standards/publications/train-trainer-introduction-ipsas-module-1-introduction.

[62] See for example UNCTAD-ISAR (forthcoming).

Bibliographic references

ACCA (2017) – IPSAS implementation: current status and challenges. [Available here; http://www.accaglobal.com/content/dam/ACCA_Global/Technical/pubsect/pi-IPSAS-implementation-current-status-and-challenges.pdf, last accessed 15 October 2022].

ADHIKARI, Pawan; KURUPPU, Chamara and MATILAL, Sumohon (2013) – Dissemination and institutionalization of public sector accounting reforms in less developed countries: A comparative study of the Nepalese and Sri Lankan central governments. Accounting Forum, 37(3), 213–230. https://doi.org/10.1016/j.accfor.2013.01.001.

ALESANI, Daniele; JENSEN, Gwenda and STECCOLINI, Ileana (2012) – IPSAS adoption by the World Food Programme: An application of the contingency model to intergovernmental organisations. International Journal of Public Sector Performance Management, 2(1), 61. https://doi.org/10.1504/IJPSPM.2012.048744.

AL-JAWAHRY, Bushra; MAHDI, Murtadha; AL-FATLAWI, Qayssar and ALMAGTOME, Akeel (2022) – The impact of IPSAS adoption on sustainable tourism development: a cross country analysis. Polish Journal of Management Studies, 25(2), 36–55. https://doi.org/10.17512/pjms.2022.25.2.03.

ALMQUIST, Roland; GROSSI, Giuseppe; van HELDEN, G. Jan and REICHARD, Christoph (2013) – Public sector governance and accountability. Critical Perspectives on Accounting, 24(7–8), 479–487. https://doi.org/10.1016/j.cpa.2012.11.005.

ANSARI, S., & EUSKE, K. J. (1987) – Rational, rationalizing, and reifying uses of accounting data in organizations. Accounting, Organizations and Society, 12(6), 549–570. https://doi.org/10.1016/0361-3682(87)90008-0.

BEKIARIS, Michalis and PARAPONTI, Thekla (2022) – Examining the status of IPSAS adoption at the country level: An analysis of the OECD member states. Journal of Accounting & Organizational Change. https://doi.org/10.1108/JAOC-02-2021-0023.

BOTZEM, Sebastian and DOBUSCH, Leonhard (2012) – Standardization Cycles: A Process Perspective on the Formation and Diffusion of Transnational Standards. Organization Studies, 33(5–6), 737–762. https://doi.org/10.1177/0170840612443626.

BRUNSSON, Nils and JACOBSSON, Bengt (2000) – A World of Standards, Oxford, 2002; online edn, Oxford Academic, 1 Jan. 2010, https://doi.org/10.1093/acprof:oso/9780199256952.001.0001.

BRUSCA, Isabel; GÓMEZ-Villegas, Mauricio and MONTESINOS, Vicente (2016) – Public Financial Management Reforms: The Role of IPSAS in Latin-America: Public Financial Management Reforms in Latin-America. Public Administration and Development, 36(1), 51–64. https://doi.org/10.1002/pad.1747.

BRUSCA, Isabel and MARTÍNEZ, Juan Carlos (2016) – Adopting International Public Sector Accounting Standards: A challenge for modernizing and harmonizing public sector accounting. International Review of Administrative Sciences, 82(4), 724–744. https://doi.org/10.1177/0020852315600232.

CHOW, Danny and AGGESTAM Pontoppidan, Caroline (2019) – The United Nations' (UN) decision to adopt International Public Sector Accounting Standards (IPSAS) – Journal of Public Budgeting, Accounting & Financial Management, 31(2), 285–306. https://doi.org/10.1108/JPBAFM-08-2018-0087.

EUROPEAN COMMISSION (2020) – Introduction and Overview to EPSAS Screening Reports. EPSAS WG 19/09rev. [available here; https://circabc.europa.eu/sd/a/dd5b0382-8304-4276-b9f7-19806af0db97/Introduction%20and%20Overview%20to%20EPSAS%20Screening%20Reports.docx.pdf].

EBERLEIN, Burkard and NEWMAN, Abraham L. (2008) – Escaping the International Governance Dilemma? Incorporated Transgovernmental Networks in the European Union. Governance, 21(1), 25–52. https://doi.org/10.1111/j.1468-0491.2007.00384.x.

GARSTEN, Christian and JACOBSSON, Kerstin (2011) – Transparency and legibility in international institutions: The UN Global Compact and post-political global ethics. Social Anthropology, 19(4), 378–393. https://doi.org/10.1111/j.1469-8676.2011.00171.x.

GÓMEZ-VILLEGAS, Mauricio and BERGMANN, Andreas (2020) – Theme: Governmental accounting and public financial management reforms in Latin America. Guest editors: Mauricio Gómez-Villegas and Andreas Bergmann: Editorial: Advances and challenges of public financial management reforms in Latin America. Public Money & Management, 40(7), 487–488. https://doi.org/10.1080/09540962.2020.1788805.

HEILING, Jens (2020) – Time to rethink public sector accounting education? A practitioner's perspective. Journal of Public Budgeting, Accounting & Financial Management, 32(3), 505–509. https://doi.org/10.1108/JPBAFM-05-2020-0059.

JENSEN, Gwenda (2018) – International Public Sector Accounting Standards (IPSAS) – In A. Farazmand (Ed.), Global Encyclopedia of Public Administration, Public Policy, and Governance (pp. 3385–3393). Springer International Publishing. https://doi.org/10.1007/978-3-319-20928-9_2280.

KARATZIMAS, Sotirios; HEILING, Jens and AGGESTAM-PONTOPPIDAN, Caroline (2022) – Public sector accounting education: A structured literature review. Public Money & Management, 1–8. https://doi.org/10.1080/09540962.2022.2066356.

LIMA, Raquel and LIMA, Diana Vaz (2019) – Brazil's experience in IPSAS implementation. Revista Contemporânea de Contabilidade, 16(38), 166–184. https://doi.org/10.5007/2175-8069.2019v16n38p166.

OECD (2017) – Accrual Practices and Reform Experiences in OECD Countries [Available here; https://www.oecd.org/publications/accrual-practices-and-reform-experiences-in-oecd-countries-9789264270572-en.htm].

PAFA (2020) – Building a bridge to a brighter Africa- International Public Sector Accounting Standards (IPSAS) implementation road map for Africa. [Available here; https://www.pafa.org.za/resources/pafa-ipsas-implementation-roadmap].

POLZER, Tobias; ADHIKARI, Pawan and GÅRSETH-NESBAKK, Levi (2020) – IPSASs Implementation – 'Walk' and 'Talk', [Available here; https://blog-pfm.imf.org/en/pfmblog/2020/09/ipsass-implementation-walk-and-talk].

POLZER, Tobias; GROSSI, Giuseppe and REICHARD, Christoph (2022) – Implementation of the international public sector accounting standards in Europe. Variations on a global theme. Accounting Forum, 46(1), 57–82. https://doi.org/10.1080/01559982.2021.1920277.

PWC (2020) – Updated accounting maturities of EU governments and EPSAS implementation cost. Paper by PwC on behalf of Eurostat, EPSAS WG 20/07rev

[Available here; https://circabc.europa.eu/sd/a/4f698875-6355-4c15-88a2-0c79c67219dd/ Updated%20accounting%20maturities%20and%20EPSAS%20implementation%20cost%20June%202020.pdf].

PONTOPPIDAN, Caroline Aggestam and BRUSCA, Isabel (2016) – The first steps towards harmonizing public sector accounting for European Union member states: Strategies and perspectives. Public Money & Management, 36(3), 181–188. https://doi.org/10.1080/09540962.2016.1133970.

SCHMIDTHUBER, Lisa; HILGERS, Dennis and HOFMANN, Sebastian (2022) – International Public Sector Accounting Standards (IPSASs): A systematic literature review and future research agenda. Financial Accountability & Management, 38(1), 119–142. https://doi.org/10.1111/faam.12265.

TAWIAH, Vincent (2022) – The Effect of IPSAS Adoption on Governance Quality: Evidence from Developing and Developed Countries. Public Organization Review. https://doi.org/10.1007/s11115-022-00625-w.

UNCTAD-ISAR (forthcoming) – International Accounting and Reporting Issues 2022. [International Accounting and Reporting Issues].

United Nations (2015) – IPSAS benefits to the UN. [Available here; https://www.un.org/ipsas/Benefits%20Realization%20Plan/IPSAS_Booklet.pdf].

UNAIDS (2013) – IPSAS benefits to UNAIDS. [Available here; https://www.unaids.org/sites/default/files/sub_landing/files/JC2513_IPSAS_en_0.pdf].

VAŠIČEK, Vesna and ROJE, Gorana (Eds.) (2019) – Public Sector Accounting, Auditing and Control in South Eastern Europe. Springer International Publishing. https://doi.org/10.1007/978-3-030-03353-8.

WORLD BANK (2021) – Technical note- First time adoption of IPSAS. [Available here; https://cfrr.worldbank.org/sites/default/files/2021-04/IPSAS.pdf].

Additional readings

BRUSCA, Isabel and MARTÍNEZ, Juan Carlos (2016) – Adopting International Public Sector Accounting Standards: A challenge for modernizing and harmonizing public sector accounting. International Review of Administrative Sciences, 82(4), 724–744. https://doi.org/10.1177/0020852315600232.

JENSEN, Gwenda R. (2018) – International Public Sector Accounting Standards (IPSAS). In A. Farazmand (Ed.), Global Encyclopedia of Public Administration, Public Policy, and Governance (pp. 3385–3393). Springer International Publishing. https://doi.org/10.1007/978-3-319-20928-9_2280.

ROCHER, Sébastien (2010) – La Genèse de la Normalisation Internationale de la Comptabilité Publique (Translation: The origins of the international standardization of public accounting)", Revue Française de Comptabilité, Vol. 438, pp. 38-41.

TAWIAH, Vincent (2022) – The Effect of IPSAS Adoption on Governance Quality: Evidence from Developing and Developed Countries. Public Organization Review. https://doi.org/10.1007/s11115-022-00625-w.

Discussion questions

- What are the barriers limiting the further adoption of IPSAS globally?
- What are some of the key lessons learned with regard to the regulatory, institutional and technical and human capacity-building aspects of the implementation of IPSAS?
- Critically discuss pros and cons of various approaches to implement IPSAS.
- Critically discuss the adoption of IPSAS in different parts of the world (for example in African countries).
- Develop research questions on the spread and use of IPSAS and highlight potentially existing research gaps.

CHAPTER 7

THE IPSASB'S CONCEPTUAL FRAMEWORK AND VIEWS ON SELECTED NATIONAL FRAMEWORKS

Susana Jorge
University of Coimbra, Portugal
susjor@fe.uc.pt
https://orcid.org/0000-0003-4850-2387

Josette Caruana
University of Malta, Malta
josette.caruana@um.edu.mt
https://orcid.org/0000-0002-6099-1577

Summary

This chapter is about conceptual frameworks in public sector accounting. While particularly taking the IPSASB's conceptual framework as a reference, the chapter also offers brief views on selected national frameworks from a group of European countries – namely the UK, Finland, Austria, Germany and Portugal – as illustrative examples of how conceptual frameworks can approximate or diverge from that of the IPSASB.

The explanations enable an understanding of the role of a conceptual framework underlying public sector accounting standards, as well as the main issues normally included in it.

Keywords

Financial information, users, qualitative characteristics, elements of financial statements, measurement criteria.

https://doi.org/10.14195/978-989-26-2464-8_7

Introduction

Financial reporting standard setters across the globe have designed a number of accounting conceptual frameworks (CFs) over time, also attempting to provide a definition. The literature has presented several definitions for a CF in accounting, emphasizing different elements, either focusing on its contents, or on its purposes.[1] A CF should be perceived as a system of practical reasoning, allowing both forward and backward reasoning. Forward reasoning by standard setters to anticipate situations that would require judgmental decisions concerning accounting concepts; and backward reasoning by preparers to relate to the intentions of the standard setters.[2]

The beginnings of accounting CFs may be found in the 1930s in the USA, originating in the accounting profession. A clear attempt to reach an accounting theory was the American Accounting Association's 1966 "*A Statement of Basic Accounting Theory*" *(ASOBAT)*[3], far beyond the development of accounting theory in Europe (see Chapter 2 in this book). However, it was not until 1973, with the creation of the Financial Accounting Standards Board (FASB), the third standard setter established by the Securities and Exchange Commission (SEC) in the United States, that accounting CFs began to be discussed and developed across countries, starting from the Anglo-Saxon world.

FASB's CF, started in 1973, was the major and most complete one, comprising several statements on a wide range of financial accounting and reporting matters (e.g., objectives of financial reporting, qualitative characteristics of accounting information, elements of financial statements, recognition and measurement in financial

---

[1] Vela Bargues (1992).
[2] Dennis (2018).
[3] Jones (1992).

statements, and presentation of financial statements). This work has inspired others, such as the Accounting Standards Committee in UK, and the International Accounting Standards Board (IASB).

As for public sector accounting (PSA), the origins of its CFs come from the USA as well, being derived from those of business accounting, at least in the last forty years. Distinguishing between federal accounting and governmental accounting for state and local level, the latter followed, since the 1930s, principles and standards issued by a national council (currently the Governmental Accounting Standards Board – GASB). However, at the beginning of the 1980s, the FASB, which was concerned explicitly with business organizations, started to concern itself with nonbusiness organizations too, issuing a statement on the objectives of financial reporting by nonbusiness organizations, conflicting with GASB's responsibilities.[4]

Nowadays, GASB focuses on state and local government accounting, including not-for-profit public sector units. Since its establishment in 1984, GASB has initiated its own CF, starting from the FASB's framework. Currently, some important pronouncements are GASB Concept Statements no. 1 (Objectives of Financial Reporting, 1987), no. 4 (Elements of Financial Statements, 2007) and no. 6 (Measurement of Elements of Financial Statements, 2014). At the federal level, there is the Federal Accounting Standards Advisory Board (FASAB) *Handbook of Federal Accounting Standards and Other Pronouncements* (last amendment in 2021), including the Statements of Federal Financial Accounting Concepts no.1 to no.9.

While, in principle, there should be only one commonly accepted (financial) accounting theory, historically derived from practice, it is acknowledged that, even within business accounting, developing a single generally accepted accounting CF is not easy. Considering

---

[4] Jones (1992).

that accounting is to be a purposive activity, aimed at producing and reporting information that must be useful for somebody to do something,[5] the development of accounting CFs has been based on approaches considering the users of financial accounting reports and their needs,[6] which, in turn, are determined by the context where they act. Environment is deemed to determine the objectives of accounting information and consequently other dimensions of the accounting CF.[7]

This explains why, although based on business accounting, specific CFs have been especially derived and developed for PSA. Even those who argue for 'one single world of accounting' recognize that there may be context specifics determining PSA particularities, hence requiring its CF to reflect differences (e.g., different concepts and different interpretations of principles), at least at a detailed level, from the one for financial accounting overall.

Accordingly, though deriving from the IASB's CF, the IPSASB (2014) published a specific CF for PSA, considering the following public sector specific characteristics:[8]

- The primary objective of delivering public services – rather than to make profits and generate a return on equity for investors; requires information beyond financial position, financial performance and cash flows, to properly evaluate the performance of public sector entities;
- Non-exchange transactions (e.g., taxes and grants) – the involuntary and compulsory nature of major contributions makes accountability an overriding purpose of GPFRs;

---

[5] Jones and Pendlebury (2010).
[6] Jones (1992).
[7] Vela Bargues (1992).
[8] See IPSASB (2014, preface).

- A budget to be accomplished – considering the budget as an instrument of public policy and a law, GPFRs must report on the budget (public policies) accomplishment;
- Nature of the programs and longevity of the public sector – financial statements have to be complemented with information allowing the assessment of sustainability in the long run, and the going concern principle cannot be assessed only by the net financial position;
- Nature and purpose of public sector assets and liabilities – there are infrastructure and other public domain assets (e.g., heritage, military assets) difficult to measure and with no market; entities assume certain liabilities in order to provide a public service (e.g., the provision of social benefits);
- The regulatory role of public sector entities – in order to safeguard public interest or bring the market to function; judgment is required to evaluate whether the regulatory role creates assets or liabilities;
- Relationship to statistical reporting – public sector accounts, namely concerning the General Government Sector, are input for the National Accounts and Government Financial Statistics – convergence is desirable but differences remain.

In the European context, some diversity can be found regarding public sector accounting CFs. While the UK is IFRS-based (e.g., *the Government Financial Reporting Manual – FReM*, revised on an annual basis), in Continental countries there are some IPSASB's adopters (e.g., Spain, Portugal, France and Austria), whereas others are based on deeply-rooted national traditions (e.g., Germany and Finland).

This chapter focuses on financial accounting and continues discussing the definition and role of a CF and the authority of the IPSASB's CF over the standards or recommended practice guidelines (RPGs). It follows by presenting and explaining the main topics addressed in the IPSASB's CF: the objectives, users and qualitative characteristics of the GPFR information; and the definitions, recognition and measurement criteria for the elements within the financial statements. Then, it presents a comparative-international analysis of the principal topics/concepts included in the frameworks of a group of European countries (Austria, Finland, Germany, Portugal and the UK) taking the IPSASB's CF as a benchmark. Finally, it briefly addresses the work currently in progress in regards to the revision of the IPSASB's CF.

2. The role of the CF *versus* the public sector accounting standards

The actual definition of a CF remains elusive.[9] There are, however, commonalities pointing to a definition of a CF that, in the first place, embraces accounting objectives that will guide the establishment of fundamental principles and key concepts. The latter will then be followed by more procedure-oriented standards.

The IPSASB's CF presents a definition as a basic theoretical structure addressing the main elements of the financial statements, which

> establishes the concepts that underpin general purpose financial reporting [...] by public sector entities that adopt the accrual basis of accounting.[10]

The elements of financial statements are assets, liabilities, revenue, expenses, net financial position, ownership contributions and ownership distributions, for which the CF also outlines recognition and measurement criteria to be considered overall in the standards.

---

[9] Dennis (2018).
[10] IPSASB (2014, CF 1.1).

The CF also defines the objectives and main users of GPFRs, and the qualitative characteristics of financial information.

The IPSASB's CF applies to GPFRs of governments at all levels, international organizations, as well as to other public sector entities (except for commercial public sector entities).

Historically, because Anglo-Saxon accounting theory has developed from practice,[11] CFs follow the standards, and not the opposite; meaning that, the CFs were published after the standards were developed. Therefore, reasons for the existence of accounting CFs include: i) the need to have harmonized concepts – a common explicit theoretical reference (set of concepts and principles based on postulates or premises) capable of giving coherence to accounting practices, and on which rules (standards) and recommendations must rest; and ii) to give legitimacy to the standards themselves and to the work of standard-setters.[12]

Therefore, the CF is not a standard. It does not offer (binding) guidance for recognizing, measuring, presenting and disclosing specific transactions or topics. Although even the IPSAS are not binding, their requirements are considered as more authoritative; and in cases of conflict between IPSAS and the CF, the standards' requirements prevail.[13]

Overall, the main purposes and importance of a CF in PSA may be summarized as:

- To support *preparers* of the financial statements, in the application of (accrual-based) PSA standards (e.g., IPSAS and future EPSAS) and in the accounting treatment of topics that become relevant as a matter of the standards;
- To help in forming an opinion about the compliance of the financial statements to the standards (*auditors'* perspective);

---

[11] Jones and Pendlebury (2000).
[12] Jones (1992); Jones and Pendlebury (2000).
[13] IPSASB (2014, CF 1.2-1.3).

- To support *users* in the interpretation of the information within the financial statements prepared by public sector entities; and
- To offer PSA *standard-setters* the proper concepts needed to prepare PSA standards.

CFs are conventionally concerned with financial accounting. They do not address management accounting, because they are concerned with accounting for external providers of finance.[14] They do not embrace budgeting either, perhaps because budget theory has much to do with political science and also with economics, particularly public finance, which do not seem so attractive for accounting theorists (academics/researchers) and even less for professionals.

Nevertheless, in some jurisdictions, like in Portugal, there was a need to create a CF also for budgetary (cash-based) accounting and reporting, defining specific principles and terms. Some terms with a similar designation in financial accounting have different meanings in budgetary accounting, for example, revenue/expenditure, current/non-current, financial assets/liabilities.[15]

The IPSASB's CF does not refer particularly to budgetary reporting. However, as explained in Chapter 3 of this book, the scope of GPFRs admittedly embraces information and statements to report also on how budgets have been accomplished.

3. The IPSASB's CF

At the time of writing, the IPSASB's CF is the only one existent for public sector accounting at an international level, with wider ge-

---

[14] Jones and Pendlebury (2000).

[15] See Decree-Law 192/2015, of 11 of September – NCP 26, PORTUGAL, DECRETO-LEI n.º 192/2015, Sistema de Normalização Contabilística para as Administrações Públicas (SNC-AP).

ographic scope and resorting to the CFs from the FASAB, the GASB, and especially that of the IASB, as sources of inspiration. Therefore, the remainder of this chapter concentrates on the IPSASB's CF as the main international benchmark.

Like the IPSAS, the CF is not obligatory at any national level, as the IPSASB does not have enforcement power; to be in force, IPSAS must be endorsed, i.e. formally and/or legally adopted by each country or jurisdiction.

3.1. Objectives and main users of financial reporting

Most of the CFs for Anglo-Saxon national governments (UK, US, Australia and NZ) developed during the 1980s took a user approach, implying that the objectives of GPFRs, hence their usefulness, have been determined by the users' needs, considering integral and differential approaches.[16] Some criticisms have been made, in regard to the fact that the users and needs considered are, in reality, potential; they do not result from empirical studies, but rather from assertions and normative approaches.[17] The lack of 'verifiability' is

> (...) symptomatic of a continuing problem with the user/user needs approach of financial reporting theory: we are still not clear that a substantial number of users exist.[18]

Due to the difficulties in identifying who the real users of public sector GPFRs are, ultimately, one could say that, in a democratic regime, everyone in the population could be assumed to be a user or

---

[16] Jones and Pendlebury (2000).
[17] Jones (1992); Rutherford (1992).
[18] Jones and Pendlebury (2000, p. 138).

potential user of the accounts of public sector organizations. This, however, would create serious problems in identifying their information needs and defining statements in order to satisfy them. Still, in democratic contexts, there is a governmental duty to be publicly accountable, so accountability is an implicit objective of public sector GPFRs, regardless of who the users are and what their needs might be.[19] In fact, various literature highlight that the objective of accountability is of paramount importance in the public sector context.[20]

Given that GPFRs in the public sector seem to be particularly oriented to external users, decision-making needs have been added and explicitly considered in CFs, also derived from business accounting in Anglo-Saxon countries. There are differences between the two objectives: accountability and decision usefulness. Accountability (past-oriented) is considered to be more generic than decision usefulness (future-oriented), which points to specific purpose financial reports, as illustrated in Figure 7.1. Balancing the two purposes is rather tricky.

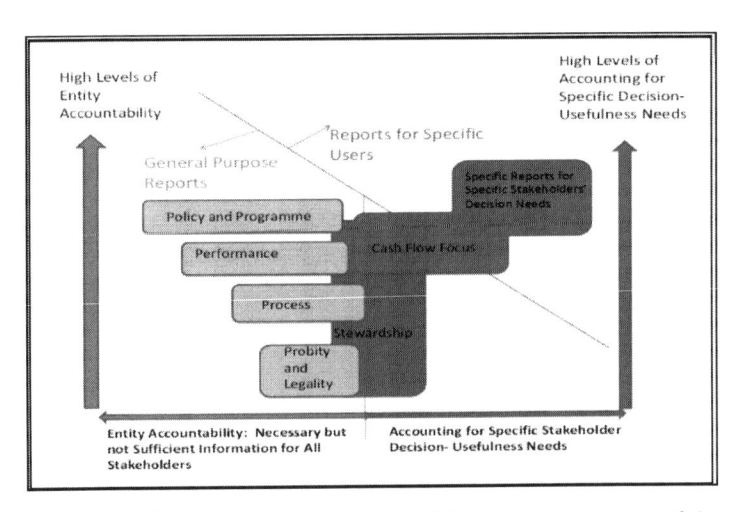

Figure 7.1: Differences between accountability and decision usefulness
Source: Laughlin (2008, p.249)

---

[19] Jones and Pendlebury (2000).

[20] See for example, Chan (2003).

Additionally, users' needs (GPFRs purposes) for accountability and decision-making seem to be rather controversial within the public sector context. For example, Jones (1992, p.260) explains that the 'accountability' notion should somehow have implicit the 'decision-making':

> (...) accountability must imply some purpose for some external user and that, however casual the decision might be, the purpose must lead to a decision: if the accountee is entirely passive, accountability surely must be an empty notion.

Moreover, even if

> There is no difficulty in identifying parties who are unequivocally external to a public sector organisation who might in principle be users of financial reports (*e.g., taxpayers, voters, service recipients, investors*). (...) There is, however, a difficulty in identifying the decisions which a rational actor falling within one of these classes might seek to take by employing the general purpose statements of any government unit. [italics provided][21]

Rutherford (1992) argues that there are no rational reasons to consider that citizens, even as voters and taxpayers, are indeed users of information for decision making, although it might be admissible that certain experts, such as the *media* and policy analysts, are users of public sector financial information on their behalf. However, in the context of control and accountability, the author admits a variety of intermediate users who might be considered internal from one perspective and external from another. Politicians in central government are an example: they are internal users as decision-makers within the government on the one hand, but they are external users while

---

[21] Rutherford (1992, p. 267).

exerting their oversight role on lower level governments or agencies. Parliamentarians are another example: in principle, they are capable of demanding any information they want; nonetheless, in practice, they exert a limited power of control, making them act as external users, using the financial reports of government and public sector entities at large for the purposes of assessing accountability and general compliance with the legislation (e.g., budgetary restrictions).

Getting around these controversies, the IPSASB has followed a normative and prescriptive approach while addressing the objectives and users of GPFRs. Accordingly,

> The objectives of financial reporting by public sector entities are to provide information about the entity that is useful to users of GPFRs for accountability purposes and for decision-making purposes.[22]

Laughlin (2008) points out that the IPSASB makes use of the word 'accountability' rather than 'stewardship'. This implies that accountability is used in order to include the concept of stewardship in the framework.

Several (potential) users are considered, distinguishing between primary users and others, as in Table 7.1.

Primary users	Other users
Service recipients and their representatives	Government statisticians
	Analysts and financial advisors
	Media
Taxpayers and their representatives	Regulators and oversight bodies
Resource providers (investors/markets, donor agencies, ...)	Audit institutions and control bodies (e.g., General Audit Office; Court of Audit, ...)
	Parliamentary or government committees
	Public interest and lobby groups and others (e.g. rating agencies; entity management, ...)

Table 7.1: Users of GPFRs
Source: IPSASB (2014, CF 2)

---

[22] IPSASB (2014, CF 2.1).

The main users of GPFRs in the public sector

> do not possess the authority to require a public sector entity to disclose the information they need for accountability and decision-making purposes.[23]

Politicians are the representatives of service recipients, taxpayers and citizens at large. They are assumed to make extensive and ongoing use of GPFRs when acting in that capacity.[24]

In view of the above discussion, questions may arise about whether all those considered by the IPSASB are, in reality, users of GPFRs in the public sector, or whether they are only 'addressees' or stakeholders. Given that the discussion about financial information users and their needs is a recurring topic in the accounting field, recently there has been another attempt to shed some light on the matter, particularly addressing the use by politicians.[25]

Despite the lack of empirical evidence, the IPSASB assumes the following as the main information needs of users of GPFRs in the public sector:[26]

1. Performance (accomplishment of operational and financial objectives; resource management; compliance with regulation and laws);
2. Liquidity and solvency of the entity;
3. The sustainability of the entity's service delivery and other operations over the long term;

---

[23] IPSASB (2014, CF 2.4).

[24] IPSASB (2014, CF 2.4).

[25] See, for example, Jorge et al. (2016) and other authors in that issue. See also Haustein et al. (2019) and other authors is that issue, and Budding and Van Helden (2022) and other authors in this theme.

[26] IPSASB (2014, CF 2.11-2.13).

4. Whether resources are used economically, efficiently, effectively and as intended;
5. Whether the volume and cost of services provided during the reporting period are appropriate;
6. Whether levels of taxes or other resources raised are sufficient to maintain the volume and quality of services;
7. How current operations are being funded (taxes, borrowing, other sources…); and
8. Future funding needs and sources.

While 1 to 3 are common to both service recipients and resource providers, 4 to 6 are more specific to the former and 7 and 8 to the latter.

3.2. Main accounting principles

There are main accounting principles constituting important postulates or assumptions in PSA, the interpretation of which may be different from that in business accounting. Even if generally developed in other chapters in this book, these principles – **accrual**, **going concern** and **substance over form** – are addressed here, within the IPSAS perspective.

Like in business accounting, in PSA under IPSAS the **accrual concept** prevails in financial accounting – transactions are recognized when they occur (and not when cash or equivalent is received or paid); transactions and events are recorded and recognized in the financial statements of the periods to which they relate. Elements to be recognized are assets/liabilities, expenses/revenues and net assets/equity.[27] Still, the application of the matching concept[28] required

---

[27] IPSASB (2022, IPSAS 1.7).

[28] The matching concept is particularly important in accrual accounting. It requires that revenues and expenses in a period to be related, so that the resulting surplus/deficit reported for a period is comprehensive. This concept is based on the

under this principle is problematic in public sector organizations, questioning the meaning of the deficit/surplus in the financial performance statement and raising a need to consider non-financial performance reporting as a complement (see Chapter 14 in this book).

Unlike IFRS-based business accounting, under IPSAS, a cash concept may also be used in financial accounting. Within most European countries, this prevails in budgetary accounting, recognizing transactions only when cash or equivalent is received or paid; statements provide information on sources of cash raised during the period, the purposes for which cash was used, and the balance at the reporting date. Elements to be recognized are cash expenditure – payments, and cash revenue – receipts.[29]

Still, overall, budgetary accounting is not a synonym of cash accounting; in fact, budgetary accounting may also be accrual-based (e.g., in UK and Austria, and in some German local governments), and in accrual-based reporting there is cash-based information too, such as in the cash-flow statement.

Another important principle is the **going concern**, by which

> Financial statements must be prepared on a going concern basis, unless there is an intention to liquidate the entity or to cease operating, or if there is no realistic alternative but to do so.[30]

While this appears to be similar to business accounting, a different interpretation is required in the public sector context: instead of considering financial viability issues (essentially reflected in the net financial position), a long-term perspective of financial

---

premise that a reporting entity must incur expenses in order to generate revenue. This does not fit to (most of) the public sector – there are no expenses needed to generate tax revenue.

[29] IPSASB (2022, Cash Basis IPSAS 1.2.2).

[30] IPSASB (2022, IPSAS 1.38).

sustainability must be considered, pointing to continuity in public service provision.

As in businesses, material uncertainty may raise doubts about an entity's ability to continue operating. Yet, in the public sector, besides the tests of liquidity and solvency, other (non-financial) issues (e.g., power to levy taxes, multi-year funding agreements, merging, restructuring, etc.) are also relevant. The going concern concept, therefore, relates to the ability of maintaining public service provision as expected.[31]

Finally, there is the **substance-over-legal-form** principle,[32] by which

> Information that faithfully represents an economic or other phenomenon depicts the substance of the underlying transaction, other event, activity or circumstance – which is not necessarily always the same as its legal form.[33]

The legal form is associated to ownership that may lead, e.g., to the legal ownership of assets, such as administrative buildings owned by municipalities.

While substance-over-legal-form has been a generally accepted accounting principle in business accounting, in the public sector it is not, as such. The legality principle is linked to traditional PSA; therefore, it has prevailed in some jurisdictions, like in Portugal, although substance over legal form was considered applicable in particular cases (for example, financial leases and public domain assets). As a general principle underlying IPSAS, it has significant

---

[31] See IPSASB (2022, IPSAS 1) and IPSASB's *Recommended Practice Guideline 1 – Reporting on the Long-Term Sustainability of an Entity's Finances*.

[32] This is an implicit principle in the IPSASB's CF, underlying the qualitative characteristics of faithful representation.

[33] IPSASB (2014, CF 3.10).

implications in jurisdictions where the legality principle used to override (e.g., Portugal). An IPSAS-based accounting system implies control criteria related to the ability to use the resources so as to derive service potential or economic benefits, to prevail over ownership and legal-based control criteria. Consequently, substantial changes in asset recognition are expected in countries where the legality principle used to prevail, because public sector entities often have control over several assets, namely buildings and infrastructures, of which they may not be legally owners.

3.3. Qualitative characteristics (and main constraints) of the financial information

To be able to achieve the objectives of accountability and decision-making usefulness, the information included in GPFRs of public sector entities must have certain attributes. The IPSASB's CF explains that these qualitative characteristics are: **relevance, faithful representation, understandability, timeliness, comparability, and verifiability**,[34] with no particular hierarchy of importance. The IPSASB's CF vastly develops these issues,[35] which may be summarized as follows.

Financial and non-financial information is said to have relevance when it 'makes a difference' in achieving the objectives of financial reporting. In order to be relevant, information must have confirmatory value, predictive value, or both; the confirmatory and predictive roles of information being interrelated (e.g., historical information helps to make judgments about the future). Materiality establishes the quantitative threshold for relevance.

---

[34] IPSASB (2014, CF 3.2).
[35] IPSASB (2014, CF 3).

Information must be a faithful representation of the economic and other phenomena that it purports to represent. The presentation of the phenomena must be neutral (neither biased, nor intentionally selected), complete (without material omissions) and as free from error as is possible.[36] Free from error does not mean complete accuracy in all respects; instead, it means there are no errors or omissions individually or collectively material in the description of the phenomenon.

Faithful representation also implies depicting the substance of the underlying transaction, using prudence while making judgments needed under conditions of uncertainty (e.g., in making estimates, such that assets or revenue are not overstated, and liabilities or expenses are not understated); these judgments might not be so neutral.

To be useful, information must also be understood by the users, implying that public sector entities should present information in a manner that responds to the needs and knowledge base of users, and to the nature of the information presented.[37] A certain balance between complexity and simplicity, using plain language, may have to be considered. Also, understandability may be enhanced by comparability. Users are assumed to have reasonable knowledge about the entity and be able to read its financial information.

Information must be made available before it loses its capacity to be useful; if it is delayed, relevance might be jeopardized, so timeliness is a critical quality of financial information. Still, some items may continue to be useful for long periods after the reporting date.

Information must also be comparable (in time and space), allowing users to identify similarities and differences between

---

[36] IPSASB (2014, CF 3.14).
[37] IPSASB (2014, CF 3.17).

two sets of phenomena. Comparability is different from consistency and uniformity, although consistency is required to assure comparability.

Finally, information must be verifiable, to help ensuring that it faithfully represents the economic and other phenomena that it purports to represent. Also referred to as 'supportability',[38] verifiability means that information must be supported by evidence, allowing independent observers to reach a consensus that it appropriately reflects the entity's reality. Verification may be done directly (e.g., counting cash), or indirectly (e.g., calculating the carrying amount of inventory).

Materiality and costs *vs* benefits are issues constraining the attainment of the above qualitative characteristics. As also acknowledged by the IPSASB's CF, the balance between the qualitative characteristics themselves is not easy, as they sometimes conflict. Figure 7.2 illustrates these constraints.

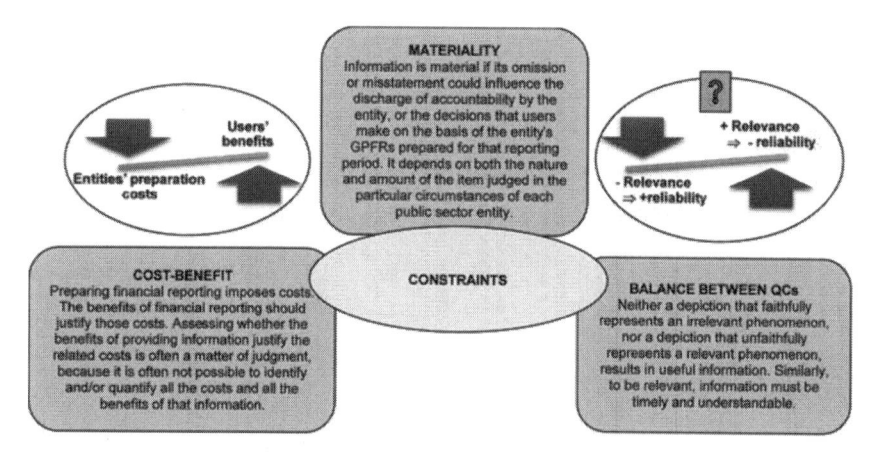

Figure 7.2: Qualitative characteristics – balance and constraints
Source: IPSASB (2014, CF 3.32-3.42)

---

[38] IPSASB (2014, CF 3.26).

3.4. Elements of the financial statements and their recognition[39]

Financial statements are demonstrations representing the financial and economic reality of a public sector entity. The main financial statements are: statement of financial position, statement of financial performance, cash flow statement, statement of changes in net assets, and notes (*IPSAS 1 – Presentation of financial statements* and *IPSAS 2 – Cash Flow Statements*). IPSAS 1 also requires the preparation of the Budget Execution Statement for public sector entities that publish their budgets. Overall, the financial statements reflect the financial effects of transactions and other events, by grouping them into broad classes which share common economic characteristics – these are called elements of financial statements.

Demonstrating the entity's financial position includes: assets (plus other resources), liabilities (plus other obligations), ownership contributions and ownership distributions. Other resources and other obligations refer to deferred expenses and revenues, respectively. The 'net financial position' presented in this statement, also called Balance Sheet, is

> (...) the difference between assets and liabilities after adding other resources and deducting other obligations recognized in the statement of financial position. Net financial position can be a positive or negative residual amount.[40]

This residual amount is then described in terms of the constituent reserves in another statement, namely, the statement of changes in net assets.

---

[39] IPSASB (2014, CF 5 and 6).
[40] IPSAS (2014, CF 5.28).

Revenue and expenses are the elements to demonstrate the entity's financial performance, in a statement where the bottom line is the (accrual-based) deficit or surplus.

Recognizing items in these elements means incorporating them in the amounts displayed on the face of the appropriate financial statements, in accordance with the criteria established in the CF.[41] Overall, recognition criteria require that the item satisfies the definition of the element, and that it can be measured with reliability. Therefore, understanding the definitions of each type of element of the financial statements in the public sector setting is critical, as these identify recognition criteria.

An **asset** is defined as a resource presently controlled by the entity as a result of a past event. A resource is an item with service potential or the ability to generate economic benefits.[42]

Consequently, as in business accounting, also considering the substance over legal form, ownership is not a requirement for an asset to be recognized by a public sector entity. Controlling the resource, instead, is critical, meaning that the entity has the ability to use the resource (or direct other parties on its use) so as to derive the benefit of the service potential or economic benefits embodied in it; or to determine the nature and the way other entities make use of the economic benefits generated by the resource.[43] For example, a police department can have a fleet of vehicles under a financial leasing contract – so not legally owned, but it has the complete control over the items, inasmuch as it defines who and how the vehicles are used, and the department is entirely responsible for maintaining the vehicles, as if these were its property. So, the vehicles under a financial leasing contract are recognized as assets.

---

[41] IPSASB (2014, CF 6).
[42] IPSASB (2014, CF 5.6-5.7).
[43] IPSASB (2014, CF 5.11-5.12).

A past transaction is also a requirement leading to the present control of an asset; it may result from internal development, an exchange (e.g., purchase) or non-exchange transaction (e.g., donation or the exercise of sovereign powers, such as the power to tax.).[44]

The service potential is the distinctive factor in the definition compared to business accounting, given that many assets in the public sector do not generate economic benefits. It refers to the asset's capacity to provide services that contribute to achieving the entity's objectives, without necessarily generating net cash inflows or equivalents for the entity (e.g., recreational, heritage, community, and defense assets),

> (...) which are held by governments and other public sector entities, and which are used to provide services to third parties. Such services may be for collective or individual consumption.[45]

Still, some assets also generate future economic benefits, i.e., cash or equivalent inflows (or a reduction in cash or equivalent outflows), derived from an asset's use in the production and sale of services (e.g., water provision), or from the direct exchange of an asset for cash or other resources (e.g., a piece of land in exchange for offices in a building).[46]

A liability is a present obligation of the entity for an outflow of resources, which results from a past event.[47] It has to be a binding obligation (either legally or non-legally), regarding which an entity has little or no realistic alternative to avoid an outflow of resources; therefore, it implies an outflow of resources from the entity for it to

---

[44] IPSASB (2014, CF 5.13).
[45] IPSASB (2014, CF 5.9).
[46] IPSASB (2014, CF 5.10).
[47] IPSASB (2014, CF 5.14).

be settled, and it is always towards a third party. The obligation may be originated by an exchange or a non-exchange transaction. The past event leading to the present obligation might be more or less straightforward to identify, depending on whether an arrangement has a legal form and is binding, or not.[48] For example, an invoice coming from a contract with a supplier undoubtedly generates a present obligation; however, a legal suit in court may require the entity to assess whether there will be a liability – the outflow might not be certain yet and/or might not be reliably measured.

Therefore, a legal obligation, enforceable in law (even if it may arise from a variety of legal constructs), gives rise to a liability. But, a non-legal (though binding) obligation, because the party to whom the obligation exists cannot take legal (or equivalent) action to enforce settlement, only gives rise to a liability under certain conditions. These are:[49]

– The entity has indicated to other parties that it will accept certain responsibilities;
– The entity has created a valid expectation of those other parties that it will discharge those responsibilities;
– The entity has little or no realistic alternative to avoid settling the obligation arising from those responsibilities.

Accordingly, in a government setting, political promises do not give rise to these types of obligations.

Ownership contributions for the net financial position are inflows of resources of an entity, contributed by external parties in their capacity as owners, which establish or increase an interest in the Net Financial Position of that entity. On the other hand, **ownership distributions**

---

[48] IPSASB (2014, CF 5.15-5.26).
[49] IPSASB (2014, CF 5.23).

from the net financial position are outflows of resources from an entity, distributed to external parties in their capacity as owners, which return or reduce an interest in the Net Financial Position of that entity.[50]

Although these notions are more related to business accounting, they may also apply in public sector organizations, for example, in business-type government entities with shareholders, applying PSA standards. The figure of 'the owner' and ownership interests may arise when one entity contributes resources to provide another entity with the capacity to start operational activities. This is the case in public hospitals in Portugal, which are companies under the business law, owned by the government and subject to the public sector accounting system (main revenues come from taxes and grants).

> In the public sector, contributions to, and distributions from, entities are sometimes linked to the restructuring of government [or of public sector organizations] and will take the form of transfers of assets and liabilities rather than cash transactions.[51]

Ownership distributions may derive from: a return on investment; a full or partial return of investment; or a return of any residual resources, in the event of the entity being wound up or restructured.[52]

Revenue and **expenses** are, respectively, increases or decreases in the net financial position of the entity, other than increases or decreases arising from ownership contributions or distributions.[53]

The entity's surplus or deficit for the period is the difference between revenue and expenses reported in the statement of financial performance (also called the Income Statement or Profit and Loss

---

[50] IPSASB (2014, CF 5.33-5.37).
[51] IPSASB (2014, CF 5.36).
[52] IPSASB (2014, CF 5.37).
[53] IPSASB (2014, CF 5.29-5.32).

Statement). Revenues and expenses are distinct from cash flows, and their matching to ascertain the surplus or deficit is rather debatable in the public sector, as will be discussed in Chapter 8 of this book.

Revenues and expenses arise from exchange and non-exchange transactions, or from other events, such as: changes in prices and unrealized increases and decreases in the value of assets and liabilities; the consumption of assets through depreciation; and erosion of service potential and ability to generate economic benefits through impairments.[54] Recognizing an item in the financial statements, apart from fulfilling the definition, requires a monetary value to be attached to it. This process entails selecting an appropriate measurement basis, ensuring that the measurement is sufficiently relevant and faithfully representative.[55]

3.5. Measurement criteria[56]

Measuring implies determining the monetary amounts to be used in the valuation of the elements to be recognized in the financial statements, by selecting specific measurement bases.

Regarding the objectives of measurement, the IPSASB instructs that an entity must select measurement bases that most fairly reflect its **cost of services, operational capacity and financial capacity**, and are useful in holding the entity to account and for decision-making purposes.[57] These measurement bases must also provide information that meets the qualitative characteristics.

The CF does not propose a single measurement basis (or combination of bases) for all transactions, events and conditions; instead,

---

[54] IPSASB (2014, CF 5.31).
[55] IPSASB (2014, CF 6.7-6.8).
[56] IPSASB (2014, CF 7).
[57] IPSASB (2014, CF 7.2-7.4).

it provides guidance on the selection of a measurement basis for assets and liabilities, based either on the **historical cost** or **current value**, and may be **entry (recognizing) values** or **exit (derecognizing) values**. From this range of criteria, each IPSAS then specifies which basis(es) is(are) to be specifically used. Furthermore, standards sometimes require measures that are not even mentioned in the CF.

Entry values and Exit values

- For **assets**, *entry values* essentially reflect the cost of purchase/acquisition (e.g., historical cost and replacement cost); *exit values* reflect the economic benefits from sale, or the amount that will be derived from use of the asset (e.g., net selling price and value in use).
- For **liabilities**, *entry values* relate to the transaction under which an obligation is received or the amount that an entity would accept to assume a liability; *exit values* reflect the amount required to fulfil an obligation or the amount required to release the entity from an obligation.

Observable and Unobservable Measures

Certain measures may be classified according to whether they are observable in an 'open, active and orderly market' (e.g., market value/fair value), or instead need to be calculated (e.g., value in use).

Observable measures are likely to be more understandable and verifiable than unobservable measures; they may also be more faithfully representative of the phenomena they are measuring.

As displayed in Figure 7.3, there is a large variety of measurement bases suggested. And even if within each standard the options may be reduced, it is a fact that there is too much flexibility and diversity, which jeopardizes the comparability claimed for the IPSAS.

```
                    MEASUREMENT OBJECTIVES
         (Most fair reflection of Cost of Services, Operational Capacity,
                         and Financial Capacity)
                                │
                       MEASUREMENT BASES
              ┌─────────────┴─────────────┐
           ASSETS                      LIABILITIES
        ┌─────┴─────┐              ┌─────┴─────┐
   Historical   Current         Historical   Current
     Cost       Value              Cost       Value
                │                             │
         ├─ Market Value              ├─ Cost of Fulfilment
         ├─ Replacement Cost          ├─ Market Value
         ├─ Net Selling Price         ├─ Cost of Release
         └─ Value in Use              └─ Assumption Price
```

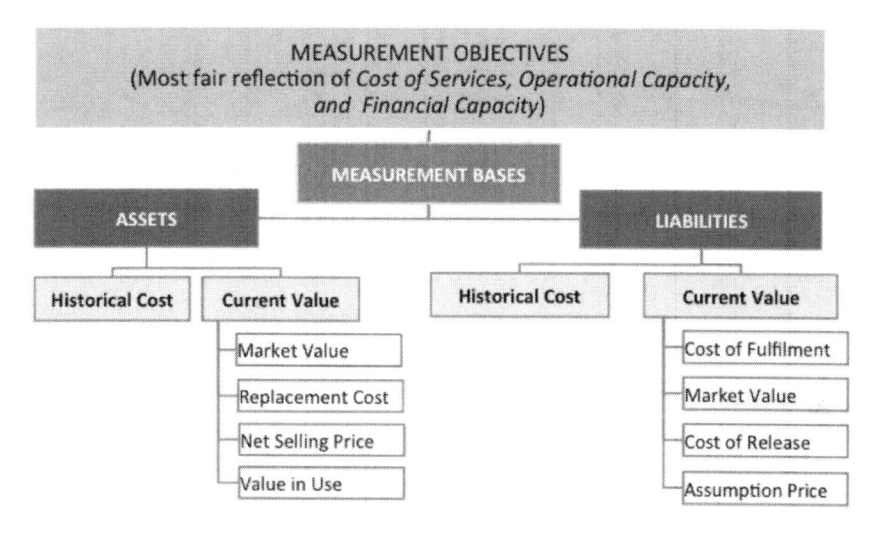

Figure 7.3: Measurement bases
Source: IPSASB (2014, CF 7)

Figure 7.3 shows different criteria regarding the current value of assets and liabilities, though some are mirrored concepts. For example, replacement cost in assets is similar to the assumption price in liabilities. Replacement cost is the amount that the entity would rationally be willing to pay to acquire the asset in its current depreciated state; while the assumption price is the amount that an entity would rationally be willing to accept in exchange for taking on an existing liability. Both are entry criteria, and they may be the most suitable for reflecting either the financial or the operational capacity of the entity.

Likewise, net selling price for assets pairs with cost of release for liabilities; both are exit criteria, and they reflect respectively the amount the entity can obtain from selling the asset (less costs of sale) and the amount the entity would be willing to pay to immediately 'get rid of' the obligation. Contrary to the market value, which may be an exit or entry criteria[58], these criteria do not require an open, active and orderly market or the estimation of a price. Because of this requirement, market value is eventually the least likely applied criterion, as for many assets in the public sector there is no market, and even less so for liabilities.

Value in use as an exit value for assets is often complex to obtain as it implies calculating the net present value of cash flows generated by the assets or, for non-cash generating assets, calculating the remaining service potential (frequently using replacement cost as a surrogate). Its complexity makes it inappropriate to reflect the entity's costs of services and reduces its usefulness in assessing its operational and financial capacity.[59]

Historical cost, an entry criterion both for assets and liabilities, is probably the most suitable for reflecting the entity's cost of services.

4. Comparative analysis of different CFs

This section presents a summarized comparative-international analysis involving the different CFs of selected European countries – Austria, Finland, Germany, Portugal and the UK – taking the one from the IPSASB as reference. These are illustrative examples on how national CFs may approximate or diverge from that of the IPSASB.

The issues to be compared are financial statements (FS) objectives and main users, main accounting principles and methodologies, FS elements and recognition criteria, and measurement criteria used in financial accounting. Table 7.2 provides a synthesis based on Brusca et al. (2015) with some additions from the countries' CFs.

---

[58] Market value is sometimes confused with fair value used for business accounting. It should be noted that, according to IFRS 13, fair value is only an exit value.

[59] IPSASB (2014, CF 7.63).

COUNTRIES	IPSASB	Portugal	UK (IFRS-based)	Austria (Central Govt)	Austria (Regional and Local Govt)	Finland	Germany (IF accrual-based accounting)
FS Objectives – provide financial information about an entity/activity for:							
Accountability	X	X	X	X	X	X	X
Decision-making	X	X		X			
Stewardship			X				
Comparability							X
Intergenerational equity							X
Regularity			X				
FS Main Users:							
Citizens (service recipients and tax payers)	X	X	X	X	X	X	X
Politicians in Parliament as representatives of citizens	X	X	X	X		X	X
Central Government					X		
Other resource providers (e.g. investors)	X	X	X	X			
Oversight authorities (e.g. SAI)	X	X		X	X	X	X
Statistics authorities	X	X		X	X	X	X
Politicians in Parliament as voters of resources			X				
Management Board			X				
Audit committees			X				
Main Accounting Principles and Methodologies:							
Accrual regime	X	X	X	X	X	X (matching and revenue realization)	X (with realization of gains and losses)
Substance over legal form	X	X	X	X			X
Going concern	X	X	X	X			X

COUNTRIES	IPSASB	Portugal	UK	Austria	Finland	Germany
True and fair view			X			X
Prudence (conservatism)					X	X
Double entry – financial accounting	X	X	X	X	X	X
Double entry – budgetary accounting		X		X		
Budgetary reporting within the financial statements	X	X				
Budgetary accounting – cash basis/commitment		X	X		X (for non-exchange transactions)	X (Central and State level[60])
Budgetary accounting – accrual basis			X	X	X (for exchange transactions)	X (Local level[61])
FS Elements:						
Assets	X	X	X	X (receivables)	X	X (including deferred expenses)
Liabilities	X	X	X	X (payables)	X	X (including deferred revenues)
Owners' contributions	X	X	X	X		X
Owners' distributions	X	X	X	X		X
Net assets/equity	X	X	X	X		X
Revenues	X	X	X	X	X	X
Expenses	X	X	X	X	X	X

[60] There may be accrual and cash-based budgeting in parallel at state level (e.g. Hesse).

[61] May not apply to all counties and municipalities.

COUNTRIES	IPSASB	Portugal	UK	Austria	Finland	Germany
Deficit/Surplus	X	X	X	X	X (income statement-led approach)	X
Recognition criteria:						
Economic control	X	X	X	X		X
Measured with reliability	X	X	X	X	X (ensured under the cost convention)	X (historical cost)
Consideration of events after the reporting date	X	X	X	X		X
Realization principle					X (for exchange transactions)	X
Cash and short-term liability for non-exchange transactions					X	
Measurement criteria in financial accounting:						
Historical cost convention	X	X	X	X	X (prudence)	X (cautious prudence)
Fair value is used for certain assets	X	X	X	X	X (for financial assets, when lower than cost)	X (when lower than cost)
Fair value is used for certain liabilities	X	X	X	X	X (when indexed, and value is higher than face value)	X (when higher than settlement amount)

COUNTRIES	IPSASB	Portugal	UK	Austria	Finland	Germany
Amortized cost is used for certain assets and liabilities	X	X	X	X		X (maximum reversal of impairment)
Revaluation for non-current assets	X		X		X (certain assets, e.g. land)	
Depreciation for non-current assets	X	X	X	X	X (excluding land)	X
Impairment review for non-current assets	X	X	X	X	X (when not depreciated, e.g. land)	X

Table 7.2: Comparative-international analysis of different CFs

Table 7.2 shows fewer differences in users than in objectives, both between countries and compared to IPSAS. Regarding the objectives, in Finland and Germany, accountability is clearly the main purpose; while in UK, providing information for decision-making is not explicitly an objective.

In the case of Austria, the reform followed a top-down process. Since 2013, central government has been going ahead with a considerable reform introducing accruals (IPSAS-based) even in the budget; while at the regional and local level, accrual based GPFS became a requirement starting from the reporting year 2020.

In the case of Germany, the reform has followed a bottom-up process. Starting in local governments (municipalities), many already using accrual accounting, but not IPSAS. At federal and state (*Länder*) levels, in 2009 a reform also started and in 2016 new legislation was passed,[62] giving the option to use either cameralistic (budgetary cash accounting and single entry) or accrual-accounting (but not IPSAS). Currently, only two states (Hesse and North-Rhine Westfalia) use accruals and double entry, plus two city states – Hamburg and Bremen. The government at federal (central) level still uses essentially modernized (extended) cameralistic accounting, meaning cameralistics including product-oriented extensions such as expenditure-revenue data for single reports and budgets (performance budgeting), KPIs built on a comprehensive cost and activity accounting system, and capital account. Therefore, the information in Table 7.2 applies only IF entities use accrual-based accounting, which may not happen in several states, neither in the federation (reforms are ongoing) and smaller municipalities, which still use cameralistic accounting.

---

[62] GERMANY, Governmental Accrual Accounting Standards (GAAS) [Standards staatlicher Doppik; SsD]; pursuant to section 7a and section 49a of the Budgetary Principles Act (HGrG); Resolution of 29 November 2016 of the committee pursuant to section 49a HGrG (to be updated on a yearly basis).

Regarding the main accounting principles and methodologies, IPSAS apply to accrual financial accounting, despite the existence of a cash-based IPSAS – *Financial reporting under the Cash Basis of Accounting*. In Table 7.2, in spite of being an IPSAS adopter (with accrual-based financial reporting), Portugal is the only country where budgetary accounting and reporting is cash and commitment-based, with double entry. The UK also uses cash-based annual budgets with some accrual additions. In the other countries (as in the IPSASB framework), an accrual basis is admitted, even in the budget. Accrual-based budgets and budgetary accounting exist in the central government in UK (three-year budget), Austria and Finland, and may be an option in Germany. In German local government, although some small municipalities in specific federal states still use only cameralistic (cash and single entry budgetary) accounting, the majority of those using accrual accounting also prepare an accrual-based budget, in addition to the cash-based one.

A striking feature is that cautious prudence (conservatism) seems to be a clearly prevailing principle in the CFs of Germany and Finland, clearly reflected in several lines in Table 7.2.

Table 7.2 additionally shows that IPSAS-compliant countries (and indirectly the UK) define the elements within the main financial statements.

Finland has an explicit focus on revenue and expenses, the annual reporting following what is called an *income statement-led approach*. The prevalence of the historical cost convention and the realization principle again evidences more conservatism in Finland and in Germany.

The German CF explicitly makes reference to deferred revenues (received in current year and perceived in the following) and expenses (paid in current year and incurred in the following), which also exist in the Balance Sheet of the IPSASB, Portugal, the UK and Austria, but they are not explicitly defined in their CFs.

As to measurement criteria in financial accounting, as expected, Table 7.2 displays (again) more prudent measurement criteria in Finland and in Germany, with no references to fair value and market value, which are admitted for use in exceptional cases only. However, while Finland allows for revaluation of non-current (non-financial) assets in some cases, this is not allowed in Portugal, Austria and Germany. In the case of Portugal, a legal instruction from the central government is required so that revaluation can be authorized.

5. Developments in the IPSASB's CF – work in progress

The IPSASB is in the process of updating its CF[63] originally published in 2014. The update is to reflect the experiences that the Board has gained over time in the process of developing and maintaining IPSAS. The update is also intended to reflect developments in international thinking about conceptual issues. Up to the end of 2022, the IPSASB has issued updates relating to three chapters of the CF, namely, Chapters 3, 5 and 7. However, no changes have been included in the 2022 Edition of the CF.

In February 2022, the IPSASB published Exposure Draft (ED) 81, aimed to revise Chapter 3 – Qualitative Characteristics, and Chapter 5 – Elements in Financial Statements.

With regards to Chapter 3, ED81 is not proposing any changes to the current six qualitative characteristics as described earlier. The ED is proposing enhanced guidance on the role of prudence and on materiality.[64] With regards to prudence, the Board highlights that the exercise of prudence under conditions of uncertainty sup-

---

[63] Agenda Item 5, Conceptual Framework – Limited Scope Update (CF-LSU) – Phase One: Measurement (Board Papers, June 2022).

[64] See also Lorson and Haustein (2019).

ports neutrality. The exercise of prudence does not imply a need for asymmetry. Individual standards may include asymmetric requirements on a case-by-case basis.[65] As for materiality, the IPSASB acknowledges that obscuring material information is a factor that can have a negative impact on users.

The IPSASB is proposing minor changes in Chapter 5, relating to the definitions of an asset and liability. An asset is defined as a resource presently controlled by the entity as a result of past events. A resource is a right to service potential and/or the capability to generate economic benefits. The ED then proceeds by explaining the definition of a resource in some depth. A liability is a present obligation of the entity to transfer resources as a result of past events. The proposed definition of a liability, thus, moves away from using the phrase "an outflow of resources". In tandem to this, in Chapter 5, ED 81 also proposes new guidance on a transfer of resources (instead of that currently provided on an outflow of resources); unit of account (which could be either singular or a group of rights and obligations); and binding arrangements that are equally underperformed by both parties.

The Board aims to finalize and publish these updates to Chapters 3 and 5 by April 2023.

Another important task was undertaken in April 2021, with the publication of ED76 relating to Chapter 7 – Measurement of Assets and Liabilities in Financial Statements. According to the IPSASB meeting held in June 2022, the Board was planning to approve the revised Chapter 7 in September 2022; however, there was no clear indication of its intended publication.

ED76 introduces a measurement hierarchy that seeks to explain how the various components required to estimate the value of an asset or liability interact in the context of IPSAS. The measurement hierarchy identifies three levels of measurement as illustrated in Figure 7.4.

---

[65] See the case study presented by Adam et al. (2022).

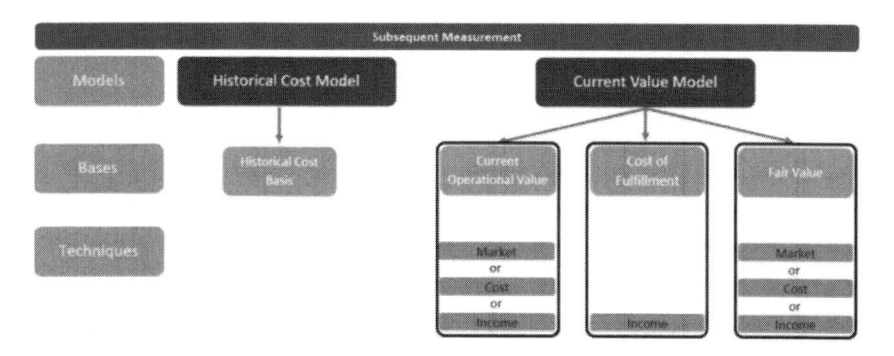

Figure 7.4: The Measurement Hierarchy proposed by ED76

The IPSASB is thus introducing a new term, namely, Current Operational Value. This measurement basis is developed to capture the unique characteristics of assets held by public sector entities, which provide challenges to the application of fair (market) value measurement. The current operational value attempts to measure public sector assets in their current use when held for their operational capacity. Operational capacity is defined as the capacity of an entity to support the provision of services in future periods through physical and other sources.

However, a degree of uncertainty underlies this new measurement basis as the ED proposes two definitions. The definition of Current Operational Value proposed by ED76 is "the value of an asset used to achieve the entity's service delivery objectives at the measurement date" (paragraph 7.48). The alternative definition is "the cost to replace the service potential embodied in an asset at the measurement date" (paragraph AV3).

Due to the mixed responses received from the constituents, further work is deemed necessary on public sector specific current value of assets primarily held for operational capacity. Some of the responses favored replacement cost, while others supported fair value (as in IPSAS 41 *Financial Instruments* / IFRS 13 *Fair Value*). Thus, at the time of writing, current operational value is an open saga for the IPSASB.

The current state of affairs on ED76 and Chapter 7 of the IPSASB's CF, according to the IPSASB's documentation, is to remove the following measurement terms from the CF: assumption price; cost of release; and net selling price. These are not considered relevant for the public sector context. Issues and contradictions also underlie measurement terms like "value in use" and "replacement cost". These arguments are being dealt with by the IPSASB as part of its ongoing Measurement Project[66]. In fact, ED76 was accompanied by three other EDs relating to measurement, namely:

- ED 77 Measurement;
- ED 78 Property, Plant and Equipment; and
- ED 79 Non-Current Assets Held for Sale and Discontinued Operations.

In May 2022, ED 79 materialized as a new standard, namely IPSAS 44. In December 2022, the IPSASB announced that it has approved the changes proposed by the other EDs relating to the CF and the Measurement project. However, the final result will be published during 2023. Of course, it is expected that the final result from these EDs is coherent with the outcome from ED 76.

6. Conclusion

While closely following the IPSASB's CF, and referring to this as much as possible, this chapter addressed CFs overall, namely their contents in the public sector setting: objectives and users, and qualitative characteristics of financial information; elements of financial statements, and their recognition and measurement criteria.

---

[66] Caruana (2021).

It called attention to the importance of a CF as an accounting theory. When standards derive from practice, there is a need to have a common theoretical basis to give consistency to practices. However, the extent that the CF does represent accounting theory is highly debatable because there is lack of consistency in the interpretation and application of certain principles. Standard-setters may have used CFs to legitimize their own activities.

The chapter likewise explained that CFs for PSA have derived from those in business accounting, but they have been adapted due to context specifics that may entail different users and users' needs of public sector organizations' financial information.

Accountability is an almost natural purpose of GPFRs of public sector entities in democratic regimes, but the IPSASB establishes that decision making is also an important purpose. Some more critical literature has raised questions not only about who the real users of public sector entities' financial statements are, but also about their needs, underlining the fact that most of the CFs have adopted prescriptive and normative, rather than empirical, approaches.

Qualitative characteristics of financial information are also a part of a CF. These attributes are crucial to determine the usefulness of that information; however, balancing between them is not an easy task, as they often conflict.

As to the elements of financial statements, although similarities can be found to those in business accounting, again public sector context specifics require particularities in the definitions, impacting on their recognition, and especially on their measurement criteria.

Acknowledging the above, the IPSASB recently embarked in revising the CF, assigning special importance to measurement issues. The IPSASB's Measurement Project promises to continue.

Finally, despite the international reference of the IPSASB's CF, not all countries necessarily follow it, as they do not follow IPSAS.

Countries with very deep-rooted accounting national traditions, such as Germany and Finland, tend to diverge from the IPSASB's perspective – even if some of their principles and concepts may approach it, a more conservative attitude is clear.

Bibliographic references

ADAM, Berit; HEILING, Jens and MEGLITSCH, Tim (2022) - The principle of prudence in public sector accounting—a comparative analysis of cautious and asymmetric prudence, *Public Money and Management*, 42(7), pp.521-529

BRUSCA, Isabel; CAPERCHIONE, Eugenio; COHEN, Sandra and MANES-ROSSI, Francesca (eds.) (2015) – Public Sector Accounting and Auditing in Europe – the Challenge of Harmonization, Basingstoke: Palgrave Macmillan, ISBN: 9781137461339.

CARUANA, Josette (2021) – The proposed IPSAS on measurement for public sector financial reporting – recycling or reiteration?, *Public Money and Management*, 41(3), pp.184-191.

CHAN, James L. (2003) – Government Accounting: an Assessment of Theory, Purposes and Standards, *Public Money and Management*, 23(1), pp.13-20.

DENNIS, Ian (2018) – What is a Conceptual Framework for Financial Reporting?, *Accounting in Europe*, 15(3), pp.374-401.

HAUSTEIN, Ellen; LORSON, Peter.; CAPERCHIONE, Eugenio and BRUSCA, I. (2019) – The quest for users' needs in public sector budgeting and reporting, *Journal of Public Budgeting, Accounting & Financial Management*, 31(4), pp. 473-477.

IPSASB (2014) – *The Conceptual Framework for General Purpose Financial Reporting by Public Sector Entities*, International Public Sector Accounting Standards Board (IPSASB) – International Federation of Accountants (IFAC), New York.

JONES, Rowan (1992) – The development of conceptual frameworks of Accounting for the Public Sector, *Financial Accountability and Management*, 8(4), pp. 249-264.

JONES, Rowan and PENDLEBURY, Maurice (2000) – *Public Sector Accounting*; Pitman, ISBN: 9780273646266, 5th ed.

JONES, Rowan and PENDLEBURY, Maurice (2010) – *Public Sector Accounting*, Pearson Education, ISBN: 9780273720362, 6th ed.

JORGE, Susana; JESUS, Maria Antónia and NOGUEIRA, Sónia (2016) – Information brokers and the use of budgetary and financial information by politicians: the case of Portugal, *Public Money and Management*, 36(7), pp. 515-520.

LAUGHLIN, Richard (2008) – A Conceptual Framework for Accounting for Public-Benefit Entities, *Public Money and Management*; 28(4), pp. 247-254.

LORSON, Peter and HAUSTEIN, Ellen (2019) – Debate: On the role of prudence in public sector accounting, *Public Money and Management*, 39(6), pp.389-390.

RUTHERFORD, Brian A. (1992) – Developing a Conceptual Framework for Central Government Financial Reporting: Intermediate Users and Indirect Control, *Financial Accountability and Management*, 8(4), pp. 265-280.

BUDDING, Tjerk and VAN HELDEN, Jan (2022) – Theme: Politicians' use of accounting information, Editorial: Unraveling politicians' use and non-use of accounting information, *Public Money and Management*, 42(3), 1pp.37-139.

VELA BARGUES, José Manuel (1992) – *Concepto y Principios de Contabilidad Pública*; Instituto de Contabilidad y Auditoría de Cuentas; Ministerio de Economía e Hacienda, Madrid, ISBN: 9788447600137.

Additional readings

AGGESTAM-PONTOPPIDAN, Caroline and ANDERNACK, Isabelle (2016) – Interpretation and application of IPSAS, Hoboken: John Wiley & Sons.

JONES, Rowan (ed.) (2011) – Public Sector Accounting, 4 volumes, Los Angeles: Sage Publications, Sage library in Accounting and Finance.

JORGE, Susana (ed.) (2008) – Implementing Reforms in Public Sector Accounting; Imprensa da Universidade de Coimbra (Coimbra University Press), Coimbra.

OULASVIRTA, Lasse (2014) – The reluctance of a developed country to choose International Public Sector Accounting Standards of the IFAC. A critical case study, *Critical Perspectives on Accounting*, 25(3), pp. 272-285.

OULASVIRTA, Lasse (2016) – Accounting principles, Global Encyclopedia of Public Administration, Public Policy, and Governance. Chapter on "Accounting, Budgeting and Financial Management", A. Farazmand (ed.), Springer International Publishing Switzerland.

Discussion topics

– What is the role of a CF compared to that of PSA standards?

– What are the main objectives and who are the main users of financial (and budgetary) information reported by public sector entities, according to the different CFs presented in this chapter (comparative-international perspective)?

– What are the main recognition criteria for assets, liabilities, expenses and revenues, according to the different

CFs presented in this chapter (comparative-international perspective)?

– Distinguish the main criteria which can be used to measure assets, liabilities, expenses and revenues within the financial statements, according to the different CFs presented in this chapter (comparative-international perspective).

– Referring to the Table 7.2 in Section 4, add data that is applicable for your jurisdiction, either at local, state or central government level.

Chapter 8
Reporting Components and Reliability Issues

Susana Jorge
University of Coimbra, Portugal
susjor@fe.uc.pt
https://orcid.org/0000-0003-4850-2387

Josette Caruana
University of Malta, Malta
josette.caruana@um.edu.mt
https://orcid.org/0000-0002-6099-1577

Summary

This chapter deals with financial reporting in the public sector, taking IPSAS as reference. Some examples of the reporting components of specific countries are presented. The chapter also highlights the role of financial reporting in promoting transparency and accountability in the public sector, and concludes by referring to the importance of auditing to ensure fair presentation and regularity of the public sector accounts, ultimately impacting on citizens' trust in public sector managers and politicians.

Keywords

IPSAS, reporting entity, financial statements, non-financial information, transparency, auditing.

https://doi.org/10.14195/978-989-26-2464-8_8

1. Introduction

Transparency and accountability have become two key aspects of sound public governance. They are two related, although different, concepts. 'Accountability' means the obligation for public officials to report on the usage of public resources and the answerability of government to the public, to meet stated performance objectives.[1] 'Transparency' refers to unfettered access, by the public and other stakeholders, to timely and reliable information on decisions and performance in the public sector. Probably the most widely discussed concept is that of accountability, which essentially relates to the obligation to explain and justify a certain conduct, for which information disclosure is indeed important.[2]

Democratic accountability requires governments to increase transparency, disclosing more budgetary and financial information to citizens and other stakeholders, promoting public expenditure scrutiny, and ultimately preventing corruption and the waste of public resources.

Consequently, budgetary and financial transparency, namely via disclosing General Purpose Financial Reporting (GPFR), has become a pillar within public (financial) management reforms.

The importance of GPFR to promote transparency in the public sector is acknowledged by the IPSASB:

> GPFRs are a central component of, and support and enhance, transparent financial reporting by governments and other public sector entities.[3]

---

[1] Accountability must be distinguished from stewardship. Stewardship is the duty of care for resources; it involves administration, management, and guardianship of public resources, without concerning about performance.

[2] Lourenço et al. (2013); Jorge et al. (2012).

[3] IPSASB (2014, CF 1.4).

Transparency is, therefore, a prerequisite for accountability, as illustrated in Figure 8.1. It is especially important in the public sector context, where principal-agent relationships prevail (citizens, investors and other stakeholders are principals, while politicians and public officials are the agents), and information needs arise from the opacity of public entities.

Accountability ⟲ Transparency ← • Principal-agent relationships • Information needs arise from the opacity of public entities

↑

Information Access/Availability
(basic requirements)

FINANCIAL TRANSPARENCY
complete disclosure of all relevant budgetary and financial information in an opportune and systematic way (e.g. GPFR online, in official websites)

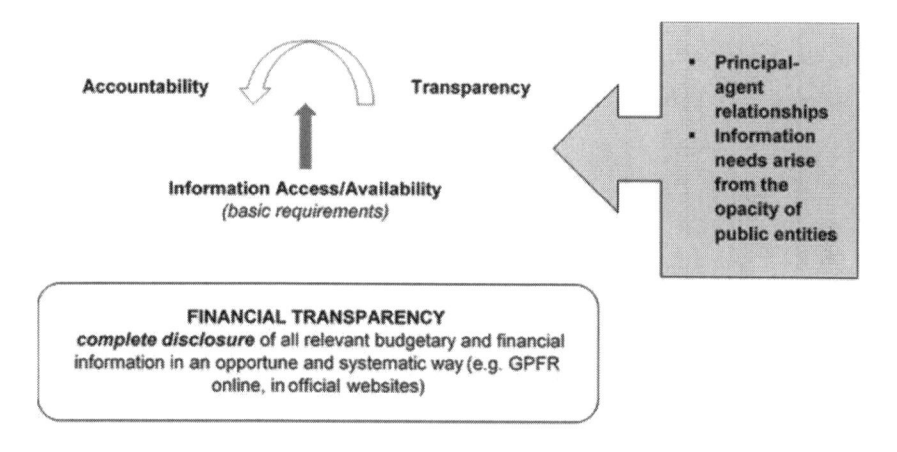

Figure 8.1: Transparency, accountability and financial information
Source: Lourenço et al. (2013).

The availability of financial information is critical for these objectives, hence GPFR must be accessible, preferably online, to all (namely citizens, *media*, investors...), under the assumption of understandability. Access to government information is a perpetual concern of citizens – it helps to improve their trust in the public sector agents and engagement in the public sector affairs.[4]

Online disclosure is nowadays a means resorted to by governments and public sector entities overall to enhance transparency and accountability. However, regarding the extension of the disclosure, one must bear in mind that more information does not

---

[4] Pina et al. (2007, 2010).

necessarily increase transparency – information overload and (lack of) understandability may jeopardize transparency, ultimately hindering accountability.

In democratic regimes, the disclosure of financial information by governments at all levels, as well as by public sector entities at large, is crucial to the promotion of transparency and increased accountability. General Purpose Financial Reports (GPFRs) are deemed to be an important means of conveying financial information to a large variety of users and stakeholders, potentially interested in such information for the purposes of accountability and decision-making (see Chapter 7 in this book).

> GPFRs are financial reports intended to meet the information needs of users who are unable to require the preparation of financial reports tailored to meet their specific information needs.[5]

This is why they are labeled 'general purpose'. Even if there are users who may have the power to require public sector entities to prepare information for their specific needs (for example, a Minister responsible for a particular project), GPFRs are not developed to respond to these, but to needs supposedly common to several types of users (mostly external to the entity, for example, the public at large), who are expected to be generally satisfied with those reports.

As this chapter will explain, GPFRs comprise several statements and different types of financial and non-financial information. Similar to the business sector, in the public sector the extent of transactions and other events to be reported in the GPFRs is determined by users' information needs, considering the objectives sought for the financial reporting. In these objectives, public sector context specificities must be taken into account.

---

[5] IPSASB (2014, CF 1.4).

Accordingly, this chapter follows by presenting an overview of the public sector financial reporting setting. Then, it addresses the notion of the reporting entity and the scope of the financial reporting, taking the IPSASB's CF as a benchmark.

The second part explains the format and contents of the main financial statements within IPSAS 1 and IPSAS 2, ending with a comparative international analysis introducing the main financial statements prepared in a number of European countries (Austria, Finland, Germany, Portugal and the UK), taking the IPSAS as a benchmark.

The last part addresses financial reporting reliability-related issues, namely referring to the importance of auditing.

2. The context of GPFR

The following sections particularly refer to the public sector financial reporting environment with multiple stakeholders, and its scope, including examples of complementary statements. The notion of reporting entity is also explained, although this chapter addresses primarily individual accounts and does not address consolidated accounts specifically (which are explained in Chapters 11 and 12 in this book).

By financial reporting one means periodical accounts, generally, the annual accounts. Therefore, other non-financial special reports, such as performance or sustainability reporting, are not addressed.

2.1. Public sector (budgetary and financial) reporting setting

Figure 8.2 illustrates the setting of governments and public sector entities' financial reporting, showing a variety of individuals and bodies as stakeholders to whom those entities report.

Despite the focus on financial issues, those addressees point to a scope of GPFR in the public sector generally wider than in the business sector, namely embracing non-financial and budgetary information (concerning the budget accomplishment).

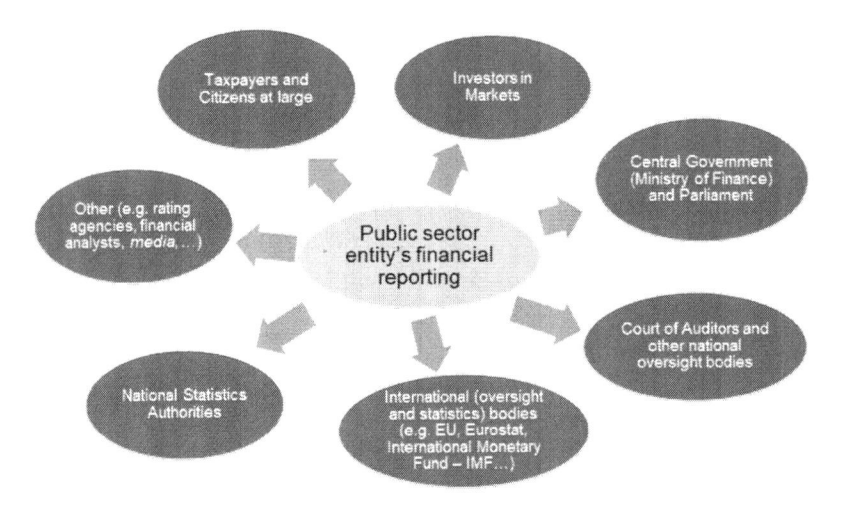

Figure 8.2: Stakeholders (deemed users) of public sector entities' financial reporting

The widely diverse nature of the stakeholders presented for the public sector financial reporting may lead them to give importance to different issues and types of information within the GPFR; there might also be some specificities – for example, Government Financial Statistics use information from GPFR as input to prepare macro/supranational reporting.

But, in spite of the likelihood of diversified information needs among these individuals and organizations, considering the 'general purpose', GPFR under IPSAS assumes that such needs can be harmonized and summarized in accountability and decision-making purposes,[6] without either purpose predominating.

---

[6] IPSASB (2014, CF 2).

As to the reporting process, i.e., the bureaucratic procedures and specific practices, while some derive from legal requirements related to monitoring processes (e.g., guidance to report to the ministries, Courts of Audit, the EU or the Eurostat), others derive from transparency practices, often not resulting from any legal requirement, but are voluntary in character. In the former case, the role of the legislator in each country or jurisdiction may be a critical factor determining the reporting practices. This then may lead to differences depending on the countries and on the addressees, users or stakeholders in the reporting process. Yet, regardless of whether reporting procedures follow legal requirements or voluntary transparency practices, including online information disclosure, the two above-stated main objectives of GPFR continue to be asserted.

2.2. Reporting entity

The IPSASB's CF defines a reporting entity as

> (...) a government or other public sector organization, program or identifiable area of activity (...) that prepares GPFRs.[7]

It may comprise two or more separate entities that present GPFRs as if they were a single entity, in this case constituting a 'group reporting entity'.[8] Independently of having legal/juridical personality or not (it may only be an administrative unit), a public sector entity is a reporting entity if it has the responsibility or capacity to raise or deploy resources, acquire

---

[7] IPSASB (2014, CF 4.1).
[8] IPSASB (2014, CF 4.2).

or manage public assets, incur liabilities, or undertake activities to achieve service delivery objectives. Additionally, there are service recipients or resource providers dependent on GPFRs of that entity to have information for accountability or decision-making purposes.[9]

In accounting terms, a reporting entity is not required to have a legal personality, but it must have operational autonomy; and it may be an identifiable area of activity within a government or organization. For example, the education and the health sectors in a central government, or the education, research, and social services areas in a university, are reporting entities. This paves the way for segment reporting.

An interesting example happened in Portugal, where in 2015, during the process of reforming public sector accounting towards IPSAS, the 'State Reporting Entity' was created, endorsing Whole-of-Government Accounts.[10] This is not a legal entity, but an 'abstract' reporting entity, recording transactions and other events related to the Portuguese State as a sovereign entity, as there are agencies acting on its behalf, such as the Taxation Authority, the Directorate-General of the Budget, the Directorate-General of the Treasury and Finance or the Agency for the Management of Public Debt. Such transactions are, e.g., general revenue (taxes), liabilities (public debt) and State's assets. This entity shall have an 'all-encompassing' GPFR, comprising financial (accrual-based), as well as budgetary (cash-based) information, prepared according to both an IPSAS-based public sector accounting system and the Portuguese Budgetary Framework Law.

---

[9] IPSASB (2014, CF 4.2-4.7).

[10] For further on the concept of Whole-of-Government Accounts, see Chapter 11 in this book.

2.3. The scope of financial reporting: financial and non-financial information

According to the IPSASB, in governments or public sector entities, GPFR encompasses the following **financial statements** as main components:[11]

- Statement of financial position (***Balance Sheet***);
- Statement of financial performance (***Income Statement by nature and/or by function***);
- Statement of **changes in the Net Assets/Equity**;
- Cash Flow Statement;
- **Comparison of budget and actual amounts** (when budgets are published), either as an additional financial statement, or as a budget column in the financial statements; and
- **Notes**.

However, users often need additional information

> (...) to better understand, interpret and place in context the information presented in the financial statements (...).[12]

Therefore, GPFR should disclose further financial and non-financial information, enhancing, complementing and supplementing the financial statements,[13] namely about:

- Compliance with approved budgets and other authority governing its operations;

---

[11] IPSASB (2022, IPSAS 1.21).
[12] IPSASB (2014, CF 2.17).
[13] IPSASB (2014, CF 2.29).

- Service delivery activities and achievements during the reporting period; and
- Expectations regarding service delivery and other activities in future periods, and the long-term consequences of decisions made and activities undertaken during the reporting period, including those that may impact expectations about the future.[14]

Usually, this additional explanatory information is included in the Notes, which also comprise a summary of significant accounting policies and further disclosures according to the requirements of each IPSAS. However, it may also be included in separate reports within the GPFRs.

For the public sector, as addressed in previous chapters, it is particularly interesting to have additional information about compliance with public budgets.

Referring to *IPSAS 24 – Presentation of Budget Information in Financial Statements*, the IPSASB explains:

> (...) entities are typically subject to budgetary limits in the form of appropriations or budget authorizations (or equivalent), which may be given effect through authorizing legislation. GPFR by public sector entities may provide information on whether resources were obtained and used in accordance with the legally adopted budget.[15]

A comparison of budget to actual amounts usually consists of a separate statement when budgets are not accrual-based.

It is equally important to disclose

---

[14] IPSASB (2014, CF 2.17).
[15] IPSASB (2022, IPSAS 1.24).

(...) additional information to assist users in assessing the performance of the entity, and its stewardship of assets, as well as making and evaluating decisions about the allocation of resources. This may include details about the entity's outputs and outcomes in the form of (a) performance indicators, (b) statements of service performance, (c) program reviews, and (d) other reports by management about the entity's achievement over the reporting period.[16]

Finally, public sector entities must also disclose in the GPFR information about compliance with legislative, regulatory or other externally-imposed regulations.[17]

The above-mentioned statements present financial information in different perspectives, which, however, complement and link each other.[18] While the Balance Sheet reflects the entity's financial position at the end of the period, the Income Statement shows the entity's financial performance over the period, leading to a certain surplus/deficit; in addition, the Cash Flow Statement displays the main cash sources (e.g., taxes, sales, borrowing, ...) and applications (e.g., purchases, investments, debt repayment, ...) during the period. The net surplus/deficit coming from the Income Statement is part of the Net Assets, and the cash and cash equivalents at the bottom of the Cash Flow Statement are included in the current assets, on the Balance Sheet.

Information about the **financial position** should enable users to identify the resources of the entity and claims on those resources at the reporting date. Information about the **financial performance** should allow for assessments about whether the entity has acquired resources economically, and used them efficiently and effectively to

---

[16] IPSASB (2022, IPSAS 1.25).

[17] IPSASB (2022, IPSAS 1.26).

[18] See, for example, Van Helden and Hodges (2015).

achieve its service delivery objectives. Finally, information about the **cash flows** should support assessments of financial performance, e.g., the entity's liquidity and solvency, and compliance with spending mandates; indicate how the entity raised and used cash during the period, including its borrowing and repayment of borrowing; and also provide evidence about the likely amounts and sources of cash inflows needed in future periods to support service delivery objectives.[19]

In summary, Figure 8.3 shows a scope of the GPFR that goes beyond that encompassed by the financial statements[20] and is generally broader than in the private sector, especially due to budgetary reporting information.

Information provided by the GPFRs				
Financial position, financial performance and cash flows	Budget information, compliance with legislation or other authority governing the resources	Service delivery	Prospective financial and non-financial information	Explanatory information

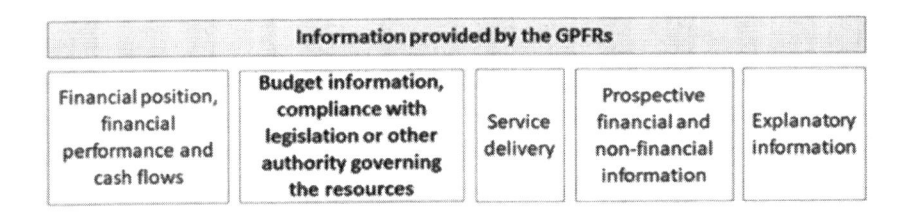

Figure 8.3: The scope of financial reporting in the public sector

Because approved budgets are public, budgetary information

> (...) is used to justify the raising of resources from taxpayers and other resource providers, and establishes the authority for expenditure of resources.[21]

---

[19] IPSASB (2014, CF 2.14-2.16); Jones and Pendlebury (2010); Van Helden and Hodges (2015).

[20] IPSASB (2014, CF 2.29). For further on the difference between GPFR and General Purpose Financial Statements (GPFS), see Chapter 1 in this book, especially Figure 1.1.

[21] IPSASB (2014, CF 2.18).

Therefore, it is important to disclose the accomplishments of the budgets finally approved.

> (...) information that assists users in assessing the extent to which revenues, expenses, cash flows and financial results of the entity comply with the estimates reflected in approved budgets, and the entity's adherence to relevant legislation or other authority governing the raising and use of resources, is important in determining how well a public sector entity has met its financial objectives.[22]

Given the main purpose of delivering public services to the citizens, governments' and public sector entities' GPFR shall also include information about the achievement of service delivery objectives. This can be done, for example, by presenting quantitative measures of outputs and outcomes, or providing an explanation of the quality of particular services provided or the outcome of certain programs. Likewise, GPFR considers explanatory information about major factors underlying the financial and service delivery performance of the government or entity during the reporting period[23] (as described in the IPSASB's RPGs, which may be applied on a voluntary basis).

Prospective and long-term information is also particularly important, given the longevity of governments and public sector programs, which determine the 'going concern', given that financial consequences of many decisions in the present may only become clear many years later.

Information within GPFR must be presented in comparative terms, particularly in relation to the preceding period, even regarding explanatory non-financial and narrative information.[24]

---

[22] IPSASB (2014, CF 2.21).
[23] IPSASB (2014, CF 2.22-2.24; 2.28).
[24] IPSASB (2022, IPSAS 1.21g), 1.53).

Finally, financial statements are usually presented annually,[25] but the reporting period can be longer or shorter than twelve months. When this is the case, the entity shall disclose the period financial statements relate to, and why it is not annual, highlighting the fact that some amounts in the statements may not be comparable.[26]

2.4. Complementary statements to the GPFR: budgetary reporting and management accounting reporting

Although there are several similarities, GPFR components in the public sector tend to differentiate across countries, as will be presented later in this chapter, namely reflecting different accounting and reporting traditions and priority purposes.

Portugal offers a noteworthy example of complementary statements to be included in the GPFR, in addition to those required by the IPSASB's CF. According to the IPSAS-based *Sistema de Normalização Contabilística para as Administrações Públicas* (SNC-AP), GPFR also comprises:

BUDGETARY REPORTING STATEMENTS (cash- and commitment-based)

- Revenue budgetary execution statement
- Expenditure budgetary execution statement
- Budgetary performance statement
- Statement of the execution of the Multiannual Investment Plan (PPI)
- Notes to the budgetary execution statements

---

[25] In some countries, the year for the accounts does not coincide with the calendar year. For example, in the UK the reporting period goes from May 1 to April 30.

[26] IPSASB (2022, IPSAS 1.66-1.68).

and MANAGEMENT ACCOUNTING REPORTING STATEMENTS (accrual-based)

- Income statement by functions/activities
- Income statement by products sold or services delivered in the period
- Costs by activities, including information of under-activity variances
- Production costs by products and services delivered, including variances
- Environmental expenses and revenues
- General revenue and expenses non-incorporated in the products and services delivered (period costs)
- Other found relevant to disclose information about management accounting

The above-mentioned *budgetary performance statement* has nothing to do with performance-based budgets but instead reports on the way the budget execution is performed, highlighting the budgetary (cash-based) deficit or surplus.

Management accounting is seen as in the business sector (i.e., relating to cost accounting), although in the public sector, the budget (especially if performance-based, as in Finland) and budgetary reporting might be also seen as management accounting. Information about management and cost accounting was found important to be included in the GPFR (if not as main statements, at least in the Notes) – for example, it is important for citizens to realize the cost of services provided compared to what they actually pay. However, management accounting statements (i.e., reporting management accounting information within the annual accounts) differ from the entity's Management Reporting, which usually accompanies the accounts.

Each of the above statements have standardized models to be used by all entities in Portugal following the accounting and reporting system SNC-AP.

3. GPFR components; comparative analysis

This section follows IPSAS 1 and IPSAS 2 especially, explaining in some detail each of the GPFR main components according to the IPSASB (2022). The comparative-international analysis involves a number of European countries, the IPSASB serving as a benchmark.

3.1. GPFR components according to the IPSASB

When preparing the financial statements, several overall considerations must be taken into account.[27]

It is assumed that if one entity's financial statements are IPSAS-compliant, they will provide a fair presentation of the entity's financial position, financial performance and cash flows.[28] Moreover, the entity's ability to continue as a 'going concern' (see Chapter 7 in this book) must be assessed when preparing the financial statements; if this is in question, such must be disclosed.[29]

Other important issues, which underly the bases for presentation of the financial statements, relate to:

– Consistency of Presentation

    The presentation and classification of items in the financial statements shall be retained from one period to the next unless (…)

---

[27] IPSASB (2022, IPSAS 1.27-1.58).
[28] IPSASB (2022, IPSAS 1.27-1.37).
[29] IPSASB (2022, IPSAS 1.38-1.41).

it is apparent, following a significant change in the nature of the entity's operations or a review of its financial statements, that another presentation or classification would be more appropriate...[30]

In the latter case, *IPSAS 3 – Accounting Policies, Changes in Accounting Estimates and Errors*, applies, in order the entity to account for the changes. Consistency is important to allow for comparability.[31]

– Materiality and Aggregation

Each material class of similar items shall be presented separately in the financial statements. Items of a dissimilar nature or function shall be presented separately, unless they are immaterial.[32]

Usually, immaterial elements appear in the statements aggregated in a residual line called «other».

– Offsetting

Assets and liabilities, and revenue and expenses, shall not be offset unless required or permitted by an IPSAS.[33]

Offsetting means some form of compensation of the amounts presented, which should be avoided, because it can lead to misrepresentations. Figures in the financial statements must be presented separately in 'gross amounts', as much as possible. For example, offsetting payables with receivables regarding a supplier, can hide information, not showing the real substance of the transaction.

---

[30] IPSASB (2022, IPSAS 1.42).
[31] IPSASB (2014, CF 3.21-3.25).
[32] IPSASB (2022, IPSAS 1.45).
[33] IPSASB (2022, IPSAS 1.48).

– and, Comparative information,[34] as previously explained.

IPSAS 1 and IPSAS 2 require minimum contents to be presented on the face of the financial statements, but a reporting entity can choose different detail, formats and presentation, as the models suggested in the standards are merely indicative and not exhaustive.

However, a universally accepted requirement is that all financial statements must be clearly identified,[35] displaying prominently the following:

a) The name of the reporting entity or other means of identification, and any change in that information from the preceding reporting date;
b) Whether the financial statements cover the individual entity or the economic entity;
c) The reporting date or the reporting period covered by the financial statements, (…);
d) The presentation currency (…); and
e) The level of rounding used in presenting amounts in the financial statements.[36]

Statement of financial position

Regarding the statement of financial position (designated in some jurisdictions as *Balance Sheet*), IPSAS 1 requires the following minimum elements to be presented on its face:

---

[34] IPSASB (2022, IPSAS 1.53-1.58).
[35] IPSASB (2022, IPSAS 1.61-1.65).
[36] IPSASB (2022, IPSAS 1.63).

a) Property, plant and equipment;
b) Investment property;
c) Intangible assets;
d) Financial assets (excluding amounts shown under (e), (g), (h) and (i));
e) Investments accounted for using the equity method;
f) Inventories;
g) Recoverables from non-exchange transactions (taxes and transfers);
h) Receivables from exchange transactions;
i) Cash and cash equivalents;
j) Taxes and transfers payable;
k) Payables under exchange transactions;
l) Provisions;
m) Financial liabilities (excluding amounts shown under (j), (k) and (l));
n) Non-controlling/minority interest, presented within net assets/equity; and
o) Net assets/equity attributable to owners of the controlling entity.[37]

Items (a) to (i) belong to Assets, while (j) to (m) belong to Liabilities. The Equity results from the difference between Assets (including other resources) and Liabilities (including other obligations) (see Chapter 7 in this book). In the public sector, the Equity would be better called 'Net Assets', but it must not be confused with net values presented on the assets side. Within the Net Assets/Equity, especially in consolidated accounts, it is im-

---

[37] IPSASB (2022, IPSAS 1.88).

portant to present separately the part belonging to the entity and that belonging to non-controlling interests ((o) and (n) above).[38]

An entity may decide to present the statement of financial position in a more synthesized or detailed format (considering additional items or subclassifications), judging the appropriateness of that to its operations,[39] but providing the accomplishment with the IPSAS 1 minimum requirements.

Table 8.1 presents the model suggested in IPSAS 1 for the statement of financial position.[40] Comparability is visible by presenting the amounts of the previous year.

Public Sector Entity—Statement of Financial Position
As at December 31, 20X2
(in thousands of currency units)

	20X2	20X1
ASSETS		
Current assets		
...	X	X
	X	X
Non-current assets		
...	X	X
	X	X
Total assets	X	X
LIABILITIES		
Current liabilities		
...	X	X
	X	X
Non-current liabilities		
...	X	X
	X	X
Total liabilities	X	X
Net assets	X	X
NET ASSETS/EQUITY		
...	X	X
Total net assets/equity	X	X

Table 8.1: Statement of financial position according to IPSAS 1

---

[38] Non-controlling interests may be zero in cases where the entity participation in the capital of other entities is 100%. For example, when a municipality wholly owns a municipal business company, there are no non-controlling interests in the municipality's consolidated accounts.

[39] IPSASB (2022, IPSAS 1.91-1.93).

[40] See IPSASB (2022, IPSAS 1 Implementation Guidance).

A distinction between current and non-current assets and liabilities is important to be considered,[41] as it affects how long the item is reported on the entity's balance sheet, ranging from short (1 year) to medium- and long-term periods of time (continuity), with differing impacts on the entity's financial balance.

Additionally, assets are broadly presented in order of liquidity, whereas liabilities are broadly presented in order of settlement.

A **current asset** must satisfy any of the following criteria:

a) It is expected to be realized in, or is held for sale or consumption in, the entity's normal operating cycle;
b) It is held primarily for the purpose of being traded;
c) It is expected to be realized within twelve months after the reporting date; or
d) It is cash or a cash equivalent (...), unless it is restricted from being exchanged or used to settle a liability for at least twelve months after the reporting date.[42]

A **current liability** must satisfy any of the following criteria:

a) It is expected to be settled in the entity's normal operating cycle;
b) It is held primarily for the purpose of being traded;
c) It is due to be settled within twelve months after the reporting date; or
d) The entity does not have an unconditional right to defer settlement of the liability for at least twelve months after the reporting date (...). Terms of a liability that could,

---

[41] IPSASB (2022, IPSAS 1.70-1.75).
[42] IPSASB (2022, IPSAS 1.76).

at the option of the counterparty, result in its settlement by the issue of equity instruments do not affect its classification.[43]

All other assets and liabilities are classified as non-current.

Examples of current assets are (available) cash, receivables, prepayments, and inventories. Non-current assets are generally capital assets, such as infrastructure, land, buildings and equipment, financial investments and intangibles. Payables, borrowings, provisions and employees' benefits owing are examples of liabilities (current if short-term, and non-current if long-term).

The model for the statement of financial position suggested in Table 8.1 highlights the Net Assets, evidenced as the difference between Assets and Liabilities. However, this difference needs to be detailed in a separate statement, namely, the Statement of changes in Net Assets/Equity. Governments and most public sector entities do not have share capital. Some public sector entities in the form of companies would have share capital. In both instances, the detail of the items in the Net Assets/Equity must be disclosed, showing separately:

a) Share capital or contributed capital, being the cumulative total, at the reporting date, of contributions from owners, less distributions to owners;

b) Accumulated surpluses or deficits [including the surplus/deficit of the current period];

c) Reserves, including a description of the nature and purpose of each reserve within net assets/equity; and

d) Non-controlling interests.[44]

---

[43] IPSASB (2022, IPSAS 1.80).
[44] IPSASB (2022, IPSAS 1.95).

The presentation of this detail must ensure that the 'Total Net Assets' equals the amount resulting from the residual difference between Total Assets and Total Liabilities.

Statement of financial performance

The statement of the financial performance displays how the entity was able to generate an accrual-based deficit/surplus from revenues obtained and expenses incurred in the period. As in the previous statement, this designation is again IPSAS language, but it is perhaps most commonly known as *Income Statement* in the public sector, and as *Profit and Loss Statement*, in the business sector. However, perhaps the reason why this label was set aside was an attempt to differentiate from business accounting, where the main goal is to highlight the 'income', anticipated as profit.

As for the statement of financial position, IPSAS 1 also suggests minimum line items to be presented on the face of the statement of financial performance, presenting the following amounts for the period:

a) Revenue;
b) Finance costs;
c) Impairment losses;
d) Share of the surplus or deficit of associates and joint ventures accounted for using the equity method;
e) Any gain or loss arising from differences in measurement criteria of financial assets;
f) Pre-tax gain or loss recognized on the disposal of assets or settlement of liabilities attributable to discontinuing operations; and
g) Surplus or deficit.[45]

---

[45] IPSASB (2022, IPSAS 1.102).

Therefore, likewise, an entity may decide to present more detail in this statement (namely additional line items and revenue subclassifications), when such presentation is relevant to a better understanding of its financial performance.[46] As in the Balance Sheet, comparability is evidenced by presenting the amounts of the previous year.

Two different presentations are allowed for the statement of financial performance, the difference basically concerning the way expenses are presented – by *nature* (origin) or by *function* (destination). In any case, expenses are deducted (shown in brackets) from revenue, as in Tables 8.2 and 8.3.[47]

Public Sector Entity—Statement of Financial Performance for the Year Ended December 31, 20X2 (Illustrating the Classification of Expenses by Nature) (in thousands of currency units)		
	20X2	20X1
Revenue		
(nature/origin of the revenues raised)	X	X
Total Revenue	X	X
Expenses		
(nature/origin of the expenses incurred)	(X)	(X)
Total Expenses	(X)	(X)
Share of surplus of associates	X	X
Surplus/(deficit) for the period	X/(X)	X/(X)
Attributable to:		
Owners of the controlling entity	X	X
Non-controlling interest	X	X
	X/(X)	X/(X)

Table 8.2: Statement of financial performance (by nature) according to IPSAS 1

---

[46] IPSASB (2022, IPSAS 1.104-1.108).

[47] See IPSASB (2022, IPSAS 1 Implementation Guidance).

Public Sector Entity—Statement of Financial Performance for the Year Ended December 31, 20X2 (Illustrating the Classification of Expenses by Function) (in thousands of currency units)		
	20X2	20X1
Revenue		
(nature/origin of the revenues raised)	X	X
Total Revenue	X	X
Expenses		
(function of the expenses incurred - program/purpose for which they are incurred)	(X)	(X)
Total Expenses	(X)	(X)
Share of surplus of associates	X	X
Surplus/(deficit) for the period	X/(X)	X/(X)
Attributable to:		
Owners of the controlling entity	X	X
Non-controlling interest	X	X
	X/(X)	X/(X)

Table 8.3: Statement of financial performance (by function) according to IPSAS 1

Expenses by nature refer to the origin of the outlays, e.g., wages, supplies and consumables, transfers and grants, depreciation, impairment losses, and finance costs; whereas by function requires a reclassification according to the destination or purpose of expenses, e.g., defense, public order, education, health, social protection, culture, housing, economic affairs, environmental affairs, and finance costs.

An entity may select the presentation that faithfully provides representative and more relevant information.[48] In some jurisdictions and/or for some smaller entities (e.g., in Portugal), only the statement by nature is obligatory.

While in the statement of financial performance by nature, no allocations of expenses to functional classifications are necessary,

---

[48] IPSAS (2022, IPSAS 1.109).

in the statement by function, expenses are presented according to the program or purpose/destination for which they were incurred.[49]

> This [latter] method can provide more relevant information to users (...), but allocating costs to functions may require arbitrary allocations and involves considerable judgment.[50]

Another problem is that, while functions might be useful for management purposes (for example, to analyze which activities absorb more expenses), they may not be comparable across entities, which make this type of statement less useful, namely, at central level to the government as a whole. Perhaps it is useful mainly as part of the management accounting reporting, as in Portugal.

Revenue in both models of the statement refers to the nature of the proceeds, e.g., from taxes, fines, fees, exchange transactions, and transfers and grants.

The statement of financial performance (either by nature or by function) must also show the allocations of the surplus/deficit between the controlling entity and non-controlling interest for the period, if any.[51] This is particularly important within a public sector group. The amounts of the surplus/deficit for the period, as signed in the tables, must be the same in both models of the statement, regardless the presentation by nature or by function.

One question that can be raised concerns the meaning of the accrual-based deficit/surplus as a measure of financial performance or efficiency,[52] considering the controversy of applying the matching principle between revenues and expenses (see Chapter 7 in this book). Given that

---

[49] IPSASB (2022, IPSAS 1.112-1.113).
[50] IPSASB (2022, IPSAS 1.113).
[51] IPSAS (2022, IPSAS 1.103)
[52] Jones and Pendlebury (2010).

most revenue comes from taxes (transfers) and grants, which do not link to the expenses incurred by the entity, the application of the matching principle underlying the meaning of the bottom line of the statement of financial performance becomes rather controversial. This has perhaps been behind many criticisms of this statement in public sector accounting, requiring the need to include service delivery and performance information in the GPFR, or even preparing a separate performance report.

Statement of changes in Net Assets

The statement of changes in Net Assets displays the changes in the financial position of an entity, from one period to the other. For the purpose of comparability, two statements must be prepared – regarding the current and the previous year. Each statement reconciles the Net Assets items carrying amounts between the two reporting dates. The suggested model by IPSAS 1 is horizontal,[53] with the Net Assets items in the columns and causes of their changes in the lines. It requires presenting the following information,[54] so that total recognized revenue and expense for the period are displayed:[55]

- Surplus/deficit for the period;
- Revenues and expenses for the period that, according to other IPSAS, are directly recognized in the Net Assets;
- Total of revenues and expenses for the period, resulting from the addition of the two previous items, separating between the amounts attributed to the controlling entity and non-controlling interests;

---

[53] See IPSASB (2022, IPSAS 1 Implementation Guidance).
[54] IPSASB (2022, IPSAS 1.118-1.119).
[55] Like an 'extended' surplus/deficit, beyond what is presented in the Income Statement, resembling the comprehensive income in business accounting.

- Eventual effects of changes in accounting policies and corrections of errors (according to IPSAS 3); and
- The amounts of transactions with owners acting as such, separating distributions to owners from contributions by owners.

The importance of the Statement of Changes in Net Assets in typical public sector entities and governments, which do not have share capital, is questionable. It does not seem so useful as in businesses. In a profit-oriented context, the principle of shareholders' protection is paramount, and this is ultimately reflected in the equity.[56] Therefore, it is important to understand the comprehensive profitability of the company and how equity has changed; but such importance is reduced in the public sector.

For this reason, it was not considered important to present here the model for this statement.

Cash Flow Statement

The Cash Flow Statement[57] informs how the entity generated cash and cash equivalents, and where and how these were applied, i.e., where the money came from and where it went. Prepared under the accrual basis regime, this statement also informs about the entity's cash needs for the period.[58]

The main concepts to be considered when preparing a Cash Flow Statement within IPSAS are:[59] cash (comprising cash on hand and demand deposits); cash equivalents (short-term, highly liquid invest-

---
[56] In some countries, like in Germany, creditors' protection is paramount.
[57] IPSASB (2022, IPSAS 2).
[58] Jones and Pendlebury (2010); Van Helden and Hodges (2015).
[59] IPSASB (2022, IPSAS 2.8).

ments that are readily convertible to known amounts of cash and which are only subject to an insignificant risk of changes in value); and cash flows (inflows/outflows of cash and cash equivalents).

Cash flows for a certain period are presented in this statement considering the classification as deriving from operating, investing and financing activities.[60]

According to IPSASB (2022, IPSAS 2.8),

> Financing activities are activities that result in changes in the size and composition of the contributed capital and borrowings of the entity.
> Investing activities are the acquisition and disposal of long-term assets and other investments not included in cash equivalents.
> Operating activities are the activities of the entity that are not investing or financing activities.

This classification

> (…) allows users to assess the impact of those activities on the financial position of the entity, and the amount of its cash and cash equivalents. [It] may also be used to evaluate the relationships among those activities.[61]

Cash flows from **operating activities** are critical, as they relate to the operational capacity of the entity, to repay obligations and to make additional investments, without needing external resources. Operational activities should be the main source of cash for most public sector entities. In particular, they indicate the extent to which the operations of the entity are funded by taxes (directly or indirectly) or by revenue raised from the recipients of goods and services

---

[60] IPSASB (2022, IPSAS 2.18).
[61] IPSASB (2022, IPSAS 2.19).

provided by the entity.[62] Deriving from principal cash-generating activities, these flows include, among others:[63]

- Cash receipts from: taxes, levies, and fines; charges for goods and services provided by the entity;
- Grants, transfers, etc., received, made by central government or other public sector entities;
- Cash receipts and cash payments of an insurance entity for premiums and claims, annuities, and other policy benefits:
- Cash payments of local property taxes or income taxes (where appropriate) in relation to operating activities; and
- Cash payments to: other public sector entities to finance their operations, e.g., grants conceded (not including loans); suppliers for goods and services; to and on behalf of employees.

When an entity holds securities for dealing or trading purposes, they must be seen as similar to inventories for resale. Therefore, cashflows deriving from these securities are included in cash flows from operating activities. Also, some interest might be included in these cash flows, if they relate to transactions generating operating revenue or expenses.[64]

As to cash flows from **investing activities**, they

> (...) represent the extent to which cash outflows have been made for resources that are intended to contribute to the entity's future service delivery. Only cash outflows that result in a recognized asset in the statement of financial position are eligible for classification as investing activities.[65]

---

[62] IPSASB (2022, IPSAS 2.21).
[63] IPSASB (2022, IPSAS 2.22).
[64] IPSASB (2022, IPSAS 2.23).
[65] IPSASB (2022, IPSAS 2.25).

Examples of cash flows deriving from investing activities include, among others:[66]

- Cash payments/receipts to acquire/from selling property, plant, and equipment, intangibles, and other long-term assets (including cash payments related to capitalized development costs and self-constructed plant, property and equipment);
- Cash payments to acquire/from the sale of equity or debt instruments of other entities and interests in joint ventures (other than for those considered cash or equivalents or held for trading purposes);
- Cash advances and loans made to other parties (other than advances and loans made by a public financial institution); and
- Cash receipts from the repayment of advances and loans made to other parties (other than advances and loans of a public financial institution).

One issue that can be questioned regards the requirement that an investment cash outflow has to result in an asset recognized on the Balance Sheet. In the public sector, there might be cash outflows to pay 'immaterial investments' (e.g., investments in democratic structures, citizen participation, or culture) not capitalized as assets according to the IPSASB's CF. According to IPSAS, these would be classified as cash outflows of operating activities.

Cash flows from **financing activities** essentially relate to borrowing (issuing and repaying), but also to ownership contributions and ownership distributions. Reporting about these cash flows is important, because they are useful in predicting claims on future cash flows by providers of capital to the entity.[67]

---

[66] IPSASB (2022, IPSAS 2.25).
[67] IPSASB (2022, IPSAS 2.26).

The following, among others, are examples of cash flows deriving from financing activities:[68]

- Cash receipts from issuing debentures, loans, notes, bonds and other short- or long-term borrowings;
- Cash repayments of amounts borrowed;
- Cash receipts/payments as contributions from an entity to another within a restructuring process; and
- Cash payments by a lessee for the reduction of the outstanding liability relating to a financial lease.

Investing and financing activities that do not require the use of cash or cash equivalents (e.g., an asset received as donation) are excluded from the Cash Flow Statement, being included in other statements or in the Notes.[69]

IPSAS 2 provides illustrative examples for models of the statement to report the above cash flows. These models differ only in the way cash flows from operating activities are compiled. Accordingly, two methods are allowed for the presentation of operating cash flows, whereby the resulting cash flows would be the same:[70]

- Direct method, which use is encouraged, whereby major classes of gross cash receipts and gross cash payments are disclosed; and
- Indirect method, whereby the accrual-based surplus/deficit coming from the Income Statement is adjusted for the effects of transactions of a non-cash nature, any deferrals or accruals of past or future operating cash receipts or payments, and

---

[68] IPSASB (2022, IPSAS 2.26).
[69] IPSASB (2022, IPSAS 2.54).
[70] IPSASB (2022, IPSAS 2.27-2.30).

items of revenue or expense associated with investing or financing cash flows.

The indirect method is useful as it shows a clear link between the net surplus/deficit for the period and the cash flows. However, although allowed, the Cash Flow Statement by the indirect method may be harder to prepare and interpret; it requires various accounting adjustments that may be difficult to explain to a non-accountant. This is why the direct method is recommended. The direct method reports operating cash flows directly from the cash/bank records. In fact, the statement of cash flows under the direct method would be easier to reconcile with the cash budget.

Table 8.4 displays the model suggested by IPSAS 2 for the Cash Flow Statement prepared using the direct method.

Cash Flow Statement (For an Entity Other Than a Financial Institution) DIRECT METHOD Cash Flow Statement Public Sector Entity—(Consolidated) Cash Flow Statement for Year Ended December 31 20X2 (In Thousands of Currency Units)		
	20X2	20X1
CASH FLOWS FROM OPERATING ACTIVITIES		
Receipts		
...	X	X
Payments		
...	(X)	(X)
Net cash flows from operating activities (1)	X	X
CASH FLOWS FROM INVESTING ACTIVITIES		
Purchases...	(X)	(X)
Proceeds...	X	X
Net cash flows from investing activities (2)	(X)	(X)
CASH FLOWS FROM FINANCING ACTIVITIES		
Proceeds...	X	X
Repayments...	(X)	(X)
Net cash flows from financing activities (3)	X	X
Net increase/(decrease) in cash and cash equivalents (1)+(2)+(3)	X/(X)	X/(X)
Cash and cash equivalents at beginning of period (4)	X	X
Cash and cash equivalents at end of period (1)+(2)+(3)+(4)	X	X

Table 8.4: Cash Flow Statement according to IPSAS 2 (direct method)

In Table 8.4, cash outflows are deducted (shown in brackets) from cash inflows; 'proceeds' are inflows. As in the other financial statements, being an illustrative model, entities can make adaptations to consider (after the net increase/(decrease) in cash), for example: value changes of cash equivalents; changes in the scope of consolidation; and effects of exchange rate variations, resulting from conversion of the financial statements in foreign currency. One interesting example of adaptation comes from the Portuguese system SNC-AP: a reconciliation between cash and cash equivalents from financial accounting (accrual-based), with cash balance from the budget execution (cash-based), was added at the end of the model for the Cash Flow Statement suggested in IPSAS 2.

The bottom-line of the Cash Flow Statement – accumulated cash and cash equivalents at the end of the period (going to the Balance Sheet) resulting from the three types of activities, plus the accumulated amount at the beginning of the period – must be at least zero, indicating that the entity overall generated enough receipts to cover the payments.

Notes

As highlighted, the Notes are very important to complement the financial statements and offer non-financial information; they might also include tables and other statements, disclosing information that is not presented on the face of the main financial statements. The financial statements must systematically refer to these Notes, for example, by adding a column to indicate the number of each note (as happens in Portugal), according to the different standard applied. The Notes tend to follow the numbers of the standards. They must start by including a declaration of compliance with IPSAS and a summary of the main accounting policies applied.[71]

---

[71] IPSAS (2022, IPSAS 1.127-1.150).

3.2. Comparative-international analysis: IPSAS as reference

This section offers a simplified comparative-international descriptive analysis, on the GPFR main components (namely the GPFS in the annual accounts), involving a number of European countries and the IPSAS. Only individual/single accounts are considered, and not consolidated accounts.

Countries	GPFR components (annual accounts)[72]		
IPSASB	Financial Statements • Statement of financial position • Statement of financial performance (nature and function) • Statement of changes in net assets/equity • Cash flow statement • A comparison of budget and actual amounts, either as a separate additional financial statement or as a budget column in the financial statements • Notes		
Portugal (C&LGov)	**Financial Statements** • Balance sheet • Income statement • Cash flow statement • Statement of changes in equity • Annex (notes)	**Budgetary Statements** • Budgetary performance statement • Revenue budgetary execution statement • Expenditure budgetary execution statement • Statement of the execution of the Multiannual Investment Plan (PPI) • Notes to the budgetary statements	**Management Accounting Statements** • Income statement by functions/ activities • Income by products sold or services delivered in the period • Costs by activities, including information of under-activity variances • Production costs by products and services delivered, including variances • Environmental expenses and revenues • Non-incorporated expense • (…)

---

[72] Excluding any mandatory management commentary.

	CENTRAL GOVERNMENT (CGov)		LOCAL GOVERNMENT (LGov)
UK	**Financial Statements** • Statement of comprehensive net expenditure • Statement of financial position • Statement of changes in taxpayer's equity • Statement of cash flows • Notes	**Budgetary Statements** Statement of Parliamentary Supply required to departments: • Comparison of outturn against the supply estimate voted by Parliament in respect of each budgetary control limit (accrual-based) • Net cash requirement, with a comparison of the outturn against voted supply estimate (cash at departmental level) • Statement of administration costs incurred, with a comparison of the administration costs limit	**Financial Statements** • Comprehensive income and expenditure statement • Movement in reserves statement • Statement of financial position • Cash flow statement • Notes
Germany (IF accrual-based accounting)	**Financial Statements** • Statement of financial position • Statement of financial performance • Cash flow statement • Statement of changes in equity (net position) • Notes	**Budgetary Statements** Operating statement by functions/activities both on accrual and on cash basis	
	CENTRAL GOVERNMENT	**REGIONAL AND LOCAL GOVERNMENTS**	
Austria	• Balance sheet • Statement of financial performance (accrual-based budgetary execution statement) • Statement of cash flow (accrual-based budgetary execution statement) • Notes		
Finland	**Financial Statements** • Balance sheet • Income sheet • Cash flow statement • Notes	**Budgetary Statements** • Statements of budgetary outturn LGov: current budget out-turn, investment budget out-turn, income statement plan outcome and cash flow statement plan outcome CGov: a combined budget out-turn report	

Table 8.5: GPFR main components (annual accounts) – comparative-international analysis

Table 8.5, while showing a diversity scenario, also shows some convergence, at least apparent.

In fact, although the names of the statements might be similar, and their contents, in some jurisdictions, be close to those required in IPSAS, it is unlikely that the formats are those suggested by the IPSASB, as the models in IPSAS are merely indicative. Financial statements in each of the countries appear to reflect different accounting traditions and the importance given to be more or less close to the reporting model within business accounting, to facilitate consolidation.

Therefore, there are countries, like Finland and Germany, where main financial statements appear to be similar to IPSAS, but in fact they are not IPSAS adopters; so, GPFR seems to have the same GPFS components as in IPSAS, but the elements are presented differently in each statement (also following different principles – see Chapter 7 in this book). On the other hand, there are other countries that, despite being IPSAS followers, have made further important adaptations of the GPFR in IPSAS (sometimes close to IFRS), to consider the specificities of the public sector. These are the cases of UK, Portugal and Austria.[73]

The UK, while not adopting IPSAS directly, refers to IFRS, which are adapted and constantly updated to the public sector scenario – both at central and at local government level. Some statements reflect this, for example, the 'statement of changes in the taxpayers' equity' and the 'movement in reserves statement'. This country also included budgetary statements in the GPFR for both levels of government, but at the local level they are not standardized. At the central level, budget-to-actual comparisons include both accruals and cash figures, reflecting what was designated as 'resource-based budgeting'.[74]

---

[73] Also, in these countries there is the Management Report that accompanies the annual accounts (GPFS), usually mandatory, which is therefore another important element of the GPFR.

[74] Jones and Pendlebury (2010); Van Helden and Hodges (2015).

As explained in section 2.4 of this chapter, in Portugal, GPFR has three main sets of statements: to the IPSAS and accrual-based financial statements, budgetary cash-based reporting statements and management accounting accrual-based reporting statements were added, as presenting seminal information to be disclosed in the public sector setting.

Austria is an IPSAS adopter at the central government level since 2013.[75] Federal (regional) states and municipalities (local government) have been obliged to produce accrual GPFS from 2020.[76] Despite the closeness to IPSAS, because the country uses accrual-based budgets and accrual-based budgetary execution statements, the statements prepared differ from the illustrative models suggested for those statements in IPSAS 1 and IPSAS 2.

Finland and Germany do not follow IPSAS, but in the public sector in these countries there is accrual-based financial reporting and, in some cases, even accrual-based budgetary reporting. In Finland, accruals in public sector accounting follow the national practice in business accounting, so the GPFR includes financial and budgetary reporting, within which the income sheet (central government) and the income statement (local government) assume special relevance, as this statement reflects the execution of accrual and performance-based budgets, somehow also combining with cash figures. Germany is a more particular case, as accrual-based financial reporting exists effectively only in some states. In fact, accrual-based and double-entry accounting only is an option for federal and state governments (see Chapter 7 in this book). Still, federal government mainly uses modernized cameralistics, for example, including performance budgeting. If accrual-based accounting is used, either in three states or roundabout over 60% of the mu-

---

[75] Rauskala and Saliterer (2015).

[76] Bundesministerium der Finanzen (2018).

nicipalities,[77] budgetary reporting is both cash and accrual-based, given that budget accomplishments have to be reported by activities/programs – comparison budget-to-actual is made within the financial statements, namely in the statement of financial performance and in the cash flow statement.

4. GPFR reliability issues: the importance of auditing

The reporting components making up the GPFR – whatever form – as detailed in this chapter, are given substance through audit. In other words, unaudited financial statements do not have the same impact as audited ones.

Perhaps even more important than in business accounting, auditing is a fundamental part of public sector accounting,[78] inasmuch as it offers the reassurance that public resources are not misappropriated, and information reported about that is reliable. Both internal and external (either by the Courts of Audit or by statutory auditors) auditing contribute to this reassurance.

One may say that citizens, namely via the Parliament, exercise democratic control over public (sector) accounts. However, this is not a professional control. Therefore, auditing professionals are needed to act in the public (citizens') interest.[79]

Regarding external auditing, two broad types of external audits may be considered[80] – financial and regularity audits, and performance audits. While the former focuses on the financial statements, the latter, which is also called 'value for money' auditing, address-

---

[77] Small municipalities basically continue using cameralistics (see Chapter 7 in this book).

[78] Jones and Pendlebury (2010).

[79] Budding et al. (2015).

[80] Jones and Pendlebury (2010).

es operational outputs and outcomes. However, the two types of auditing (financial and regularity, and performance audits) tend to be increasingly linked.

> It is not possible to give an opinion on accrual-based financial statements without giving an opinion on the going concern status of the government, which is strictly a matter of performance. Neither is it possible, strictly, to give an opinion about propriety and probity without giving an opinion about outputs and outcomes.[81]

Therefore, as much as financial and performance auditing tend to be separated, the auditor's opinion on fair presentation and financial regularity increasingly requires assessing economy, efficiency and effectiveness.

Financial statement (GPFS) audits, are part of the financial and regularity auditing. GPFS audit ensures: 1) fair presentation (fighting exaggerating or underestimating certain figures in the reporting); and 2) financial regularity and legality (ensuring conformity with the law, namely the budget, and fighting fraud and corruption).

In the public sector, financial statement auditing is usually exercised by professional auditors, internal or external to the entities (for example, auditing firms) and is based on professional pronouncements, namely auditing standards. The assurance of financial regularity and legality is also a very important role of auditing in the public sector context, usually carried out by oversight auditing bodies, namely Supreme Audit Institutions (SAI), such as Courts of Audit or General Audit Offices. Financial statement auditing aims at assessing conformity with accounting

---

[81] Jones and Pendlebury (2010, p.133).

and reporting standards (financial matters), financial statements being audited at least once a year[82] for fair presentation, and producing the auditor's report. Regularity auditing (also called compliance auditing), aims at ensuring conformity with legal form, i.e. propriety and probity (explicit in the law) of records of transactions and of transactions themselves. As budgets are law, regularity audits also include assessing whether transactions conform to the budget or not.[83]

Even before the existence of financial statement auditing, auditing in governments and public sector entities overall already assessed the propriety of the transactions and the transactions records.

> The propriety of spending and collection of income, the safeguarding of assets and the appropriateness of liabilities, as well as the accuracy and completeness of the records, are judged in the context of public money. (...) Propriety and probity mean the records of transactions have been found to be free of error and not fraudulent, and the transactions themselves have been neither wasteful nor extravagant.[84]

In this case, the auditor (usually a SAI) gives an opinion on whether or not transactions conform to the law. In the case of financial statement auditing, the auditor's report is the

> (...) auditor's opinion on whether or not the general purpose financial statements fairly present what they purport to present

---

[82] There are *ad-hoc* audits, also related to financial matters, but these audits provide lower levels of assurance, merely 'attesting' – for example, an auditor can certify grant claims (Jones and Pendlebury, 2010).

[83] Jones and Pendlebury (2010); Van Helden and Hodges (2015).

[84] Jones and Pendlebury (2010, p.132).

and conform to the law related to financial statements [i.e., the reporting standards].[85]

The auditor's report is usually published with the accounts[86] (referring to the records of transactions and whether the recognition, measurement and disclosure criteria and requirements were properly applied to the specific context). Fair presentation can vary across jurisdictions, being expressed as 'presents fairly', 'true and fair view' and 'properly presents'.[87]

Overall, auditing and auditors should reveal whether the reported financial information is reliable or not, highlighting why (for example, via *reservations* and *emphases* in the financial auditing reports) financial information cannot be trusted.[88]

Consequently, the citizens' trust (in the figures, hence in the public sector officials and politicians, as upper level decision-makers about the public resources entrusted to them) should be increased by auditing and auditors (or decreased, if unreliability is highlighted).

> Financial auditing (...) will enhance the confidence of the intended users of (...) financial statements.[89]

External financial auditors may rely on some work of internal auditors, namely in assessing the systems used to record the transactions and produce the financial statements.[90]

---

[85] Jones and Pendlebury (2010, p.132).

[86] This is not the case in Germany, where there is no obligation to publish this audit report and only very few German public entities do this.

[87] Jones and Pendlebury (2010).

[88] Jones and Pendlebury (2010).

[89] Van Helden and Hodges (2015, p. 185).

[90] Van Helden and Hodges (2015).

5. Conclusion

This chapter made clear that, considering the setting of governments and public sector entities overall, the scope of the GPFR is different and broader than in businesses. Given that, in the public sector, budgets are commonly published, there is an additional requirement, compared to business enterprises, to, at least, report on the budget accomplishment. Moreover, reporting additional non-financial information, namely service performance-related information, is an important complement to financial statements, inasmuch as the deficit/surplus reported in the Statement of Financial Performance is questionable as a financial performance measure, due to problems relating to applying the matching concept between public revenue and expenses.

Another remark to be made is that, despite standardized models for the statements suggested in the IPSAS, these models, and even the components within GPFR, may diverge across countries, including between those that are IPSAS-compliant; divergence is more striking in countries not following IPSAS. Countries' specificities and national accounting traditions are considered for this divergence, which may jeopardize the international harmonization sought in IPSAS for the GPFR.

But, from the comparative-international analysis carried out in this chapter, a commonality was identified: in all jurisdictions already using accrual-based accounting in the public sector, GPFR presents financial (and budgetary) information in different perspectives – financial, economic, cash and budget execution (regardless of whether budgets are cash- commitment- or accrual-based). Therefore, GPFR seeks fair presentation of the financial position, performance, cash flows and budget accomplishment, of a government or a public sector entity.

Finally, GPFR is generally acknowledged as a crucial means to promote transparency (and accountability), enhanced by the fact that financial statements are audited for reliability assurance, and may easily be made accessible online.

Bibliographic references

BUDDING, Tjerk, GROSSI, Giuseppe and TAGESSON, Torbjorn (2015) – *Public Sector Accounting*, London: Routledge, ISBN: 9780415683159.

BUNDESMINISTERIUM DER FINANZEN (2018) – Voranschlags- und Rechnungsabschlussverordnung – VRV 2015. BGBl. II Nr. 17/2018 vom 23.01.2018.

IPSASB (2022) – *Handbook of International Public Sector Accounting Pronouncements*, New York: IFAC, ISBN: 9781608154913, 2022 Edition, Vols. 1-3.

IPSASB (2014) – *The Conceptual Framework for General Purpose Financial Reporting by Public Sector Entities*, International Public Sector Accounting Standards Board (IPSASB), International Federation of Accountants (IFAC), New York.

JONES, Rowan and PENDLEBURY, Maurice (2010) – *Public Sector Accounting*, New York: Pearson Education, ISBN: 9780273720362, 6th ed.

JORGE, Susana, PATTARO, Anna Francesca, MOURA E SÁ, Patricia and LOURENÇO, Rui Pedro (2012) – *Local Government financial transparency in Portugal and Italy: a comparative exploratory study on its determinants*; XVI IRSPM Conference "Contradictions in Public Management. Managing in volatile times"; Rome (Italy), April 11-13.

LOURENÇO, Rui Pedro, MOURA E SÁ, Patricia, JORGE, Susana and PATTARO, Anna Francesca (2013) – Online transparency for accountability: one assessing model and two applications, *The Electronic Journal of e-Government*, 11(1), pp.280-292.

PINA, Vicente, TORRES Lourdes and ROYO, Sonia (2007) – Are ICTs improving transparency and accountability in the EU regional and local governments? An empirical study, *Public Administration Review*, 85(2), pp. 449-472.

PINA, Vicente, TORRES Lourdes and ROYO, Sonia. (2010) – Is e-Government leading to more accountable and transparent local governments? An overall view, *Financial Accountability and Management*, 26(1), pp. 3-20.

RAUSKALA, Iris and SALITERER, Iris. (2015) – Public Sector Accounting and Auditing in Austria, in Isabel Brusca, Eugenio Caperchione, Sandra Cohen, Francesca Manes Rossi (Eds.), *Public Sector Accounting and Auditing in Europe – the Challenge of Harmonization*. Palgrave Macmillan: London, Chapter 2, pp. 12-26.

VAN HELDEN, Jan and HODGES, Ron (2015) – *Public Sector Accounting for Non-Specialists*, London et al.: Palgrave Macmillan, ISBN: 9781137376985.

Additional readings

JORGE, Susana (2015) – Public Sector Accounting and Auditing in Portugal, in Isabel Brusca, Eugenio Caperchione, Sandra Cohen and Francesca Manes Rossi (Eds.), *Public Sector Accounting and Auditing in Europe – the Challenge of Harmonization*. Palgrave MacMillan: London, Chapter 11, pp. 173-190.

LOURENÇO, Rui Pedro, MOURA E SÁ, Patrícia and JORGE, Susana (2017) – Transparency and accountability in municipalities: an analysis of 40-year evolution in Portugal; In Beatriz Cuadrado-Ballesteros and Isabel María García-Sánchez (Eds.), *Local Governments in the Digital Era: Looking for Accountability*, Nova Science Publishers, NY, USA, Chapter 13, pp. 219-241.

LOURENÇO, Rui Pedro, JORGE, Susana and ROLAS, Helena (2016) – Towards a transparency ontology in the context of open government, *Electronic Government, an International Journal*, 12(4), pp. 375-394.

NOGUEIRA, Sónia and JORGE, Susana (2017) – The perceived usefulness of financial information for decision-making in Portuguese municipalities: the importance of internal control, *Journal of Applied Accounting Research*, 18(1), pp. 116-136.

Discussion topics

- What is the scope of public sector entities' financial reporting? What information may it embrace, generally going beyond that reported by business entities?
- What are the main financial (and possibly budgetary and management) accounting statements that are part of the GPFR of public sector entities, according to the different frameworks presented in the comparative-international analysis in this chapter? What are the main differences to the GPFR components within the IPSAS?
- What is the role expected for GPFR to have as a tool to improve public sector entities' transparency, enhanced by the fact that those accounts are audited, both for legal form and fair presentation?

CHAPTER 9
OVERVIEW OF IPSAS ON PUBLIC SECTOR SPECIFIC TOPICS

Ellen Haustein, Peter C. Lorson
both University of Rostock, Germany
ellen.haustein@uni-rostock.de
https://orcid.org/0000-0002-1218-1043
peter.lorson@uni-rostock.de
https://orcid.org/0000-0002-2699-5451

Christophe Vanhee, Johan Christiaens
both Ghent University, Belgium
Christophe.Vanhee@UGent.be
https://orcid.org/0000-0002-7917-856X
Johan.Christiaens@UGent.be
http://orcid.org/0000-0003-4939-8331

Summary

This chapter sets forth the IPSAS content by reviewing relevant norms. The hierarchy of IPSASB announcements and the set of IPSAS financial statements are briefly explained. Still, the focus of this chapter is on selected IPSAS referring to specific balance sheet items, namely property, plant and equipment (IPSAS 17, 21, 26), revenues and expenses from non-exchange transactions (IPSAS 23, 42, ED 72) and service concessions and the related assets and liabilities (IPSAS 32). Each standard is summarized in brief and for each accounting field, the definition, initial recognition and subsequent measurement is introduced.

Keywords

Public sector specific standards, IPSAS, non-cash generating assets, concessions, social benefits, non-exchange transactions, transfer expenses

1. Introduction and background

As IPSASs, their spread and use, and also objectives and users of IPSAS financial statements, have already been introduced in previous chapters of this book, this chapter directly turns to the delimitation of selected thematic areas of IPSASs. It was made clear that, in general, the IPSASB uses standards issued by the International Accounting Standards Board (IASB) (IAS & IFRS[1]) and interpretations from the International Financial Reporting Interpretations Committee (IFRIC) and the Standing Interpretations Committee (SIC) as basis of reference for IPSAS development. However, for some public sector specific topics, there are no corresponding standards and interpretations, so that the IPSASB pronounced self-standing IPSASs. These public sector specific standards are in the focus of this and the subsequent chapter: whereas Chapter 9 aims to introduce accounting for certain balance sheet items by using selected IPSAS, Chapter 10 reviews a case study that applies these standards. Therefore, the original texts of the standards and other pronouncements of the IPSASB are used[2].

---

[1] IAS (International Accounting Standards), IFRS (International Financial Reporting Standards)

[2] The chapters rely on the 2022 Handbook of IPSAS Pronouncements.

This section will provide some background to IPSASs, whereas in Section 2 the IPSASs selected for Chapters 9 and 10 are briefly derived. The main sections of this chapter will then explain the accounting rules for accounting for property, plant and equipment (PPE, Section 3), revenue from non-exchange transactions (Section 4), non-exchange expenses (Section 5) and service concessions from the perspective of the grantor (Section 6). The final section gives a short conclusion. Chapter 10 then proceeds with a case study corresponding to the IPSASs introduced here.

Before, however, the hierarchy of IPSASB pronouncements needs to be reviewed in order to clarify their degree of bindingness. Four levels of bindingness are distinguished as shown in Figure 9.1. In the first level, only the accrual-based standards and the annual improvements to IPSASs, if effective yet, or the cash-based standard are binding. If a specific economic transaction is not addressed in a corresponding IPSAS, on a second level, requirements of other IPSASs that deal with similar or related topics are to be used. If still fruitless, the Conceptual Framework (CF) can be consulted on level 3, to find information with respect to definitions, accounting criteria and measurement methods. If the accounting treatment of an economic transaction cannot be handled by using the previously named sources, on the least binding level 4, pronouncements of other standard setters can be applied, if these are consistent with the IPSASB CF (e.g., those of the IASB[3]); or (other) authoritative literature (including the IPSAS Preface); or accepted best practices in the public and private sectors (including IPSASB's Recommended Practice Guidelines – RPG) can be applied.

---

[3] Some national frameworks would not fit since these rely on different reporting objectives or focus on different user groups e.g. the German Standards of Governmental Accrual Accounting, the Belgian and Finnish governmental accounting frameworks.

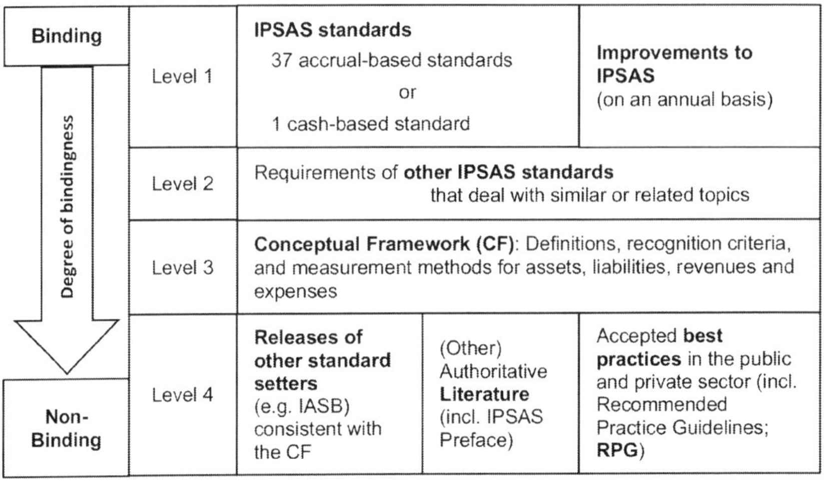

Binding	Level 1	IPSAS standards 37 accrual-based standards or 1 cash-based standard		Improvements to IPSAS (on an annual basis)
↓ Degree of bindingness ↓	Level 2	Requirements of **other IPSAS standards** that deal with similar or related topics		
	Level 3	**Conceptual Framework (CF)**: Definitions, recognition criteria, and measurement methods for assets, liabilities, revenues and expenses		
Non-Binding	Level 4	**Releases of other standard setters** (e.g. IASB) consistent with the CF	(Other) **Authoritative Literature** (incl. IPSAS Preface)	Accepted **best practices** in the public and private sector (incl. Recommended Practice Guidelines; **RPG**)

Figure 9.1: Hierarchy of IPSAS Pronouncements

In total (as of April 2023), 44 IPSASs were published by the IPSASB, of which IPSAS 6, 7, 8, 15 and 25 have been superseded by other standards. IPSAS 13 will be withdrawn as soon as IPSAS 43 becomes effective (at the latest for the annual financial statements covering periods beginning on or after January 1, 2025) As shown by the Table 6.1, the majority of standards in force, namely nineteen, focus on specific balance sheet items. There are three general standards on accounting recognition and measurement and sixteen general standards on reporting.

According to IPSAS 1.66, financial statements have to be presented by the reporting entities at least annually. A set of IPSAS financial statements consists of (IPSAS 1.21): a) a statement of financial position[4], b) a statement of financial performance[5], c) a statement of changes in net assets/equity, d) a cash flow statement, e) a comparison of budget and actual amounts if an entity makes publicly available its approved budget,

---

[4] Also called balance sheet or statement of assets and liabilities.

[5] Also known as statement of revenues and expenses or income statement, operating statement or profit and losses.

and f) the notes, compromising a summary of significant accounting policies and other explanatory notes. According to IPSAS 1.53 an entity shall, for all amounts reported in the financial statements, present comparative information at least in respect of the preceding period.

Further information about the content of some components is provided in other chapters (e.g. statement of financial position in Chapter 8 and comparison of budget and actual amounts in Chapter 3).

2. Selected public sector specific IPSASs

As mentioned in the first section, most IPSASs are based on existing standards of the IASB and interpretations from the IFRIC and SIC.[6] However, for some accounting issues in the public sector there are no corresponding private sector norms. Thus, the following standards were developed by the IPSASB without an equivalent private sector standard:

- IPSAS 21: Impairment of non-cash generating assets;
- IPSAS 22: Disclosure of financial information about the general government sector;
- IPSAS 23: Revenue from non-exchange transactions;
- IPSAS 24: Presentation of budget information in financial statements;
- IPSAS 32: Service concession arrangements: Grantor;
- IPSAS 40: Public sector combinations;
- IPSAS 42: Social benefits.

Also, to some extent, IPSAS 33 (First-time adoption of accrual basis IPSASs) can be seen as public sector specific IPSAS, as the transition from cash to accrual accounting is not addressed in the

---

[6] See IPSASB (2022), Introduction to the IPSASB, p. 1.

standards of the IASB. On the other hand, in some IPSASs that are based on other IASs/IFRSs, paragraphs have been included from time to time to address some public sector specific issues (e.g. accounting treatment of heritage assets in IPSAS 17).

In the following, IPSASs 21, 23, 32 and 42 will be considered as these are related to accounting for specific balance sheet items. A such, when introducing the impairment of non-cash and cash generating assets, IPSAS 21 and 26 are respectively used. When an entity receives (gives) resources and no or nominal considerations are provided (received), IPSAS 19, IPSAS 23, IPSAS 42 and a forthcoming IPSAS on transfer expenses[7] need to be applied, i.e. when non-exchange transactions occur. Also, service concessions are a typical transaction in the public sector, in which an operator uses an asset to provide a public service on behalf of a public entity (grantor), for a specified period of time, being compensated by the public entity. The topic of IPSAS 22 is partially discussed in Chapters 1, 6 and 12. IPSAS 24 is partially also addressed in Chapter 3 on budgetary accounting and IPSAS 40 is referred to in Chapter 12 and are not discussed further in this chapter. IPSAS 17 is not strictly public sector specific, but used here as an introduction to PPE accounting.

Examples of how to handle the accounting treatment for PPE, revenue from exchange transactions, non-exchange expenses and service concessions are provided in Chapter 10.

3. Accounting for property, plant and equipment

This section introduces accounting for property, plant and equipment (PPE) and will refer to IPSAS 17 for the definition, rec-

---

[7] Expected December 2022 (IPSASB Board Paper, July 2022), but as of April 2023, not yet published.

ognition, initial and subsequent measurement of PPE, and IPSAS 21 and 26 for impairment.

3.1. Definition of PPE

According to IPSAS 17.13, PPE are defined as tangible (i.e. physical) assets for the purposes of production or supply of goods or services, for administrative purposes or for rental to others, and which are expected to be used during more than one reporting period (i.e. as non-current assets). PPE also include specific public sector assets such as specialized military equipment and infrastructure assets (IPSAS 17.5). Some assets are out of scope of IPSAS 17, e.g. investment property, construction contracts, leases, inventories (see IPSAS 17.6-8) for which other standards may apply (e.g. IPSAS 11 for inventories, IPSAS 43 for leases or IPSAS 16 for construction contracts).

It is important to add that for heritage assets, IPSAS 17 can be voluntarily used (IPSAS 17.9). Basically, heritage assets are assets with a (1) cultural, environmental, educational or historical value, which are additionally characterised by (2) sale prohibitions or restrictions laid upon the assets, (3) the difficulty to estimate their useful lives, and (4) their irreplaceability. Typical examples are historical buildings, archaeological sites, nature reserves, and works of art (IPSAS 17.10). If heritage assets are accounted for, the disclosure requirements for PPE of IPSAS 17 are mandatory, whereas the measurement requirements of IPSAS 17 can be complied with optionally. An IPSASB project is currently under development to update guidance for reporting heritage assets and infrastructure assets. It proposes (IPSASB's ED 78) to recognise the heritage assets that satisfy the definition of PPE as an asset when they meet the recognition criteria. Thus, the principles on accounting for PPE should also apply to heritage assets. It also suggests adding application guidance, implementation guidance to clarify application of existing principles to heritage assets. However, there is still much debate amongst academics and accounting practitioners about the recognition, measurement and disclosure criteria for heritage assets[8].

The structure of PPE presentation in the statement of financial position is not explicitly prescribed by IPSAS. According to IPSAS 1.93, subclasses of assets have to be presented either in the statement of financial position or in the notes, depending on the size, nature and functions of the amounts (IPSAS 1.94). Examples for these subclasses are provided in IPSAS 17.52, such as land, operational buildings, and administrative equipment. These classes are particularly relevant for initial and subsequent measurement such as using the revaluation model. Individually insignificant items (e.g., chairs or cutlery parts in a school) can be presented as an aggregate value according to IPSAS 17.18.

3.2. Recognition of PPE

An item of PPE is to be recognised in the balance sheet if and only if: a future flow of economic benefits or service potential is expected from that item, and its cost or fair value can be measured reliably (IPSAS 17.14). In this context, reliable means free from material error and bias, so that the measurement faithfully represents what it purports or could reasonably be expected to represent. The reliance on the service potential, i.e. an asset's capacity to provide services that contribute to the entity's objectives (without necessarily generating net cash inflows) (IPSAS CF 5.8), is a public sector specific divergence of the IPSAS CF from the IASB CF (see also Chapter 7).

---

[8] See for a discussion on heritage assets in particular and the asset definition more generally Anessi-Pessina, E./Bisogno, M./Lorson, P. (2022); Aversano N., Christiaens, J./Tartaglia, P./Sannino, S. (2020); Aversano, N./Christiaens J./Van Thielen, T. (2019) and Task force IRSPM A&A SIG, CIGAR Network, EGPA PSG XII (2017).

In the private sector definition of an asset, only future flows of economic benefits in terms of cash flows determine an asset. This, however, is often not applicable in the public sector for, e.g., the majority of infrastructure assets such as streets or school buildings.

Also, the public entity needs control over the item, in order to recognise the item as an asset (IPSAS CF 5.11). This does not necessarily refer to legal ownership, but economic ownership is relevant. The date of recognition thereby is the point in time of transfer of the economic ownership (= control), i.e. the date on which the risks and rewards pertaining to ownership get transferred. This generally corresponds to the acceptance of an asset.

3.3 Initial recognition of PPE

3.3.1 General principle

For the recognition of PPE in the accounts, the initial value is to be determined. According to IPSAS 17.26, measurement at recognition of PPE has to be undertaken at cost. In order to determine the cost, the way how the public entity gained control of the asset needs to be distinguished:

Acquisition of the asset can, on the one hand, be realised through either (1a) an exchange transaction or through (1b) a non-exchange transaction. Here, the acquisition or purchase costs need to be determined. On the other hand, (2) self-construction of an asset is also possible. Here, the costs, also called conversion or production or manufacturing costs[9], are relevant (IPSAS 17.36). In the following, determination of the cost according to these three variants are explained.

---

[9] According to IPSAS 12.20 ff., about Inventories.

3.3.2 Acquisition through an exchange transaction

Initial measurement of an item received by an **acquisition through an exchange transaction,** i.e. a typical purchase, is at cost (IPSAS 17.26). For determining the acquisition cost, three phases are distinguished (acquisition itself, use and end of useful life) of which each is important. The "acquisition cost" contains the sum of (IPSAS 17.30):

1) Purchase price (cash price equivalent) including non-refundable duties and purchase taxes less trade discounts and rebates,
2) Costs directly attributable to bring the item into service,
3) Costs of obligations for dismantling and removing the item and restoring the site at the end of the useful life, if recognised as provision (IPSAS 19), and
4) Optionally, borrowing costs of qualified assets (IPSAS 5).

As highlighted in 4), borrowing costs, i.e. interest or other expenses related to the borrowing of funds, can be optionally added to the initial value only, if the asset acquired meets the definition of a qualified asset. Qualified assets necessarily take a substantial time to be ready for their intended use or sale (IPSAS 5.5), such as administrative buildings, hospitals and infrastructure assets.

In addition, also during the use of the item, a replacement of significant components can lead to additional costs. However, it is prohibited to capitalize general cost such as administration and other general overhead cost, cost of opening a new facility, introducing a new product, etc. (IPSAS 17.33). Particularly relevant are also costs that are expected to occur at the end of the useful life of the asset. For expected costs for dismantling and restoring, a provision needs to be recognised (IPSAS 19.22).[10] The provision is to be measured at the best estimate of the cost expected (IPSAS 19.44). If there is a large number of items of the asset type acquired, the expected value of the provision is determined by "weighting all possible outcomes by their associated probabilities" (IPSAS 19.47). If there is a continuous range of possible outcomes, the midpoint of the range is used, if each point in that range is as likely as any other (IPSAS 19.47). In order to assess the best estimate for a single obligation, as a matter of principle, the individual most likely outcome is used according to IPSAS 19.48. The present value of the initially estimated costs is then capitalized.

3.3.3 Acquisition through a non-exchange transaction

For an **acquisition through a non-exchange transaction**, i.e. an item acquired at no cost or at nominal cost[11] (IPSAS 17.29), the item is initially measured at fair value as at the date of acquisition (IPSAS 17.27). As such, according to IPSAS 23.44, an increase in assets (e.g. PPE) is recognised and, at the same time, a revenue (except to the extent a liability may be recognised at the same time). This will be explained in more detail in section 4 of this chapter.

---

[10] "A provision shall be recognized when: (a) An entity has a present obligation (legal or constructive) as a result of a past event; (b) It is probable that an outflow of resources embodying economic benefits or service potential will be required to settle the obligation; and (c) A reliable estimate can be made of the amount of the obligation" (IPSAS 19.22).

[11] Nominal cost should not be mixed up with terms from economics. Nominal cost for such transaction means insignificant or symbolic cost.

3.3.4 Self-construction

If control for the asset is gained by **self-construction**, according to IPSAS 17.36 the cost has to be measured based on IPSAS 12.20 ff., which is the standard for inventories. The "construction cost" contains the sum of:

1) Costs directly related to the item (e.g. direct labour) include a systematic allocation of fixed and variable production overheads (IPSAS 12.20);
2) Costs directly attributable to bring the item into service;
3) Costs of obligations for dismantling and removing the item and restoring the site at the end of the useful life, if recognised as provision (IPSAS 19); and
4) Optionally, borrowing costs of qualified assets (IPSAS 5).[12]

According to IPSAS 12.25 and IPSAS 17.36, it is prohibited to capitalize some cost as, e.g., abnormal production costs, storage costs, and general administrative overheads.

3.4. Subsequent measurement of PPE

3.4.1 Cost versus revaluation model

After an asset has been initially recognised, its subsequent measurement is to be determined at the end of each following reporting period. According to IPSAS 17.42 and as illustrated in Table 9.1

---

[12] The cost components 3) and 4) have already been explained for the acquisition cost.

below, public entities have the option to choose between (1) the cost model, and (2) the revaluation model, whereas the latter can only be applied if the asset's fair value can be measured reliably. However, often, in the public sector the fair value is hardly measurable. The selected approach is to be applied to the entire class of PPE (IPSAS 17.51). Using the cost model, the asset is carried at its cost, less any accumulated depreciation and less any accumulated impairment losses (IPSAS 17.43). When the revaluation model is applied, the asset is carried at its revalued amount, i.e. its fair value at the date of the revaluation, less any accumulated depreciation and less any accumulated impairment losses (IPSAS 17.44). Using the revaluation model provides more relevant and better information for decision-making as the depreciation reflects the true cost of using assets. It also improves asset management. However, the revaluation model is complex (high administrative costs), results in volatility in reported results and the revalued amounts do not reflect the renewal costs required to sustain service levels.[13] Also, compared to the cost model, the revaluation method is more prone to management judgement.

	Cost Model	**Revaluation Model**
Initial measurement	Cash price or equivalent or fair value at date of acquisition	
Subsequent measurement	*Each balance sheet date*: Amortized cost, i.e. historical cost less accumulated depreciation and accumulated impairment losses (net of reversals of impairment) since initial measurement	*On revaluation date*: Revalued amount (fair value at the date of revaluation) *On balance sheet dates, where no revaluation takes place*: Revalued amount less accumulated depreciation and accumulated impairment losses (net of reversals of impairment) since revaluation date

Table 9.1: Cost versus Revaluation Model

---

[13] See IPSASB (2020).

3.4.2 Depreciation

As such, for both methods, depreciation needs to be deducted for assets with a definite useful life. Depreciation is an accounting technique of systematically allocating the expected depreciable amount of an asset over its useful life (IPSAS 17.13), in order to reflect the reduction of the PPEs' future economic benefits or service potential due to wear, aging or other similar factors. Depreciation is recognised even if the fair value is higher than the carrying amount of the asset, as long as the asset's residual value does not exceed its carrying amount (IPSAS 17.68). Consequently, the depreciable amount is the difference between the initial cost of an asset and its residual value (IPSAS 17.13). The useful life is the expected period of use or number of production units, i.e. the period of time of consumption of a specified portion of the asset's future economic benefits or service potential (IPSAS 17.13). Useful life can be shorter than the economic life of the asset, e.g. if the disposal of the asset is planned earlier. It is to be judged building on experiences with similar assets. The depreciation charge is an expenditure which is to be recognised in surplus or deficit (IPSAS 17.64).

For determining the depreciation, when applicable, the asset is to be broken down into its components, i.e. the initially recognised cost of the item is to be allocated to its significant parts and thereby an individual depreciation of those parts over the parts' useful lives takes place (IPSAS 17.59). This is also known as **component approach**. The significant parts or costs are to be assessed in relation to the total costs of the item. Therefore, the useful lives may differ between the components, so that e.g. of a road system, parts such as pavements, formation, curbs, channels, footpaths and bridges, and lighting are depreciated or exchanged separately (IPSAS 17.60), but disclosed in the statement of financial position as one single item. A further example are the components of airplanes. Still, land and buildings are independent of the component approach as these are accounted for separately even if they are acquired together (as land has an unlimited useful life) (IPSAS 17.74).

In addition, the depreciation method needs to be determined. For each asset, the public entity has to select a method that best reflects the consumption of the future economic benefits or service potential (IPSAS 17.76). The method selected has to be applied consistently, given that the pattern of consumption remains as planned. IPSAS 17.78 proposes three depreciation methods, even though other methods could be used:

a) Straight-line method: an easy to use method with a constant charge over the useful life. The depreciation charge is calculated by dividing the depreciable amount by the useful life.
b) Diminishing balance method: the depreciation charge decreases over the useful life, as it is accounted for by multiplying a previous reporting date's carrying amount with a constant percentage-based depreciation rate.
c) Units of production method: the depreciation charge is based on the expected use or output of the asset by dividing the depreciable amount by the total units of production, multiplied by the production in the respective reporting period.

3.4.3 Revaluation

When the **revaluation model** is applied for subsequent measurement of assets, the revalued amount is to be determined, being its fair value at the date of the revaluation, less any subsequent accumulated depreciation, and subsequent accumulated impairment losses (IPSAS 17.44). Thereby, the revalued amount of the item may even exceed the initial carrying amount. This fact is a remarkable difference to some other national accounting systems, e.g. the German one. The fair value is usually derived from a market value, e.g., by an actuary in terms of quoted prices in an active and liquid market. If no active market is prevalent, which will often be the case (not only) in the public sector, for items of property (such as land) the price of items with similar characteristics can be used. In case of an item of plant and equipment, relying on IPSAS 21 for non-cash generating assets, there is a choice to use the depreciated replacement cost, restoration cost, or service unit approaches for measuring the fair value (IPSAS 17.47).

The general principles of using the revaluation model are outlined in IPSAS 17.44 ff. These refer, e.g., to the frequency of revaluation, items with a definite useful life, and classes of assets. Revaluation has to be undertaken with sufficient regularity, building on the question how often significant changes in fair value occur. If significant annual changes are expected, then a revaluation is to be done annually. If insignificant annual changes occur, then a revaluation every 3-5 years is sufficient. Even if using the revaluation model, items with a definite useful life still need to be depreciated. Also, it needs to be stressed that the revaluation model applies to the entire class of PPE to which the revalued asset belongs (IPSAS 17.51, with the exception of impairments under IPSAS 21 and 26). Thus, a simultaneous revaluation of all assets in that class of PPE has to be undertaken. Also, the adjustment of the accumulated depreciation after revaluation is to be done for the entire class of assets (IPSAS 17.50).

The accounting treatment of the revaluation method can be a sophisticated matter. An example is shown in Figure 9.2 with the reporting periods depicted on the abscissa and the carrying amount on the ordinate axis.

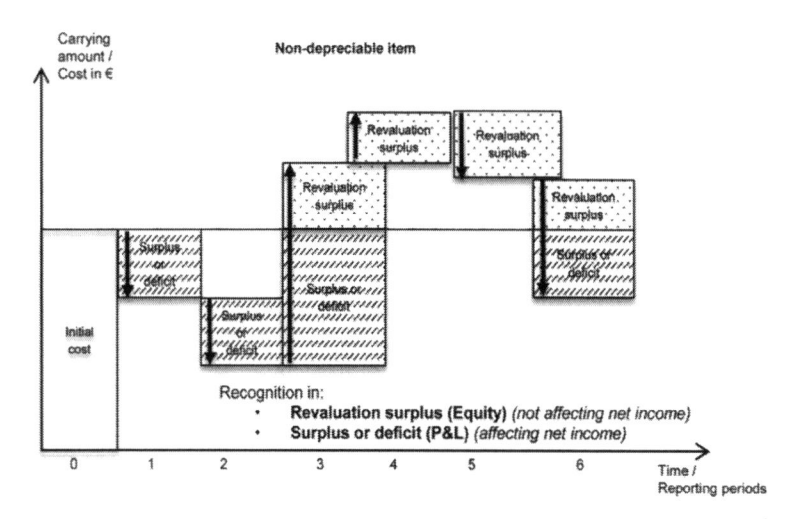

Figure 9.2: Revaluation model: Accounting treatment of revaluation surpluses / deficits

For reasons of simplicity, an example of a non-depreciable item is drawn, which might be, e.g., a piece of land, as land has an unlimited useful life. The graph shows revaluation amounts that have to be accounted for directly in equity without changing net income in the dotted areas ("Revaluation surplus"). The diagonally striped areas depict revaluation amounts that are accounted for through "surplus or deficit" (i.e. profit and loss), and thus will change net income. In this example, after initial recognition in the first two reporting periods, the revalued amount lies below the initial cost of the item, i.e. there is an impairment loss. In this case, the revaluation decrease shall be recognised in the surplus or deficit, leading to a reduction in the net income of the public entity in these years. In years 3 and 4, the value of the item increases, so that the revalued amount even lies above the initial cost. In this case the revaluation surplus has to be split. First, to the extent that the revaluation reverses a revaluation decrease (i.e. impairment loss) previously recognised in surplus or deficit, it has to be recognised in surplus or deficit. The remaining amount, i.e. the difference that exceeds the initial cost, is to be recognised directly in net assets. Here, the reverse of revaluation even does not only refer to one specific asset, but to the entire class of assets (IPSAS 17.54). If in year 5 the revalued amount goes down below the initial cost again, first the revaluation surplus is to be reversed, and second the remaining amount is to be recognised in surplus or deficit.

To summarize subsequent measurement so far, for both assets with a definite useful life and those with an indefinite useful life, there is the option to choose between the cost model or the revaluation model. Regardless of the approach for subsequent measurement selected, for assets with a definite useful life, a scheduled depreciation has to be accounted for. When using the revaluation method, for both assets with a definite useful life and those with an indefinite useful life, a revaluation depending in the determined frequency has to take place.

3.4.3 Impairment

In addition, to each of the two models and regardless of the useful life of an asset, it has to be tested for impairment, i.e. whether there is a loss in the future economic benefits or service potential of an asset, over and above the systematic recognition of the loss of the asset's depreciation. With respect to impairment, IPSAS 17.79 distinguishes between cash generating and non-cash generating assets and this differentiation is a public sector specific one, because IAS/IFRS do not regard such situations. Cash generating assets are held by the public entity with the intention to generate cash inflows independent of other assets (IPSAS 21.16). Therefore, the asset is deployed in a manner consistent with that adopted by a profit-oriented company, such as rented buildings or managed forests. For impairment of these assets IPSAS 26 has to be applied. Non-cash generating assets are all assets other than cash generating assets (IPSAS 21.14), as these are acquired with the intention to deliver services to the public (IPSAS 21.18): e.g., streets, public buildings, and fire trucks. Specifically, for the impairment of non-cash generating assets, IPSAS 21 has been developed by the IPSASB, as there was no comparable IAS/IFRS to be referenced to.

The general procedure of testing for impairment is basically the same under IPSAS 21 and 26. In a first step, at the reporting date, a check for an indication of impairment has to be done. Accordingly, external and internal sources of information are listed in IPSAS 21.27 and 26.25[14]. The check for such indications is not to be conducted for intangible assets with indefinite useful lives or intangible assets not yet available for use or goodwill, as for these assets there is an obligation for an impairment test once a year (IPSAS 26.26A). Secondly, if there is any indication of impairment, the impairment test is initiated by measuring the recoverable service amount (IPSAS 21) or the recoverable amount (IPSAS 26), respectively. Thirdly, the recoverable (service) amount is compared with the carrying amount of the asset: if the recoverable (service) amount lies below the carrying amount, an impairment is to be recognised.

For non-cash generating assets, the recoverable service amount is the higher of the fair value less costs to sell and the value in use (IPSAS 21.14). If one of the amounts exceeds the asset's carrying amount, the other does not need to be calculated (IPSAS 21.36). For the fair value less costs to sell, the best evidence would be the asset's price in a binding sale agreement in an arm's length transaction, or current bid price at an active market (IPSAS 21.40 ff.). As this will hardly be measurable for typical public sector assets, an alternative is a disposal amount, e.g. recent transactions for similar assets not within a forced sale. The value in use, i.e. the present value of an asset's service potential, can, according to IPSAS 21 be determined by using one of three methods:

---

[14] Including the respective Implementation Guidance (IG).

1) **Depreciated replacement cost approach:** Cost to replace the asset's gross service potential, which is determined as the lower of the reproduction or replacement cost (less accumulated depreciation) (IPSAS 21.45 ff.);
2) **Restoration cost approach:** Cost of restoring the service potential to its pre-impaired level, which is determined by subtracting the estimated restoration cost of the asset from the current cost of replacing the remaining service potential of the asset before impairment (IPSAS 21.48);
3) **Service units approach**: Value of the reduced number of service units from the asset in its impaired state, determined by reducing the current cost of the remaining service potential of the asset before the impairment to conform with the reduced number of service units expected from the asset in its impaired state (IPSAS 21.49).

For cash generating assets, the recoverable amount is the higher of the fair value less costs to sell (comparable to the IPSAS 21 definition) and the value in use (IPSAS 26.13). The value in use is determined by an estimation of the future cash in- and outflows expected to be derived from the use of the asset and its ultimate disposal. Here the appropriate discount rate to those future cash flows has to be applied, which is a sophisticated issue (IPSAS 26.AG3).

If the (accumulated) impairment loss of the previous period has decreased in the next period, a reversal of impairment is to be recognised (IPSAS 21.67/26.102). However, the maximum of reversal is the amount as if no impairment loss existed (IPSAS 21.68/26.106). A reversal of impairment is to be recognised in surplus or deficit (IPSAS 21.68/26.108). Also, the depreciation charge needs to be adjusted afterwards.

4. Accounting for revenue from non-exchange transactions

IPSAS 23 addresses accounting for revenue from non-exchange transactions, which is a specific public sector matter. Whereas in the private sector, the majority of transactions has an exchange character, the public sector mainly finances its activities by means of taxes or transfers,[15] i.e. by non-exchange transactions. Due to this reason, there is no IAS/IFRS that deals with this type of transactions and therefore the IPSASB developed an own standard as the accounting treatment of revenue from non-exchange transactions is not trivial.

4.1. Definition of non-exchange transactions

The scope of IPSAS 23 and the corresponding definitions are provided in IPSAS 23.5-23.7. Here, non-exchange transactions are defined as transactions in which a public entity receives/pays resources and provides/receives no or nominal consideration directly in return (IPSAS 23.9). Nominal costs are either insignificant or symbolic. The scope of IPSAS 23 covers (1) taxes and (2) transfers. Non-exchange expenses are discussed in section 5.

(1) Taxes are economic benefits or service potential compulsorily (imposed by law and/or regulations) paid or payable to the public entity other than fines or other penalties (IPSAS 23.7). Taxes represent revenues to the public sector entities. **(2) Transfers** are inflows from non-exchange transactions, other than taxes, such as cash or non-cash assets (grants), debt forgiveness, bequests, donations, goods and services in-kind (IPSAS 23.77).

---

[15] IPSASB (2022) Preface to the IPSASs, §10.(b).

4.2 Recognition of elements to be recorded for revenue from non-exchange transactions

In order to account for revenue from non-exchange transactions, the following flowchart can be applied as shown in Figure 9.3[16].

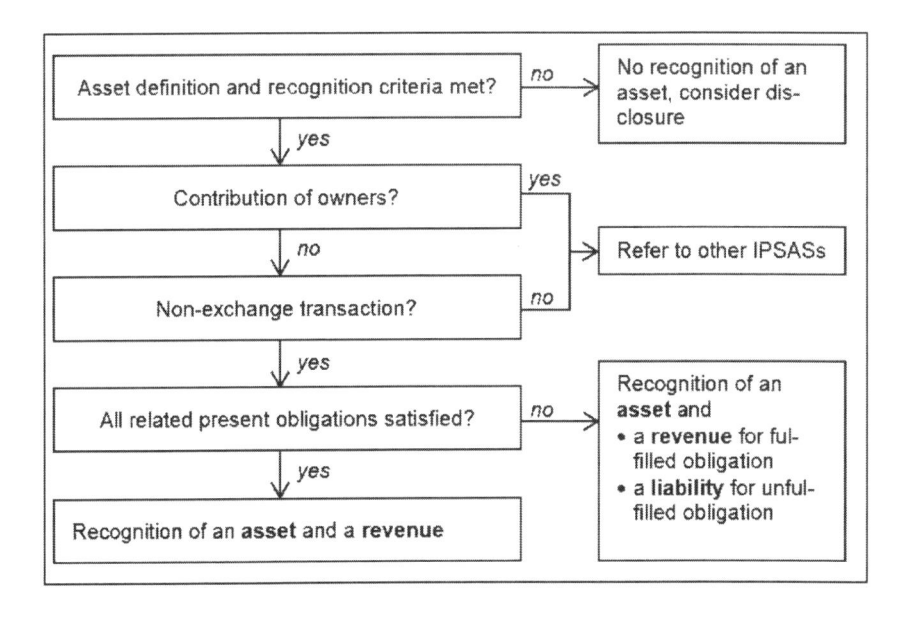

Figure 9.3: Flowchart of accounting for non-exchange transactions (IPSAS 23.29)

First, an assessment is needed, whether for the item acquired the asset definition (IPSAS 1.7) and recognition criteria (IPSAS 23.31) are met. If this is not the case, an asset is not recognised, but maybe a disclosure is to be done. If an asset was acquired, it needs to be verified whether it was a contribution of owners (IPSAS 23.37-38) as defined in IPSAS 1.7. If so, other IPSASs are referred to. In the opposite case, it is necessary to check whether

---

[16] See also IPSAS 23.29 and Müller-Marques Berger and Wirtz (2018) in Adam (2018), p. 398.

it was a non-exchange transaction as otherwise different IPSASs apply. If the transaction meets the definition of a non-exchange transaction (IPSAS 23.9-10), the next question is whether all related obligations to the transaction have been fulfilled, i.e. if there are not any conditions on the transferred asset (IPSAS 23.17). If there are no conditions, i.e. no present obligations, or the conditions are satisfied an asset and a revenue in the surplus or deficit is to be recognised (IPSAS 23.44). Otherwise (conditions are not satisfied), an asset and a revenue for the fulfilled obligation and a liability for unfulfilled obligations are to be recorded. In fact, a liability is a deferred revenue, i.e. a revenue with conditions. It becomes revenue in the surplus or deficit as the obligations are accomplished.

A specific question with respect to recognition is the point of time in which to recognise particular taxes and transfers. According to IPSAS 23.59, taxes are to be recognised at the taxable event, i.e. the event that the public entity has determined to be subject to taxation (IPSAS 23.7). This is, e.g., the event of earning of assessable income during taxation period for income tax, undertaking of a taxable activity during a taxation period for the value added tax, the movement of dutiable goods across customs boundary for customs duty, or passing of the date on or for which the tax is levied for property tax (IPSAS 23.65). As the taxable event and the payment of taxes often take place at different points in time, in the statement of financial position, also advance receipts – revenue deferrals (for prepayments) and tax receivables – revenue accruals (for subsequent payments) need to be considered (IPSAS 23.27-28). The timing of revenue recognition of transfers is determined by the nature of the stipulations and their settlement (IPSAS 23.47). These stipulations could be either conditions (e.g. consume as specified or return) or restrictions (consume as specified) (IPSAS 23.15).

4.3. Measurement of the elements to be recorded for revenue from non-exchange transactions

The asset is to be initially measured when the public entity gains control over the asset, at fair value (IPSAS 23.42). Assets arising from taxation transactions should be measured at the best estimate of the inflow of resources to the public entity (IPSAS 23.67). Public entities should develop accountancy policies for the measurement of assets arising from taxation transactions, taking into account of both the probability that the resources arising from taxation transactions will flow to the government, and the fair value of the resulting assets. For subsequent measurement, other IPSASs, e.g., IPSAS 17 (PPE) or 16 (Investment Property) apply. The revenue is to be measured at the amount of the increase in net assets (also fair value) (IPSAS 23.48). The liability is recognised if its definition and recognition criteria are fulfilled; it is measured at the amount to settle the obligation as of the reporting date (IPSAS 23.57).

5. Accounting for non-exchange expenses

The accounting treatment of non-exchange expenses is addressed by IPSAS 19 (Provisions, Contingent Liabilities and Contingent Assets) with respect to collective and individual services, IPSAS 42 (Social Benefits) and a forthcoming IPSAS on transfer expenses[17]. Those expenses result from non-exchange transactions as defined in section 4.1. Non-exchange expenses can, as illustrated in Table 9.2 below, be divided into (1) expenses for collective and individual services, (2) transfer expenses and (3) social benefits.

---

[17] In the following the stipulations of Exposure Draft (ED) 72 – Transfer Expenses are taken into account.

	Category			
	Transfer expenses	**Collective services**	**Individual services**	**Social benefits**
Transactions with performance obligations?	Yes or No	No	No	No
Provided as cash transfers to specific individuals/household?	Sometimes	No	No	Yes
Provided to specific individuals/households who meet eligibility criteria?	Sometimes	No	Sometimes	Yes
Mitigates effect of social risks?	No	No	Sometimes	Yes
Addresses needs of society as a whole?	Sometimes	Yes	Yes	Yes

Table 9.2: Boundaries of different types of non-exchange expenses (IPSASB's ED 72)

5.1 Expenses for collective and individual services

5.1.1 Definition

Expenses for **collective services** are expenses incurred to deliver services simultaneously to all members of the community that are intended to address the needs of society as a whole (IPSAS 19.18). Examples include defence, street lighting, and offering sport infrastructure. Expenses for **individual services** on the other hand are incurred to provide goods and services to individuals and/or households that are also intended to address the needs of society as a whole. Examples of such expenses relate to universal education and universal health care. Expenses for collective and individual services differ from social benefits in the fact that beneficiaries of the services should not satisfy eligibility criteria (e.g., being unemployed, handicapped or having children).

5.1.2 Recognition

With respect to collective and individual services, IPSAS 19 (AG1-AG20) states that no provisions should be recorded for collective or individual services as they are considered to be on-going activities of a public sector entity that delivers the services. The intention to deliver individual services, budget approval to deliver such services, or the existence of legislation in respect to those services are not sufficient per se as there is no post event that gives rise to a liability. Only when the resources to deliver the services are acquired (for example the purchase of pharmaceuticals for delivering healthcare), an expenses and liability is incurred.

5.1.3 Measurement

As no provisions should be recorded for collective or individual services, there are no specific measurement issues for these transactions. The assets acquired to deliver the services should be reported at the cost incurred on their acquisition.

5.2 Transfer expenses

5.2.1 Definition

Transfer expenses are expenses arising from a transaction, other than taxes, in which an entity provides a good, service, or other asset to another entity (which may be an individual) without directly receiving any good, service, or other asset in return (IPSASB's ED 72.8). Examples are transfers to other public sector entities or charities. Transfer expenses can be **with or without performance obligations**. In the case of performance obligations, the transfer recipient is required to provide goods or services to a third-party beneficiary or to the transfer provider (e.g. in order to get a grant a research university has to transfer the results of the research to the transfer provider).

5.2.2 Recognition

In the case of transfer expenses with no binding arrangement, the expenses should be recognised as the public sector entity (transfer provider) transfers the resources (i.e. the moment the transfer provider loses control of the transferred resources). In the case, there is a binding arrangement and the transfer recipient has performance obligations, a five-step approach should be applied (= the **Public Sector Performance Obligation Approach**; IPSASB's ED 72.12):

- Step 1: Identifying the binding arrangement with a transfer recipient;
- Step 2: Identifying the transfer recipient's performance obligations in the binding arrangement;
- Step 3: Determining the transaction consideration;
- Step 4: Allocating the transaction consideration to the transfer recipient's performance obligations in the binding arrangement;
- Step 5: Recognising expenses when (or as) the transfer recipient satisfies the performance obligation.

If there are no performance obligations the expenses should be recognised at the earlier of the following dates (IPSASB's ED 72.91):

- when the transfer provider has a present obligation to transfer resources to a transfer recipient. In such cases, the transfer provider shall recognise a liability representing its obligation to transfer the resources; and
- when the transfer provider ceases to control the resources. This will usually be the date at which the transfer provider transfers the resources to the transfer recipient. In such cases, the transfer provider derecognises the resources it ceases to control in accordance with other standards. If for example a public sector entity waives its right to collect a debt owed by a non-profit organization, an expense should be recognised at the date the public sector entity derecognises (in accordance with IPSAS 41) the financial asset (or a portion of it).

5.2.3 Measurement

In case of a transfer expense with a binding arrangement, the transfer provider should recognise as an expense, the amount of the transaction consideration that is allocated to the performance obligation (IPSASB's ED 72.47). The transaction consideration is the value of the resources that the transfer provider expects to transfer to the transfer recipient, in exchange for transfer recipient transferring the promised goods or services to the third-party beneficiary.

When there is no binding arrangement and the transfer is recognised at the date the public entity transfers the resources to the transfer recipient, the expense should be measured at the carrying amount of the resources transferred (IPSASB's ED 72.102). If the transfer is not in cash, but in non-current assets, inventory, or services, the expense should be measured at the carrying amount of resources transferred. In the case of services, this will be the cost of providing the services. Where a transfer provider recognises an expense prior to transferring the resources to the transfer recipient, it measures the expense and liability at the best estimate of the costs that the transfer provider will incur in settling the liability. These costs may include fixed costs, variable costs, or both (IPSASB's ED 72.103).

5.3 Social benefits

5.3.1 Definition

Social benefits finally are defined as cash transfers provided to specific individuals and/or households who meet eligibility criteria. They are intended to mitigate the effect of social risks and address the needs of society as a whole (IPSAS 42.5). Social risks are events or circumstances that relate to the characteristics of individuals and/or households – for example, age, health, poverty and employment status and that may adversely affect the welfare of individuals and/or households, either by imposing additional demands on their resources or by reducing their income (IPSAS 42.5).
Examples of social benefits are state pensions, unemployment benefits, income support.

5.3.2 Recognition

According to IPSAS 42.6, a liability for a social benefit should be recognized when the eligibility criteria to receive the next social benefit have been satisfied. At the same point that a liability is recognised, an expense should be recorded (IPSAS 42.10). If the social benefit payment is made prior to the moment all eligibility criteria for the next payment are satisfied, a payment in advance should be booked (and not an expense). If for example a person becomes unemployed, a liability occurs for the public sector entity in the case of an unemployment benefit without a waiting period. If there is a waiting period, the liability occurs when the person was unemployed for a specific period.

For the sake of completeness, it should be mentioned that IPSAS 42 allows an alternative insurance approach for the recognition and measurement of social benefit schemes that meet certain criteria (e.g. the scheme is intended to be fully funded from contributions). This approach, that should adopt the principles of IFRS 17, will not be discussed further.

5.3.3 Measurement

An entity should recognise an expense for a social benefit scheme, measured at the amount of the next (maybe monthly) payment following satisfaction of the eligibility criteria (IPSAS 42.21) as unemployment. Where the entity makes a social benefit payment prior to all eligibility criteria for the next payment being satisfied, it measures the payment in advance (or expense recognized where the payment is irrecoverable) at the amount of the cash transferred. The liability for a social benefit scheme should be measured at the best estimate of the costs (i.e. the social benefit payment) (IPSAS 42.12) that the entity will incur in fulfilling the present obligations represented by the liability. The liability is reduced as social benefit payments are made. Any difference between the cost of making the social benefit payments and the carrying amount of the liability is recognized in surplus or deficit in the period in which the liability is settled.

6. Accounting for service concession arrangements: Grantor

IPSAS 32 is a further standard developed for the specific use by public sector entities that act as the grantor in such constellations.[18]

6.1 Definition of service concession arrangements and assets

A **service concession arrangement** is defined as a binding agreement between a grantor and an operator, whereby the operator uses an asset to provide a public service on behalf of the grantor for a specified period of time, and the operator is compensated over the service concession period (IPSAS 32.8). Thereby, the so called service concession asset can alternatively either be provided by a) the operator, who constructs, develops or acquires the asset for the grantor or is an existing asset of the operator, or b) the grantor as an existing asset of the grantor or an upgrade to such an asset (IPSAS 32.8).

Table 9.3 provides an overview of examples of service concession agreements and assets based on IPSAS 32.

Agreements	Assets
Provision of toll roads	Roads, bridges, tunnels, etc.
Hospital operation	Hospitals (land & buildings, etc.)
Facility management, e.g. cleaning services	Machines as cleaning facilities, etc.
Transportation services	Busses, trains, etc.
Utilities, e.g. water supply, telecommunication services	Water pipelines, telecommunication networks

Table 9.3: Examples for service concession arrangements (IPSAS 32 IE)

---

[18] Still, it mirrors IFRIC 12 for the private sector and the operators.

6.2 Recognition of elements to be recorded in service concession arrangements

A service concession asset has to be recognized by the **grantor** if the following conditions are cumulatively fulfilled (IPSAS 32.9). The grantor controls or regulates which services are provided with the asset, to whom these are provided, and what is the price of delivery. In addition, the grantor must control any significant residual interest in the asset, at the end of the term of the arrangement. A liability is recognized together with a new service concession asset, except for cases in which the service concession asset is an existing asset of the grantor, and therefore only requiring reclassification (IPSAS 32.14).

6.3 Measurement of elements to be recorded in service concession arrangements

6.3.1 Initial measurement

Initial measurement of the service concession asset is at fair value at the time of recognition (IPSAS 32.11), except for cases in which an existing asset of the grantor is only reclassified (IPSAS 32.12). For its subsequent measurement, the IPSASs relevant for the specific asset are to be applied, namely IPSAS 17 for PPE or IPSAS 31 for intangible assets.

The liability is initially measured at the same amount as the asset. The subsequent measurement depends on the type of compensation the operator receives for the service concession. **Two alternative models** have to be distinguished: (1) the financial liability model, and (2) the grant of a right to the operator model.

In the following, the models[19] are explained and two examples are drawn to highlight the differences in accounting treatment for the grantor, i.e. a public entity.

6.3.2 The financial liability model

The **financial liability model** is prevalent if the grantor (public sector entity) has an unconditional obligation to pay for the construction, development, acquisition or upgrade of the asset (IPSAS 32.18). As such, the operator is compensated for the asset by a payment of the grantor, and not by the parties who receive the service delivered with the asset. The subsequent measurement is recorded as follows: the payment of the grantor is distinguished between an asset component, which also leads to a reduction of the liability, a finance charge, i.e. the cost of capital and a service component, which covers the charge for delivering the service (IPSAS 23.21). Finance charge and service component are accounted for as expenses (IPSAS 23.22). If the service charge and the finance charge are not separately identifiable, the payment is to be allocated relative to the fair values of the asset and the revenues or by using estimation techniques (IPSAS 23.23). Applying this model approximates the recognition of a financial leasing contract.

An example

> A private operator provides transportation services on behalf of a public entity, using busses controlled by the public entity.

---

[19] Also, a mixed model by dividing the agreement is possible (IPSAS 32.27). In such cases, the parts of the contract need to be accounted for separately. See Aggestam-Pontoppidan and Andernack (2016), p. 181 for an example.

The operator receives fixed payments from the public entity, which prescribes the services and prices. As such, the financial liability model is prevalent and the asset and a liability have to be recognised. The initial measurement of the asset, i.e. the busses, takes place at fair value of the busses, whereas for subsequent measurement, according to IPSAS 17, there is the option to choose between the cost or the revaluation model. The busses are assets with a definite useful life, so these are to be depreciated and regularly assessed for indications of impairment. Correspondingly to the asset, also the liability is to be initially measured at the fair value of the busses. In each reporting period, the payment to the operator is divided into an asset component and a service component (plus interest), whereas the asset component annually reduces the liability.

6.3.3 Grant of a right to the operator model

For the **grant of a right to the operator model**, there is no unconditional obligation to pay by the grantor to the operator. Instead, the operator is given the right to earn revenue from third-party users of the service concession asset or the access to another revenue-generating asset for the operator's use (e.g. a private parking facility adjacent to a public facility (IPSAS 32.24). Thereby a revenue is earned by the operator. Together with the asset and a liability (which is a deferred revenue) at the initial recognition, a revenue is afterwards recorded by the grantor in combination with a reduction of the liability (IPSAS 32.25).

An example

> A private operator provides ferry services on behalf of a public entity using a cable ferry which is controlled by the grantor. For

the service delivery, the operator is granted the right to charge the ferry users. Thus, the grant of a right to the operator is to be applied and the asset and a liability (deferred revenue) have to be recognised. Also, the grantor recognises a revenue in each reporting period during the term of the contract. However, a question remains whether the initial values of the asset and the liability are the fair value of the asset received (i.e. the concession asset) or of the revenues foregone by the public entity. Thus, the revenue recorded by the grantor does not necessarily equal the revenue of the operator. The sophisticated question of measuring the fair value of the asset and the revenue of the grantor has also been addressed in a Question and Answer document of the IPSASB:

"generally, it will be appropriate to determine the fair value of the asset received (the service concession asset). This is because the right to earn revenue from third-party users (which is the asset given up under the grant of a right to the operator model) will not have been previously recognised in the grantor`s statement of financial position. Consequently, the fair value of the asset received (the service concession asset) will be more clearly evident than the fair value of the asset given up (…)."[20]

Thus, the initial measurement of the asset, i.e. the cable ferry, is at its fair value. Subsequent measurement is done according to IPSAS 17, as done for the busses. The liability is to be initially measured at the fair value of the cable ferry. In the following reporting periods, for determining the reduction in the liability and the recording of a revenue, the liability is allocated over the term of the agreement, e.g., on a straight-line basis. Other allocation methods can be used if these better reflect the earned portion of the liability.[21]

---

[20] IPSASB, Q&A, February 2016, Q1, p.2.
[21] IPSASB, Q&A, February 2016, Q2, p.3.

7. Conclusion

For almost each line item in the financial statement, there is at least one specific IPSAS to be applied. In addition, there are reporting specific IPSASs and IPSASs on accounting recognition and measurement. This chapter focused on the accounting treatment of PPE, non-exchange transactions (revenues and expenses) and service concession arrangements, thus particularly addressing IPSASs 17, 21, 23, 26, 32 and 42 and a forthcoming IPSAS on transfer expenses (based on ED 72, as of April 2023).

Summarizing, not only PPE, many long-term assets can be measured at cost or revalued amounts/fair values. For potential revenue from non-exchange transactions, a specific procedure has to be undergone to verify (1) whether the definition of a non-exchange transaction is fulfilled and thus whether an asset has to be recognised and (2) whether all related present obligations are satisfied. Revenue from non-exchange transactions that are not bound to an unfulfilled obligation are to be recorded as revenues, either in the surplus of deficit or directly in the equity. If there are unfulfilled obligations a liability should be recorded of that obligation. As to non-exchange expenses a distinction has to be made between expenses for collective and individual services, transfer expenses and social benefits. Whereas for collective and individual service no provisions should be recorded, the recognition and measurement of transfer expenses depends on the existence of a binding arrangement and performance obligations. Social benefits give rise to an expense and liability when the eligibility criteria to receive the next social benefit are met. For service concession contracts, the substance of the transaction needs to be considered in order to select the appropriate model for recognizing the liability; it may imply a deferred revenue if a right is granted to the operator.

Nevertheless, IPSASB already tackled many public sector specific issues, many issues, for which there is no matching IAS/IFRS, are still open for debate and require further guidelines (e.g. natural resources, heritage assets, infrastructure assets, retirement benefit plans and different measurement issues).

The next chapter presents a case study in which the IPSASs introduced in this chapter will be used and the accounting records are shown.

Bibliographic references

ADAM, Berit (Ed.) (2015) – Praxishandbuch IPSAS, Berlin: Erich Schmidt Verlag, ISBN: 9783503163991.

AGGESTAM-PONTOPPIDAN, Caroline and ANDERNACK, Isabelle (2016) – Interpretation and Application of IPSAS, Chichester: Wiley, ISBN: 978111900319.

ANESSI-PESSINA, Eugenio/BISOGNO, Marco/LORSON, Peter (2022) – Debate: Accounting for Public Sector Assets – the implications of 'service potential', in: Public Money & Management, Vol. 42 2022, Issue 7 (accepted for publication); https://doi.org/10.1080/09540962.2022.2107286.AVERSANO, Nathalia/ CHRISTIAENS, Johan/ VAN THIELEN, Tine (2019) - "Does IPSAS meet heritage assets' user needs?," INTERNATIONAL JOURNAL OF PUBLIC ADMINISTRATION, vol. 42, no. 4, pp. 279–288, 2019.

AVERSANO, Nathalia/ CHRISTIAENS, Johan/ TARTAGLIA POLCINI, Paolo/ SANNINO, Giuseppe (2020) - "Accounting for heritage assets : an analysis of governmental organization comment letters on the IPSAS consultation paper," INTERNATIONAL JOURNAL OF PUBLIC SECTOR MANAGEMENT, vol. 33, no. 2–3, pp. 307–322, 2020.

IPSASB (2016) – Staff Questions and Answers on IPSAS 32, The „Grant of a Right to the Operator Model" in IPSAS 32, Service Concession Arrangement: Grantor, New York: IFAC.

IPSASB (2018) – Handbook of International Public Sector Accounting Pronouncements, New York: IFAC, ISBN: 9781608153626, 2018 Edition, Vol. 1. and 2.

IPSASB (2020) - Property, Plant and Equipment IPSAS® 17 – Presentation, IFAC, https://www.ifac.org/system/files/uploads/IPSASB/2020_02b_Assets_PPE_PP.pptx

MÜLLER-MARQUES BERGER, Thomas (2018) – IPSAS Explained: A Summary of International Public Sector Accounting Standards, Chichester: Wiley, ISBN: 9781119415060. 3rd ed.

KPMG (2016) – IFRS visuell, Stuttgart: Schäffer Poeschel, ISBN 9783791036434, 7th ed.

Task force IRSPM A&A SIG, CIGAR Network, EGPA PSG XII (2017) - Comments and suggestions IPSAS Consultation Paper Financial Reporting for Heritage in the Public Sector, https://www.ifac.org/sites/default/files/publications/exposure-drafts/comments/Comm_and_sugg_IPSAS_CP_HA_task_forcefinal.pdf

Additional readings

AGGESTAM-PONTOPPIDAN, Caroline / ANDERNACK, Isabelle (2016) – Interpretation and Application of IPSAS, Chichester: Wiley, ISBN: 978-1-119-0031-9.

MÜLLER-MARQUES BERGER, Thomas (2018) – IPSAS Explained: A Summary of International Public Sector Accounting Standards, Chichester: Wiley, ISBN: 978-1-119-41506-0, 3rd ed.

Discussion topics

- Heritage assets in the public sector – Challenges for accounting and differences between IPSAS and local accounting norms
- Revaluation model in the public sector – PROs and CONs from the perspectives of preparers and users
- Options in PSA – PROs and CONs from the perspectives of preparers and users
- Measurement of assets arising from taxation transactions and assets held for their operational capacity
- Accounting and reporting by retirement benefit plans
- Recognition, measurement, presentation and disclosure of natural resources and infrastructure assets

CHAPTER 10
IPSAS: CASE STUDY

Ellen Haustein, Peter C. Lorson
both University of Rostock, Germany
ellen.haustein@uni-rostock.de
https://orcid.org/0000-0002-1218-1043
peter.lorson@uni-rostock.de
https://orcid.org/0000-0002-2699-5451

Christophe Vanhee, Johan Christiaens
both Ghent University, Belgium
Christophe.Vanhee@UGent.be
https://orcid.org/0000-0002-7917-856X
Johan.Christiaens@UGent.be
http://orcid.org/0000-0003-4939-8331

Summary

This chapter sets forth the Chapter 9 by presenting the accounting treatment of selected economic transactions. By using a case study of a municipality, specific accounting issues will be worked through using the standards and other pronouncements of the IPSASB.

Thereby this chapter provides insights into selected accounting issues dealt by public sector entities and the process to prepare financial reports in conformity with IPSAS. Thereby, also the accounting records and the changes in the accounts will be entered. The focus is on selected public sector relevant IPSAS, namely

IPSAS 17, 21, 23, 32 and 42 and IPSASB ED 72. As a result of this chapter, a closing balance sheet, a statement of financial performance and a statement of financial position are developed.

Keywords

Public sector specific standards, IPSAS, non-cash generating assets, non-exchange transactions, service concessions, social benefits, transfer expenses

1. Introduction

This chapter sets forth the Chapter 9 by presenting the accounting treatment of selected economic transactions. By using a case study of a municipality, specific accounting issues will be worked through using the standards and other pronouncements of the IPSASB.

Thereby this chapter provides insights into selected accounting issues dealt by public sector entities and the process to prepare financial reports in conformity with IPSAS. The aim of this chapter is to deepen the readers' knowledge about certain areas of IPSAS accounting by resolving specific real life accounting cases. The focus will be on selected public sector relevant IPSAS, namely IPSAS 17, 21, 23, 32 and 42 and IPSASB's ED 72 on transfer expenses.

Relying on the IPSAS that have been introduced, initial and (the options for) subsequent measurement of property, plant and equipment (PPE) according to IPSAS 17 is exemplified and complemented by an impairment of non-cash generating assets (IPSAS 21). Furthermore, differences in the application of IPSAS 23 (revenues from non-exchange transactions) are highlighted by using examples with and without an obligation. With respect to non-exchange expenses the accounting treatment of a collective and individual service, transfer expenses and a social benefit will be illustrated. Finally, the two models of service concession arrangements (IPSAS 32) are characterised by two transactions.

The chapter is structured as follows: Section 2 introduces the case study. The subsequent sections are devoted to the accounting transactions of PPE (Section 3), revenues from non-exchange transactions (Section 4), non-exchange expenses (Section 5) and service concession arrangements (Section 6). In each section, the background of the transactions is explained and tasks to be resolved are formulated. In general, for each transaction, the reader is expected to set up the accounting records, to edit the accounts and the balance sheet, and to identify whether the transaction has an impact on the cash flow (C) or the financial performance (FP). In the corresponding lecture material[1], also the entire task description can be found, as well as the respective booking entries and updated balance sheets after each transaction. However, in this chapter, only in Section 7 the completion of the balance sheet, statement of financial performance and cash flow statement will be presented.

2. Description of the case study

Municipality "Eucity" is a public sector entity fully adopting the accrual basis IPSAS since 5 years, with 300,000 inhabitants and 300 employees in the municipal administration. The reporting period is equal to the calendar year. The following transactions take place in the year 20X1.

For each transaction, specific tasks have to be completed, such as developing the accounting records and indicating the potential impacts on the cash flow statement (C for cash flow) and the state-

---

[1] See Lecture 11, as of the 1st edition of the textbook available at https://www.uni-rostock.de/weiterbildung/offene-uni-rostock/onlinekurse/european-public-sector-accounting/

ment of financial performance (FP for financial performance; i.e. surplus and deficit). At the end, a closing balance sheet, cash flow statement and the statement of financial performance (nature of expense method) have to be prepared.[2]

At the beginning of the reporting period, inventory lists of assets and balance confirmations for bank accounts and liabilities have been created, which conform with the balance sheet at the end of 20X0.

Item	Remaining useful life / maturity	Opening balance 20X1
City hall	20 years	200 kEUR
Land of city hall		100 kEUR
Machines	10 years	50 kEUR
Mainframe computer	3 years	112.5 kEUR
Office wear (desks, chairs, IT)	4 years	44.5 kEUR
Software licenses	5 years	10 kEUR
Raw materials (mineral aggregates, bitumen)	To be used in 20X1	8 kEUR
Cash		25 kEUR
Bank account		250 kEUR
Accounts receivable	50% due in 20X1, remaining due in 20X4	40 kEUR
Non-exchange recoverables	Due in 20X1	30 kEUR
Bank liabilities	Annuity loan until 20X1+8, of which 12.5% due in 20X1	Total 240 kEUR
Pension for the mayor	Due in 20X1+30	50 kEUR
Accounts payable	Due in 20X1	11.75 kEUR
Non-exchange payables	Due in 20X1	3.25 kEUR

Table 10.1: Inventory list to compile the opening balance sheet

---

[2] For didactic purposes, the balance sheet and some accounting information is simplified and presented e.g. without comparative prior year information.

The introductory task is to assign these items to the respective balance sheet positions and to compile the opening balance sheet 20X1 starting with non-current items.

The opening balance sheet 20X1 is composed as shown in Table 10.2. Assets[3] that are expected to be used during more than one reporting period are assigned as non-current assets. Most of these non-current assets belong to the category of PPE.[4] Also liabilities have to be distinguished between current and non-current depending on their maturity. This also means that e.g. the accounts receivable and the bank liabilities have to be split and disclosed separately. The net assets are determined as the residual value between the total assets (870 kEUR) and the total liabilities (305 kEUR). As the reporting period starts with the opening balance sheet, the net surplus/(deficit) is zero, so that the net assets (565 kEUR) are recorded in the reserves.

ASSETS	kEUR	LIABILITIES AND NET ASSETS	kEUR
NON-CURRENT ASSETS		**NON-CURRENT LIABILITIES**	
Intangible assets	10	Pensions, other employee benefits	50
Property, plant and equipment	507	Financial liabilities	210
Accounts receivable	20	**CURRENT LIABILITIES**	
CURRENT ASSETS		Financial liabilities	30
Accounts receivable	20	Accounts payable	11.75
		Non-exchange payable	3.25
Non-exchange recoverables	30	**TOTAL LIABILITIES**	305
Inventories	8	**NET ASSETS**	
Cash and cash equivalents	275	Reserves	565
		Net surplus/(deficit)	0
		TOTAL NET ASSETS	565
TOTAL ASSETS	870	**LIABILITIES AND NET ASSETS**	870

Table 10.2: Opening balance sheet 20X1

---

[3] See Chapter 8 for a review of the asset definition.

[4] As defined in Chapter 9.

Taking the opening balance sheet as starting point, in the following the transactions of Eucity in 20X1 will be analysed and accounted for.

3. Selected transactions of property, plant and equipment

This chapter deals with initial and subsequent measurement of property, plant and equipment (PPE) according to IPSAS 17. In particular, the options for subsequent measurement of PPE are shown and also how an impairment of non-cash generating assets can be accounted for by applying IPSAS 21, addressing the three methods for determining value in use.

Transaction 1: Purchase of assets

In order to establish a public library, Eucity buys a building together with its lot of land on April 1st, 20X1. Both assets are ready for use as a library. Details of the transaction are presented in Table 10.3.

Costs	Amount	Financing / Payment
Purchase price land	50 kEUR	Bank loan (due in 20X1+20)
Purchase price building	147 kEUR	
Land transfer tax (for land only)	4 kEUR	Bank account
Notary fees (allocation: 25% land, 75% building)	4 kEUR	
Costs for establishing disabled access and parking on the land	5 kEUR	
General administration cost for setting up the library (already recorded as expenses)	3 kEUR	

Table 10.3: Details for Transaction 1

> **The tasks for Transaction 1** at initial recognition are to determine the acquisition cost and to set up the accounting records for 20X1.

In a first step to determine the acquisition cost, the assets purchased need to be identified. IPSAS 17 does not prescribe the unit of measure for recognition[5]. However, these assets belong to different classes: the lot of land (library building) belongs to the asset class of land (buildings). The acquisition cost is to be determined separately, also because the lot of land has an unlimited useful life, whereas the building has a definite useful life and is to be depreciated. Both are non-current assets and PPE.

In the second step, the acquisition cost components (IPSAS 17.30) as shown in Chapter 9 are determined. The purchase price and the fees have to be allocated to both assets whereas, according to Table 10.3, the costs for establishing the access for the disabled is recorded for the land only. The general administration cost cannot be capitalized (IPSAS 17.33). Table 10.4 and Table 10.5 show the allocation of cost.

Elements of cost	Application to Transaction 1	Amount
Purchase price	Purchase price	50 kEUR
+ Non-refundable import duties and purchase taxes	+ Land transfer tax + Notary fees (75% of 4 kEUR)	4 kEUR 1 kEUR
- Trade discounts and rebates	(none)	
+ Costs directly attributable to bringing the item into service	+ Making land accessible for disabled persons	5 kEUR
= **Acquisition cost**	= **Acquisition cost land**	**60 kEUR**

Table 10.4: Transaction 1: Acquisition cost of lot of land

---

[5] See Müller-Marques Berger (2018), p. 155.

Elements of cost	Application to Transaction 1	Amount
Purchase price	Purchase price	147 kEUR
+ Non-refundable import duties and purchase taxes	+ Notary fees (75% of 4 kEUR)	3 kEUR
- Trade discounts and rebates	(none)	
+ Costs directly attributable to bringing the item into service	(none)	
= Acquisition cost	= Acquisition cost building	150 kEUR

Table 10.5: Transaction 1: Acquisition cost of library building

According to IPSAS 5, also borrowing cost for the acquisition of qualified assets can optionally be capitalized. However, the benchmark treatment is to recognize borrowing costs as expenses (IPSAS 5.5). Presumably, both assets do not meet the definition of a qualified asset as these do not necessarily take a substantial time to be ready for their intended use or sale, but are ready for use. Thus, the borrowing cost are expenses. After determining the acquisition cost, the accounting records are set up separately for both assets, also indicating that part of the transaction influenced the cash flow[C]. The changes in the accounts will be considered when setting up the closing balance sheet in Section 7.

Debit		to	Credit	
Land	60 kEUR	to	Non-current financial liabilities	50 kEUR
			Bank account[C]	10 kEUR
Building	150 kEUR	to	Non-current financial liabilities	147 kEUR
			Bank account[C]	3 kEUR

Transaction 2: Self construction of a road

Due to (another) larger construction project, Eucity builds a by-pass road that will be used for 3 years only. The road is completed at the end of June 20X1. After 3 years, the road has to be closed and removed. Details are shown in Table 10.6.

Costs	Amount	Additional information
Costs for raw materials	8 kEUR	Taken from inventories
Personnel cost for own staff*	19 kEUR	Paid from bank account
Best estimate for cost of removing the road (Pre-tax discount rate: i = 3.57422% p.a.)	10 kEUR	In June 20X4

Table 10.6: Details for Transaction 2

* Simplified, including the employer's social security contributions, not yet recorded as expenses.

The tasks for Transaction 2 at initial recognition are to determine the construction cost of the item and to set up the accounting records for 20X1.

Again, the item is a non-current asset belonging to the class road network and balance sheet line item PPE. The construction cost calculation is shown in Table 10.7.

Elements of costs	Application to Transaction 2	Amount
Costs directly related to the unit of production	Raw material + Personnel cost	8 kEUR 19 kEUR
+ Systematic allocation variable and fixed production overheads	(none)	
+ Costs directly attributable to bringing the item into service	(none)	
+ Costs of obligations for dismantling, removing and restoring (DRR) the site after the end of use	(Discounted) Present value of the best estimate	9 kEUR
= Construction cost	= Construction cost road	36 kEUR

Table 10.7: Transaction 2: Acquisition cost of road

In order to determine the DRR cost after the end of use[6] the present value of the expenditures expected to settle the obligation has to be calculated (IPSAS 19.53). Therefore, the best estimate of future costs for dismantling the road in June 20X4 (10 kEUR) is discounted by 3 years, for which the pre-tax discount rate (i) is used:

$$\frac{10\ kEUR}{(1+i)^{years}} = \frac{10\ kEUR}{1.0357442^3} = 9\ kEUR$$

Thus, 9 kEUR are capitalized at initial recognition and at the same amount, a provision for DRR cost is accounted for. The accounting record is the following:[7]

Debit		to	Credit	
Road network	36 kEUR	to	Inventories	8 kEUR
			Bank account[C]	19 kEUR
			Provision for DRR costs	9 kEUR

After the initial measurement of the three items of PPE, their subsequent measurement at the end of the reporting year 20X1 is subject of Transactions 3-5 differentiated between the assets.

Transaction 3: Subsequent measurement of the library building

At the end of 20X1, the library building is to be subsequently measured. As shown in Transaction 1, the initial costs were 150 kEUR in April

---

[6] See Chapter 9 for more explanations.

[7] Simplified, the effects on financial performance due to the use of raw materials and personnel costs are neglected.

20X1. For buildings, as one class of assets, Eucity applies the cost model. Eucity expects that the acquisition cost will decrease with a constant charge over the useful life of 30 years to a residual value of 10 kEUR.

The library building contains an elevator for access of the disabled. The elevator makes up 20 kEUR of the initial costs of the building, has an expected useful life of only 10 years with no residual value and will be used by 600,000 persons with 30,000 persons using the elevator in the first year. This is based on the assumption that the number of passengers per year will increase over the useful life of the elevator.

> **The tasks for Transaction 3** are to determine the depreciation method and calculate the depreciation and to set up the accounting records for 20X1.

According to IPSAS 17.59, each part of an "item of PPE with a cost that is significant in relation to the total cost of the item shall be depreciated separately", i.e. the component approach is to be used. Thus, the building and its elevator are depreciated separately, but still disclosed together. The calculation of depreciation starts in April 20X1 with the availability for use, according to IPSAS 17.71. In this example, the useful life is considered in months and using the duodecimal method. Otherwise, in the first year, despite just being used for 9 months, the entity might choose to depreciate the whole year, and not to depreciate in the final. The calculation of the depreciation in 20X1 using the straight-line depreciation for the building and the units of production method (IPSAS 17.78) for the elevator is shown in Table 10.8.

	Library building	Elevator
Useful life	30 years	10 years
Residual value	10 kEUR	0 kEUR
Depreciation method	Straight-line method	Units of production method

Depreciable amount	Initial costs - elevator - residual value = 150 kEUR - 20 kEUR - 10 kEUR = **120 kEUR**	Initial costs of elevator - residual value = 20 kEUR - 0 = **20 kEUR**
Calculation of depreciation in 20X1	$= \dfrac{\text{Depreciable amount}}{\text{Useful life}} \cdot \dfrac{\text{Months in 20X1}}{12 \text{ months}}$ $= \dfrac{120 \text{ kEUR}}{30 \text{ years}} \cdot \dfrac{9 \text{ months}}{12 \text{ months}}$ $= 3 \text{ kEUR}$	$= \dfrac{\text{Depreciable amount}}{\text{Total production}} \cdot \text{Production 20X1}$ $= \dfrac{20 \text{ kEUR}}{600{,}000 \text{ persons}} \cdot 30{,}000 \text{ persons}$ $= 1 \text{ kEUR}$

Table 10.8: Transaction 3: Subsequent measurement for Transaction 1

Thus, for the first 9 months of use, the building is depreciated by 3 kEUR and the elevator by 1 kEUR, which is recorded as an expense (and therefore affects the statement of financial performance[FP]) as shown in the accounting records below. Depreciation expense refers to accumulated depreciation, that allow to decrease the assets value in the balance sheet every year. The component approach only concerns valuation of assets, but not their presentation in the balance sheet. As such, the elevator remains a part of the building, but is depreciated separately.

Debit		to	Credit	
Depreciation expense[FP]	3 kEUR	to	Building	3 kEUR
Depreciation expense[FP]	1 kEUR	to	Building	1 kEUR

Transaction 4: Subsequent measurement of library's lot of land

At the end of reporting period 20X1, the lot of land of the library (Transaction 1) is to be subsequently measured. For land, as one class of assets, Eucity applies the revaluation model. In general, land has an unlimited useful life. The library's lot of land lies in a prosperous area in Eucity. As such, significant changes in fair value are expected, so that Eucity undertakes an annual revaluation. For the other property hold by Eucity (the lot of land of the city hall (100 kEUR)), no revaluations are necessary as no change in fair value incurred. The fair value of the library's lot of land is reliably determined from market-based evidence by appraisal. The following fair values were assessed at the respective revaluation dates:

Revaluation date; end of	Fair value of the lot of land
20X1	75 kEUR
20X2	50 kEUR
20X3	60 kEUR

Table 10.9: Details for Transaction 4: Fair values of the lot of land

The tasks for Transaction 4 are to determine the carrying amount of the lot of land at the end of the years 20X1, 20X2 and 20X3, to set up the accounting records for the same years, but to update the accounts and the balance sheet for the year 20X1 only.

As the lot of land is an asset with an unlimited useful life, the asset is not depreciated. Therefore, the asset can be immediately revalued, i.e. it is subsequently measured at fair value: above (below) its initial costs in revaluation reserve (allocated to deficit or surplus). This is shown in Table 10.10. For year 20X1, the revaluation effect of 15 kEUR are accounted for through the revaluation reserve (IPSAS 17.44 ff.). In year 20X2, the revaluation reserve is reduced until zero value (i.e. 15 kEUR) and the remaining amount of 10 kEUR is allocated to surplus or deficit (i.e. affecting financial performance). In year 20X3, the increase in the carrying amount is also recorded in surplus or deficit[FP] because the initial costs are not exceeded.

Year	Carrying amount beginning of year	Fair value of the lot of land	Carrying amount end of year	Revaluation recognized in	
				Revaluation reserve	Surplus or deficit (Profit/ Loss)
20X1	60 kEUR	75 kEUR	75 kEUR	+15 kEUR	
20X2	75 kEUR	50 kEUR	50 kEUR	-15 kEUR	-10 kEUR
20X3	50 kEUR	60 kEUR	60 kEUR		+10 kEUR

Table 10.10: Transaction 4: Revaluation of lot of land

The accounting records for the revaluations are shown below.

Year	Debit		to	Credit	
20X1	Land	15 kEUR	to	Revaluation reserve	15 kEUR
20X2	Revaluation reserve	15 kEUR	to	Land	25 kEUR
	Impairment expenses[FP]	10 kEUR			
20X3	Land	10 kEUR	to	Reversal of impairment[FP]	10 kEUR

Notabene: No deferred taxes are to be booked, because Eucity is not subject to income taxes or the like.

Transaction 5: Subsequent measurement of the road and its provisions for DRR costs

At the end of year 20X1, also the self-constructed road and the provision for DRR costs (initial recognition 9 kEUR at end of June 20X1, 3 years, discount rate 3.57442% p.a.) are subject to subsequent measurement (Transaction 2). Eucity applies the cost model with a straight-line depreciation for the 3 years of useful life with no residual value.

The tasks for Transaction 5 are to calculate the carrying amount of the road at the end of 20X1 and of the provision at the end of the years 20X1 to 20X3, but to set up the accounting records for 20X1 only.

The road was capitalized at an amount of 36 kEUR in June 20X1. Thus, it needs to be depreciated for 6 months until the end of 20X1 by using the straight-line method. Like in Transaction 4, the duodecimal system is used, i.e. considering the precise months of use:[8]

$$\frac{Depreciable\ amount}{Useful\ life} \cdot \frac{Months\ in\ 20X1}{12\ months} = \frac{36\ kEUR}{3\ years} \cdot \frac{6\ months}{12\ months} = 6\ kEUR$$

Just like the road (the asset), also the provision needs to be subsequently measured (IPSAS 19.54). Presumably, the expected DRR costs do not change. This means that for year 20X1 the provision is to be compounded by 6 months (until the end of 20X1) by using the underlying monthly pre-tax interest rate i_m of 0.293097% p.m.[9] Thus, as shown in Table 10.11 below, at the end of the first year, the provision increases by 159 EUR, which is accounted for as an interest expense (i.e. through surplus or deficit). The process of compounding is repeated for the years 20X2 and 20X3 for 12 months and for 20X4 for 6 months only. In June 20X4, the present value of the provision equals 10 kEUR which is the best estimate for the cost of removing the road (see Table 10.6 of Transaction 2), as the estimation was not subject to revision.

Date	Present value at beginning of reporting period	Calculation: Compounding of provision Present value$_{20XX}$ x (1+i_m) months	Present value at end of reporting period of the provision	Interest expense
31 Dec 20X1	9,000 EUR	9,000 EUR × 1.002930976	9,159 EUR	159 EUR
31 Dec 20X2	9,159 EUR	9,159 EUR × 1.0029309712	9,487 EUR	328 EUR
31 Dec 20X3	9,487 EUR	9,487 EUR × 1.0029309712	9,825 EUR	338 EUR
30 June 20X4	9,825 EUR	9,825 EUR × 1.002930976	10,000 EUR	175 EUR

Table 10.11: Transaction 5: Subsequent measurement of the provision

---

[8] In some countries, it is also possible to consider the whole year (i.e. Germany and Portugal).

[9] $\sqrt[12]{1.0357442} - 1 = 0.293097\%$ p.m. See in the online lecture material, Lecture 11 Appendix A for the calculation.

Accordingly, the accounting records for 20X1 for this transaction are the following:

Debit		to	Credit	
Depreciation expense[FP]	6 kEUR	to	Road network	6 kEUR
Interest expense[FP]	0.2 kEUR	to	Provision for DRR	0.2 kEUR

Transactions 6-8: Impairment of non-cash generating assets

After the acquisition and construction of assets and their subsequent measurement has been completed according to IPSAS 17, the following three transactions relate to the impairment of assets, which is a further step in subsequent measurement. As non-cash generating assets are a public sector specific matter, IPSAS 21 has no IAS/IFRS-equivalent. Due to the high importance of these assets in the public sector, the following transactions focus on the application of IPSAS 21 only.[10]

The case study proceeds as follows: At the end of the reporting year 20X1, straight-line depreciation has been recorded for all assets with a limited useful life. The indication whether non-cash generating assets may be impaired has been checked by assessing internal and external indicators (IPSAS 21.27). The results are shown in Table 10.12.

Asset	Indicator & Description	Details
Mainframe computer	**Significant long-term change with adverse effect on use:** Usage of mainframe computer declined by 80% as Eucity increasingly relies on cloud computing technologies. The mainframe computer has an estimated useful life of 5 years and is in 20X1 at the end of its 3rd year of use. A smaller (new) computer that can provide the remaining service potential has a market price of 30 kEUR. Reproduction is not possible by Eucity.	Carrying amount: 75 kEUR Asset's market price: 50 kEUR Costs of disposal: 5 kEUR

---

[10] See Chapter 9 for a definition of non-cash generating assets.

Road (Trans- actions 2 & 5)	**Physical damage of the asset:** Several severe Winter caused road holes, plans to conduct road repair in Spring 20X2. The road has been built and completed at the end of June 20X1. Restoring the road to a usable condition would require 10.5 kEUR. To build a new road (incl. costs of obligations for DRR after the end of use) would now cost 39 kEUR. The restoration will not affect the useful life of the road.	Carrying amount: 30 kEUR Fair value less costs to sell: no reliable estimate available
Scanner for books	**Cessation of the demand or need for services provided by the asset:** Library users do rarely use scanning service in the library. The scanner was acquired and recorded on 1st January 20X0 for 15 kEUR (included in office wear). Its use was estimated to be 100,000 scans per year for 6 years of its useful life. Citizens used the service only 60,000 times in each year, i.e. the number of service units decreased by 40%. A new scanner would cost 13.5 kEUR.	Carrying amount: 10 kEUR Asset's market price: 10.5 kEUR Costs of disposal: 0.5 kEUR

Table 10.12: Details for Transactions 6-8

> **The tasks for Transactions 6-8** are to explain the general rule for impairment and to describe for each of the three assets, which method for measuring value in use is appropriate. Afterwards, the value in use for each of the three assets is to be determined and the necessity of an impairment is to be assessed and (if applicable) at which amount. Then, the accounting records for the year 20X1 are to be completed.

The general rule of impairment is explained in details in Chapter 9, Section 3 with the respective references. To put it short: An asset is to be impaired, if the recoverable (service) amount lies beyond the asset's carrying amount. Before, the recoverable (service) amount needs to be determined, which is the higher of the fair value less costs to sell (FVLCTS) and the value in use (VIU). In the following, the procedure is described for each of the assets separately.

Transaction 6: Depreciated replacement cost approach

With respect to the mainframe computer, drawing on the information shown in Table 10.12, the FVLCTS and VIU are to be calculated. The

FVLCTS is the difference between the asset's market price and its costs of disposal, i.e. 45 kEUR. As it is lower than the carrying amount of the asset (75 kEUR), also the VIU needs to be determined. In this example, the mainframe computer is an overcapacity asset: its capacity is greater than necessary to meet the demand, also as no standby or surplus capacity is needed. As such, in order to determine the VIU, the depreciated replacement cost approach is appropriate (IPSAS 21.45-.47) with the calculation shown in Table 10.13 (see also IPSAS 21.IE2, IE4, IE6 and IE8). Hereby, the replacement by another computer is assumed that has the required (lower) capacity to fulfil the demand. As the mainframe computer has been used for 3 years already, also the replacement computer needs to be depreciated for 3 years. Therefore, the VIU is 12 kEUR.

Carrying amount, end of 20X1	75 kEUR
Replacement cost (new computer)	30 kEUR
Accumulated depreciation 30 kEUR × $\frac{3}{5}$ years	-18 kEUR
Depreciated replacement cost = Value in use	12 kEUR

Table 10.13: Transaction 6: Depreciated replacement cost approach

The recoverable service amount of the mainframe computer is the higher amount of the FVLCTS (45 kEUR) and the VIU (12 kEUR). As 45 kEUR lies below the carrying amount of the asset (75 kEUR), an impairment by 30 kEUR is required and recorded as follows:

Debit		to	Credit	
Impairment expense[FP]	30 kEUR	to	Computer	30 kEUR

Transaction 7: Restoration cost approach

As shown in Table 10.12, the road is physically damaged. It needs to be repaired to restore its service potential to its pre-impaired level.

Therefore, the restoration cost approach is suitable to determine its VIU (IPSAS 21.48) with the calculation shown in Table 10.14 (see also IPSAS 21.IE10 and IE12). Thereby, the VIU is based on the costs of an undamaged new road, also in order to reflect potential changes in prices, it needs to be depreciated by 6 months to have a comparative level of use (see information in Table 10.12). The VIU of the road is 22 kEUR.

Carrying amount, end of 20X1		30 kEUR
Replacement cost (new road)		39 kEUR
- Accumulated depreciation	$\frac{39 \text{ kEUR} \times 6}{3 \quad 12}$	-6.5 kEUR
Depreciated replacement cost (undamaged)		32.5 kEUR
- restoration cost		-10.5 kEUR
Value in use		22 kEUR

Table 10.14: Transaction 7: Restoration cost approach

In order to find the recoverable service amount, in general, the FVLCTS would be needed as well, but is not available for the public road. Therefore, the VIU of 22 kEUR may be used as recoverable service amount (IPSAS 17.37). As it is lower than the carrying amount of the asset (30 kEUR), the road is to be impaired by 8 kEUR:

Debit		to	Credit	
Impairment expenses^{FP}	8 kEUR	to	Road network	8 kEUR

Transaction 8: Service units approach

For the book scanner, as shown in Table 10.12, the number of service units to be produced by the asset has reduced, as the demand for this asset ceased. As the service units are measurable, the service units approach is most appropriate for measuring the asset's VIU (IPSAS 21.49). The scanner was acquired and recorded on 1st January 20X0 for 15 kEUR. Its number of service units needed decreased by 40%. A new scanner would cost 13.5 kEUR. The calculation of the VIU based on the service units approach is shown in Table 10.15 (see also IPSAS 21.IE14).

Carrying amount, end of 20X1	15 kEUR - $\frac{15\text{ kEUR}}{6} \times 2$	10 kEUR
Replacement cost (new scanner)		13.5 kEUR
- Accumulated depreciation	$\frac{13.5\text{ kEUR}}{6} \times 2$	-4.5 kEUR
Depreciated replacement cost (before adjustment for remaining service units)		9 kEUR
- Reduction of remaining service units (40%)		-3.6 kEUR
Value in use		5.4 kEUR

Table 10.15: Transaction 8: Service units approach

Thus, the VIU of the scanner is 5.4 kEUR and lower than the FVLCTS (market price less costs of disposal), so that the recoverable service amount is 10 kEUR. Therefore, no impairment is required, as the FVLCTS equals the carrying amount. In general, a VIU calculation was not necessary as the FVLCTS was determinable more easily and not below the carrying amount. Therefore, for this transaction, no accounting record is needed.

With respect to Transactions 6-7, in the future, Eucity will have to check whether there are indications that the impairment for both assets has increased, decreased or does not exist anymore (IPSAS 21.64). In such latter cases Eucity may potentially have to record a reversal of impairment to the maximum of the carrying amount of the asset without prior impairment (i.e. taking net depreciation or amortization of the original acquisition or production costs into account) (IPSAS 21.68).

4. Selected transactions of non-exchange transactions

Section 4 explains the application of IPSAS 23 Revenue from non-exchange transactions (by drawing two transactions one with a taxation and one with a donation) and Section 5 selected expenses from non-exchange transactions.

Transaction 9: Taxation of citizens

For any conveyance and disposition of land in its territory, Eucity imposes a 10% land transfer tax. In June 20X1, Citizen A acquired a lot of land for 500 kEUR (effective date of the transfer). Eucity issues a tax statement, which will probably be paid by Citizen A in July 20X1.

> **The tasks for Transaction 9** are to determine whether this is a non-exchange transaction and when it has to be recognized. If applicable, the accounting records are to be developed followed by an update of the accounts and the balance sheet.

In a first step, it needs to be checked whether the inflow of cash represents an asset. According to IPSAS CF 5.6 an asset is a resource presently controlled by the entity as a result of a past event. In this case, the payment by Citizen A represents a resource, which is controlled by Eucity, because Eucity has an enforceable claim (= the tax statement issued). The past event, here the taxable event, is the acquisition of land according to tax law. As the inflow of resources is probable and the inflow can be reliably measured, an asset is to be recognised with the IPSAS to be applied in question.

IPSAS 23 only applies to revenues from non-exchange transaction, which means that there is no exchange of approximately equal values. This is the case here, as Citizen A pays the tax, but does not receive an asset from Eucity in exchange. Through the tax, Eucity receives a revenue (IPSAS 23.12), i.e. is a gross inflow of economic benefits or service potential, which represents an increase in net assets, other than increases relating to contributions of owners.

IPSAS 23.14-18 also provides information about potential stipulations (conditions or restrictions) on the transferred assets. However, this does not apply to tax payments. Therefore, it can be concluded that the payment is to be recognised as a revenue according to IPSAS 23, after determining the taxable event and the tax amount. The taxable event (subject to taxation; IPSAS 23.7) is June 20X1, in which the transfer of land has been conducted. The tax amount is 50 kEUR (10% of 500 kEUR).

The accounting records are the following. First when the tax statement is issued, non-exchange recoverables are booked and the transaction is recorded in a revenue account, here called land transfer taxes, which affects the financial performance of Eucity. After Citizen A completed the payment, non-exchange recoverables are decreased.

Debit		to	Credit	
Non-exchange recoverables	50 kEUR	to	Land transfer taxes[FP]	50 kEUR
Bank account[C]	50 kEUR	to	Non-exchange recoverables	50 kEUR

Transaction 10: Donation of an asset with obligation

On December 31st, 20X1, Citizen B voluntarily transfers a building, which was the birthplace of a famous person, to Eucity. The transfer, however, underlies a contractual agreement: Eucity needs to open the house to the public for the next 10 years. If the condition is not met, the initially recognized value of the building – reduced pro rata temporis over 10 years – is to be retransferred.

The carrying amount of the building is 80 kEUR, whereas its fair value is 100 kEUR. As a public sector entity, Eucity is not subject to tax over donations received.

> **The tasks for Transaction 10** are to assess the measurement of the asset, the obligation and the revenue from the non-exchange transaction. Afterwards, the accounting records are to be set up.

Again, as for Transaction 9, it needs to be considered whether there is an asset to be recognised. In this case, also, an asset is prevalent, as Eucity gains control over the building by completing its transfer together with an agreement which is based on a past event, i.e. the donation of Citizen B. Here, the building is a heritage asset, for which there is an option for recognition (IPSAS 17.9), which Eucity decided to use. The asset is to be measured at fair value, i.e. 100 kEUR. As Eucity does not provide a value in exchange for the building, IPSAS 23 is to be applied for this non-exchange transaction.

However, compared to Transaction 9, it needs to be considered that this is a transaction with a condition (making open to the public for at least 10 years). Therefore, for Transaction 10, a performance obligation due to this condition has to be recognised in the form of a liability (IPSAS 23.17, 23.23 and 23.55). In future reporting periods, the liability is reduced on a straight-line basis, and revenue is progressively recognised for each reporting period in which the condition is fulfilled (i.e. 10 kEUR per year) (IPSAS 23.BC11). Initially, the liability is measured at 100 kEUR and split up in its current and non-current part. Here, it is presumed that there is no material time value of money, so the liability it is not discounted (IPSAS 19.53). The first year's accounting records are as the following:

Debit		to	Credit	
Buildings	100 kEUR	to	Non-current financial liability	90 kEUR
			Current financial liability	10 kEUR

5. Selected transaction of non-exchange expenses

In this section transaction related to non-exchange expenses will be discussed. Hereby Eucity receives no nominal consideration in return for the expenses it makes. The transactions are inspired by the illustrative examples that accompany IPSAS 19, 42 and IPSASB ED 72.

> **The tasks for Transactions 11-15** are first to determine which type of non-exchange expense it represents and which aspects should be recorded. Thereafter, the timing of recognition and measurement of the expenses should be defined and finally the accounting records for the year 20X1 are to be prescribed.

Transaction 11: Expenses for municipal education

Eucity organizes education for primary school students in a public school. It pays the salaries of the teachers assigned in the school (a total of 3 kEUR/month, paid at the end of each month).

As these expenses are intended to provide services to individuals (i.e. pupils) to address the educational needs of society as a whole, they are considered **expenses for individual services**. According to IPSAS 19 AG 15-16, these expenses are considered as expenses for ongoing activities of Eucity and not as transfer expenses or social benefits (students do not have to satisfy eligibility criteria).

Notwithstanding that Eucity, e.g. by law, has the obligation to continue to offer educational services, no provision should be recognized for those future services after the balance sheet date as they give no rise to a present obligation (IPSAS 19 AG 14).

Consequently, only the salaries could, according to IPSAS 39.11, be recognized as an expense and a liability when the teachers have rendered service to the public school, if and only if, service-delivery and payment periods would differ. As the salaries are paid by the end of each month in which the services were rendered, the liability will be deducted each time by this payment. Thus, every month salary expenses will be recognized in surplus or deficit (for the due amounts from January 20X1 until December 20X1). Subsequently a payment will be recorded at the end of every month (for the due amounts from January 20X1 until December 20X1). As a result, no due amount for salary expenses will be recorded in the accounts payable in the closing balance sheet 20X1.

	Debit		to	**Credit**	
Jan 20X1 - Dec 20X1	Salary expenses^{FP}	3 kEUR	to	Bank^C	3 kEUR

Transaction 12: Payments for making available sport infrastructure

As of the beginning of 20X1 Eucity has a binding arrangement with a sport facility entity that owns and manages a swimming pool. According to this arrangement, children from Eucity under 12 years of age should have access to the pool free of charge. In return, Eucity pays 1 kEUR per month (paid in the month following the month in which the children had free access to the pool).

As Eucity does not directly receive any goods or services in return, the expense is considered **a transfer expense with a performance**

obligation as the owner and manager of the swimming pool has to provide services to a third-party beneficiary.

According to IPSASB ED 72.33 and 72.47 Eucity has to recognize a transfer expense when the performance obligation is satisfied. As the extent to which the children use the pool does not affect the monthly payment, Eucity will recognize a transfer expense on a straight-line basis throughout the year at 1 kEUR per month (as long as the pool remains available for the children). Thus, every month a transfer expense will be recognised in the accounts (for the due amounts from January until December X1). Also a payment will be recorded every month (for the due amounts from January 20X1 until November 20X1). As a result, the due amount for December 20X1 (1 kEUR) will be recorded in the account payable in the closing balance sheet 20X1.

	Debit		to	Credit	
Jan 20X1 - Dec 20X1	Transfer expenses^{FP}	1 kEUR	to	Accounts payable	1 kEUR
Feb 20X1 - Dec 20X1	Accounts payable	1 kEUR	to	Bank^C	1 kEUR

Transaction 13: Cash transfer for social housing

Eucity enters into an agreement with a social housing entity to make a one-off cash transfer of 50 kEUR to a social housing entity. The agreement specifies that the social housing entity must:

(a) Increase the number of social housing units by 5; or
(b) Use the cash transfer to make the existing social housing units more eco-friendly.

If none of these requirements are satisfied, the social housing entity must return the cash to Eucity. On September 15th 20X1 Eucity transfers the 50 kEUR to the housing entity.

As the social housing entity has no obligation to provide goods or services to a third-party beneficiary, there is **no performance obligation** for the social housing entity. However, there is **a binding arrangement** in which the rights and obligations for both parties are stipulated. Consequently, Eucity should (IPSASB ED 72.91) recognize **a transfer expense** at the earlier of the point at which it has a present obligation to transfer the 50 kEUR or the point at which it transfers the amount. As Eucity has paid out the amount on September 15th 20X1, it has to record at that time a transfer expense.

	Debit		to	Credit	
Sep 15th 20X1	Transfer expenses^{FP}	50 kEUR	to	Bank^{C}	50 kEUR

Any return of the funds is conditional on a future event (due to non-compliance with the binding arrangement). As long as Eucity has no enforceable right to claim the return of the funds, no assets should be recorded for the possible return of the fund (IPSASB ED 72 AG94).

Transaction 14: Grant for a culture association

The municipal council of Eucity decided to grant a culture association an amount of 7.5 kEUR to support its operations. No further arrangements have been settled between Eucity and the association. Eucity pays on May 1st 20X1. In this case, there is **a transfer expense without performance obligation and no**

binding arrangement. Those transfers should be recognized as an expense when the cash transfer to the culture association is performed. At that time Eucity loses control of the transferred resources (IPSASB ED 72.91).

	Debit		to	Credit	
May 1st 20X1	Transfer expenses[FP]	7.5 kEUR	to	Bank[C]	7.5 kEUR

Transaction 15: Disability pensions

Eucity pays disability pensions to individuals, inhabitants of Eucity, who have a permanent disability (certified by a doctor) that prevents them from working, regardless of their age. The pensions, equal to 2.5 kEUR/month for the period January 20X1 until June 20X1; 2.75 kEUR for the period July 20X1 until November 20X1 and 3.25 kEUR for December 20X1, is paid in the month following the month in which the eligibility criteria were met. At 31 December 20X0 Eucity recognized a liability of 2.25 kEUR (non-exchange payable) for disability pensions payable to those who satisfied the eligibility criteria at that date. As the disability pensions are cash transfers, provided to specific individuals, who meet an eligibility criteria, and are intended to mitigate the effect of social risks and address the need of society as a whole, they meet the definition of **a social benefit** (IPSAS 42.5).

According to the general approach of IPSAS 42, the pensions should be recognized monthly as an expense and a liability when the eligibility criteria to receive the next amount are satisfied (IPSAS 42.6 & 42.10). A payment will also be recorded every month (for the due amounts of the previous month).

	Debit		to	**Credit**	
Jan 20X1 - June 20X1	Social Benefit^{FP}	2.5 kEUR	to	Accounts payable	2.5 kEUR
Jan 20X1	Accounts payable	2.25 kEUR	to	Bank^C	2.25 kEUR
Feb 20X1 - July 20X1	Accounts payable	2.5 kEUR	to	Bank^C	2.5 kEUR
July 20X1 - Nov 20X1	Social Benefit^{FP}	2.75 kEUR	to	Accounts payable	2.75 kEUR
Aug 20X1 - Dec 20X1	Accounts payable	2.75 kEUR	to	Bank^C	2.75 kEUR
Dec 20X1	Social Benefit^{FP}	3.25 kEUR	to	Accounts payable	3.25 kEUR

6. Selected transactions of service concession arrangements

Public sector entities increasingly use partnerships with private sector entities for their service delivery. Some of these partnerships are service concession arrangements, in which a private sector entity uses or develops an asset of a public sector entity in order to provide public services (for a definition see Chapter 9). Here, IPSAS 32 applies if certain criteria are met. Under IPSAS 32, there are two different models of how to account for service concession arrangements. They are introduced by Transactions 16 and 17 in the following.

Transaction 16: Construction and fixed-payment operation of a tunnel by an operator

Eucity commissioned an external operator to construct a tunnel running under a river in 20X0. The tunnel is completed and accepted by Eucity on 1st January 20X1. The construction cost of the tunnel is 250 kEUR and has been financed by the operator. The expected useful life of the tunnel is 20 years and the residual value after a straight-line depreciation is 50 kEUR. The arrangement also specifies that from 20X1 onwards for the next 10 years, the operator delivers the following free of access services to the public:

- operation of the transit through the tunnel;
- maintenance works at the tunnel.

Thereby, Eucity controls the services to be provided by the operator and pays an unconditional fixed amount of 40 kEUR at the end of each year to the operator of which the service charge is 10 kEUR. After the end of the term, the operator will transfer the operation of the tunnel to Eucity. By then, Eucity also controls the residual interest in the tunnel.

The rate implicit in the service concession arrangement specific to the asset is 3.46% p.a.

The tasks for Transaction 16 are to determine the type of service concession contract, (if applicable) to recognize and measure the elements to be recorded and to set up the accounting records in 20X1.

In this transaction, Eucity has an unconditional obligation to pay for the construction of the asset. Therefore, the **financial liability model** applies according to IPSAS 32.18. This means that in January 20X1 an asset and a liability have to be recognised. The asset is the tunnel, which is part of the asset class PPE. According to IPSAS 32.11 initial measurement is to be done at the fair value of the tunnel, which are the construction costs of the tunnel (IPSAS 32.AG30, IPSAS 17.26). Therefore, the tunnel is initially measured at 250 kEUR. According to IPSAS 32.15 the liability is to be initially measured at the same amount as the asset, i.e. also 250 kEUR.

At the end of the reporting year, i.e. December 20X1, also the payment of 40 kEUR is to be accounted for. According to the financial liability model the payment is to be distinguished between (1) a service component (here the service charge of 10 kEUR) and (2) an asset component, which is related to the liability and needs to be further distinguished into a finance charge and the reduction in liability. First, the finance charge is determined, which is the borrowing cost of ca. 8.7 kEUR (250 kEUR × 3.46%).[11] The calculation of the reduction in liability in 20X1 is shown in Table 10.16.

Annual payment	40 kEUR
– Service charge	10 kEUR
– Finance charge	8.7 kEUR
Reduction in liability	**21.3 kEUR**

Table 10.16: Transaction 16: Calculation of reduction in liability

Besides the payment of 40 kEUR, at the end of the reporting year also the depreciation of the tunnel has to be considered. In this case the cost model according to IPSAS 17.43 is applied:

$$\frac{(250 \text{ kEUR} - 50 \text{ kEUR})}{20 \text{ years}} = 10 \text{ kEUR.}$$

Summarising Transaction 16, the following accounting records have to be set up. The first concerns the beginning of the year, when the tunnel is acquired and the liability is recognised. The two remaining are for the depreciation of the tunnel and the payment of Eucity to the operator at the end of 20X1.

---

[11] See in the online lecture material, Appendix B for the calculation for the entire term of the contract.

	Debit		to	Credit	
Jan 20X1	Road network	250 kEUR	to	Non-current financial liability	250 kEUR
Dec 20X1	Depreciation expense^{FP}	10 kEUR	to	Road network	10 kEUR
	Service expense^{FP}	10 kEUR	to	Bank^C	40 kEUR
	Financial charge^{FP}	8.7 kEUR			
	Non-current financial liability	21.3 kEUR			

For reporting of liabilities, it has to be distinguished between current and non-current liabilities (IPSAS 1.80). For this transaction, the financial liability has to be split into one part with a longer duration and one part that is due within the next operating cycle. So for the next reporting year, the amount due is to be calculated for this transaction. By the end of the reporting year 20X1, the liability has a carrying amount of 228.7 kEUR (250 kEUR − 21.3 kEUR). So in the next reporting year, a financial charge of 7.9 kEUR (228.7 kEUR × 3.46%) is due. The reduction of the non-current liability consequently is 22.1 kEUR (40 kEUR − 10 kEUR −7.9 kEUR)[12], which requires the following accounting record:

Debit		to	Credit	
Non-current financial liability	22.1 kEUR	to	Current financial liability	22.1 kEUR

Transaction 17: Construction and operation of a tunnel by an operator with the right to earn revenue from third-party users

Eucity commissioned an external operator to construct another tunnel running under a railtrack in 20X0. The tunnel is completed and accepted by Eucity (= grantor obtains control) on 1st January 20X1.

---

[12] See calculation for the previous year in the text ahead.

The construction cost of the tunnel is 250 kEUR and has been financed by the operator. The expected useful life of the tunnel is 20 years and the residual value after a straight-line depreciation is 50 kEUR.

The arrangement also specifies that from 20X1 onwards for the next 10 years, the operator delivers the following services by collecting tolls from users:

- operation of the transit through the tunnel;
- maintenance works at the tunnel.

There is no direct payment from Eucity to the operator, but the operator will receive revenue from car drivers' tolls. A constant number of users is expected with a collection of tolls of 40 kEUR per year.

The tasks for Transaction 17 are to determine the type of service concession contract, (if applicable) to recognize and measure the elements to be recorded and to set up the accounting records for 20X1.

This transaction is different from Transaction 17, as the operator is not compensated by Eucity, but granted the right to earn revenues from the users of the tunnel. Therefore, the **grant of a right to the operator model** (IPSAS 32.24) is to be used here. This means that in January 20X1, an asset (i.e. the tunnel) and also a liability (i.e. the unearned revenue) is to be recognised. The asset is to be initially measured like an exchange of non-monetary assets (IPSAS 32.AG25b) that means to its fair value at the date of acquisition (IPSAS 17.27), here 250 kEUR. The liability is to be measured at the same amount as the asset (IPSAS 32.15). Even the IPSASB considered the question of measuring the liability: It concluded that "generally it will be appropriate to determine the fair value of the asset received (the service concession asset). This is because the right to earn revenue from third-party users (which is the asset given up under the grant of a right to the operator model) will not have been previously recognized in the grantor's statement of financial position. Consequently, the fair value of the asset received (the service concession asset) will be more clearly evident that the fair value of the asset given up"[13] (the right to collect tolls).

At the end of year 20X1, the depreciation amount of the tunnel on a straight-line basis is determined: $\frac{(250 \text{ kEUR} - 50 \text{ kEUR})}{20 \text{ years}}$

For this asset, there would have been the subsequent measurement choice between applying the cost or the revaluation model (IPSAS 17.42), however, assets with a limited useful life need to be depreciated either way. Eucity applies the cost model. As there are no indications for impairment, their assessment and a test for impairment are obsolete (IPSAS 21.26).

It is assumed that the time value of revenue recognition is not significant, therefore the liability needs not to be discounted. As such, the reduction in liability equals the pattern of revenue recognition which depends on the access to the service concession asset:

$$\frac{250 \text{ kEUR}}{10 \text{ years}} = 25 \text{ kEUR}$$

Therefore, the accounting records for the year 20X1 are the following: The first refers to initial recognition in January 20X1, whereas the remaining two relate to subsequent measurement at the end of 20X1:

		Debit		to	Credit	
Jan 20X1	Road network	250 kEUR		to	Non-current service concession liability	250 kEUR
Dec 20X1	Depreciation expense^{FP}	10 kEUR		to	Road network	10 kEUR
	Non-current service concession liability	25 kEUR		to	Service concession revenue^{FP}	25 kEUR

---

[13] IPSASB Q&A, February 2016, Q1.

As discussed under transaction 16, a distinction should be made between the current and non-current liabilities (IPSAS 1.80). So, for this transaction, the service concession liability has to be split once again into one part with a longer duration (200 kEUR) and one part that is due within the next operating cycle (25 kEUR). This requires the following accounting record:

Debit		to	Credit	
Non-current service concession liability	25 kEUR	to	Current service concession liability	25 kEUR

7. Conclusion

After the accounting for the 17 transactions in 20X1 have been completed, Eucity's financial statements[14] can be compiled. Here, the completion tasks are not to compile and present the entire set of financial statements required by IPSAS 1.21[15], but a closing balance sheet, a cash flow statement and a statement of financial performance for the reporting year 20X1, only.

After closing all the accounts, the balance sheet as shown in Table 10.17 is derived.

ASSETS (in kEUR)	20X1	20X0	LIABILITIES AND NET ASSETS (in kEUR)	20X1	20X0
NON-CURRENT ASSETS			NON-CURRENT LIABILITIES		
Intangible assets	10	10	Pensions, other employee benefits	50	50

---

[14] In the corresponding lecture material, also the transactions in the accounts and balance sheet are to be recorded. As of the 1st edition of the textbook, see Lecture 11, available at https://www.uni-rostock.de/weiterbildung/offene-uni-rostock/onlinekurse/european-public-sector-accounting/

[15] See also Chapter 3 & 8 for further explanations of the different statements.

Property, plant and equipment	1,300	507	Financial liabilities	703.6	210
Accounts receivable	20	20	Service concession liability	200	0
CURRENT ASSETS			Provisions (…) DRR	9.2	0
Accounts receivable	20	20	**CURRENT LIABILITIES**		
Non-exchange recoverables	30	30	Financial liabilities	62.1	30
Inventories	0	8	Accounts payable	11.75	11.75
Cash and cash equivalents	117.5	275	Non-exchange payable	5.25	3.25
			Service concession liability	25	0
			TOTAL LIABILITIES	1,066.9	305
			NET ASSETS		
			Reserves	580	565
			Net surplus/(deficit)	(149.4)	0
			TOTAL NET ASSETS	430.6	565
TOTAL ASSETS	1,497.5	870	**LIABILITIES AND NET ASSETS**	1,497.5	870

Table 10.17: Closing balance sheet 20X1 (simplified)

For setting up the statement of financial performance (Table 10.18) and the cash flow statement (Table 10.19), the indications of FP and C in the accounting records can be used to find all relevant transactions. For guidance, also the relevant transactions for setting up the statements are shown in the tables, which is however not needed in real life. From the statement of financial performance, it can be seen that the difference of total revenues and total expenses equals the change in net surplus/(deficit) in the balance sheet. The net decrease in cash and cash equivalents equals the change in cash and cash equivalents between the opening and the closing balance sheet.

	kEUR	Relevant transactions
Revenue from non-exchange transactions		
Taxes	50	9 (50 kEUR)
Property, plant and equipment acquired in non-exchange transactions		
Revenue from exchange transactions		
Revenue from service concession arrangement	25	17 (25 kEUR)
Total revenue	75	
Expenses		
Depreciation and amortisation	68	3 (4 kEUR) 5 (6 kEUR) 6-7 (38 kEUR) 16 (10 kEUR) 17 (10 kEUR)
General expenses	10	16 (10 kEUR)
Salary expenses	36	11 (36 kEUR)
Transfer expenses	69.5	12 (12 kEUR) 13 (50 kEUR) 14 (7.5)
Social benefits	32	15 (32 kEUR)
Interest expenses	8.9	5 (0.2 kEUR) 16 (8.7 kEUR)
Total expenses	224.4	
Net deficit	**(149.4)**	
Surplus attributable to non-controlling interest	0	
Surplus attributable to Eucity	**(149.4)**	

Table 10.18: Statement of Financial Performance 20X1[16]

---

[16] The right column is for reproducibility only; the column is not part of the statement of financial performance.

	kEUR	Relevant transactions
Cash flows from operating activities		
Receipts from taxes	50	9 (50 kEUR)
Receipts from transfers		
Payments to suppliers	(10)	16 (10 kEUR)
Payments for non-exchange expenses	(135.5)	11 (36 kEUR) 12 (11 kEUR) 13 (50 kEUR) 14 (7.5 kEUR) 15 (31 kEUR)
Net cash flows from (used in) operating activities	**(95.5)**	
Cash flows from investing activities		
Purchase of property, plant and equipment	(32)	1 (13 kEUR), 2 (19 kEUR)
Net cash flows from (used in) investing activities	**(32)**	
Cash flows from financing activities		
Cash repayments of amounts borrowed	(30)	16 (8.7 kEUR + 21.3 kEUR)
Net cash flows from (used in) financing activities	**(30)**	
Net increase/(decrease) in cash and cash equivalents	**(157.5)**	
Δ Cash and cash equivalents 20X1 – 20X0	**(157.5)**	117.5-275 kEUR

Table 10.19: Statement of Cash Flows 20X1[17]

Bibliographic references

ADAM, Berit (2013) – Einführung in IPSAS, Berlin: Erich Schmidt Verlag, ISBN: 9783503154029. ADAM, Berit (Ed.) (2015) – Praxishandbuch IPSAS, Berlin: Erich Schmidt Verlag, ISBN: 9783503163991.

AGGESTAM-PONTOPPIDAN, Caroline and ANDERNACK, Isabell (2016) – Interpretation and Application of IPSAS, Chichester: Wiley, ISBN: 978111900319.

---

[17] The right column is for reproducibility only; the column is not part of the statement of cash flows. For deriving the cash flow from operations, Eucity chooses the direct method.

IPSASB (2016): Staff Questions and Answers on IPSAS 32, The „Grant of a Right to the Operator Model" in IPSAS 32, Service Concession Arrangement: Grantor: http://www.ifac.org/publications-resources/staff-questions-and-answers-ipsas-32

IPSASB (2018) – Handbook of International Public Sector Accounting Pronouncements, New York: IFAC, ISBN: 9781608153626, 2018 Edition, Vol. 1 and Vol 2.

MÜLLER-MARQUES BERGER, Thomas (2018) – IPSAS Explained: A Summary of International Public Sector Accounting Standards, Chichester: Wiley, ISBN: 9781119415060. 3rd ed.

Additional readings

AGGESTAM-PONTOPPIDAN, Caroline and ANDERNACK, Isabelle (2016) – Interpretation and Application of IPSAS, Chichester: Wiley, ISBN: 978111900319.

MÜLLER-MARQUES BERGER, Thomas (2018) – IPSAS Explained: A Summary of International Public Sector Accounting Standards, Chichester: Wiley, ISBN: 9781119415060, 3rd ed.

Discussion topics

- Non-cash generating assets vs. cash-generating assets – Implications for accounting
- Differences between cost for acquisition and self-construction
- Challenges in determining the taxable event according to IPSAS 23
- Collective vs. individual services, transfer expenses and social benefits – Implications for accounting
- Performance obligation vs. binding arrangement – Implications for accounting
- Heritage assets vs. natural resources – Implications for accounting

Chapter 11
Consolidated Financial Statements

Ellen Haustein, Peter C. Lorson
both University of Rostock, Germany
ellen.haustein@uni-rostock.de
https://orcid.org/0000-0002-1218-1043
peter.lorson@uni-rostock.de
https://orcid.org/0000-0002-2699-5451

Eugenio Anessi-Pessina
Università Cattolica del Sacro Cuore, Milan, Italy
eugenio.anessi@unicatt.it
https://orcid.org/0000-0002-4660-5457

Summary

This chapter introduces consolidated financial reporting in general and highlights public sector specifics. The aim is to provide insights into the concept of 'group' or 'economic entity', the reasons for consolidation, the peculiarities of the public sector, and the underlying theories of consolidation. The different types of influences and consolidation methods are explained. The chapter outlines the differences between consolidated financial statements and whole of government accounts and shows organisational challenges for preparing consolidated financial statements. Finally, a short overview about consolidated financial reporting in selected European countries is presented.

Keywords

Consolidation, consolidated financial reporting, whole of government accounting

https://doi.org/10.14195/978-989-26-2464-8_11

1. Introduction: The group as an accounting phenomenon

The preceding chapters have focused on the financial statements (FS) of individual public sector entities (single entity FS). To perform their functions, however, public sector entities often rely on other entities in which they have equity interests, voting rights, or other sources of influence. This is particularly true for primary governments, i.e., public sector entities which have "a separately elected governing body – one that is elected by the citizens in a general, popular election".[1] A municipality, for example, may provide public services not only through its own departments, but also by means of separate, legally independent entities such as public utility companies, municipal housing companies or wastewater associations. These arrangements have become particularly common following New Public Management (NPM), which has encouraged the disaggregation of formerly monolithic public entities[2] and the establishment of legally separate authorities, agencies, and government-owned enterprises (state-owned businesses) as well as the development of public-private partnerships. Hence, **a need exists for an "appropriate accounting tool" that provides financial information on the "group of entities" as a whole**[3].

In general, a **'group'** or **'economic entity'** is composed of at least two legally independent entities: a focal entity representing the group's nucleus (commonly referred to as the 'parent' and generally represented, in the public sector, by a primary government) and at least one affiliated entity (called a 'subsidiary' or a 'special purpose entity' in the private sector). The criteria whereby an entity can be qualified as being affiliated to another entity have been extensively discussed

---

[1] GASB 14.13.

[2] Hood (1995)

[3] Santis, Grossi, and Bisogno (2019), p. 230.

both in the academic literature and by accounting standard setters. The most widespread approach makes reference to the **principle of control**, so that **a group is generally conceptualized as being composed of a controlling entity and at least one controlled entity.**

For any given economic entity, **consolidated financial statements (CFS)**, if prepared, will **present the assets, liabilities, net assets/ equity, revenues, expenses, and cash flows of the controlling entity and its controlled entities as if they were a single entity.** This reference to a virtual single entity is often referred to as the 'single entity fiction'.[4] As a first approximation, consolidation is achieved by summing up like items of the controlling and the controlled entities line-by-line. For example, if the value of Property, Plant and Equipment (PPE) – or accounts payable, or fee revenues, or labour expenses – is 100 EUR for the controlling entity and 200 EUR for the controlled entities, the corresponding amount in the CFS will generally be 300 EUR. In fact, however, **CFS do not merely sum up the FS** of the single entities belonging to the same economic entity. Rather, they aggregate such FS using specific consolidation techniques which eliminate the effects of intra-group transactions (i.e., the transactions that occurred between entities belonging to the group and are thus inconsistent with the single entity fiction) and deal with the possible presence of non-controlling interests (i.e., the remaining interests that are held by third parties in controlled entities, as in the case of outside investors – investors not belonging to the group – holding minority shares in a government-owned corporation controlled by a primary government).

The first CFS were prepared by U.S. private sector entities around the turn of the 20th century.[5] Since then, for private companies, CFS

---

[4] Aggestam-Pontoppidan and Andernack (2016), p. 308.

[5] J.P. Morgan is attributed to have insisted on consolidated accounts for his steel holding company in 1901, see Mueller; Gernon and Meek (1997), p. 103.

have become the norm, especially if the company's debt or equity instruments are traded in a public market. IFRS 10.2, in particular, "requires an entity (the parent) that controls one or more other entities (subsidiaries) to present consolidated financial statements". In the public sector, on the contrary, this is not always the case. Reforms, primarily in Anglo-Saxon countries, have indeed driven the adoption of 'consolidated accounts' or even 'whole of government accounts'.[6] However, as consolidated accounting creates several organizational challenges, some jurisdictions have not yet introduced the legal requirement for consolidated financial reporting in the public sector, while others introduced it only to later withdraw it. This latter case occurred, for example, in some federal states of Germany, where small local governments no longer need to prepare CFS.[7] This decision was attributed to the costs of preparing CFS being greater than the corresponding benefits. Still, both practice and research are predominantly of the view that CFS foster accountability and support decision-making – for example, because CFS reveal the 'true' extent of the primary entity's indebtedness when liabilities are spread over several public sector entities belonging to the same economic entity[8].

The aim of Chapter 11 is to introduce the fundamental concepts concerning CFS. To some extent, these concepts are comparable with those used in the private sector; however, the chapter is also intended to highlight specific issues related to the public sector. Chapter 12 is specifically devoted to consolidation under IPSASs. Thereby, both chapters take accrual-based financial statements as a starting point. Conversely, the consolidated presentation of budgets

---

[6] See Brusca and Montesinos (2009), p. 243.

[7] For instance, in the German federal state Mecklenburg-Vorpommern: Kommunales Haushaltsrecht - Regierungsportal M-V (regierung-mv.de)

[8] See e.g. Chapter 8 for the terms accountability and decision-making support.

lies outside the scope of these chapters, regardless of whether the budgets are cash or accrual-based.[9] Horizontal peer groups, where two or more entities have strong and continuous relationships, but lack a parent entity, are similarly scoped out of these chapters.

This Chapter 11 is structured as follows. Section 2 presents the objectives of consolidated financial reporting. Section 3 introduces the group as a fictional entity and discusses its perimeter, i.e., the 'area of consolidation'. Section 4 presents the methods for consolidated accounting and the theories of consolidation. Section 5 introduces the procedures for full consolidation, which are further addressed in Chapter 12 with IPSASs-based examples. Organizational challenges are discussed in Section 6. Finally, a conclusion is provided in Section 7 together with a comparative table showing the status quo of consolidated public sector financial reporting in selected European countries.

2. The objectives of consolidated financial reporting

Consolidated financial reporting is intended to "provide relevant and undistorted financial information to internal and external stakeholders that encompasses every subsidiary or department and clears out any internal transactions, as well as mutual assets and liabilities".[10] To offer such view, CFS have long been argued to be necessary also in the public sector context.[11] This necessity, in fact, has become even stronger following NPM-inspired public sector reforms. One element of NPM is that it fragments the public sector

---

[9] See Bergmann et al. (2016), p. 772 for a short explanation of cash-based traditional approaches.

[10] Bergmann et al. (2016), p. 766.

[11] See e.g. Heald and Georgiou (2000) and Lande (1998).

into smaller organizations. Such disaggregation is claimed to improve both efficiency and accountability, but it may end up obscuring the broader picture. Hence the importance of consolidation both for overall system control and for public accountability.[12] In the absence of consolidation, in fact, primary governments may be encouraged to pursue an "escape out of the budget [...] for the purpose of hiding public debt"[13] by shifting expenses and liabilities to affiliated entities. However, Walker (2009) warns that, for some information needs (e.g., to inform about the efficiency of service delivery), other financial statements or budget reports may be more suitable.

Based on theoretical considerations, Walker (2009) puts forward a list of routinely made judgements, for which CFS prepared at the central government level may deliver useful information.[14] The list includes:

1. Results and sustainability of a government's financial management practices;
2. Capacity to continue to deliver existing levels of services (or to enhance those services);
3. Manner in which a government is pricing services;
4. Extent to which a government is funding or delivering subsidized services;
5. How government has spent taxpayers' funds and any borrowings;
6. Whether a government is incurring obligations which will impose burdens on future generations;
7. Attractiveness of investing in government securities;
8. Attractiveness of maintaining investment in government securities;

---

[12] Heald and Georgiou (2009).
[13] Bergmann et al. (2016), p. 764.
[14] See Walker (2009), p. 200, Table 3.

9. Financial circumstances of regional governments vis-à-vis other regional (state) governments; and
10. Financial circumstances of nations vis-à-vis other nations.

This list, however, refers to a specific category of CFS and does not apply to CFS at all government levels. Thereby, Walker (2009) stresses the need to first identify the **addressees and users of CFS**, to then figure out their information needs and thus adjust the objectives and features of CFS. He also suggests that several kinds of CFS may be necessary depending on information needs. Multi-column CFS might even be required, so as to consolidate different sets of entities (e.g., only general government entities or also financial and non-financial government-owned enterprises; only controlling and controlled entities or also other types of affiliated entities) or to consolidate a given set of entities using different methods (e.g., full, proportional or equity/one-line consolidation)[15].

The addressees and users of public sector CFS are strongly debated in practice and research.[16] Usually, the following users/stakeholders are discussed to benefit from CFS through greater transparency and better support for decision-making: **internal users** such as politicians, managers, and employees as well as **external stakeholders** including citizens in their capacities as voters, taxpayers, and users of public services, but also suppliers, other public administrations, and financial institutions.[17] For internal users, CFS can represent a tool for "steering and controlling the direct and indirect provision of public services" and for "public decision-making in programming and controlling the different public policies".[18] With respect to ex-

---

[15] See Sections 3 and 5 for a discussion of the scope and methods of consolidation.
[16] See e.g. Walker (2009) and Bergmann et al. (2016).
[17] Santis, Grossi and Bisogno (2018), p. 242.
[18] Bergmann et al. (2016), p. 766.

ternal stakeholders, for example, banks could use CFS in order to assess the creditworthiness of the economic (fictitious single) entity while, for rating agencies, CFS may be useful to assess solvency and financial risks.[19] However, empirical findings about the actual usefulness of CFS remain sparse, especially with respect to citizens.[20]

3. The group as a fictional entity and the area of consolidation

The concept of economic entity is based on the observation that a set of single entities, which are legally independent, may represent one entity from an economic point of view. Thereby, an 'economic entity' or 'group' is created where the single entities fictitiously lose their legal independence and are treated in accounting as dependent operations of the focal entity. Thus, the economic entity exists and is accounted for based on the single entity fiction. Accordingly, the group does not legally exist and may also not be subject to tax law in many jurisdictions.[21] In a public sector context, Clarke and Dean (1993) stress that groups of governments with their controlled entities are "a fictitious structure, without legal power to exercise rights or incur physical or financial damage."[22] For the public sector, the term 'economic entity' may be somehow misleading since government entities do not strive for profits and have other purposes than private sector entities. In this regard, the term '**service providing entity**' would be more suitable. However, for consistency within the commonly used accounting terminology, this textbook uses 'economic entity' in the following.

---

[19] Bergmann et al. (2016), p. 766.
[20] Walker (2009); Bergmann et al. (2016).
[21] Küting and Weber (2018), p. 92.
[22] Clarke and Dean (1993) cited by Grossi et al. (2014).

When preparing CFS, a crucial decision is the identification of the entities that must be classified as being part of the group and whose accounts must consequently be consolidated. In other words, the **area of consolidation** or **scope of consolidation needs to be clarified**. For accounting standard setters, this translates into the need to define appropriate criteria concerning the scope of consolidation.

Chapters 11 and 12 of this textbook draw on the **concept of control as the leading principle to define the scope of consolidation**, because control is the principle predominantly used both in the private sector and in European public sector accounting (PSA), as also shown in Table 11.3 with specific reference to selected European countries.

Control is seen as the strongest form of influence of one entity over another. The definition of control is complex in general and even more so in the public sector.[23] A frequently used presumption is that an entity controls another if it holds more than 50 percent of voting rights in the other entity. Control can be exerted **directly** by the controlling entity and/or **indirectly** through one or more controlled entities. Indirect control occurs when the economic entity consists of a chain of controlling relationships whereby a controlled entity holds control of another entity, i.e., it is itself a controlling entity. Such indirect control is also called 'pyramiding control'. A mixed direct and indirect control occurs when a majority of voting rights in an entity is held in part directly by the controlling entity and in part by one or more of its other controlled entities. Importantly, under mixed control, the total voting rights held by the controlling entity correspond to the unweighted sum of the rights held directly and indirectly. This is because the controlling entity has control over all the rights held indirectly via controlled companies, regardless of the presence of non-controlling interests.

---

[23] See also Brusca and Montesinos (2009). Chapter 12 presents the definition provided by IPSASs.

For example, for assessing the control criterion, assume that Alpha owns 80% of Beta and 30% of Gamma, while Beta owns another 25% of Gamma. The total voting rights controlled by Alpha in Gamma are 30% + 25% = 55%, not 30% + 25% x 80% = 50%. This is because, by controlling Beta, Alpha controls the entirety of Beta's voting rights in Gamma. Due to the 55%, Gamma is included in the CFS as a controlled entity. Nevertheless, Alpha's share in Gamma's net assets is 50%, which is relevant when consolidating the entities' financial reports.

Figure 11.1 exemplifies the identification of the consolidation area when control is chosen as the leading principle.

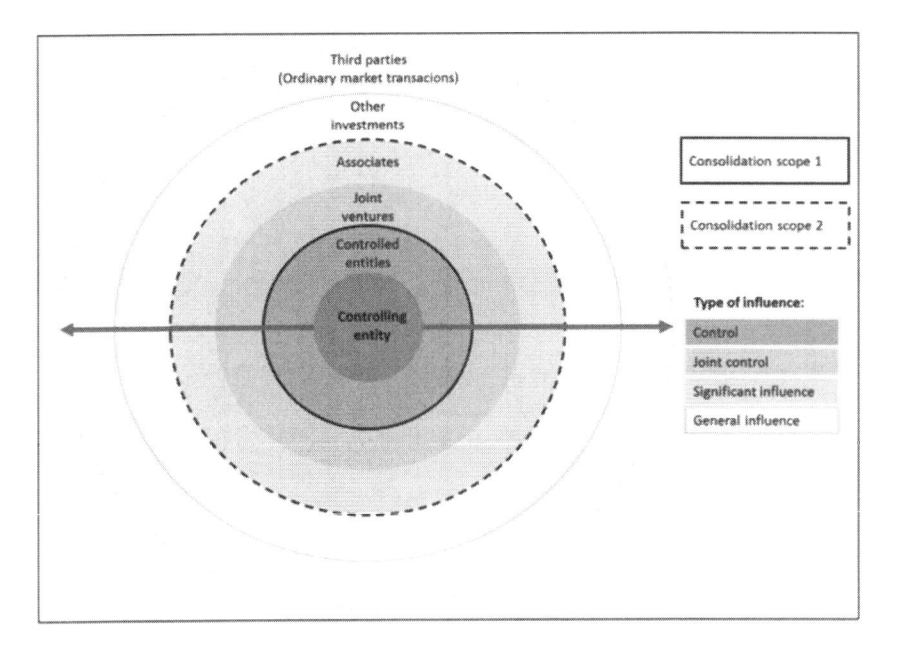

Figure 11.1: Scope of consolidation – between hierarchy and market

In a **narrow sense** (consolidation scope 1), the area of consolidation will encompass the parent entity as well as the entities that are controlled by the parent entity. Thus, it consists of controlled entities and the controlling/parent entity. In a **broader sense** (consolidation scope 2), the area of consolidation will also encompass two further types of entities, that is, joint ventures and associates. In a **joint venture**, two or more independent parties (not relating to the same group) have **joint control** over an entity and share rights to the entity's net assets,[24] so that decisions about the entity's activities require the unanimous consent of the parties sharing control. An **associate** is an entity over which the parent has **significant influence**. Significant influence exists if the parent entity has neither control nor joint control over another entity, but it has the power to participate in the financial and operating policy decisions of such entity. In terms of voting power (if applicable), the investing entity is presumed to have significant influence if it holds at least 20% of the voting power in an investee, but not more than 50%, which would confer control. If influence is weaker, (almost) normal arm's length relationships are assumed, so that no consolidation is required or appropriate. The parent's and the controlled entities' (almost) normal investments in other entities are included in the CFS as financial assets, in the same way as an individual entity would present its equity investments in its own FS.

Using the concept of control to define the scope of consolidation, however, is not uncontested in public sector research and practice. Accounting standards that rely on the concept of control generally prescribe full consolidation[25] only for the entities that fall into the (narrow) consolidation scope 1. As a consequence, the assets, liabilities, revenues, expenses and cash flows of associates and joint ventures are not included in the CFS. Even more critically, as highlighted by e.g. Grossi and Steccolini (2015) and Bisogno et al. (2015), the public sector is characterized by "alternative control forms, funding and financial dependence relationships", and bailout expectations which

---

[24] For the distinction between joint operations and joint ventures as variants of joint arrangements, see Chapter 12.

[25] See Section 4 of this Chapter for an explanation of full consolidation and Chapter 12 for examples.

"are not only or mainly based on the concept of ownership" and are not properly captured by traditional control indicators.[26] Under these circumstances, using the concept of control to define the scope of consolidation may have a "negative effect in terms of financial disclosure". This is especially true in the presence of "fragmented ownership, contractual relationships, and use of significant municipal subsidies", as "some entities that are not controlled but significantly funded by the government budget, or are only able to survive on contract with the government, are not included in the area of consolidation", although the focal public sector entity is retaining financial responsibility.[27]

Other perspectives and approaches could therefore be more appropriate to define the scope of consolidation in the public sector. **Suggestions include the risk perspective, the organizational and legal perspective, the budget or budgetary perspective, and the statistical perspective**,[28] with the last two being particularly influential.

According to the **budget or budgetary perspective** CFS should include all the entities that receive significant financial support from the focal government's budget. This perspective is particularly consistent with a view of CFS as predominantly serving accountability purposes. In the U.S., for example, GASB 14.10 highlights that "the concept underlying the definition of the financial reporting entity is that elected officials are accountable to their constituents for their actions". In particular, "the elected officials are accountable to those citizens for their public policy decisions, regardless of whether those decisions are carried out directly by the elected officials through the operations of the primary government or by their designees through the operations of specially created organizations"

---

[26] Grossi and Steccolini (2015), p. 332.

[27] Grossi and Steccolini (2015), pp. 330 and 332.

[28] See Bergmann et al. (2016), p. 769 for a detailed description of these perspectives.

(GASB 14.8). Therefore, "the financial reporting entity consists of (a) the primary government, (b) organizations *for which the primary government is financially accountable* [italics added] and (c) other organizations for which the nature and significance of their relationship with the primary government are such that exclusion would cause the reporting entity's financial statements to be misleading or incomplete" (GASB 14.12). Financial accountability generally entails the primary government's appointment of "a voting majority of an organization's governing body", but "a primary government may also be financially accountable for governmental organizations that are fiscally dependent on it". With respect to the European public sector context, a frequent suggestion is that **financial dependence should supplement** rather than replace **control**. Carini and Teodori (2021), for example, argue that control "will not grasp all the nuances of the public group" and that "the budget approach is more effective in providing a complete representation of the resources entrusted to and managed by [...] governments". However, they also acknowledge that "the control approach better approximates financial results"[29].

Under the **statistical perspective**, the scope of consolidation overlaps with the so-called general government sector (GGS)[30]. GGS is defined as including "all institutional units which are non-market producers controlled by government, whose output is intended for individual and collective consumption, and are financed by compulsory payments made by units belonging to other sectors; it also includes institutional units principally engaged in the redistribution of national income and wealth, which is an activity mainly carried out by government"[31]. GGS includes all levels of government, even

---

[29] Carini and Teodori (2021), p. 432.

[30] See Chapter 1 for a definition.

[31] Eurostat. Manual on Government Deficit and Debt. Implementation of ESA 2010. 2019 edition. Section 1.2.1, para. 1.

in a federal setting, where states are clearly not controlled by the national government. Conversely, it "excludes market public producers [...], which are classified in the non-financial corporations [...] or financial corporation [...] sectors"[32]. Because of this focus on the GGS, CFS prepared according to the statistical perspective are close to Government Finance Statistics (GFS), whose main goal is to provide macroeconomic information concerning each of the different sectors of the economy[33]. Figure 11.2 shows the financial reporting entity[34] from a macroeconomic point of view, with its differentiation between the GGS on the hand, public non-financial and financial corporations (in bold rectangles) on the other.[35]

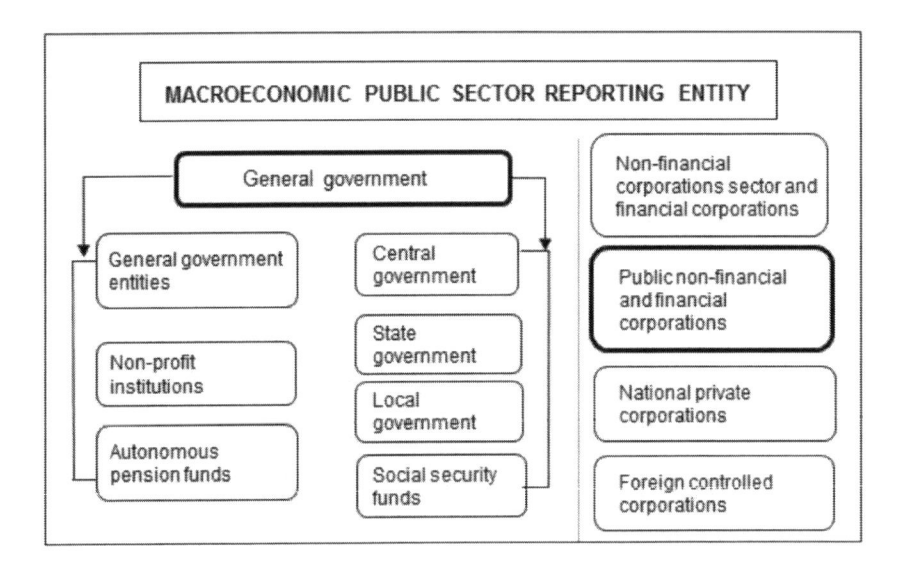

Figure 11.2: Macroeconomic public sector reporting entity
(Source: Brusca and Montesinos, 2009)

---

[32] Eurostat. Manual on Government Deficit and Debt. Implementation of ESA 2010. 2019 edition. Section 1.2.1, para. 2.

[33] Bisogno et al. (2015), p. 313.

[34] See glossary for a definition and for further references in the book.

[35] See Brusca and Montesinos (2009) for more detailed explanations.

Comparisons are often drawn between GFS on the one hand, and the concepts of **whole of government accounting (WGA)** or **whole of government financial reporting (WGFR)** on the other[36]. WGFR aims to present "the overall financial position of the government of a particular jurisdiction [...] via the consolidation of the financial statements and transactions of all the entities controlled by the jurisdiction's government"[37] and the resulting preparation of "statements encompassing the whole of a specific tier of government" (e.g., the central government, all state / regional governments or all local governments) or, in fact, the whole of all tiers of government, as in the UK.[38]

Similar to GFS, WGFR does not focus on individual economic entities (e.g., a municipal government and its controlled entities); rather, it takes a broader approach by including the whole of one or more tiers of government. GFS, however, measure financial position and performance according to their own statistical methodologies and conventions, while WGFR generally relies on IPSASs, IFRSs or the relevant national adaptations. GFS, moreover, pursue international harmonisation and comparability; WGFR, conversely, presents significant national specificities in the actual scope of consolidation[39]. This is also because, in some countries, the national government has control over its state and local governments, whereas in other countries it does not, due to different constitutional arrangements. As a result, whole-of-government reports are not standardized and internationally comparable. In other words, disparities exist as to what parts of the public sector (as depicted in Figure 11.3) are encompassed by WGFR in different countries.

---

[36] See Chapter 5 for more details.
[37] Santis, Grossi and Bisogno (2018), p. 231 with further references.
[38] Chow et al. (2019).
[39] Brusca and Montesinos (2009), p. 243.

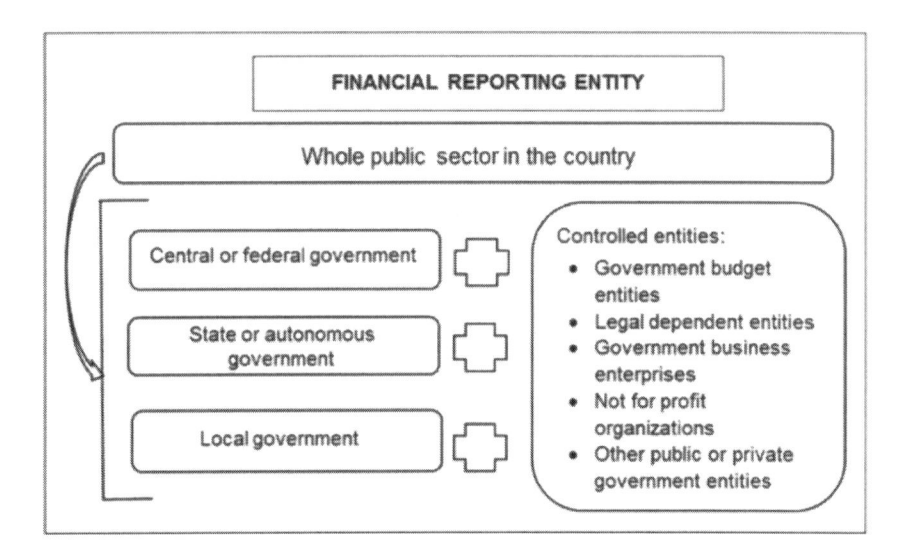

```
┌─────────────────────────────────────────────────────────────┐
│                  FINANCIAL REPORTING ENTITY                  │
│                                                              │
│          Whole public sector in the country                  │
│                                                              │
│     ┌──────────────────────────┐                             │
│     │ Central or federal       │    Controlled entities:     │
│     │ government               │    • Government budget      │
│     └──────────────────────────┘      entities               │
│     ┌──────────────────────────┐    • Legal dependent        │
│     │ State or autonomous      │      entities               │
│     │ government               │    • Government business    │
│     └──────────────────────────┘      enterprises            │
│                                     • Not for profit         │
│     ┌──────────────────────────┐      organizations          │
│     │ Local government         │    • Other public or        │
│     └──────────────────────────┘      private government     │
│                                       entities               │
└─────────────────────────────────────────────────────────────┘
```

Figure 11.3: Financial reporting entity
(Source: Brusca & Montesinos, 2009)

As mentioned, the country with the most extensive whole-of-government scope of consolidation is the UK. In the UK, whole-of-government accounts are viewed as the "most consequent approach to CFS"[40]. They comprise all tiers of government as well as public corporations. Notable exclusions are "entities that are not responsible to an executive arm of government"[41], among which Parliament and the National Audit Office. Nationalized banks are also excluded.[42] Significantly, Heald and Georgiou (2009) highlight that "there is no mention of 'control' as a criterion for determining whether an organization is included in the UK's WGA"[43]. This is because the Government Resources and Accounts Act 2000 "requires HM Treasury to consolidate entities that appear to HM Treasury to 'exercise functions of a public nature' or

---

[40] Bergmann et al. (2016), p. 776.
[41] UK Whole of Government Accounts, 2019-20, Annex 2.
[42] Chow et al. (2015).
[43] Heald and Georgiou (2009), p. 224.

to be 'substantially funded from public money'". This is achieved by making reference to "the Office for National Statistics (ONS) classification of the public sector", so as "to ensure the accounts are consistent and comparable to other measures of financial performance, such as the National Accounts". An indirect reference to the control concept is included by highlighting that the ONS takes "account of the degree of control that government has over each entity"[44]. In other words, the UK's WGA has been combining the control and the statistical perspectives to meet the need for a "clear line of sight" from WGFR to CFS, lest "the practical impact of the former on policy formation and fiscal surveillance [...] be greatly reduced [...] given that macroeconomic policies and obligations generally depend on national accounts definitions"[45].

The process of WGFR is very data intensive and complex.[46] In addition, for federal countries, it is argued to be very challenging, but "less useful".[47] As a consequence, WGFR is not very widespread, but only applied by few countries.[48] In the UK, WGFR has traditionally been criticized by both politicians and academics due to ongoing qualified audit opinions (i.e., audit reports highlighting certain quality issues) and to delays in the preparation and publication of the statements.[49] Recently, however, its merits have begun to be recognised. The UK's Public Accounts Committee has described it as the most "complete and accurate of pictures to the UK's public sector finances"[50]. According to Stewart and Connolly, WGFR has highlighted assets and liabilities that are not captured by GFS, such as future pension liabilities, clin-

---

[44] UK Whole of Government Accounts, 2019-20, Note 1.3.
[45] Heald and Georgiou (2009), p. 220.
[46] Brusca and Montesinos (2009).
[47] Bergmann et al. (2016), p. 776.
[48] Brusca and Montesinos (2009), p. 243.
[49] Stewart and Connolly (2022).
[50] UK Public Accounts Committee. (2021), p. 4.

ical negligence claims, and public private partnership obligations; it has also seemingly started to support planning, facilitate decisions on the use of assets, increase transparency, and stimulate debates on long-term risk management and fiscal policy[51].

4. Consolidation methods and theories of consolidated accounts

Once the scope of consolidation has been defined, another crucial decision is the **choice of consolidation method(s)**, with specific reference to (1) full consolidation, (2) proportional consolidation and (3) the equity method.[52]

Under **(1) full consolidation** (also called "line-by-line consolidation"), the assets, liabilities, revenues, expenses and cash flows of the controlling entity and its controlled entities are fully included in the CFS on a line-by-line basis, irrespective of the controlling entity's share in the equity of the controlled entities. In the presence of non-controlling interests (NCI), such interests are presented in the consolidated balance sheet as a separate item within liabilities or equity. Accordingly, in the consolidated statement of financial performance, the share of surplus or deficit attributable to NCI must be separately disclosed. Transactions between the group's entities are eliminated in full. This includes the offsetting of mutual receivables and payables (in the balance sheet), revenues and expenses (in the statement of financial performance), and cash flows (in the cash flow statement). It also includes the elimination of both double counting and economic transactions not yet realized with third parties (in the three statements mentioned). The procedures associated with full consolidation are explained in detail in Section 5.

---

[51] Stewart and Connolly (2022).

[52] See e.g. Mori (2016) and Krimpmann (2015) for detailed explanations.

Under **(2) proportional consolidation**, the assets, liabilities, revenues, expenses and cash flows of the controlling entity are once again fully included in the CFS. Those of the controlled entities, however, are included only to the extent of the controlling entity's portion in the equity of such controlled entities. Transactions between the group's entities are eliminated only to that same extent. Correspondingly, NCI are excluded from the CFS.

Strictly speaking, the **(3) equity method** (also called "one-line consolidation") is not a method of consolidation. Under this method, the equity investments held by an entity continue to be disclosed as financial assets in that entity's balance sheet, but they are measured in a particular manner. Initially, they are recognised at fair value, which normally coincides with cost at the point of acquisition. Subsequently, their carrying amount is increased or decreased to recognise the investor's share of the investee's surplus or deficit after the date of acquisition, the distribution of dividends from the investee to the investor, as well as other changes in the investee's equity that are not recognised in the investee's surplus or deficit (e.g., changes arising from the revaluation of PPE) – converging towards the investment's fair value. For the purposes of consolidation, using the equity method for an affiliated entity implies that, in the consolidated balance sheet, the controlling entity's interest in such affiliated entity is reported as a financial asset and that the value of such asset will change over time to reflect changes in the affiliated entity's equity. The affiliated entity's assets, liabilities, revenues, expenses and cash flows, conversely, will not be included in the consolidated statements. Hence, the label 'one-line consolidation'.

The impact of the three methods is exemplified in Table 11.1. The example deliberately ignores which method would be required by existing accounting standards and is only intended to highlight the differential impact of the three methods. In particular, the example shows that, even in a very simple situation, the resulting representations of an economic entity's financial position and performance are significantly different across the three methods.

Example of consolidation methods

Alpha is a primary government which holds 70% of the shares in Company Beta. Table 11.1 shows simplified statements of financial performance and balance sheets for Alpha and Beta. It also shows the relevant CFS under full consolidation, proportional consolidation, and the equity method. The example relies on several simplifying assumptions, including that (i) Alpha acquired the shares in Beta at the beginning of the financial year for which the statements are shown; (ii) the consideration paid by Alpha to purchase 70% of Beta's shares (700 EUR) coincides with 70% of the value of Beta's reported equity (70% * 1000 EUR); (iii) Alpha measures its financial investments at cost; and (iv) no mutual transactions occurred between Alpha and Beta.

For most items (cash, other non-cash assets, liabilities, revenues and expenses), the consolidated amount equals: (1) the sum of Alpha's and Beta's amounts under full consolidation; (2) the sum of Alpha's amount and 70% of Beta's amount under proportional consolidation, (3) Alpha's amount under the equity method. Alpha's investment in Beta is not presented in the consolidated balance sheet under full or proportional consolidation; with the equity method, conversely, it continues to be disclosed and its amount is adjusted to reflect Alpha's share of Beta's net income, with the adjustment being recorded as a revenue labelled "share of surplus of affiliated entities". Contributed capital and accumulated surplus / deficit are the same across the three methods. The presence of NCI is reported in the balance sheet only under full consolidation. Correspondingly, the 30 EUR portion of surplus attributable to NCI is included in net income only under full consolidation.

	Financial Statements		Consolidated financial statements		
	Alpha	Beta	Full	Proportional	Equity
---------- STATEMENT OF FINANCIAL PERFORMANCE ----------					
Revenues	8,000	900	8,900	8,630	8,000
Share of surplus of affiliated entities					70
Expenses	7,500	800	8,300	8,060	7,500
NET INCOME (*)	500	100	600	570	570
(*) Of which attributable to parent			570		
(*) Of which attributable to NCI			30		
---------- BALANCE SHEET ----------					
Alpha's equity investment in Beta	700	-	-		770
Other non-cash assets	10,000	1,500	11,500	11,050	10,000
Cash	1,000	500	1,500	1,350	1,000
TOTAL ASSETS	11,700	2,000	13,000	12,400	11,770
Contributed capital	3,700	1,000	3,700	3,700	3,700
Accumulated surpluses / deficits	800	-	800	800	800
Net income attributable to parent	500	100	570	570	570
NCI at the beginning of the period			300		
Net income attributable to NCI			30		
Liabilities	6,700	900	7,600	7,330	6,700
TOTAL LIABILITIES AND EQUITY	11,700	2,000	13,000	12,400	11,770

Table 11.1. Impact of different consolidation methods

The selection of consolidation methods is guided by accounting standards which, in turn, are inspired by specific **accounting theories**.

Accounting theories have already been addressed in Chapter 4 by explaining that they represent "a set of broad principles that provide a general frame of reference by which accounting practice can be evaluated and guide the development of new practices and procedures"[53]. Accounting research has relied on several theories to discuss the users and usefulness of CFS, including legitimacy, institutional, agency, and stakeholder theory.[54]

With respect to the choice of consolidation methods, reference is commonly made to three specific theories: (i) proprietary theory, (ii) parent company theory and (iii) entity theory. These theories were developed in the private sector, but they have also been discussed with reference to the public sector context.[55]

---

[53] See Chapter 4, p. 124.
[54] Santis, Grossi and Bisogno (2018).
[55] See also Chapter 4.

Proprietary theory views the group through the eyes of its ultimate owners only, that is, the shareholders of the controlling entity. The group's assets and liabilities are considered to be those of the owners and the CFS is viewed as an extension of the controlling entity's FS. Since NCI are not ultimate owners of the group, their share of equity is disregarded.[56] In terms of consolidation methods, this theory results in proportional consolidation.[57]

Parent company theory moves from the premise that, even in the presence of NCI, the controlling entity has control over the subsidiaries' assets and liabilities in full, rather than on a proportionate basis. In terms of consolidation methods, this theory results in full consolidation in the variant of disclosing partial goodwill. Variations exist as to the status of NCI and consequently their classification.[58] In particular, the holders of NCI can be alternatively viewed as a secondary set of owners or a particular class of lenders, with NCI being correspondingly classified within equity, among liabilities, or even in a dedicated class.[59]

Entity theory, finally, takes the perspective of the economic entity as a whole, as separate from its owners. The economic entity is viewed as having two classes of proprietary interests (controlling and non-controlling) which, however, are treated consistently for consolidation purposes, with no special treatment accorded to either. This perspective serves for all considerations of classification, measurement, and netting of assets and liabilities of the controlling and the controlled entities. In terms of consolidation methods, this

---

[56] See Kell (1953).

[57] See specifically for PSA e.g. Bisogno et al. (2015), p. 312.

[58] Measurement alternatives arise when the fair values of the subsidiary's assets and liabilities differ from the carrying values and in the presence of goodwill. These issues are tackled in Chapter 12.

[59] See e.g. Huefner & Largay III (1990) and specifically for PSA e.g. Bisogno et al. (2015), p. 312.

theory also results in full consolidation, with NCI being presented as a component of equity and full goodwill being disclosed.[60]

Traditionally, accounting standard setters have mainly found inspiration in parent company theory[61]. **Entity theory, however, is becoming increasingly influential** for being "fundamental to modern accounting as well as more appropriate, especially in the public sector".[62] CFS prepared in accordance with proprietary theory, on the contrary, are generally regarded as inappropriate information and decision-making tools[63] as they do not provide a complete insight into the fictitious single entity's financial position, performance and cash flows.

Consequently, **national and international accounting standards that prescribe consolidation on the basis of the control principle generally require the full consolidation of controlled entities. Proportional consolidation is usually limited to joint ventures, while the equity method may apply to associates and joint ventures**[64]. For the public sector, however, some national standard setters have extended the equity method to the consolidation of controlled entities. In some cases (e.g., Austria and France), the equity method has been introduced as an intermediate step towards full consolidation, while in others (e.g., Sweden and Switzerland) it appears to be a longer-term choice. The equity method has also been recommended for the consolidation of immaterial entities as well as entities whose activities are dissimilar from the controlling entity's. In this last respect, the full consolidation of controlled entities performing dissimilar activities and often characterized by 'strong balance sheets', such as national banks, financial intermediaries, or insurance companies, would mean

---

[60] See Moonitz (1942). Specifically for PSA, see e.g. Bisogno et al. (2015), p. 312.

[61] See e.g. Bergmann et al. (2016), p. 767.

[62] See e.g. Bisogno et al. (2015), p. 312.

[63] See e.g. Bisogno et al. (2015).

[64] Bergmann et al. (2016), p. 771. See example provided in Chapter 12.

that all the assets of these entities are included in the consolidated balance sheet. This could produce a misleading representation of the resources controlled by the economic entity. For this reason, Canada consolidates these entities using the equity method, while Austria and France outright exclude them from the CFS.[65]

Depending on the theory, the **objectives of consolidated financial reporting** are also different. Under entity theory, CFS are intended to provide a true and fair view of the group's position, performance and cash flows. Under parent company or proprietary theory, conversely, the true and fair view is largely limited to the parent's perspective, that is, the parent's own share or controlled part of assets, liabilities and net assets.

Generally, CFS have a pure **information function**. In contrast, according to some national accounting standards, FS also have a profit/revenue distribution function. In the municipal context, in particular, the frequent outsourcing of service delivery to public corporations hampers the transparency of local governments' FS. This stems from the fact that those unconsolidated (single entity) reports only present a partial view of the municipality's economic and financial activities, as the financial conditions of controlled entities, joint ventures and associates are not adequately considered.[66]

5. Procedures for full consolidation

As mentioned in Section 3, national and international accounting standards generally require the **full consolidation of controlled entities**.

---

[65] See e.g. Bergmann et al. (2016), p. 777 and 780; Bisogno at al. (2015), p. 321; Walker (2011) pp. 487 and 492-493.

[66] Tagesson (2009).

Usually, the economic entity will not have a common accounting system. Moreover, the entities to be consolidated may not be required or even allowed by local legislation to apply the same set of accounting standards in the preparation of their own single-entity FS. Therefore, at the end of each reporting period, the original FS (henceforth labelled '**FS I**') of the entities to be consolidated must preliminarily be[67]:

– harmonised to comply with the group's accounting policies, the reporting date of the group, and its currency, hence producing '**FS II**';
– prepared for consolidation, which may entail a remeasurement of the controlling entity's and/or the controlled entities' assets and liabilities. Different alternatives exist as to this remeasurement, including the acquisition method, the pooling of interest method, and the fresh start method. These three methods are depicted in Table 11.2. The most commonly used alternative is the acquisition method. The acquisition method requires the remeasurement of the controlled entities' assets and liabilities at their acquisition-date fair values, thus revealing hidden reserves (e.g., items of PPE for which the fair value exceeds the carrying value) and hidden burdens (e.g., underestimated provisions). In subsequent consolidation periods, it also requires the recognition of the relevant changes in value, as in the depreciation of hidden reserves. Importantly, the remeasurement may also add assets and liabilities that were not included in the original FS of the entities to be consolidated – typically, intangible assets and further provisions. The end result is labelled '**FS III**'.

---

[67] See Krimpmann (2015), pp. 116 ff.

Entity	Controlling entity	Controlled entity
Method	Valuation of assets/liabilities	
Pooling of interest method	Book value	Book value
Acquisition (or purchase) method	Book value	Fair value
Fresh start method	Fair value	Fair value

Table 11.2: Remeasurement alternatives for the purposes of consolidation

Subsequently, **consolidation procedures** (sometimes also called '**consolidation steps**' in the literature) are performed as specified in the remainder of this section. Importantly, at the end of each reporting period, the previous years' consolidation procedures must be repeated to establish the status quo at the beginning of the current reporting period, followed by the consolidation procedures for the current period. This is because, each year, the CFS will be based on the FS I for the current period, which do not incorporate the harmonisations and remeasurements performed in the previous periods to produce FS II, FS III and, on that basis, CFS.

Full consolidation, in particular, encompasses **four different consolidation procedures**, which are shortly explained in this section by also highlighting public sector specificities:[68]

1) Net assets/equity consolidation;
2) Debt consolidation;
3) Consolidation of revenues and expenses; and
4) Elimination of unrealized gains or losses.

(1) Net assets/equity consolidation is also known as 'capital consolidation'. Its purpose is to prevent the equity of the controlled

---

[68] IPSASs-based examples are presented in Chapter 12.

entities from being double-counted on the consolidated balance sheet: on the one hand, as the difference between the controlled entity's assets and liabilities; on the other hand, as the controlling entity's equity investment in the controlled entity, which already incorporates the value of the controlled entity's assets and liabilities. To this end, the (a) carrying amount of the controlling entity's investment in each controlled entity, as reported in the controlling entity's balance sheet, must be offset against (b) the controlling entity's portion of each controlled entity's equity. In this process, it is important to highlight that consolidation procedures operate on FS III. Under the acquisition method, as mentioned, this entails the remeasurement of the controlled entities' assets and liabilities at their acquisition-date fair values, which will also produce a remeasurement of the controlled entities' equity. Any difference between (a) and (b) is recognised as goodwill (if positive) or badwill/bargain purchase (if negative). Goodwill is an asset, while the nature and treatment of badwill/bargain purchase varies across sets of accounting standards.

In the course of **(2) debt consolidation**, intra-group receivables and payables must be eliminated. These include accounts receivable and payable stemming from the exchange of goods and services within the group as well as loans and interest receivable and payable stemming from intra-group financing relationships. Accruals and deferrals relating to intra-group transactions may also be involved. The aim is to avoid double counting and to eliminate the effects of intra-group transactions on the presentation of the economic entity's financial position, as such transactions would not exist if the single-entity idea was not a fiction.

In the simplest case, mutual receivables and payables have identical amounts and can be neutralized by simply 'omitting' them. When differences exist, they must be recognised in surplus or deficit in the period in which they occur (and rebooked in subsequent consolidation periods in net assets/equity). In this respect, a distinction can be drawn between 'real' and 'unreal' offsetting differences:[69]

- **Real offsetting differences** arise when the group's entities apply different recognition and measurement rules. Most of these differences are identified and reconciled at the beginning of the consolidation process, when the original FS of the groups' entities (FS I) must be adjusted to the group's accounting policies, as required by the principles of uniformity (FS II).
- **Unreal offsetting differences** are caused by accounting deficiencies such as wrong journal entries, incorrect uses of intra-group accounts, and timing differences whereby the two entities recognise the effects of a mutual transaction in different accounting periods (possibly due to different lengths of booking stop periods before the same balance sheet date).

Under the **(3) consolidation of revenues and expenses**, intra-group revenues and expenses must be eliminated. This procedure is similar to debt consolidation, but it relates to the statement of financial performance as opposed to the balance sheet/statement of financial position.

During this procedure, a particular offsetting difference in the public sector can result from **consumption taxes** such as a sales tax or VAT. The correct consolidation of intra-group transactions in which the seller must charge a consumption tax, but the buyer is not eligible for consumption tax deduction, is largely unclear. Various solutions are discussed and applied in practice. For example, the offsetting difference may remain in the expenses after consolidation, or it may be eliminated.[70]

---

[69] See Krimpmann (2015), pp. 278 ff.
[70] See e.g. Lorson et al. (2016), Note 715.

More generally, a public sector specific case of revenues and expenses consolidation is **tax consolidation**, which occurs whenever one of the consolidated entities pays taxes to another consolidated entity (e.g., a local authority).[71] To prepare CFS, the tax revenues (or expenses from tax refunds) of the local authority must be offset against the corresponding tax expenses (or income from tax refunds) of the other consolidated entity. Special features for tax consolidation arise, e.g., from combined federal, state and local taxes, whereby a public sector entity is entitled to collect a tax, but the relevant proceeds are shared among public sector entities at different government levels on a pro-rata basis. Combined federal, state and local taxes can be shown as liabilities from tax distribution. A further challenge in tax consolidation may arise from differences in the timing of recognition across the consolidated entities. These differences can result, for example, from the principle of asymmetric prudence: while the paying entity must recognise a corporate income tax expense as a provision (reduced by advanced tax payments) in the financial year when the taxed income (related to a taxable event) was earned, the receiving government may only recognise the relevant revenue once it has been sufficiently specified (e.g., with the publication of the tax assessment notice). In the course of consolidation, these offsetting differences of the current period will need to be reconciled, with an effect on surplus or deficit in the CFS (and, in subsequent consolidation periods, they will need to be rebooked in net assets/equity).

Another specific public sector application of revenues and expenses consolidation refers to **investment grants**, depending on how these grants are recorded by their recipient and by their provider. The provider will recognise a payable and, usually, an expense. The recipient will recognise a receivable; as for the account to be

---

[71] See e.g. Lorson et al. (2016), Notes 720 ff.

credited, depending on the underlying accounting norms, investment grants may alternatively be deducted from the acquisition or production cost of the subsidized items (net method) or recognised on the liabilities side as special items for investment grants or as deferred government grants (gross method). During consolidation, the provider's payable must be offset against the recipient's receivable. In addition, the provider's expense must also be eliminated. Correspondingly, when using the net method, the recipient's asset is to be remeasured to show its value without the grant's deduction; when using the gross method, the recipient's special item for investment grants or deferred government grants is to be eliminated. If any expenses or revenues arose from the investment grant in the reporting period, these also have to be reversed, with an effect on surplus or deficit.

As for grants in the form of **income subsidies**, the offsetting follows the general procedure for the consolidation of revenue and expenses.

Finally, the **4) elimination of unrealized gains or losses** deals with situations where a consolidated entity, after purchasing goods and services from another consolidated entity, capitalizes them as inventories, fixed assets, or intangible assets. In the preparation of its FS, the purchasing consolidated entity will measure these assets at its own acquisition costs. These costs will correspond to the selling consolidated entity's revenues, but not necessarily to the selling consolidated entity's acquisition or production costs. From the group's perspective, the selling consolidated entity's FS will incorporate a gain (or a loss) from the sale, but such gain or loss is unrealized because it was not generated in a sale to a third party. Correspondingly, the purchasing entity's FS will overstate (or understate) the value of the relevant assets because such assets were measured using the purchasing entity's acquisition cost (i.e., their book values include the gain/loss of the selling entity) as opposed to the selling entity's (and thus the group's) acquisition or production costs. During consolidation, the unrealized gain or loss must be eliminated, and the corresponding overstatement or understatement must be removed from the assets' book values.

6. Organizational challenges

The preparation and presentation of CFS pose several organizational challenges. The range and severity of these challenges will also depend on the local legal requirements with which a public sector entity must comply. This section presents a (non-exhaustive) list of challenges, with a particular focus on the public sector context:[72]

1) Implementation of consolidated financial reporting;
2) Initial consolidation;
3) Requirements of uniformity;
4) Timely organization of the consolidation process;
5) Coordination of audits.

The **(1) implementation of consolidated financial reporting** needs adequate planning. Consolidated financial reporting (CFR) can be viewed as the supreme discipline of accounting and financial reporting as it covers all kinds of economic transactions at several layers of an economic entity. Therefore, the tasks to be carried out by the controlling entity and by the other entities to be consolidated must be specified in advance, together with the relevant methodologies and responsibilities. Skilled personnel is needed,

---

[72] See also Krimpmann (2015) or Lorson, Poller and Haustein (2019) for more detailed explanations.

with experience in the application of consolidation methods and the ability to oversee the relevant consolidation areas in the economic entity. This creates a high demand for qualified personnel, especially for the public sector. It also implies increased labour, training and consulting expenses. The volume of data for consolidated accounting and the complexity of the relevant treatments also require significant investments on enhanced information technology systems and accounting software.[73]

With respect to **(2) initial consolidation**, a public sector peculiarity is that consolidation requirements are recent and so are, in fact, the requirements regarding the preparation of accrual-based financial reports. As a consequence, controlling entities will begin to produce CFS long after having obtained control of their affiliated entities. Moreover, they will generally have incomplete records of the relevant transactions; hence the frequent need for strong assumptions and simplifications, as the strict application of consolidation rules would require the remeasurement of the controlled entities' assets and liabilities at their fair value as of the acquisition date.

As mentioned in the previous section, the preparation of CFS involves specific **(3) requirements of uniformity** in that the financial statements of the individual entities to be consolidated must be adjusted to comply with the group's accounting policies, reporting date, and currency. In the public sector, the harmonisation of accounting policies can be particularly cumbersome. Not only can rules, standards and practices vary across entities.[74] Public sector groups exist where some entities still use only cash accounting, while others

---

[73] Bergmann et al. (2016), p. 766.

[74] See e.g. Walker (2011) for an in-depth analysis of the different (non-) recognition and valuation rules and practices across the jurisdictions that are consolidated in the Australian government's financial report.

use accrual accounting.[75] Alternatively, a primary government using accrual accounting may be required to apply PSA standards while its controlled entities, being established as joint stock corporations, must comply with private sector accounting standards.

To enforce uniformity, streamline the consolidation process, and improve the resulting quality of CFS, the controlling entity can issue a **consolidated accounts manual**. The manual should consider the group's overall features as well as its accounting structures and environment. On this basis, it should provide guidelines regarding the group's reporting date as well as its recognition, measurement, and disclosure policies. It may also prescribe a common chart of accounts. In the presence of foreign controlled entities, it will establish guidelines on language (of the report and of all communications concerning the report's preparation and presentation) and on currency conversion. Due to the importance and complexity of these issues, the manual should be documented in writing (at least in the group's main language) and agreed upon with the auditors.

A further challenge lies in the **(4) timely organization of the consolidation process** to comply with preparation, auditing and disclosure obligations and deadlines. To this end, a binding timetable should be drawn up and enforced for all controlled entities, joint ventures and associates.

Finally, with respect to the **(5) coordination of audits**, the audits of the FS of all controlled entities, joint ventures and associates must be coordinated with the audits of the controlling entity's FS and of the CFS, while ensuring compliance with national and local audit laws and regulations.

To conclude, it is important to notice that these challenges include one-off issues such as the initial consolidation and the initial

---

[75] Brusca and Montesinos (2009).

	Country					
	Austria	Finland	Germany	Italy	Portugal	UK
State of consolidated financial reporting	• Mandatory CFS at central level only • Ongoing transition to accrual accounting for all government levels. After completion: Mandatory CFS for central, state, and local governments[76]	• Central level: Consolidated central government financial statement (CCGFS) (less than 90 accounting entities) • Mandatory CFS for municipalities using the acquisition method or pooling of interest method[77]	Heterogeneous at central, state and local level (if accrual only): • Voluntary CFS at central and state level (currently prepared by only 3 federal states); • Mandatory CFS for municipalities[78] located in 12 of 16 federal states	• Mandatory CFS at regional and local level only • Ongoing transition to accrual accounting for all government levels. After completion: Mandatory CFS for central, regional, and local governments	• Mandatory CFS at central and local level	• Mandatory CFS at central and local level
WGA/WGFR	No	No	No	No	No (future plans)	Yes
Principle for scope of consolidation	Control	Control	Control	Control and financial dependence	Control	Control

[76] https://www.ris.bka.gv.at/GeltendeFassung.wxe?Abfrage=Bundesnormen&Gesetzesnummer=20009319 §23

[77] Referred to as "parity method": no goodwill or gains are recorded in the consolidation (See Oulasvirta in Brusca et al (2015), p. 73).

[78] With recently implemented exceptions for small local governments in some federal states.

| Notable exceptions | Only consolidation of directly controlled entities | CCGFS do not contain government funds, government utilities, state owned companies or universities | Controlled entities with dissimilar activities to those of the controlling entity in most jurisdictions are not consolidated | The conditions for the identification of controlled entities include references to financial dependence. Affiliated, non-controlled entities are included (with exceptions) in the CFS using proportional consolidation | | WGA does not include: Parliament, National Audit Office, Nationalised Banks WGA combines control and statistical perspectives to define scope of consolidation |

Table 11.3: Status quo of consolidated accounting in selected European countries (Adapted from: Brusca et al. (2015))

preparation of the consolidated accounts manual, but also recurring issues such as the maintenance of the manual. If accounting policies change or new accounting standards become effective, moreover, the manual must be updated and the transition procedures explained. These updates may also introduce modifications to CFR-related processes in terms of timing, performance, responsibilities, and auditing.

7. Conclusion

This chapter provides an introduction to terminology and processes related to the preparation of CFS. Due to the increased fragmentation of the public sector and the network of relationships connecting each public sector entity with other entities, CFS can enhance transparency and support decision-making in the public sector much better than FS can do.

Despite its complex technical nature, consolidated financial reporting can be seen as an important development in PSA and reporting. However, on an international scale, many different approaches exist to the definition of the consolidation scope, the definition of the reporting entity and the choice of consolidation methods.

As a summary of this chapter, Table 11.3 provides an overview about consolidated financial reporting in selected European countries. Similar to the status quo of financial reporting by individual entities as shown in Chapter 1, the current situation is quite heterogeneous. However, commonalities lie in the definition of the consolidation area according to the control concept. As stressed in this chapter, the UK can be seen to pursue the most consequent approach to CFS, that is, WGA/WGFR. Chapter 12 continues to explain consolidation methods by specifically drawing on IPSASs and providing some numerical examples.

Bibliographic references

AGGESTAM-PONTOPPIDAN, Caroline and ANDERNACK, Isabelle (2016) – Interpretation and application of IPSAS. Chichester: Wiley, ISBN: 978-1-119-01029-6.

BERGMANN, Andreas; GROSSI, Giuseppe; RAUSKALA, Iris and FUCHS, Sandro (2016) – Consolidation in the public sector: methods and approaches in Organisation for Economic Co-operation and Development countries. International Review of Administrative Sciences, 82(4), pp. 763-783.

BERGMANN, Andreas (2009) – Public Sector Financial Management, Harlow et al.: Prentice Hall, ISBN: 9780273713548.

BERGMANN, Andreas; GROSSI, Giuseppe; RAUSKALA, Iris and FUCHS, Sandro (2016) – Consolidation in the public sector: methods and approaches in Organisation for Economic Co-operation and Development countries. International Review of Administrative Sciences, 82(4), pp. 763-783.

BISOGNO, Marco; SANTIS, Serena and TOMMASETTI Aurelio (2015) – Public-Sector Consolidated Financial Statements: An Analysis of the Comment Letters on IPSASB's Exposure Draft No. 49, International Journal of Public Administration, 38, pp. 311-324.

BRUSCA, Isabel and MONTESINOS, Vicente (2009) – International experiences in whole of government financial reporting: lesson-drawing for Spain, Public Money & Management, 29(4), pp. 243-250.

BRUSCA, Isabel and MONTESINOS, Vicente (2010) – Developments in financial information by local entities in Europe, Journal of Public Budgeting, Accounting & Financial Management, 22(3), pp. 299-324.

BRUSCA, Isabel; CAPERCHIONE, Eugenio; COHEN, Sandra and MANES-ROSSI, Francesca (eds.) (2015) – Public Sector Accounting and Auditing in Europe – the Challenge of Harmonization, Basingstoke: Palgrave Macmillan, ISBN: 9781137461339.

CARINI, Cristian and TEODORI, Claudio (2021) – Debate: Public sector consolidated financial statements—the hybrid approach, Public Money & Management, 41(6), 432-433 https://doi.org/10.1080/09540962.2021.1883286

CHOW, Danny; DAY, Ronald; BASKERVILLE, Rachel; POLLANE, Raili and AGGESTAM, Caroline (2015) – Consolidated government accounts: How are they used?, Association of Chartered Certified Accountants.

CHOW, Danny; POLLANEN, Raili, BASKERVILLE, Rachel; AGGESTAM-PONTOPPIDAN, Caroline & DAY, Ronald (2019) – Usefulness of consolidated government accounts: A comparative study, Public Money & Management, 39(3), 175-185, DOI: 10.1080/09540962.2018.1535034

EUROSTAT. Manual on Government Deficit and Debt. Implementation of ESA 2010. 2019 edition.

GROSSI, Giuseppe and STECCOLINI, Ileana (2015) – Pursuing private or public accountability in the public sector? Applying IPSASs to define the reporting entity in municipal consolidation. International Journal of Public Administration, 38(4), pp. 325-334.

GROSSI, Giuseppe; MORI, Elisa and BARDELLI, Federica (2014) – From Consolidation to Segment Reporting in Local Government: Accountability Needs, Accounting Standards, and the Effect on Decision-Makers, Journal of Modern Accounting and Auditing, 10(1), pp. 32-46.

HEALD, David and GEORGIOU, George (2009) – Whole of government accounts developments in the UK: Conceptual, technical and timetable issues. Public Money & Management 29(4), pp. 219-227.

HOOD, Christopher (1995) – The New Public Management in the 1980s: Variations on a theme. Accounting, Organizations and Society 20(2-3): 93-109.

HUEFNER, R. J., & LARGAY, J. A. (1990) – Consolidated Financial Reporting: Accounting Issues, Financial Reporting Choices, And Managerial Implications. Journal of Managerial Issues, 2(1), 26-40.

KELL, Walter G. (1953) – Should the Accounting Entity Be Personified? The Accounting Review, 28(1), 40–43.

KRIMPMANN, Andreas (2015) – *Principles of Group Accounting under IFRS*. Chichester: Wiley, ISBN: 978-1-118-75141-1.

KUETING, Karlheinz and WEBER, Claus-Peter (2018) – Der Konzernabschluss, 14th ed., Stuttgart: Schäffer Poeschel, ISBN: 978-3-7910-3730-1.

LANDE, Eveline (1998) – The scope of accounting consolidation in the local public sector. In: CAPERCHIONE, Eugenio and MUSSARI, Riccardo (eds.) Comparative Issues in Local Government Accounting. London: Kluver, pp. 227-239. ISBN: 978-1-4615-4581-1.

LORSON, Peter; DOGGE, Bianca, HAUSTEIN, Ellen and WIGGER, Christina (2016) – Kommentierung zu Standards staatlicher Doppik (SsD), in: HOFBAUER, Peter & KUPSCH, Max (eds.): Rechnungslegung. Aufstellung, Prüfung und Offenlegung des Jahresabschlusses, Kommentar, 85. Ergänzungslieferung, Bonn: Beck, ISBN: 978-3-08-255800-3.

LORSON, Peter; POLLER, Jörg and HAUSTEIN, Ellen (2019) – Fallstudie zur Rechnungslegung – Vom nationalen Einzelabschluss zum IFRS-Konzernabschluss, Düsseldorf: Handelsblatt Fachmedien, ISBN: 978-394-7711147.

MOONITZ, Maurice (1942) – The Entity Approach to Consolidated Statements. The Accounting Review, 17(3), 236–242.

MUELLER, Gerhard G.; GERNON, Helen and MEEK, Gary K. (1997) – Accounting: An International Perspective, 4th ed., Boston MA: Irwin/McGraw-Hill, ISBN: 0-256-17082-7.

MUNTER, Paul (1999) – Business Combinations: Are You Ready for Purchase Accounting?, Journal of Corporate Accounting & Finance, Spring 1999, pp. 19-25.

PUBLIC ACCOUNTS COMMITTEE (2021) – Whole of Government Accounts 2018– 19. https://committees.parliament.uk/publications/4339/documents/ 44418/default/

SANTIS, Serena; GROSSI, Giuseppe and BISOGNO, Marco (2018) – Public sector consolidated financial statements: a structured literature review, Journal of Public Budgeting, Accounting & Financial Management, Vol. 30 Issue: 2, pp. 230-251.

SANTIS, Serena; GROSSI, Giuseppe and BISOGNO, Marco (2019): Drivers for the voluntary adoption of consolidated financial statements in local governments, Public Money & Management, DOI: 10.1080/09540962.2019.1618072

STEWART, Elaine and CONNOLLY, Ciaran (2022) – New development: Ten years of consolidated accounts in the United Kingdom public sector—taking stock, Public Money & Management https://doi.org/10.1080/09540962.2022.2031647

TAGESSON, Torbjörn (2009) – Arguments for proportional consolidation: The case of the Swedish local government. Public Money and Management, 29(4), pp. 215-216.

WALKER, Robert Graham (2009) – Public sector consolidated statements - An assessment, Abacus, 45(2), pp. 171-220.

WALKER, Robert Graham (2011) – Issues in the Preparation of Public Sector Consolidated Statements, Abacus, 47(4), pp. 477-500.

Additional readings

BRUSCA, Isabel; CAPERCHIONE, Eugenio; COHEN, Sandra and MANES-ROSSI, Francesca (eds.) (2015) – Public Sector Accounting and Auditing in Europe – the Challenge of Harmonization, Basingstoke: Palgrave Macmillan, ISBN: 978-1-137-46133-9.

Discussion topics

- Reasons for consolidated financial reporting in the public sector
- Information needs fulfilled by public sector CFS
- Consolidation methods: Which suits best the public sector?
- Single entity fiction versus the group as an economic (and service delivery) entity

CHAPTER 12
CONSOLIDATION METHODS

Ellen Haustein, Peter C. Lorson
both University of Rostock, Germany
ellen.haustein@uni-rostock.de
https://orcid.org/0000-0002-1218-1043
peter.lorson@uni-rostock.de
https://orcid.org/0000-0002-2699-5451

Eugenio Anessi-Pessina
Università Cattolica del Sacro Cuore, Milan, Italy
eugenio.anessi@unicatt.it
https://orcid.org/0000-0002-4660-5457

Summary

This chapter aims to illustrate consolidated financial reporting (CFR) under IPSAS. Public sector combinations according to IPSAS are introduced. The process of CFR is explained by illustrating full consolidation comprising the four consolidation procedures. The relevant steps are illustrated by short case examples. The application of the equity method is also presented and exemplified. This IPSAS-focused chapter informs about when consolidated financial statements (CFS) must be prepared, which entities must be included and by which methods, how to set up the accounting records for consolidation, and what consolidation procedures must be applied.

Chapter 12 complements Chapter 11 in a special regulated (IPSAS) setting.

Keywords

Consolidation, consolidated financial reporting, consolidation methods, full consolidation, equity method, public sector combinations, goodwill

1. Introduction

The preceding Chapter 11 introduced important notions and terms with respect to consolidated financial statements (CFS). It also highlighted conceptual problems related to the public sector. The consolidation methods and accompanying procedures were shortly introduced and explained, but without a focus on any specific set of accounting standards.

This chapter, conversely, is devoted to consolidation under International Public Sector Accounting Standards (IPSASs). Thereby, the terms explained in Chapter 11 serve as a basis. The steps in the consolidation process are illustrated by short case examples drawn from the municipality of Eucity, which has already been the subject of the case study presented in Chapter 10, which focused on single entity financial statements. Whereas the financial statements (FS) presented in Chapter 10 made reference to the municipality of Eucity *per se*, this chapter focuses on the CFS for Eucity's economic entity[1], i.e., the municipality and its controlled entities, joint ven-

---

[1] The term 'economic entity' might be somewhat misleading in the public sector context since these entities do not strive for profits and have other purposes than private sector entities. In this regard, the term 'service providing entity' would be more suitable. To stay within the commonly used accounting terminology, however 'economic entity' is used throughout the chapter.

tures, and associates. The complexity of the consolidation process prevents the presentation of a full case study. Therefore, the chapter includes only selected examples.

After this IPSAS-focused chapter, readers will know when IPSAS CFS must be prepared, which entities must be included and by which methods, how to set up the accounting records for consolidation and what consolidation procedures must be applied.

The chapter is structured as follows. Section 2 provides further definitions and background information about consolidated financial reporting according to IPSAS. In particular, public sector combinations (PSC) are introduced. Section 3 gives an overview about the IPSASs that are relevant for consolidated financial reporting. The process of consolidated financial reporting is the subject of Section 4, which presents the IPSAS' control concept, the principles of uniformity, and the steps for initial and subsequent consolidation. In Section 5, full consolidation and its relevant consolidation procedures are explained through examples. Section 6 introduces the application of the equity method. Section 7 concludes the chapter.

2. Definitions and background

Public sector entities prepare and present their own single-entity FS. For a public sector entity which prepares its accounts in accordance with the accrual-based IPSASs and holds investments in one or more controlled entities, (significantly influenced) associates, or (jointly controlled) joint ventures, these single-entity FS are called **separate financial statements** (SFS) (IPSAS 34.8). In the entity's SFS, such investments are accounted for at cost, as financial instruments according to IPSAS 29/41, or using the equity method as described in IPSAS 36 (IPSAS 34.12).

If the public sector entity controls one or more entities, moreover, it must also prepare and present CFS for the economic entity (i.e., group) as a whole (IPSAS 35.5)[2]. CFS are FS of an economic entity in which the assets, liabilities, net assets/equity, revenues, expenses, and cash flows of the controlling and the controlled entities are presented as those of a single economic unit (single entity fiction; IPSAS 35.14).

Similar to FS,[3] **a complete set of IPSAS CFS consists of:**

a) A statement of financial position;
b) A statement of financial performance;
c) A statement of changes in net assets/equity;
d) A cash flow statement;
e) A comparison of budget and actual amounts (either as a separate FS or as a budget column in the FS), if the underlying/combined entities make their approved budgets publicly available;
f) Notes, and
g) Comparative information.

In general, **an economic entity is formed through a public sector combination (PSC)**.[4] A PSC is the bringing together of separate operations into one – possibly fictitious – public entity (IPSAS 40.5), where such separate operations may or may not retain their legal form. An operation is an "integrated group of activities and assets and/or liabilities that is capable of being managed or

---

[2] For entities that prepare CFS, in fact, the preparation of SFS is not required by IPSAS, but it may be mandatory under local regulations (IPSAS 34.2).

[3] See Chapter 8.

[4] However, mostly in the public sector, the group will already exist before initial consolidation.

conducted for the purpose of achieving an entity's objectives, by providing goods and/or services" (IPSAS 40.5).[5]

PSC may occur either by mutual agreement or by compulsion (e.g., through legislation). IPSAS 40 contains no provisions or restrictions regarding the legal structure of PSC or the abandonment of the legal capacity of the entities to be combined (IPSAS 40 AG1). The public entity that is formed through a PSC can be either a new single reporting entity or an economic reporting entity consisting of several reporting entities retaining their legal form (IPSAS 40 AG2). Depending on which type of entity results from the PSC, the combination will be accounted for at the level of FS or CFS.

Two forms of PSC need to be distinguished: amalgamations and acquisitions (IPSAS 40.5). This distinction also affects how consolidation is performed.

An **amalgamation** is a PSC (IPSAS 40.5) in which:

a) no party to the combination gains control of one or more operations; or
b) one party to the combination gains control over one or more operations, and the economic substance of the combination is that of an amalgamation.

As a special case, a combination under common control is also considered as an amalgamation. This case occurs if all entities or operations involved in the combination are controlled by the same entity before and after the combination (IPSAS 40.5).

---

[5] In this respect, there is a terminological difference to IFRS 3, as the term business is used in IFRS 3 instead of operation. Also, in contrast to IFRS 3.2c, also combinations under common control are within the scope of IPSAS 40.4/13c.

An **acquisition** occurs when a party to the combination obtains control of one or more operations and there is evidence that the combination is not an amalgamation (IPSAS 40.5).

The classification of a PSC as an amalgamation or an acquisition, therefore, is performed in two steps (Figure 12.1). The first step is to assess whether control over the operations is gained by one of the parties involved. For the definition of control, reference is made to IPSAS 35 (see Subsection 4.1). If no party gains control, the PSC is an amalgamation. Otherwise, a second step is required to analyse the economic substance of the combination. This analysis is based on two criteria relating respectively to the consideration paid and to the decision-making process which led to the PSC (IPSAS 40.12 and .13).

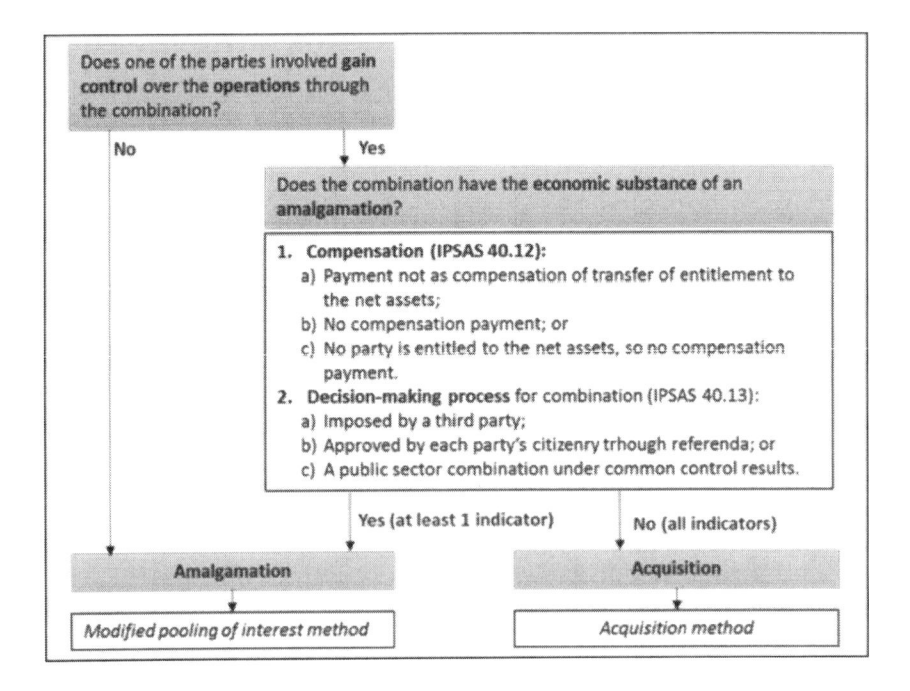

```
Does one of the parties involved gain
control over the operations through
the combination?
       │                    │
       No                   Yes
       │                    │
       │         Does the combination have the economic substance of an
       │         amalgamation?
       │         
       │         1. Compensation (IPSAS 40.12):
       │            a) Payment not as compensation of transfer of entitlement to
       │               the net assets;
       │            b) No compensation payment; or
       │            c) No party is entitled to the net assets, so no compensation
       │               payment.
       │         2. Decision-making process for combination (IPSAS 40.13):
       │            a) Imposed by a third party;
       │            b) Approved by each party's citizenry through referenda; or
       │            c) A public sector combination under common control results.
       │                    │
       │        Yes (at least 1 indicator)    No (all indicators)
       │                    │                        │
   Amalgamation                              Acquisition
       │                                             │
Modified pooling of interest method          Acquisition method
```

Figure 12.1: Indicators to distinguish between amalgamations and acquisitions (IPSAS 40)

Each criterion is operationalized by three indicators to be fulfilled either individually or jointly (IPSAS 40.9). If at least one indicator is true (1.a to 1.c or 2.a to 2.c), evidence exists that the PSC is an amalgamation. This is the case, for example, when a PSC is enforced by third parties without the involvement of the combined entities (IPSAS 40 AG32). Conversely, if the entities involved participate voluntarily in the decision (IPSAS 40 AG32) in order to exert a certain influence on the conditions for the combination (IPSAS 40 AG33), the classification of the PSC as an amalgamation is less straightforward. Importantly, there can be PSC in which no consideration is paid (Indicator 1.b), but which have the economic substance of an acquisition ('non-exchange acquisitions'), as in the case of forced nationalizations, donations, bequests, or bailouts (IPSAS 40.93, IPSAS 40 AG 29-30).

An **amalgamation** is accounted for by applying the **modified pooling of interest method** (IPSAS 40.15) when presenting the FS of the new reporting entity. Conversely, for an **acquisition**, the use of the **acquisition method** is prescribed (IPSAS 40.58). The difference between these two methods lies primarily in the remeasurement of assets and liabilities, as already addressed in Chapter 11. This Chapter 12 refers specifically to those PSC that (i) qualify as acquisitions and (ii) bring together into one public economic entity separate operations that retain their legal capacity, consequently requiring the preparation of CFR. Subsection 5.1 illustrates the application of the acquisition method.

3. Overview about relevant IPSASs

Table 12.1 provides an overview of the IPSASs that are relevant for consolidated financial reporting.

IPSAS	Scope	Excluded from the scope	Corresponding IAS /IFRS
35. Consolidated financial statements	Preparation and presentation of **CFS for the economic entity** (*inter alia* by reference to IPSAS 40)	Accounting requirements for PSCs Postemployment benefit plans (IPSAS 39) Controlling entities that are investment entities	IFRS 10
36. Investments in associates and joint ventures	Accounting for investments in **associates** and **joint ventures** which are based on quantifiable ownership interests	Investments which are not based on a quantifiable ownership interest	IAS 28
37. Joint arrangements	Determining the type of joint arrangement in which the entity is involved and accounting for the rights and obligations of a **joint operation**	None	IFRS 11
38. Disclosure of interests in other entities	Disclosing information about **interests in controlled** consolidated and unconsolidated entities, **joint arrangements**, **associates** as well as **unconsolidated structured entities**	Postemployment benefit plans (IPSAS 39) Separate financial statements (with exceptions) Interest in another entity that is accounted for in accordance with IPSAS 41	IFRS 12
40. Public sector combinations	Accounting for PSC, i.e., the **bringing together of separate operations into one public sector entity,** which can be a single entity or a (fictitious) economic entity. Classification of PSC as **amalgamations** or **acquisitions** and corresponding accounting treatments	Accounting for the formation of a joint arrangement in the FS of the joint arrangement Acquisition or receipt of an asset /group of assets or assumption of a liability / group of liabilities that do not constitute an operation Acquisition of investment entities	IFRS 3

Table 12.1: Overview of IPSASs relating to consolidation

The most relevant rules for consolidation can be found in IPSASs 35, 36, and 37. Each of these standards was issued in

2015 and has been effective since reporting periods beginning from 1st Jan 2017. These three standards, however, do not specify how to perform net assets/equity consolidation, that is, offsetting the carrying amount of the controlling entity's investment in each controlled entity against the controlling entity's portion of net assets/equity of such controlled entity. These prescriptions are contained in **IPSAS 40**, which became effective on 1st Jan 2019 and requires the use of the "acquisition method of accounting" (IPSAS 40.58). Of course, the IPSAS conceptual framework serves as a guideline for the definition, recognition, and measurement of FS items, although its use is not mandatory.[6]

4. Process of consolidated financial reporting

From a legal and organizational perspective, the process of consolidated financial reporting for a public sector entity that presents IPSAS CFS comprises the following **steps for initial consolidation**:

1. **Verify that the entity is required by IPSAS to prepare and present CFS** (i.e., check for the existence of at least one controlled entity);
2. **Define the consolidation area**[7] (i.e., determine which entities are to be included in the CFS and by which consolidation methods);
3. **Develop a consolidated accounts manual** to achieve and maintain uniformity by stating the group's reporting date and detailing its recognition, measurement, and disclosure policies (esp. when IPSASs provide explicit options);

---

[6] See Chapters 1 and 8.

[7] Also referred to as scope of consolidation.

4. **Assign responsibilities**, e.g.: at the individual entity's level, harmonisation of the entity's FS with the group's reporting date and accounting policies (FS II); at the group's level, currency conversion of FS (FS II), remeasurement of assets and liabilities at fair value with the identification of hidden reserves and burdens (FS III), and consolidation procedures;
5. **Perform initial consolidation** by applying the consolidated accounts manual (Step 3) and completing the required consolidation procedures (according to the distribution of responsibilities decided in Step 4).

In the **subsequent reporting periods**, the controlling entity:

6. May **review** and **update** the consolidation area (Step 2), the consolidated accounts manual (Step 3), and the allocation of responsibilities (Step 4);
7. **Complies with the need for continuity in CFS** over successive periods. Similar to FS, the CFS for any given period are conceptually the result of the consolidated balance sheet for the previous period and the transactions of the current period. In the absence of a consolidated accounting processing system which ensures the continuity of consolidated accounting data,[8] however, the preparation of CFS for any given period must be based on the FS I for the current period, which do not incorporate the harmonisations and remeasurements performed in the previous periods to produce FS II, FS III and, on that basis, CFS. Therefore, the need for continuity in CFS requires the **repetition of all consolidation steps performed in the previous reporting periods** (i.e., initial consolidation as well as subsequent consolidation for the previous reporting

---

[8] This will be the usual case for public sector groups.

periods in net assets/equity) in order to achieve the status quo as at the end of the previous reporting period;
8. **Implements the subsequent consolidation** for the current reporting period.

This section addresses Steps 1 to 4. More specifically, the requirement to prepare and present CFS (i.e., Step 1) is explained in Subsection 4.1; the scope of consolidation (i.e., Step 2) is addressed in Subsection 4.2; and the principles of uniformity (as a key component of the consolidated accounts manual and as enforced through the allocation of responsibilities, i.e., Steps 3 and 4) are covered in Subsection 4.3. In addition, Subsection 4.4 provides an overview of the consolidation procedures under full consolidation (Steps 5 to 8, see Figure 12.2). Such procedures are then presented in more detail in Section 5.

4.1. Requirement to prepare and present CFS

A controlling public sector entity is required to present CFS (IPSAS 35.5). Therefore, a public sector entity needs to verify whether it controls at least one other entity (IPSAS 35.18). According to IPSAS 35.20, three conditions must be jointly fulfilled for **control** to exist. Specifically, the entity must have:

a) **Power** over another entity;
b) **Exposure**, or **rights**, to **variable benefits** from its involvement with the other entity; and
c) The **ability** to **use** its **power to affect** the nature or amount of the **benefits**.

Power is defined as arising from existing rights that give the controlling entity the current ability to **direct the relevant financial**

and operating activities of the controlled entity (IPSAS 35.24), that is, the activities that significantly affect the nature or amount of the benefits that the controlling entity can derive from its involvement with the controlled entity. The rights can lie in voting rights, e.g. granted by equity instruments, but they can also result from binding agreements. Power may exist even if the rights to direct are not exercised in the reporting period (IPSAS 35.27). However, IPSAS 35.26 explicitly states that rights stemming from regulatory control or economic dependence[9], *per se*, do not give rise to power. In other words, budget dependence, by itself, is not a sufficient condition for inclusion in the area of consolidation.

Benefits are variable when they may vary as a result of the controlled entity's performance. The **variable benefits can be positive or negative, financial or non-financial** (IPSAS 35.30). Examples of **financial benefits** are the typical returns on investment such as dividends or similar distributions (IPSAS 35.32). Also, the possibility that a payment may not be made is considered a variable benefit. **Non-financial benefits** can lie, for example, in specialized knowledge, improved outcomes or more efficient delivery of outcomes, or higher levels of service quality (IPSAS 35.33).

The third and final criterion is the **link between power and benefits.** This means that the controlling entity must have the ability to use its power to affect the nature or amount of the benefits from its involvement with the controlled entity (IPSAS 35.35). In this respect, the mere existence of congruent objectives is insufficient. For control to exist, the controlling entity must have the ability to direct the controlled entity to further the controlling entity's objectives (IPSAS 35.36).

---

[9] "Economic dependence may occur when: (a) An entity has a single major client and the loss of that client could affect the existence of the entity's operations; or (b) An entity's activities are predominantly funded by grants and donations and it receives the majority of its funding from a single entity" (IPSAS 35 AG41).

A controlling entity must present CFS, but it is **exempted from this obligation** if it jointly meets all of the following conditions (IPSAS 35.5):

a) It is itself a controlled entity – provided that the information needs of users are met by its controlling entity's CFS and that none of its other owners (if they exist) objects;
b) Its debt or equity instruments are not traded in a public market;
c) It did not file, nor is it in the process of filing, its FS with a securities commission in order to issue any class of instruments in a public market; and
d) It has an ultimate or any intermediate controlling entity that produces publicly available FS that comply with IPSAS.

4.2. Scope of consolidation

To present CFS, a controlling entity must define its **consolidation area in a narrow and a broad sense**, as well as choose the appropriate **consolidation methods**[10]. The relevant IPSAS prescriptions are summarized in Table 12.2.

Type of influence	Type of entity	IPSAS	Method of consolidation
Controlling influence	Controlled entity	35	Full consolidation
Joint controlling influence	Joint venture (as defined in IPSAS 37)	36	Equity method
Significant influence	Associate entity		

Table 12.2: Overview of IPSAS prescriptions concerning consolidation area and methods

---

[10] See Chapter 11.

Controlled entities must be consolidated in full regardless of whether control is direct or indirect and regardless of the presence of non-controlling interests (NCI). The definition of control was presented in Subsection 4.1 and full consolidation according to IPSAS 35 is explained in Section 5.

Joint control is defined by IPSAS 37.12 as "the **sharing of control of an arrangement**, which exists only when decisions about the relevant activities require the **unanimous consent** of the parties sharing control." A prerequisite is a binding arrangement (IPSAS 37.10) between at least one entity inside and another outside the area of consolidation. This binding arrangement can be in the form of a contract or documented discussions between the parties, but it can also result from statutory mechanisms such as legislative or executive authority (IPSAS 37.8). A **joint arrangement** gives at least two parties joint control of the arrangement (IPSAS 37.10) and it can qualify as either a joint operation or a joint venture (IPSAS 37.11). In a **joint operation**, the jointly controlling parties have rights to the assets, and obligations for the liabilities, relating to the arrangement (IPSAS 35.7). In contrast, for a **joint venture**, the parties have **rights to the net assets** of the arrangement (IPSAS 35.7). A joint arrangement that is not structured through a separate vehicle is always classified as a joint operation (IPSAS 37 AG16). A joint arrangement that is structured through a separate vehicle is classified as either a joint operation or a joint venture depending on the legal form of the separate vehicle, the terms of the binding arrangement and, when relevant, any other facts and circumstances (IPSAS 37 AG19-21). In the presence of joint operations, each joint operator will proportionally recognize its share of the operation's assets, liabilities, revenues, and expenses in its own FS (IPSAS 37.23). Conversely, **investments in joint ventures will be recognized in the joint venturer's CFS using the equity method** in accordance with IPSAS 36 (IPSAS 37.27 and IPSAS 36.22).

Significant influence "is the power to participate in the financial and operating policy decisions of another entity, but is not control or joint control of those policies". An entity over which another entity exercises significant influence is said to be the latter entity's **associate** (IPSAS 36.8). Significant influence is assessed based on judgement on the nature of the relationship between the investor and the investee. Its presence is **presumed** if the investor **holds**, directly or indirectly, **at least 20% of the voting power** of the investee. Conversely, if it holds less, a rebuttable presumption must be considered: significant influence is presumed not to exist, unless the opposite can be clearly demonstrated (IPSAS 36.11). Besides voting power, **other indicators of significant influence** are e.g. representation on the investee's board of directors, participation in policy-making processes, or interchange of managerial personnel (IPSAS 36.12). IPSAS 36 only applies to "those associates in which an entity holds a quantifiable ownership interest either in the form of a shareholding or other formal equity structure or in another form in which the entity's interest can be measured reliably" (IPSAS 36.10). Under these circumstances, **the investment in an associate is recognized by applying the equity method** (IPSAS 36.16), with exemptions similar to IPSAS 35.5 (IPSAS 36.23).

Finally, **investments** providing no controlling influence, joint control, or significant influence are recognized in the CFS as financial instruments according to IPSAS 29/41, which is not further addressed in this chapter.

From the date on which the controlling entity obtains control, joint control, or significant influence over another entity, this latter entity must be included in the CFS. The obligation to present CFS starts when the reporting entity becomes a controlling entity and ceases when the entity is no longer a controlling entity (IPSAS 35.39), regardless of whether it continues to hold investments in joint ventures or associates.

4.3. Principles of uniformity

CFS present the group as a fictitious single entity and must consequently comply with uniformity principles. As described in Chapter 11[11], the consolidated accounts manual prepared by the controlling entity can support this requirement. The principles of uniformity usually encompass:

1. Uniform reporting dates;
2. Uniform accounting policies (recognition, measurement, and disclosure); and
3. Uniform reporting currency.

The **(1) reporting dates** of the controlling entity's FS, the controlled entities' FS, and the CFS should be the same. If the reporting date of a controlled entity differs, either (i) additional FS for that controlled entity are prepared, solely for the purpose of consolidation, as of the same date as the CFS, or (ii) the controlled entity's most recent FS are used, despite the different date, but only after adjusting them for the effects of significant transactions and events that occurred between the dates of the controlled entity's FS and of the CFS (IPSAS 35.46). Should an associate or a joint venture have a different reporting date, the most recent available FS are to be used, but again only after (i) obtaining additional information as of the same date as the CFS or (ii) adjusting for the effects of significant transactions or events that occurred between the two dates (IPSAS 36.36).

When preparing CFS, the controlling entity is required to use **(2) uniform accounting policies** "for like transactions and other events in similar circumstances" (IPSAS 35.38, IPSAS 36.37). Thereby, the consolidated entities must either (i) adopt these **uniform recognition, measurement, and disclosure policies** in the preparation

---
[11] See Chapter 11.6.

of their (original) FS (i.e., FS I), to the extent that this is possible under existing (national/local) regulations, or they need to (ii) make appropriate adjustments to their FS in preparation for consolidation (FS II).[12] Although IPSAS 35.38/36.37 require the use of uniform accounting policies, there are no clear prescriptions that this also includes uniform presentation, such as the use of common classifications and denominations in the FS as well as a common definition of what falls into each FS item. Under the fiction of the single entity (IPSAS 35.14), however, an explicit regulation is unnecessary and uniform presentation is understood to be mandatory. In this respect, IPSAS 1 applies, with its guidelines on the general features, structure, and content of FS, including that the presentation and classification of items must be maintained consistently over all reporting periods (IPSAS 1.42 f.). The uniformity principle for recognition, measurement, and disclosure applies equally to explicit and factual options, where the latter result from regulatory gaps, the interpretation of indefinite IPSAS terms, and the use of estimates or other discretionary decisions.

Finally, whenever a consolidated entity's reporting currency differs from the CFS's reporting currency, a **(3) currency conversion** is required. Basically, IPSAS 4 applies.

After the uniformity of the FS has been ensured by preparing **FS II** for each entity to be consolidated, Steps 1-4 as described in the introduction of this Section 4 are completed and the proper consolidation process can start.

4.4. Overview about the process of full consolidation

Before presenting full consolidation in Section 5 and the equity method in Section 6, Figure 12.2 provides an overview of full consolidation over

---

[12] See Chapter 11 for further explanations about the different levels of FS.

two consecutive reporting periods, with a focus on the balance sheet (BS). The figure assumes that the reporting period coincides with the calendar year and that the controlled entity is acquired on Jan 1, 20X1. On such date, the controlled entity's BS (BS I) must be adjusted to comply with the principles of uniformity, which yields BS II. Subsequently, the acquisition method of capital consolidation (according to IPSAS 40) requires that the assets and liabilities of the controlled entity be remeasured at fair value, which results in BS III of the controlled (not the controlling) entity. On this basis, the BS items of all consolidated entities are added up line by line, resulting in an 'aggregated' or 'combined' BS. From this, the procedures of full consolidation are implemented to produce the consolidated BS as at Jan 1, 20X1. As described in Step 7 of the consolidation process, these procedures need to be repeated at the end of every reporting period to then proceed with that period's subsequent consolidation. This is also depicted in Figure 12.2, which additionally shows that the controlled entity is usually responsible only for the preparation of its own BS I and II.

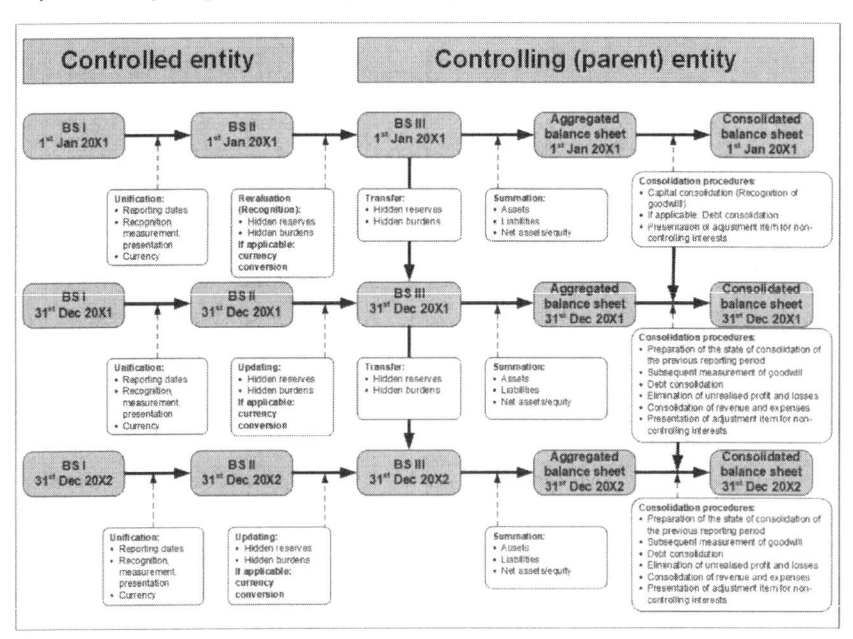

Figure 12.2: Process of full consolidation
(Source: Lorson, Poller and Haustein, 2019)

5. Full consolidation (initial and subsequent consolidations)

IPSAS 35.40 outlines the consolidation procedures for controlled entities. Full consolidation is required. To this end, the first step is that all like items of assets, liabilities, net assets/equity, revenues, expenses, and cash flows of the controlling entity's FS II are summed line by line with those of the controlled entities' FS III (IPSAS 35.40a). As shown in Figure 12.2, this results in an 'aggregated' or 'combined' FS. The next step is net assets/equity consolidation (also called 'capital consolidation') (IPSAS 35.40b), which is explained in Subsection 5.1. Finally, all intra-economic entity assets, liabilities, net assets/equity, revenues, expenses, and cash flows (i.e., those relating to transactions within the group) must be eliminated (IPSAS 35.40c), as described in Subsections 5.2 to 5.4. Each of these consolidation procedures was already introduced in Chapter 11. In this chapter, the focus is on providing further details and short examples.

5.1. Capital consolidation

As explained in Section 2, for PSC that are categorized as acquisitions, the **acquisition method of accounting** must be used for initial recognition (IPSAS 40.58). This method includes four steps (IPSAS 40.59):

a) Identification of the acquirer;
b) Determination of the acquisition date;
c) Recognition and measurement of the identifiable assets acquired, of the liabilities assumed, and of any NCI in the acquired operation;
d) Recognition and measurement of goodwill.

The **acquirer** is the party that obtains control of the acquired operations (IPSAS 40.60).

The **acquisition date** is the date on which control of the acquired operations is obtained (IPSAS 40.62). This is generally the "closing date", that is, the date on which the acquirer legally transfers the relevant consideration and/or acquires the transferred assets and liabilities (IPSAS 40.63).

All the **identifiable assets acquired** and the **liabilities assumed** – including assets and liabilities that were not recognized in the acquired entity's balance sheet (e.g. intangible assets such as patents that were developed internally with the related costs being charged to expense (IPSAS 40.67)) – must be recognized and **measured at their fair values at the date of acquisition** (IPSAS 40.72), separately from any goodwill (IPSAS 40.64). Specific rules exist for:

- The recognition of contingent liabilities (IPSAS 40.76-77);
- The recognition and measurement of (i) taxation items waived as part of the terms of the acquisition (IPSAS 40.78-79), (ii) liabilities and assets from employee benefit arrangements (IPSAS 40.80), (iii) indemnification assets (IPSAS 40.81-82), and (iv) leases in which the acquiree is the lessee (IPSAS 40.82A-82B); and
- The measurement of (i) reacquired rights (IPSAS 40.83) and (ii) share-based payment transactions (IPSAS 40.84).

As for **NCI**, a choice is offered between the **partial goodwill method** and the **full goodwill method** (IPSAS 40.73). The partial goodwill method measures NCI according to their "share in the recognized amounts of the acquired operation's identifiable net assets", as remeasured at their acquisition-date fair values. The full goodwill method measures NCI according to their fair value at the acquisition date, which can be determined on the basis of a quoted price on an active market or, if not available, using other valuation techniques (IPSAS 40 AG91). In this last respect, an extrapolation based on the purchase price paid by the acquirer or the fair value of the acquirer's interest may be inappropriate as these amounts may include a control premium (IPSAS 40 AG92). Importantly, the underlying difference between the partial and the full goodwill methods is that the latter recognizes goodwill in full (including the portion pertaining to NCI), while the former recognizes it only to the extent that it pertains to the controlling entity.

Concerning **goodwill**, finally, its amount is determined on the basis of the previous steps by using the following computation:

+ Controlling entity's interest in the acquired entity (consideration paid)	A
– Controlling entity's share of acquired entity's remeasured net assets	$B = b1 \pm b2$
+ Controlling entity's share of acquired entity's net assets, at book value	$b1$
± Controlling entity's share of acquired entity's hidden reserves/burdens	$b2$
= Goodwill pertaining to controlling entity (Partial Goodwill)	$C = A - B$
+ Goodwill pertaining to NCI	$D = d1 - d2$
+ Fair value of NCI at acquisition	$d1$
– NCI's share of acquired entity's remeasured net assets	$d2$
= Full Goodwill	$E = C + D$

More precisely, goodwill (regardless of whether it is calculated according to the partial or the full method) is recognized as such only (i) if the computation yields a positive amount (IPSAS 40.85) and (ii) to the extent that the acquisition is estimated to produce future favourable changes to the acquirer's net cash flows (IPSAS 40.86). Goodwill related to service potential rather than cash flows cannot be recognized (IPSAS 40 AG93). In subsequent periods, goodwill is not amortized, but it must be tested for impairment in accordance with IPSAS 26 "Impairment of Cash-Generating Assets" (IPSAS 26.76-97).

If the computation yields a positive amount, but to the extent that the acquisition is not estimated to produce future favourable changes to the acquirer's net cash flows, the amount is recognized as a loss in surplus or deficit (IPSAS 40.86).

Finally, should the computation yield a negative amount, a review must be performed to ensure that all the assets and liabilities involved in the acquisition were identified and measured correctly (IPSAS 40.90). If the amount is confirmed to be negative, the acquisition is recorded according to the '**bargain purchase**' fiction and the amount is recognized as a gain in surplus or deficit (IPSAS 40.88).

In the public sector, acquisitions may occur without the transfer of consideration. Examples include forced nationalizations, donations and bequests, and bailouts. In these cases, no goodwill is recognized. Rather, a gain (or a loss, e.g., if the liabilities of a bailed-out operation exceed its assets) is recognized in surplus or deficit (IPSAS 40.94). Acquisition-related costs (e.g., professional and consulting fees as well as general administrative costs) are recognized as expenses when incurred (IPSAS 40.111).

In the remainder of this subsection, examples are presented of initial and subsequent consolidation under 100% ownership and thus no NCI (Examples 1 and 2) as well as under 80% ownership (Examples 3 and 4). The examples apply the full goodwill method. Only the balance sheets are shown; therefore, no consolidation entries are presented for the statements of financial performance[13]. Moreover, all the examples assume the absence of intra-economic

---

[13] Those entries will be necessary if no group IT booking system exists. Under such circumstances, the different FS such as balance sheet and statement of financial performance are not linked through the underlying bookkeeping system and the accounts. All transactions that affect accounts both at the balance sheet level and the statement of financial performance level, therefore, are to be recorded twice, as one would do if the balance sheet and statement of financial performance were on paper and had to be modified. Two sets of entries become necessary, using surplus/deficit as a sort of transfer position.

entity receivables and payables, revenues and expenses, and unrealized gains and losses, so that the consolidation procedures other than capital/equity consolidation (i.e., debt consolidation, consolidation of revenues and expenses, and elimination of unrealized gains and losses) are not necessary and capital/equity consolidation is sufficient to produce the consolidated BS.

Example 1: Net assets/equity initial consolidation without NCI

On 1st Jan 20X1, municipality Eucity acquires 100% of company CE (controlled entity) for 100 kEUR. Eucity thus gains control of CE. The PSC is an acquisition according to IPSAS 40.5. The simplified balance sheets for the two entities, which comply with the consolidated accounts manual (BS II), are shown in Table 12.3. The surpluses shown in Examples 1 and 3 are to be understood as accumulated surpluses.

Eucity (BS II) 1st Jan 20X1 in kEUR			
Assets		Net assets & liabilities	
PPE	800	Reserves	300
Investment	100	Surplus	100
Inventories	50	Liabilities	550
Total	950	Total	950

CE (BS II) 1st Jan 20X1 in kEUR			
Assets		Net assets & liabilities	
PPE	250	Reserves	40
Inventories	100	Surplus	10
Cash	50	Liabilities	350
Total	400	Total	400

Table 12.3: Balance sheets II for Eucity and CE at initial consolidation date

At 1st Jan 20X1, a scan of CE's accounted-for assets and liabilities unveiled the following measurement issues:

- The fair value of property, plant, and equipment (PPE) is 300 kEUR, with a remaining useful life of 5 years and straight-line depreciation.
- The fair value of inventories is 110 kEUR.
- Liabilities are understated. An additional 20 kEUR will be needed to settle them.

This information provides the basis for the net assets/capital consolidation as part of initial consolidation.

At initial consolidation, according to the acquisition method, the acquirer (Eucity) and the acquisition date (1st Jan 20X1) have been determined. Next, the controlled entity's identifiable assets and liabilities must be remeasured at fair value. There are hidden reserves of 50 kEUR in PPE (300 kEUR fair value – 250 kEUR book value) and 10 kEUR in inventories (110 kEUR fair value – 100 kEUR book value) as well as 20 kEUR of hidden burdens in the liabilities. The effects of these remeasurements are cumulated in a dedicated reserve within equity.[14] The consolidation entry is as follows:

Debit		to	Credit	
PPE	50 kEUR	to	Liabilities	20 kEUR
Inventories	10 kEUR		Reserves	40 kEUR

The remeasured assets and liabilities of CE are shown in its level III balance sheet (BS III) in Table 12.4. Eucity's (the controlling entity) BS II and CE's (the controlled entity) BS III are then added up line by line to produce the aggregated BS (last column to the right).

---

[14] For this and the following examples, deferred tax is neglected because it depends on national tax systems and because public entities will probably not be subject to tax.

Item in kEUR	Eucity BS II	CE BS II	Remeasurement		CE BS III	Aggregated BS
			Debit	Credit		
PPE	800	250	50		300	1,100
Investment in CE	100	0			0	100
Inventories	50	100	10		110	160
Cash	0	50			50	50
Total assets	**950**	**400**	**60**		**460**	**1,410**
Reserves	300	40		40	80	380
Surplus	100	10			10	110
Liabilities	550	350		20	370	920
Total net assets & liabilities	**950**	**400**		**60**	**460**	**1,410**

Table 12.4: Example 1: Determination of the aggregated balance sheet as at 1st Jan 20X1

However, the aggregated BS cannot serve as the consolidated BS because of double counting: the aggregated BS includes both (i) CE's remeasured assets and liabilities and (ii) Eucity's equity investment in CE, which already incorporates the value of CE's assets and liabilities. Net assets/equity consolidation is thus performed by offsetting Eucity's equity investment in CE against CE's remeasured equity. The remeasured equity of CE is already shown in CE's BS III (Reserves kEUR 80 + Surplus kEUR 10 = kEUR 90), but for verification it can be recalculated as follows:

Reserves	40 kEUR
+ Surplus	+ 10 kEUR
= Net assets of CE, at book value	= 50 kEUR
+/ − Hidden reserves/burdens (+60 kEUR / - 20 kEUR)	+ 40 kEUR
= Remeasured net assets of CE	**= 90 kEUR**

Offsetting the carrying amount of Eucity's investment in CE against the remeasured net assets of CE yields a positive difference of 10, which is to be capitalized as goodwill based on the expectation of positive future net cash flows. Notice that, in the absence of NCI, the distinction between partial and full goodwill becomes moot.

Eucity's investment in CE (consideration transferred)	100 kEUR
– Remeasured net assets of CE	- 90 kEUR
= Goodwill	**= 10 kEUR**

Net assets/equity consolidation is completed by the following consolidation entries:

Debit		to	Credit	
Reserves	80 kEUR			
Surplus	10 kEUR	to	Investment in CE	100 kEUR
Goodwill	10 kEUR			

In the consolidated BS (Table 12.5), Eucity's investment in CE is no longer presented, the consolidated net assets coincide – in acquisitions without any NCI – with Eucity's net assets, and goodwill appears as an additional asset item.

Item in kEUR	Aggregated BS	Consolidation entries		Consolidated BS
		Debit	Credit	
PPE	1,100			1,100
Goodwill	0	10		10
Investment in CE	100		100	0
Inventories	160			160
Cash	50			50
Total assets	**1,410**	**10**	**100**	**1,320**
Reserves	380	80		300
Surplus	110	10		100
Liabilities	920			920
Total net assets & Liabilities	**1,410**	**90**	**0**	**1,320**

Table 12.5: Example 1: Consolidation table as at 1st Jan 20X1

Example 2: Net assets/equity subsequent consolidation without NCI

After one year, on 31st Dec 20X1, the subsequent consolidation is to be performed. The BS II of the two entities are the following, whereby the surplus was earned in period 20X1, while the accumulated surplus from previous years is included in the reserves:

Eucity (BS II) 31st Dec 20X1 in kEUR			
Assets		Net assets & liabilities	
PPE	800	Reserves	300
Investment	100	Surplus	100
Inventories	50	Liabilities	550
Total	950	Total	950

CE (BS II) 31st Dec 20X1 in kEUR			
Assets		Net assets & liabilities	
PPE	250	Reserves	50
Inventories	100	Surplus	40
Cash	50	Liabilities	310
Total	400	Total	400

Table 12.6: Balance sheets II for Eucity and CE at subsequent consolidation date

Preliminarily, the initial consolidation must be repeated by rolling forward the relevant remeasurements and consolidation entries. To some extent, the remeasurements may also need to be reversed.

To repeat the remeasurements, the entries to be rolled forward are as follows, considering that the accumulated surplus as at the initial consolidation date is now part of the reserves:

Debit		to	Credit	
PPE	50 kEUR	to	Liabilities	20 kEUR
Inventories	10 kEUR		Reserves	40 kEUR

These entries must then be reviewed and possibly reversed. In this respect, at the end of the reporting period (i.e., 31st Dec 20X1), assume the following: (i) the hidden reserves in CE's inventories (10 kEUR) have been realized and included in CE's surplus; (ii) the higher value of CE's PPE (50 kEUR) needs to be depreciated[15] on a straight-line basis as per the group's policies over a remaining useful life of five years; and (iii) the 20 kEUR hidden burdens in CE's liabilities have remained unchanged. Hence, another set of entries is required to record the relevant reversals and charge their effects to surplus or deficit in CE's BS III:

Debit		to	Credit	
Surplus	20 kEUR	to	PPE	10 kEUR
			Inventories	10 kEUR

These two sets of entries (i.e., the remeasurements rolled forward and the relevant reversals) yield the BS III for CE, which is then used to produce the aggregated BS as at 31st Dec 20X1, as shown in Table 12.7:

Item in kEUR	Eucity BS II	CE BS II	Remeasurements rolled forward and reversals		CE BS III	Aggregated BS
			Debit	Credit		
PPE	800	250	50	10	290	1,090
Investment in CE	100	0			0	100
Inventories	50	100	10	10	100	150

---

[15] See Chapters 9 and 10 for explanations about depreciation.

Cash	0	50			50		50
Total assets	950	400	60	20	440		1,390
Reserves	300	50		40	90		390
Surplus	100	40	20		20		120
Liabilities	550	310		20	330		880
Total net assets & liabilities	950	400	20	60	440		1,390

Table 12.7: Example 2: Determination of the aggregated balance sheet as at 31st Dec 20X1

On this basis, the initial net assets/equity consolidation must also be repeated, taking into account that, for CE, the initially consolidated accumulated surplus is now part of the reserves. Therefore, the consolidation entry to be rolled forward is slightly different from the one presented in Example 1:

Debit		to	Credit	
Reserves	90 kEUR	to	Investment in CE	100 kEUR
Goodwill	10 kEUR			

With respect to goodwill, an annual impairment test must be performed for the cash-generating unit to which goodwill has been allocated (IPSAS 26.90 f.). Assuming that no impairment loss has occurred, the consolidation table is shown in Table 12.8.

Item in kEUR	Aggregated BS	Consolidation entries		Consolidated BS
		Debit	Credit	
PPE	1,090			1,090
Goodwill	0	10		10
Investment in CE	100		100	0
Inventories	150			150
Cash	50			50
Total assets	1,390	10	100	1,300

Reserves	390	90		300
Surplus	120			120
Liabilities	880			880
Total net assets & liabilities	**1,390**	**90**	**0**	**1,300**

Table 12.8: Example 2: Consolidation table as at 31st Dec 20X1

Examples 1 and 2 have assumed that the controlling entity holds 100% of the ownership rights of the controlled entity. The following Examples 3 and 4 use the same data, but they assume 80% ownership in order to show the accounting treatment of NCI under the full consolidation method.

Example 3: Net assets/equity initial consolidation with NCI

On 1st Jan 20X1, municipality Eucity acquires 80% of company CE (controlled entity) for 100 kEUR. All other information provided in Example 1 applies, with the BS II shown in Table 12.3. The fair value of the NCI on 1st Jan 20X1 is assumed to be 25 kEUR.

As in Example 1, as a first step in the initial consolidation, CE's assets and liabilities must be remeasured at their acquisition-date fair values, producing CE's BS III.

Debit		to	Credit	
PPE	50 kEUR	to	Liabilities	20 kEUR
Inventories	10 kEUR		Reserves	40 kEUR

Once again, moreover, the aggregated BS must be compiled from Eucity's BS II and CE's BS III. It is important to highlight that, although Eucity only acquired 80% of CE, all asset and liability items are still added in full to produce the aggregated BS, as shown in

Table 12.4. This is because 80% ownership allows Eucity to control CE's assets and liabilities in their entirety.

To offset the carrying amount of Eucity's investment in CE against the remeasured net assets of CE, however, Eucity's ownership share needs to be taken into consideration. This step consequently differs from Example 1. The total remeasured equity of CE is already shown in CE's BS III (Reserves 80 kEUR + Surplus 10 kEUR = 90 kEUR, see Table 12.4). Eucity's share is 80%, hence 72 kEUR. For verification, these amounts can be recalculated as follows:

Reserves	40 kEUR
+ Surplus	+ 10 kEUR
= Net assets of CE, at book value	= 50 kEUR
+/ − Hidden reserves/burdens (+60 kEUR / - 20 kEUR)	+ 40 kEUR
= Remeasured net assets of CE	**= 90 kEUR**
of which Eucity group's share (80%)	72 kEUR
of which NCI (20%)	18 kEUR

The difference between the carrying amount of Eucity's investment in CE (100 kEUR) and Eucity's share in CE's net assets (kEUR 72) is positive and is capitalized as goodwill based on the expectation of positive future net cash flows. This goodwill is labelled as 'partial' as it is only associated with Eucity's group:

Eucity's investment in CE (consideration transferred)	100 kEUR
− Eucity's share in remeasured net assets of CE	- 72 kEUR
= Partial Goodwill pertaining to Eucity	**= 28 kEUR**

The resulting consolidation entry is as follows:

Debit		to	Credit	
Reserves	64 kEUR (80 * 80%)	to	Investment in CE	100 kEUR
Surplus	8 kEUR (10 * 80%)			
Goodwill	28 kEUR			

As for NCI, they account for 20% of CE's remeasured net assets and they must be presented separately in the consolidated BS. Hence the need for the following consolidation entry:

Debit		to	Credit	
Reserves	16 kEUR (80 * 20%)	to	Non-controlling interests	18 kEUR
Surplus	2 kEUR (10 * 20%)			

As mentioned in Section 5.1, NCI can either be measured at fair value (full goodwill method) or "at the present ownership instruments' proportionate share in the recognized amounts of the acquired operation's identifiable net assets" (partial goodwill method). In the latter case, no further consolidation entries are needed. If the full goodwill method is applied, the NCI must be adjusted to their fair value which, according to the case description, is 25 kEUR. A difference of 7 kEUR (= 25 kEUR fair value − 18 kEUR proportionate share of CE's remeasured net assets) results, which is recognized as goodwill. Thus, an additional consolidation entry is needed. The consolidation Table 12.9 shows the results for the initial net assets/equity consolidation in the case of 80% ownership under the full goodwill method.

Debit		to	Credit	
Goodwill	7 kEUR	to	Non-controlling interests	7 kEUR

Item in kEUR	Aggregated BS	Consolidation entries		Consolidated BS
		Debit	Credit	
PPE	1,100			1,100
Goodwill	0	28 7		35
Investment in CE	100		100	0
Inventories	160			160
Cash	50			50
Total assets	**1,410**	**35**	**100**	**1,345**
Reserves	380	64 16		300
Surplus	110	8 2		100
Non-controlling interests	0		18 7	25
Liabilities	920			920
Total net assets & liabilities	**1,410**	**90**	**25**	**1,345**

Table 12.9: Example 3: Consolidation table as at 1st Jan 20X1

In the consolidated BS (Table 12.9), the consolidated net assets (425) exceed Eucity's net assets (400) because of the additional net asset portion related to NCI (25).

Example 4: Net assets/equity subsequent consolidation with NCI

Similar to Example 2, after one year, on 31st Dec 20X1, the subsequent consolidation must be performed. Unlike Example 2, Eucity's ownership share is now 80%. The same information provided in Example 2 applies, with the BS II shown in Table 12.6. The fair value of the NCI on 31st Dec 20X1 is assumed to have increased to 30 kEUR.

As in Example 2, it is preliminarily necessary to repeat the initial consolidation by rolling forward the relevant remeasurements (reversing them where appropriate) and consolidation entries.

To repeat and reverse the remeasurements, the entries are the same as those presented in Example 2:

Debit		to	Credit	
PPE	50 kEUR	to	Liabilities	20 kEUR
Inventories	10 kEUR		Reserves	40 kEUR

Debit		to	Credit	
Surplus	20 kEUR	to	PPE	10 kEUR
			Inventories	10 kEUR

So far, therefore, there are no differences in CE's BS III between cases with and without NCI. Consequently, the aggregated BS is the same shown in Table 12.7.

Next, the initial net assets/equity consolidation must also be repeated, keeping in mind that CE's initially consolidated accumulated surplus is now part of the reserves. Under the full goodwill method, the goodwill pertaining to the NCI continues to reflect the fair value of the NCI at the acquisition date (25 kEUR) and is not updated to the fair value at the reporting date. The consolidation entries to be rolled forward are as follows:

Debit		to	Credit	
Reserves	72 kEUR	to	Investment in CE	100 kEUR
Goodwill	28 kEUR			

Debit		to	Credit	
Reserves	18 kEUR	to	Non-controlling interests	18 kEUR

Debit		to	Credit	
Goodwill	7 kEUR	to	Non-controlling interests	7 kEUR

As for subsequent consolidation, it is important to notice that CE's BS III surplus for 20X1 is 20 kEUR. Of this, 20% pertains to NCI and must be classified accordingly. This is achieved with the consolidation entry shown below. The consolidation table is presented in Table 12.10.

Debit		to	Credit	
Surplus	4 kEUR	to	Non-controlling interests	4 kEUR

Item in kEUR	Aggregated BS	Consolidation entries		Consolidated BS
		Debit	Credit	
PPE	1,090			1,090
Goodwill	0	28 7		35
Investment in CE	100		100	0
Inventories	150			150
Cash	50			50
Total assets	**1,390**	**35**	**100**	**1,325**
Reserves	390	72 18		300
Surplus	120	4		116
Non-controlling interests	0		18 7 4	29
Liabilities	880			880
Total net assets & liabilities	**1,390**	**94**	**29**	**1,325**

Table 12.10: Example 4: Consolidation table as at 31st Dec 20X1

5.2. Debt consolidation

According to the single entity fiction, the mutual liabilities and receivables between the group's entities do not count as group liabilities and receivables and must consequently be eliminated by means of debt consolidation. Thus, debt consolidation only affects the BS. Debt consolidation is carried out during initial consolidation to the extent that intra-economic entity liabilities and receivables already exist at the date of acquisition. It is also performed during subsequent consolidation to eliminate the mutual liabilities and receivables that are recognized in the controlling entity's BS II and the controlled entities' BS III at the relevant reporting date. Usually, intra-economic entity liabilities and receivables will balance, but offsetting differences may occur.[16] Two examples are introduced in the remainder of this subsection. In both examples, Eucity is assumed to have acquired 100% of CE on 1st Jan 20X1 and the reporting period coincides with the calendar year. The same assumptions apply to the examples presented in the next subsections.

Example 5: Debt consolidation without offsetting differences

On 15th Nov 20X1, Eucity ordered goods from CE and made a 50 kEUR advance payment (at no interest) for delivery in two months. From an accounting viewpoint, Eucity recognized advances to suppliers as a current receivable and CE recognized unearned revenues as a current liability, each in the amount of 50 kEUR.

Debt consolidation is carried out as at 31st Dec 20X1. The mutual receivables and liabilities have the same amount. Therefore, there are no offsetting differences. The elimination is carried out with the following consolidation entry:

Debit		to	Credit	
Current liabilities	50 kEUR	to	Current receivables	50 kEUR

---

[16] Explained in Chapter 11.

Example 6: Debt consolidation with offsetting differences

On 20th May 20X1, Eucity lent CE 100 kEUR to be repaid after three years. For simplicity, assume that the loan carried no interest[17]. From an accounting viewpoint, Eucity recognized a non-current receivable and CE recognized a non-current payable, each in the amount of 100 kEUR. However, due to pessimistic expectations at the end of 20X1, Eucity wrote down the receivable in its FS by recognizing an impairment loss for 8 kEUR in surplus or deficit.

Debt consolidation is conducted as at 31st Dec 20X1. Due to the write-down, the mutual receivables and payables do not balance. To reconcile the resulting real offsetting difference[18], Eucity's write-down entry is reversed as if it had not taken place. The relevant consolidation entry is as follows:

Debit		to	Credit	
Non-current liability	100 kEUR	to	Non-current receivable	92 kEUR
			Surplus (Impairment loss)	8 kEUR

In the course of the **subsequent debt consolidation** for the next period, a similar entry will be needed. However, the impairment loss will not be reversed against surplus, but rather against the reserves, as it did not affect the surplus of the current period 20X2, but that of the prior period 20X1.

---

[17] Should the loan carry interest, the relevant revenues and expenses would be eliminated during the 'Consolidation of revenues and expenses' (see subsection 5.3).

[18] See the explanation of real and unreal offsetting differences in Chapter 11.5.

5.3 Consolidation of revenues and expenses

As the group can only realize revenues and expenses with outside parties, all economic transactions that produced intra-economic entity revenues and expenses must be eliminated. The consolidation of revenues and expenses is not relevant for initial consolidation, but it must be carried out during subsequent consolidation periods.

Example 7: Consolidation of revenues and expenses

Eucity rented one of CE's buildings. Rent for the current accounting period totalled 3 kEUR, which Eucity paid in full before 31st Dec 20X1.

Consolidation is carried out as at 31st Dec 20X1. Because rent was paid in full, there are no mutual receivables and payables to be eliminated in the course of debt consolidation (at the balance sheet level). However, at the level of the consolidated statement of financial performance, CE's rent revenues must be offset against Eucity's rent expenses by means of the following consolidation entry:

Debit		to	Credit	
Rent revenues	3 kEUR	to	Rent expenses	3 kEUR

5.4 Elimination of unrealized gains or losses

As explained in Chapter 11, after purchasing goods and services from another consolidated entity, a consolidated entity may capitalize them as inventories, fixed assets, or intangible assets. From the group's perspective, this may result in the overstatement (or understatement) of assets and the corresponding recognition of unrealized gains (or losses). During consolidation, these unrealized gains or losses must be eliminated and the affected assets must be remeasured at group acquisition or production cost.

Example 8: Elimination of unrealized gains for inventories

In 20X1, CE purchased merchandise from third parties for 38 kEUR and sold it to Eucity for 45 kEUR. Eucity paid for the merchandise, but did not sell it to third parties, so that such merchandise is presented as inventory in Eucity's BS as at 31st Dec 20X1 at Eucity's acquisition cost.

Consolidation is carried out as at 31st Dec 20X1. Because the purchase was paid in full, there are no mutual receivables and payables to be eliminated in the course of debt consolidation. However, by purchasing at 38 kEUR and selling for 45 kEUR, CE recorded a gain of 7 kEUR. From the group's perspective, this gain is still unrealized because the merchandise has not yet been sold to third parties. Correspondingly, the carrying value of Eucity's inventory is 45 kEUR, but the group (through CE) purchased it for 38 kEUR. The following consolidation entries are needed to eliminate the revenues and expenses from the intra-economic entity sale of merchandise, the unrealized gain, and the overstatement of Eucity's inventories:[19]

Debit		to	Credit	
Consolidated balance sheet				
Surplus	7 kEUR	to	Inventories	7 kEUR
Consolidated statement of financial performance				
Sales revenues	45 kEUR	to	Cost of goods sold	38 kEUR
			Surplus	7 kEUR

---

[19] Separate accounting records for the balance sheet and the statement of financial performance are illustrated here, because it is assumed that there is no group accounting system and the FS have to be booked separately (see Footnote 13 for a more detailed explanation).

If Eucity's ownership were less than 100%, a portion of the adjustment to CE's surplus would relate to NCI and would need to be classified accordingly. The relevant consolidation entry would be similar to the one presented at the end of Example 4.

Example 9: Elimination of unrealized gains for depreciable PPE

At the beginning of 20X1, CE produced equipment and sold it to Eucity for 45 kEUR. CE's production cost (measured in compliance with the group's accounting policies) was 38 kEUR. Eucity paid for the equipment and began using it. Useful life is five years and the group's accounting policies require straight-line depreciation.

Consolidation is carried out as at 31st Dec 20X1. This example is similar to Example 8 in that: (i) there are no mutual receivables and payables since the purchase was paid in full; (ii) by producing equipment at a cost of 38 kEUR and selling it to Eucity for 45 kEUR, CE recorded an unrealized gain of 7 kEUR; (iii) the gross carrying value of Eucity's PPE is 45 kEUR even if the group's production cost was 38 kEUR. In addition, in 20X1 Eucity depreciated the equipment by 9 kEUR (45 kEUR / 5 years) whereas, from the group's perspective, depreciation is only 7.6 kEUR (38 kEUR / 5 years). The following consolidation entries are needed to eliminate the revenues and expenses from the intra-economic entity sale of PPE, the unrealized gain, and the overstatement of Eucity's gross value of PPE, as well as to adjust the amount of depreciation expenses:[20]

---

[20] The reasons for separate accounting records for the balance sheet and the statement of financial performance are explained in Footnote 13.

Debit		to	Credit	
Consolidated balance sheet				
Surplus	7 kEUR	to	Equipment	7 kEUR
Consolidated statement of financial performance				
Sales Revenues	45 kEUR	to	Cost of goods sold/ Own work capitalised	38 kEUR
			Surplus	7 kEUR
Consolidated balance sheet				
Equipment (Accumulated depreciation)	1.4 kEUR	to	Surplus (BS)	1.4 kEUR
Consolidated statement of financial performance				
Surplus	1.4 kEUR	to	Depreciation expenses	1.4 kEUR

As in Example 8, the presence of NCI would require a further consolidation entry to allocate the adjustments to CE's surplus.

In the course of the **subsequent consolidation** for the next period 20X2, these consolidation entries will need to be repeated to re-establish the status quo at the beginning of 20X2. However, reserves will be debited and credited instead of surplus, as these entries affect the surplus for 20X1, which in 20X2 has become part of accumulated surplus within the reserves. Conversely, the new entry needed to adjust the depreciation expense for 20X2 will be recorded in surplus.

6. Equity method (initial and subsequent consolidations)

The equity method is similar to capital consolidation. It is a 'one-line' consolidation method to be used for the subsequent measurement of the book value of investments in **associates** (IPSAS 36.16) and **joint ventures** (IPSAS 37.28). Similar to full consolidation, its application requires the existence of uniform accounting policies (IPSAS 36.37). In the CFS, an investment in an associate or a joint venture accounted for using the equity method is classified among non-current financial assets (IPSAS 36.21).

Initially, the investment is measured at cost. However, in an auxiliary calculation, the difference between the cost of the investment and the pro-rata book net assets of the associate / joint venture is calculated and explained in terms of (i) the remeasurement of the associate's / joint venture's assets and liabilities at their acquisition-date fair values, with the resulting identification of hidden reserves and burdens, as well as (ii) a residual amount which, if positive, is qualified as goodwill in the auxiliary calculation, but not disclosed separately from the investment in the associate/joint venture on the consolidated balance sheet. Should the residual amount be negative, it must be accounted for as revenue in surplus or deficit in the period when the investment is acquired, without the need of reassessing the calculation (IPSAS 36.35b). The purpose of this auxiliary calculation is to provide the basis for the adjustments to be carried out in the subsequent reporting periods.

In subsequent reporting periods, the carrying value of the investment is increased or decreased to reflect the investor's share of the investee's surplus or deficit after the date of acquisition; such increase or decrease is recognized in the investor's surplus or deficit as a financial gain or loss from investments in associates or joint ventures. Dividends and similar distributions received from an investee reduce the investee's equity and thus the carrying amount of the investment. Adjustments to the carrying amount of the investment may also be necessary to reflect other changes in the investee's equity that are not recognized in the investee's surplus or deficit (e.g., those arising from the revaluation of PPE); the investor's share of those changes is recognized in the investor's net assets/ equity (IPSAS 36.16). Finally, further adjustments may be needed to capture the effects of the initial difference between the cost of the investment and the pro-rata book net assets of the associate or joint venture; these adjustments (e.g., the depreciation of hidden reserves such as those arising from remeasured PPE) are similar to the reversals of remeasurements performed under full consolidation to achieve subsequent net assets / equity consolidation.

A general structure for the subsequent adjustments to the carrying value of the investment according to the equity method is presented in Table 12.11. In the structure, a distinction is drawn according to whether the adjustments must be recognized in the investor's surplus or deficit.

When using the equity method and in contrast to full or proportionate consolidation, therefore, the investment in associates or joint ventures is not replaced line-by-line by the underlying assets and liabilities in the consolidated BS. The assets and liabilities presented in the consolidated BS, in other words, do not include the associate's or joint venture's assets and liabilities. Instead, **only one line is affected**. In particular, the carrying value of the investment, as initially recognized in the consolidated BS for an amount corresponding to the consideration paid by the investor, is subsequently adjusted to reflect the changes in the associate's or joint venture's remeasured net assets, so that over time it approximates the investment's fair value. **Similarly, the consolidated statement of financial performance does not include line-by-line the revenues and expenses of the associate or joint venture. Rather, it only includes an item reflecting the investor's (adjusted) share of the associate's or joint venture's surplus or deficit.** Notably, according to IPSAS 1.102(c), this "share of the surplus or deficit of associates and joint ventures accounted for using the equity method" must be presented as a separate line item on the face of the statement of financial performance.

Starting point	**Book value of investment in associates or joint ventures** at acquisition cost or at the beginning of the current reporting period
Adjustments through surplus or deficit	+ Pro-rata surplus of the associate or joint venture
	- Pro-rata deficit of the associate or joint venture
	- Pro-rata dividend paid[21]
	- Depreciation and other adjustments to initially recognized reserves
	- Adjustment of hidden burdens
	+ / - Alignment of the associate's / joint venture's balance sheet items to the group's accounting policies affecting net income
	+ / - Deferred taxes on depreciation and adjustments (if applicable)
Adjustments through net assets (i.e., not through surplus and deficit)	+ / - Revaluations and adjustments to PPE that are not recognized by the associate or joint venture through surplus or deficit (e.g., due to use of revaluation method)
	+ / - Changes in the participation quota that result from any under- or over proportionate increase or decrease in net assets
	+ / - Capital contributions by the investor /paid to the investor
	= **Book value of investment in associates or joint ventures** at end of reporting period

Table 12.11: Adjustment of the investment's book value according to the equity method[22]

Due to the procedure described above, the equity method is often perceived as a valuation or measurement method rather than a true consolidation method.[23] Notably, such procedure only ensures net assets/equity consolidation. Transactions with associates and joint ventures may also require the elimination of unrealized gains and losses (IPSAS 36.29 ff.), which is not explained here due to technical complexity.[24] Differences may lie, for example, in the consolidation of gains and losses between downstream and upstream transactions (see IPSAS 36.31).

---

[21] Assuming that dividends are recognized as revenue and only later deducted from the carrying value of the investment (see Example 10).

[22] See e.g. Krimpmann (2015), pp. 427.

[23] Stolowy and Lebas (2006), p. 468.

[24] See for detailed explanations e.g. Krimpmann (2015), pp. 450 ff.

Example 10: Application of the equity method

On 1st Jan 20X1, Eucity acquired 25% of the shares in company AE (associated entity). The acquisition cost was 50 kEUR. The book value of AE's equity at the time of acquisition was 120 kEUR. At the time of acquisition, AE had hidden reserves worth 32 kEUR in PPE with a remaining useful life of 5 years. In 20X1, AE reported a deficit of 8 kEUR and distributed dividends of 4 kEUR.

Initial recognition is at cost:

Debit		to	Credit	
Investments in Associates	50 kEUR	to	Bank	50 kEUR

The auxiliary calculations are as follows:

Acquisition cost	50 kEUR
- Pro rata net assets acquired, at book value (25% of 120 kEUR)	30 kEUR
= Difference	20 kEUR
- Pro-rata hidden reserves (25 % of 32 kEUR)	8 kEUR
= Goodwill	12 kEUR

The pro-rata hidden reserves and the goodwill are not recognized separately in the consolidated BS, but they will cumulatively affect subsequent measurement.

For the subsequent measurement as at 31st Dec 20X1, the relevant parts of Table 12.11 are shown below:

Acquisition cost = Investment's carrying value at 1st Jan 20X1	50 kEUR
- AE's pro rata deficit (25% of 8 kEUR)	2 kEUR
- Pro rata dividend paid by AE (25% of 4 kEUR)	1 kEUR

- Pro rata depreciation of AE's hidden reserves (25% of 32 kEUR/5 years)	1.6 kEUR
= Investment's carrying value at 31st Dec 20X1	45.4 kEUR

The carrying value of the investment must be adjusted accordingly. In addition, the investor must verify whether the investment is impaired, in which case an impairment loss would need to be recognized (IPSAS 36.43).

The accounting entries for the reduction in the carrying value of the investment and the dividend received are shown below. The net result from the investment in the associate is a loss of 3.6 kEUR.

Debit		to	Credit	
Deficit of associates accounted for using the equity method	4.6 kEUR	to	Investments in associates	4.6 kEUR
Bank	1 kEUR	to	Surplus of associates accounted for using the equity method	1 kEUR

7. Conclusion

The aim of this chapter was to present consolidated financial reporting according to IPSAS, with a specific focus on consolidation methods and procedures. It was shown that controlled entities must be fully consolidated, whereas investments in associates and joint ventures are consolidated using the equity method, which is also different from measurement as financial assets (IPSAS 29/41). Proportionate consolidation was not addressed since it is not allowed by current IPSASs.

To explain the consolidation methods, this chapter used short examples. Given the introductory character of this chapter, such examples were rather simplified. Still, upon completion of this chapter, readers should be familiar with the basic techniques and challenges of consolidation.

Bibliographic references

AGGESTAM-PONTOPPIDAN, Caroline and ANDERNACK, Isabelle (2016) – Interpretation and application of IPSAS. Chichester: Wiley, ISBN: 978-1-119-01029-6.

BERGMANN, Andreas (2009) – Public Sector Financial Management, Harlow et al.: Prentice Hall, ISBN: 9780273713548.

KRIMPMANN, Andreas (2015) – *Principles of Group Accounting under IFRS*. Chichester: Wiley, ISBN: 978-1-118-75141-1.

KUETING, Karlheinz and WEBER, Claus-Peter (2018) – Der Konzernabschluss, 14th ed., Stuttgart: Schaeffer Poeschel, ISBN: 978-3-7910-3730-1.

LORSON, Peter; POLLER, Joerg and HAUSTEIN, Ellen (2019) – Fallstudie zur Rechnungslegung – Vom nationalen Einzelabschluss zum IFRS-Konzernabschluss, Düsseldorf: Handelsblatt Fachmedien, ISBN: 978-394771114.

STOLOWY, Hervé and LEBAS, Michel (2006) – Financial Accounting and Reporting: A Global Perspective, London: Cengage learning, ISBN: 978-1-84480-250-0.

Additional readings

GALLIMBERTI, Carlo Maria (2013) – Consolidation. Preparing and Understanding Consolidated Financial Statements under IFRS, Boston: McGraw-Hill, ISBN-13: 978-0077160968.

KRIMPMANN, Andreas (2015) – *Principles of Group Accounting under IFRS*. Chichester: Wiley, ISBN: 978-1-118-75141-1.

Discussion topics

– Relevance of accounting for goodwill in the public sector and its interpretation
– Relevance of the full goodwill method in public sector accounting
– Typical examples of public sector specific revenues and expenses and unrealised gains and losses
– Consolidation issues in financial statements, other than financial position and financial performance

Chapter 13
The Accounting Harmonization Challenge in the European Union and the EPSAS

Sandra Cohen
Athens University of Economics and Business – Athens, Greece
scohen@aueb.gr
https://orcid.org/0000-0002-4795-0527

Isabel Brusca
University of Zaragoza, Zaragoza, Spain
ibrusca@unizar.es
https://orcid.org/0000-0002-2897-1744

Francesca Manes-Rossi
University of Napoli Federico II, Italy
manes@unina.it
https://orcid.org/0000-0001-9617-4379

Summary

The European Commission decided in 2013 that a new set of accrual-based standards named European Public Sector Accounting Standards (EPSAS), which would have International Public Sector Accounting Standards (IPSAS) as a reference, should be developed for the EU Member States (MS). This signalled the beginning of the public sector harmonization journey in the European Union that is still in progress despite the long time that has already elapsed. In this chapter, we present the process that the development of

EPSAS has followed so far, and we discuss the structures created to deal with EPSAS development, the content of the EPSAS conceptual framework and the EPSAS governance issues. Moreover, we analyze the issue papers and the screening reports developed during the process. Finally, the EPSAS implementation challenges are addressed, concentrating on the cost of implementation and the ambiguous relation between IPSAS and EPSAS.

Keywords:

European Public Sector Accounting Standards (EPSAS), EPSAS Conceptual Framework, EPSAS Governance, EPSAS Working Group

1. Introduction to the EU harmonization challenge and EPSAS

The financial crisis of 2008 underlined the relevance of public sector accounting and the need for comparable financial reporting in the European Union (EU) Member States (MS), which could lead to high-quality government finance statistics (GFS) data and make it easier to compare deficit and debt indicators among the countries. The situation was characterized by heterogeneity among accounting systems in place in EU MS. However, heterogeneity existed even within the same country at different levels of government and different types of public sector entities.[1]

In this context, the Council of EU adopted in 2011 a set of five regulations and the Council Directive 2011/85/EU on requirements for budgetary frameworks with the intention to reinforce economic governance and stability (commonly called the "Six Pack"). The Directive calls for the MS to have accounting systems that cover all sub-sectors of general government and produce the information

---

[1] See Ernst and Young (2012) and European Commission (2013b).

needed to generate accrual data to prepare the National Accounts. Comparable data could help to ensure high-quality government financial statistics. At the same time, the Directive asked the European Commission (EC) to assess the suitability of the International Public Sector Accounting Standards (IPSAS) for the MS.[2]

On behalf of the EC, Eurostat launched a public consultation in 2012 to assess the suitability of implementing IPSAS in the MS. The public consultation was a tool to allow stakeholders to give their opinion about the advantages and disadvantages of the potential adoption of IPSAS. Considering the responses to the public consultation as well as the report prepared by Ernst and Young (EY) in 2012 (EY, 2012), the Commission announced that the harmonization policy should be based on the development of a new set of European Public Sector Accounting Standards (EPSAS) that would have IPSAS as a reference point and they would be, of course, accrual accounting based.

In this realm, it was proposed that accrual IPSAS could be classified into three categories[3] in relation to EPSAS

- Standards that might be implemented with minor or no adaptation;
- Standards that need adaptation or for which a selective approach would be needed; and
- Standards that are seen as needing to be amended for implementation.

The assessment of IPSAS as a relevant framework for public sector accounting in the EU marked the origin of the harmonization process to deal with the heterogeneity of public sector accounting systems in EU MS.

The reason why Europe decided to move on with the development of a European set of standards, the EPSAS, has been justified

---

[2] European Commission (2012).

[3] European Commission (2013a).

as an appropriate alternative that permits the EU to create its own conceptual framework, developed for the European context, and maintain sovereignty for issuing accounting standards.[4] The development of the EPSAS based on the IPSAS allows the advantages of *glocalization*[5], that is, the adoption of global standards but with local adaptations, maintaining the local identity and at the same time gaining legitimacy and prestige for the acceptance of the global standards. The key objective of EPSAS is to achieve the necessary minimum level of financial transparency and comparability of financial reporting between and within the EU MS.

The process for EPSAS development is still in progress as there are no EPSAS created yet. While the benefits of EPSAS have been adequately advocated, EPSAS are also encountering challenges.

In this chapter, we present the process that the development of EPSAS has followed so far (as of October 2022). In the next section, we discuss the structures created to deal with EPSAS development, examining the different documents issued, such as the EPSAS first-time implementation guidelines, the conceptual framework (CF), the governance issues, the issue papers and the screening reports. We analyze the EPSAS implementation challenges and possible next steps in the third section. Finally, the conclusions of this chapter are presented in the fourth section.

2. The process

The economic and financial crisis that started in 2008 highlighted the importance of controlling the deficit and debt in the EU, where budgetary stability is fundamental. One of the aims of the European

---

[4] Caruana et al. (2019).

[5] Baskerville and Grossi (2019).

Union was to reinforce the Stability and Growth Pact (SGP), initiating a process of negotiation with MS that led to the called "Six Pack", which contains a set of rules for economic and fiscal surveillance (five regulations and one Directive).

In this context, accounting data was considered very relevant to achieve this objective. The EU realized that countries need adequate accounting systems that allow the control of debt and deficit. Also, harmonized accounting could provide a solution to the problems that resulted from the lack of data comparability among the different MS. Debt and deficit are calculated with reference to the European System of Accounts (ESA), but the data for all sub-sectors of the general government are compiled from individual financial reports that, in many countries, correspond to the budgetary reports that are the initial input to obtain macro-economic data. Because of this, in the negotiations of the Six Pack, the reform of the accounting systems was included, particularly in the form of a Directive on Requirements for Budgetary Frameworks of the MS.

During the development of the Directive, in a report issued by the European Parliament on the Proposal of the Directive in May 2011, it was stated that[6] "The Member States' provisions of the budgetary surveillance framework established by the Treaty on the Functioning of the European Union (TFEU) and in particular the Stability and Growth Pact should be updated to International Public Sector Accounting Standards". In line with this, the European Parliament introduced the following amendment to the EC's proposal for the Council directive regarding the requirements for the budgetary frameworks of the MS[7]: "Member States shall move to adopt International Public Sector Accounting Standards within three years of this Directive coming into force".

---

[6] European Parliament (2011, p.16).

[7] European Parliament (2011, Art. 3).

EU Economic governance "Six-Pack" (2011)	CONTRACTS WITH EXPERTS AND CONSULTANTS
Council Directive 2011/85/EU of 8 November 2011 on requirements for budgetary frameworks of the Member States. It calls the Commission to assess the suitability of the	
Public Consultation on IPSAS suitability (2012)	EY Study about practices in Member countries (2012)
2013 Report from the Commission to the Council and the European Parliament. *Towards implementing harmonised public sector accounting standards in Member States*.	
2013 Eurostat conference in Brussels on the implementation of EPSAS	
2013 (Oct) Task Force EPSAS governance principles and structures	
2013 (Nov) Public consultation on future EPSAS governance principles and structures	
2013-2015. Task Force EPSAS governance principles and structures	PwC Study about EPSAS impact assessment (2014)
	EY Study about potential impacts of implementing accruals accounting in the public sector (2016)
2015 (Sept)-October 2022. EPSAS Working Group (12 meetings)	
EPSAS Cell First Time Implementation	
EPSAS Cell on Governance Principles	
EPSAS Cell on Principles related to EPSAS Standards	
	EY Study regarding the collection of additional and updated information related to the potential impacts of EPSAS
Final Report of Cell on First Time Implementation (2016)	
	PwC Issues Papers for developing and implementing EPSAS (2017-2018)
Final Report of Cell on Governance: Principles underlying EPSAS governance (2017)	
Guidance for the First Time Implementation of Accrual Accounting (2017)	PwC Study on potential impacts of accruals implementation (2018)
Final Report of Cell on Principles related to EPSAS standards (2018)	PwC-Eurostat EPSAS Screening reports (2019-2022)
EPSAS Conceptual Framework (2018)	PwC Study: Updated accounting maturities of EU governments and EPSAS implementation cost (2020)

Figure 13.1: The process in the EPSAS project

However, this requirement was removed in the final text approved.[8] Article 3 of the Directive requires MS to "have in place public accounting systems comprehensively and consistently covering all sub-sectors of general government and containing the information needed to generate accrual data with a view to preparing data based on the ESA 95 standard. Those public accounting systems shall be subject to internal control and independent audits".

As a consequence, accrual accounting systems were considered necessary for public administrations but there was not a final decision about whether IPSAS were the best way to achieve data comparability. Instead, the Directive requires the Commission to assess the suitability of the IPSAS for the MS. To this end, the Commission opened a Public Consultation on the suitability of the IPSAS for EU MS, followed by another public consultation about EPSAS governance. These facts are presented in Figure 13.1, which summarizes all the processes of the EPSAS project.

Eurostat has been in charge of leading the EPSAS project on behalf of the European Commission since the beginning, with the specific mandate to comply with the requirements of the Council Directive 2011/85. Eurostat is the statistical office of the European Union and coordinates all the statistical activities at EU level, including National Accounting. For example, it produces national accounts with data from the EU MS, which provides aggregated information about the country's economy, such as Gross Domestic Product (GDP) aggregates. In particular, Eurostat elaborates the national accounts, which include the information necessary for fiscal control, such as debt and deficit, essential for the SGP. Although statistical information is produced using the European System of National and Regional Accounts (ESA)[9], the information used by

---

[8] Council Directive 2011/85/EU, 8 November 2011.

[9] Eurostat (2013).

the MS is based on financial and budgetary accounting. Thus, as Eurostat is responsible for coordinating all the financial information of the MS, it has assumed this leading role in the EPSAS project.

The first step in the process was a public consultation about the suitability of IPSAS, aiming at collecting the opinions of the relevant stakeholders within the EU on the advantages and disadvantages of a potential adoption of IPSAS. The public consultation process (between February and May 2012) received 68 contributions, showing a limited interest of potential stakeholders on the matter. 82% of responses were received from EU countries and 18% from non-EU countries and international institutions and organizations[10]. German stakeholders represented a majority, and their responses disagreed with the implementation of IPSAS[11]. The position of respondents about the suitability of the IPSAS was as follows[12]:

- 38% of the total responses considered IPSAS to be suitable for implementation. They argued mainly for the need to improve public sector accounts' accountability, transparency and comparability, especially in light of the sovereign debt crisis.
- 31% of the total responses considered that IPSASs were partly suitable. They agreed on the need for a set of accrual-based public sector accounting standards for the EU, but had reservations as to whether IPSAS was entirely suitable. For example, they argued that the IPSAS were based on private sector accounting standards and they were insufficiently adapted to public sector requirements.
- 28% of the total answered that IPSAS was unsuitable. The majority also agreed about the need for a set of accrual-based

---

[10] European Commission (2012).

[11] Aggestam and Brusca (2016).

[12] European Commission (2012).

public sector accounting standards, but they were against IPSAS. They argued about its incompleteness with respect to public sector accounting requirements, such as taxation or social benefits, its complexity, its strong link to IFRS or their governance arrangements. Of the 19 "No" responses, 10 were received from Germany, 4 from France, 3 from Austria and 1 each from the Netherlands and Poland.

To sum up, the opinions gathered revealed different positions about the IPSAS adoption. However, the views in favour of introducing a set of accrual-based standards triggered the decision of the EPSAS development. The official position of the Eurostat and the EC was that harmonized public sector accounting standards were needed for the EU MS. In the report entitled[13] "Towards implementing harmonized public sector accounting standards in the Member States. The suitability of IPSAS for the Member States", the EC recognizes that "IPSAS is currently the only internationally recognized set of public sector accounting standards. As a consequence, the IPSAS standards represent an indisputable reference for potential EU harmonized public sector accounts", however, "it seems that IPSASs cannot easily be implemented in the EU Member States as they currently stand".

The reasons given at that moment (2013) for moving towards a European set of standards were the following[14]:

- The IPSAS standards did not describe sufficiently precisely the accounting practices to be followed, considering that some of them offer the possibility of choosing between alternative accounting treatments, which would limit harmonization in practice;

---

[13] European Commission (2013a, p. 8).

[14] European Commission (2013a).

- The suite of standards was not complete in terms of coverage or its practical applicability to some important types of government flows, such as taxes and social benefits. A major issue was the capacity of IPSAS to resolve the problem of consolidating accounts on the basis of the definition used for general government, which is a core concept of fiscal monitoring in the EU;
- IPSAS were also regarded as insufficiently stable since they were expected to be occasionally updated;
- The governance of IPSAS suffered from insufficient participation from EU public sector accounting authorities.

EPSAS would initially be based on the IPSAS principles but EU would have the capacity to develop its own standards to meet its own requirements. This process would offer a set of harmonized accrual-based public sector accounting standards adapted to the specific requirements of the EU MS. As stated before, the adoption of global standards but with local adaptations *or "glocalization"*[15] allows for maintaining the local identity while gaining the legitimacy and prestige for the acceptance of the global standard.

It was proposed that the IPSAS standards would be classified into three categories: standards that might be implemented with minor or no adaptation; standards that need adaptation, or for which a selective approach would be needed; and standards that are seen as needing to be amended for implementation.

After the first consultation, the EC organized a conference in Brussels in May 2013 to address the issues of the suitable governance structure, the definition of the EPSAS framework, the specification of a first set of core EPSAS and the planning of the implementation.

---
[15] Baskerville and Grossi (2019).

A second public consultation on the EPSAS governance was launched in November 2013 by Eurostat following the conference in Brussels. Eurostat prepared a summary draft report[16] based on the 203 responses received during this second public consultation. The responses to the public consultation revealed some disappointment with the proposals about the principles for the EPSAS governance and structure, so no consensus was achieved. Consequently, rather than continuing a public consultation process, two task forces (TFs) supported the process: the TF on EPSAS Governance and the TF EPSAS standards.

The TF on EPSAS Governance (set in October 2013) started working on the development of a suitable model for the EPSAS governance structure, while the TF EPSAS standards (set in February 2014) had the role of providing an arena where representatives of MS could discuss technical aspects of the standards both by adapting existing IPSAS and developing new standards suitable for the European context.

One of the issues that emerged at that point was about the governance of the EPSAS and the necessary tools to introduce EPSAS in the European regulatory space. Options such as a Directive or a Regulation for MS were initially considered. However, one of the questions that arose was about the sovereignty power of MS on the matter, as public sector accounting systems form part of the administrative organization of MS. In this realm, the capacity of EC to act as a regulator in public sector accounting is restricted[17] and the support of all MS would be needed, which seemed to be difficult considering the position of some countries, as the case of Germany as evidenced in both public consultations.

In September 2015, the TFs were substituted by the newly developed EPSAS Working Group (WG). Experts from the member countries were selected to support the EC in elaborating and implementing

---

[16] European Commission (2014).

[17] Helldorff and Christiaens (2021).

the new set of standards. Each MS was invited, in consultation with the national standard-setting authorities for public sector accounting, to nominate up to three delegates to the WG. It was expected that the delegates would represent the views of their MS within the WG and present their national experience and viewpoints, introducing proposals and contributing to the debate. The WG maintained the option to invite other experts and institutions to support the process, which has been the case during the meetings of the WG.

Intending to simplify the preparation of the EPSAS, in September 2015 – during the first meeting of the WG – Eurostat decided to split the project between different 'cells', a small group of experts with the duty of making some preparatory work on specific topics, to facilitate the work of the WG. The cells created were the following: the EPSAS Cell First Time Implementation, the EPSAS Cell on Governance Principles, and the EPSAS Cell on Principles related to the EPSAS Standards.

As for the process for introducing the EPSAS, in the first meeting of the EPSAS WG, Eurostat proposed two possible approaches: (a) legally binding EPSAS implemented step-by-step and (b) a more gradual approach developing EPSAS in the medium to long term. The EPSAS Cell on First Time Implementation prepared a Guidance for the First Time Implementation of Accrual Accounting in 2017, where Eurostat highlighted[18] that "the Commission is convinced that a progressive and voluntary approach seems appropriate to begin with in order to first achieve increased fiscal transparency in the short to medium term and then ensure comparability in the medium to the longer term".

In the fifth EPSAS WG meeting (November 2017), Eurostat outlined four options to move forward: a) Discontinuing EPSAS, b) Recommended Conceptual Framework and EPSAS, c) Binding

---

[18] Eurostat (2017, p. 2).

Conceptual Framework and recommended EPSAS, and d) Binding both Conceptual Framework and EPSAS. At the moment (October 2022), the controversy about how to implement the EPSAS continues and the options considered are still the same: from entirely voluntary to partly or fully mandatory.

The EPSAS Cell on Principles was in charge of preparing a draft regarding the accounting principles that would serve as a basis to guide the formulation of EPSAS and their interpretation. Considering these materials, Eurostat prepared a draft of the *EPSAS Conceptual Framework* that was presented at the sixth EPSAS WG in May 2018.

Up to October 2022, the EPSAS WG has convened thirteen meetings (the first meeting in September 2015 - the thirteenth meeting in May 2022)[19].

In parallel to the above actions, the EC opened several calls for tenders for developing some studies and documents useful for the preparatory works for EPSAS. For example, in 2014, PricewaterhouseCoopers (PwC) developed a study about the Potential Impact, Including Costs, of Implementing Accrual Accounting in the Public Sector and Technical Analysis of the Suitability of Individual IPSAS Standards. The study contains an evaluation of the accounting maturity of EU MS. The study was updated in 2020.

In 2016 the EC requested a set of (topical) issue papers commissioned to EY and PwC, two of the Big Four auditing companies, in which a selection of specific accounting topics is analyzed with reference mainly to the provisions of the IPSAS (see more about the issue papers in the dedicated section).

In 2019 the EC commissioned PwC to elaborate the EPSAS screening reports on IPSAS, aiming at assessing the consistency of individual

---

[19] European Commission (2022a).

IPSAS standards against the draft EPSAS CF and the principle of European Public Good to inform future EPSAS standard setting.

In the following paragraphs, we analyzed the main documents issued by Eurostat related to the preparation of the EPSAS framework: Guidance for the First Time Implementation of Accrual Accounting, Draft EPSAS Conceptual Framework, the issue papers and the EPSAS screening reports.

2.1 Guidance for the First Time Implementation of Accrual Accounting

The EPSAS Cell on *First Time Implementation* was in charge of preparing a draft report about the First Time Implementation of Accrual Accounting, which was then discussed in the three first EPSAS WGs meetings, and a final version was presented by Eurostat in April 2017. The guidance contains the EC's opinion as for the EPSAS implementation. The EC was in favour of a progressive and voluntary approach to achieve increased fiscal transparency in the short to medium term and ensure comparability, as a later step, in the medium to the longer term. For this purpose, it suggested a dual phase approach[20].

Phase 1: Increasing fiscal transparency in the EU MS in the short to medium term by promoting accrual accounting, e.g. IPSAS, in the period 2016 to 2020, and in parallel developing the EPSAS framework (i.e. EPSAS governance, accounting principles and standards).

Phase 2: Addressing comparability within and between the EU MS in the medium to longer term, by implementing EPSAS by 2025.

In the first phase, MS would implement accrual accounting for example by adopting or adapting IPSAS while EPSAS would be un-

---

[20] European Commission (2017).

der development. In order to support MS with the process, Eurostat provided financial support for MS to carry out preparatory analyses on the modernization of their public sector accounting systems on an accrual basis. In this line, two calls for proposals were open for the MS[21]. One of them in 2017 for Co-financing of preparatory work for the modernization of public sector accounting systems on an accrual basis of accounting, and another in 2018 for Modernization of public sector accounting on an accrual basis in support of EPSAS.

In the second phase the goal of comparability could be achieved by the EPSAS adoption. Under this planning the move to EPSAS was scheduled for 2025 (the initial plan was for 2020 but it has been postponed). The process and governance about how to implement the EPSAS is strongly debated and up to now has not been decided.

In this context, the character of the EPSAS being either binding or non-binding standards was (and still is) another issue begging for a decision in the process of EPSAS, as we mentioned before. Furthermore, taking into account that a regulatory procedure of the EU requires an impact assessment to justify the decision, in the fifth meeting of the EPSAS WG, Eurostat presented the EPSAS impact assessment considerations, following a request of the Council and endorsed by ECOFIN in November 2017[22]. Impact assessments are prepared for Commission initiatives expected to have significant economic, social or environmental impacts. Imact assessment is a tool to analyze the potential advantages and disadvantages of different available solutions for a particular problem.

In line with the options presented in the fifth EPSAS WG (November 2017), Eurostat outlined that the impact assessment would analyze four options under discussion in EU in relation to EPSAS:

---

[21] https://ec.europa.eu/eurostat/web/epsas/grants

[22] Eurostat (2017).

- Option 1: Binding European Conceptual Framework (CF) and binding EPSAS, accompanied by technical and financial support to MS.
- Option 2: Binding European CF with recommended but voluntary EPSAS, accompanied by technical and financial support to MS, and with a further review based on an assessment after some time of the effectiveness of the approach.
- Option 3: Recommended but voluntary European CF with recommended but voluntary EPSAS, accompanied by technical and financial support to MS and a further review based on an assessment after some time of the effectiveness of the approach.
- Option 4: Discontinue work completely on EPSAS.

Considering the implications of these different options on the objective of comparability of accounting information between EU MS, it can be envisaged that:

Option 1): the objective of harmonization could be achieved but requires more changes to achieve the objectives of EPSAS project with also more efforts and costs necessary.

Option 2): as the EPSAS would be voluntary, MS could adapt their standards to EPSAS and then different national variants would come up, that would diverge from the original ones, which would end up with a questionable comparability in accounting reporting.

Option 3): in this case, MS could decide whether to follow the recommended framework and EPSAS and then heterogeneity would persist across EU.

Option 4): countries would continue with their national standards, but probably most of them would already have implemented accrual accounting, in many cases adapted to IPSAS, but not necessarily harmonized among EU MS and the problems of comparability would not be solved.

The guidance for the first time implementation of accrual-based financial statements intended to support accounting reforms toward accrual accounting and IPSAS adoption in order to improve fiscal transparency, as the first step. As clarified by Eurostat, it is not meant to implement EPSAS as such but to support improvements to fiscal transparency while preparing the ground for implementing EPSAS at a later point in time. As the aim is supporting the preparation of general purpose financial statements under the accrual basis, the guidance is focused on first accrual-based opening balance sheet. Its preparation is based primarily on the experiences of the countries that participated in the EPSAS Cell on *First Time Implementation,* considering also the IPSAS 33 (First time adoption of accrual basis IPSAS).

The guidance contains recommendations for first time recognition of assets and liabilities.

The recommendations of the guidance intend to achieve the most comprehensive coverage possible of assets and liabilities and significant events and transactions in the accrual financial statements, also considering cost effectiveness. Then, a main issue is the recognition of assets and liabilities, for example property, plant and equipment, accepting that problems of initial and subsequent measurement could be dealt with progressively.

2.2 EPSAS Conceptual framework

The work of the EPSAS Cell on Principles related to EPSAS lead to a first draft of the EPSAS CF, which was presented at the sixth EPSAS working group in May 2018. The report defines the general purpose and objectives of financial reports under the EPSAS, their users, qualitative characteristics, application principles and constraints as well as the elements of the financial statements and recognition and measurement criteria. The CF of the EPSAS tries to keep a balance among all existing forces affecting public sector accounting in the realm of EPSAS development. The document proposes that the EPSAS should take into account the standards applied in the EC, the private sector, the nationally developed General Accepted Accounting Principles (GAAP) for the public sector, and the rules of the statistical accounting framework adopted under ESA. Moreover, continuing with the decision adopted in 2013,

> *The EPSAS should be aligned with internationally accepted accounting standards for the public sector where such standards exist.*[23]

The draft EPSAS CF, therefore, provides a set of concepts and definitions for the development, adoption, and publication of EPSAS, and provides guidance for the preparation and the presentation of financial accounting information by public sector entities under the EPSAS basis of accounting.

The structure and elements of the CF are the following (Figure 2)[24]:

> **General Purpose Financial Reports (GPFR) under the EPSAS**
- GPFR: comprise General Purpose Financial Statements (GPFSs) and other reports presenting financial and non-financial information.
- Objectives of GPFR: to provide financial information for accountability and decision making. These are the objectives traditionally defined for accounting systems, both in the private and in the business sector, with some exceptions[25]. In particular, the IPSASB conceptual framework defines the objectives of financial reporting in this line.

---

[23] European Commission (2018, p. 13).

[24] European Commission (2018).

[25] For example, in Germany, the accounting system is focused mainly on accountability purposes (See Mann et al., 2019).

- Objectives of GPFS: to provide a true and fair view of the financial position, financial performance and cash-flows for accountability and decision making purposes, and under the accrual basis of accounting, in the context of sustainability and inter-generational equity.
- Accrual basis of accounting: transactions and other events are recognized in financial statements when they occur and not when cash or its equivalent is received or paid.
- True and fair view: In order to provide a true and fair view GPFRs should conform with the qualitative characteristics, the application principles and the resulting EPSAS deriving therefrom, subject to the constraints.
- Users of GPFR: Resource providers and their representatives as well as service recipients and their representatives – ultimately the citizens.

> **Qualitative Characteristics, Application Principles, Constraints**
- Qualitative characteristics: Relevance, Faithful representation/Reliability, Completeness, Prudence[26], Neutrality, Verifiability, Substance over form, Understandability, Timeliness, Comparability.
- Application principles: Going concern, Consistency, Offsetting/Aggregation, Presentational sensitivity, Reporting period, Compliance.
- Constraints: Materiality, Cost-benefit, Balance between the individual qualitative characteristics and application principles objectives of financial reporting.

---

[26] The EPSAS CF defines prudence "the inclusion of a degree of caution in the exercise of the judgments needed in making the estimates required under conditions of uncertainty, such that assets or revenue are not overstated while liabilities or expenses are not understated". This means that expenses and revenues must be considered with neutrality, while in some jurisdictions prudence has a conservatism orientation, that means that possible future losses are recognized but not future gains (this is the case for example of Germany, see Mann et al., 2019).

It has to be mentioned that the order of the qualitative characteristics, the application principles and the constraints does not imply a hierarchy.

> **Definition of Elements**
- Assets: An asset is a resource, an item with service potential or the ability to generate economic benefits,- presently controlled by the entity as a result of past events or transactions.
- Liabilities: A liability is a present obligation of the entity for an outflow of resources that results from past events or transactions.
- Expenses: An expense is a decrease in the net financial position of the entity, other than a decrease arising from ownership distribution.
- Revenues: A revenue is an increase in the net financial position, other than an increase arising from ownership contribution.
- Ownership contributions: Ownership contributions are inflows of resources to an entity, contributed by external parties in their capacity as owners, which establish or increase an interest in the net financial position of the entity.
- Ownership distributions: Ownership distributions are outflows of resources from the entity, distributed to external parties in their capacity as owners, which return or reduce an interest in the net financial position of the entity.

> **Recognition and Derecognition of Elements**
- Recognition: process of incorporating and including an item on the face of the appropriate financial statement.
- Recognition criteria: An item should be recognized when it satisfies the definition of an element; and can be measured in a way that achieves the qualitative characteristics and takes account of constraints on information in GPFRs.

- Derecognition: Process of evaluating whether changes have occurred since the previous reporting date that would warrant removing an element that had been previously recognized from the financial statements

➢ **Measurement**
- It should reflect the objectives of financial reporting under the EPSAS basis of accounting, as well as comply with qualitative characteristics, application principles and constraints of information in financial reports.
- Measurement concepts for assets: historical costs and current value.
- Measurement concepts for liabilities: historical costs and current value.
- Measurement bases: The selection of a measurement basis for assets and liabilities in order to meet the objectives of financial reporting would be provided in EPSAS.

➢ **GPFS**. A complete set of GPFS should comprise: A statement of financial position, a statement of financial performance, a statement of changes in net assets/ equity, a cash flow statement, Notes to the financial statements and *Other comprehensive statements*[27].

➢ **Public Sector Reporting Entity**. GPFS under the EPSAS basis of accounting should serve *the public interest and be conducive to the European public good*. This implies that every entity which is held accountable for receiving resources, and for the use it makes of them for delivering public goods, public services or public programmes, is considered as a public sector entity.

---

[27] As for other comprehensive statements, the body of the text of the EPSAS CF does not provide any examples. It just mentions this type of statements in italics and brackets in the original text, i.e. [*other comprehensive statements*]. However the topic has been discussed with the use of examples in the WG meetings.

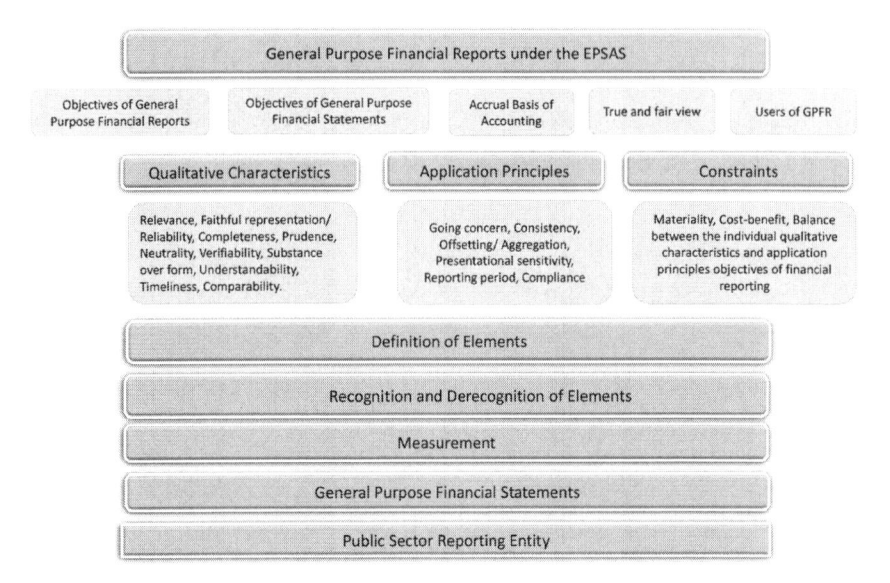

Figure 13.2: Elements of the Draft EPSAS Conceptual Framework

The CF is structured in a less expected way as the elements of the financial statements are defined before the GPFS. Moreover, the objectives of the GPFR should consider the users of financial reports and their needs that should be at the core of the CF.

2.3 EPSAS Governance

The issue of the governance for the future EPSAS was identified as a priority since the beginning of the project and a TF on EPSAS Governance (set in October 2013) worked on the development of a suitable model for the EPSAS governance structure. Considering the discussion of the TF, Eurostat decided to launch a second public consultation on EPSAS governance in order to ensure that views are collected from the widest possible range of stakeholders. Figure 13.3 contains the proposed structured of EPSAS Governance in the public consultation, which included a high-level Committee- supervised by European Institutions-and two WGs and TFs, as well as a technical advisory group.

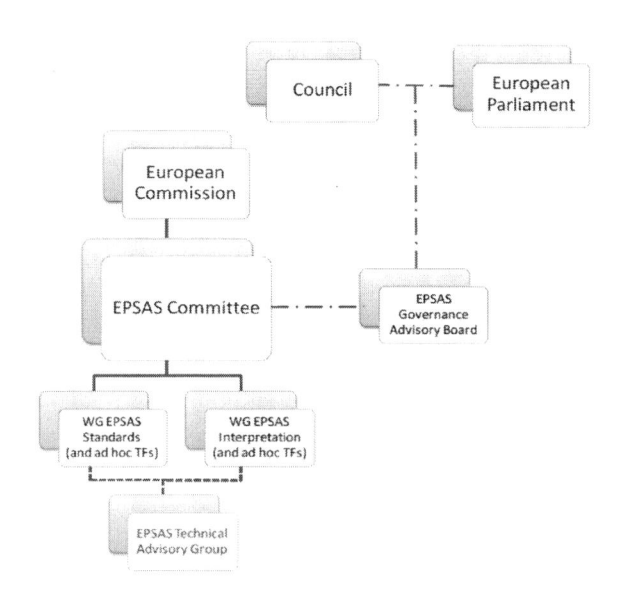

Figure 13.3: Proposed EPSAS governance structure in the Public Consultation[28]

In total, 203 responses were received in this consultation, with a high percentage of contributions coming from Germany. The main conclusion after analyzing the responses was that the proposed model was not considered suitable enough and many comments reaised concerns about it, forcing in this sense the EC to continue working on it.

In 2015, the EPSAS Cell on Governance Principles assumed this task. In the fourth EPSAS WG meeting (April 2017), Eurostat presented the report of the Cell, dealing with the objectives as well as the users of the EPSAS and the GPFRs, *Other comprehensive*

---

[28] European Commission (2014).

statements, the governance principles and the functional analysis (e.g., functions for oversight/monitoring and technical advice). As for the objectives of GPFRs and the users, as analyzed before, they have been included in the Draft CF.

With respect to the governance principles, the report identified the following characteristics necessary for EPSAS governance: professional independence and integrity, transparency and openness of procedures, legitimacy, competence and capacity, efficiency and effectiveness and accountability. For the moment, there is not a final decision regarding the bodies that would assume the standard-setting function, oversight and technical advisory, and it seems that they have to be agreed upon in the context of the EPSAS due process where legitimacy issues should be taken into consideration[29]. In this respect, it can be useful to look at the IPSASB experience, where the due process for standards includes consultation with stakeholders through public consultations and transparency. The communication about the EPSAS project has been already established through two public consultations, the TFs and the WGs, where MS and different observers have participated. Nevertheless, the high implications and impact of the EPSAS can require to open the discussion to all stakeholders, and in particular to academics[30]. In parallel, it would be important to clarify what will be the regulatory tool to be used as well as the character of the EPSAS for MS, considering potential legal issues that emerge as fas as the EU capacity to establish compulsory accounting standards is concerned.

It can be also mentioned that the EPSAS governance influenced the governance of the IPSAS, as some of the comments to the first public consultation shown concerns about the governance and oversight of the IPSASB, arguing that the IPSASB governance was

---

[29] Dabbicco and Steccolini (2021).

[30] Manes-Rossi et al. (2021).

not totally suitable for the EU. In 2014, it was created an IPSASB Governance Review Group to recommend future governance and oversight arrangements for the international standards for the public sector, in which Eurostat participated as an observer.[31]. This initiative carried out by the IPSASB about the governance and monitoring of the standard setting process could also be useful for defining the EPSAS governance.

2.4 EPSAS issue papers

The EC requested a set of *issue papers* commissioned to EY and PwC, two of the Big Four auditing companies, on issues that have been raised as particularly important by experts and stakeholders participating in the WGs and cells.

In the issue papers, the topics are analyzed with reference mainly to the provisions of the IPSAS (both specific IPSAS and the IPSAS CF), the ESA including the Manual on Government Deficit and Debt (MGDD) when applicable, the IFRS, the Government Finance Statistics Manual (GFSM), the EC accounting rules and selected MS accounting standards. The national accounting standards considered are not the same in all issue paper. The examples mainly come from countries with accrual accounting standards or countries that have adapted to IPSAS, such as Austria, Belgium, Estonia, Finland, France, Latvia, Slovak Republic or United Kingdom. For each of

---

[31] After a public consultation to gather views from stakeholders and the public, the Governance Review Group made some recommendations intended at ensuring neutrality in the process. In particular, the Review Group proposed the establishment of the Public Interest Committee, in order to ensure that the public interest is served by the standard setting activities of the IPSASB. The Committee oversights the IFAC and IPSASB activities and nominations around three pillars: rigorous due process, qualified and inclusive appointments and relevant and timely standards; https://www.oecd.org/gov/budgeting/oecd-public-interest-committee.htm

the topics, the issue paper analyses the problems with regards to definition, recognition, measurement and disclosure, the advantages and disadvantages of the existing approaches and possible ways forward for EPSAS.

The list of the papers prepared by the two consulting firms is provided in Table 13.1. The full list of EPSAS issue papers is available at https://ec.europa.eu/eurostat/web/epsas/key-documents/technical-developments

N.	EPSAS Issue paper	Producer	Date
1	Approach for narrowing down of options within IPSAS	EY	June 2016
2	Relief for smaller and less risky entities from financial reporting requirements under the future EPSAS	EY	June 2016
3	Accounting treatment of taxes with a view to financial reporting requirements under the future EPSAS	EY	Oct. 2016
4	Accounting treatment of employee benefits (pensions) with a view to financial reporting requirements under the future EPSAS	EY	Nov. 2016
5	Accounting treatment of social benefits with a view to financial reporting requirements under the future EPSAS	EY	Nov.2016
6	Accounting treatment of infrastructure assets with a view to financial reporting requirements under the future EPSAS	EY	Feb. 2017
7	Segment reporting under the future EPSAS	EY	March 2017
8	Accounting treatment of heritage assets with a view to financial reporting requirements under the future EPSAS	EY	March 2017
9	Accounting treatment of military assets with a view to financial reporting requirements under the future EPSAS	EY	April 2017

N.	EPSAS Issue paper	Producer	Date
10	Member States' approaches to harmonizing charts of accounts formational purposes with a view to financial reporting requirements under the future EPSAS	PwC	Sept. 2017
11	Accounting treatment of social contributions with a view to financial reporting requirements under the future EPSAS (After Comments of WG)	EY	Oct. 2017
12	Accounting treatment of intangible assets with a view to financial reporting requirements under the future EPSAS	PwC	Jan.2018
13	Applying discount rates under the future EPSAS	PwC	March 2018
14	Accounting treatment of grants and other transfers with a view to financial reporting requirements under the future EPSAS	PwC	March 2018
15	Principal approach to disclosures with a view to financial reporting requirements under the future EPSAS	PwC	March 2018
16	Accounting treatment of provisions, contingent assets, contingent liabilities and financial guarantees with a view to financial reporting requirements under the future EPSAS	PwC	August 2018
17	Accounting treatment of loans and borrowings with a view to financial reporting requirements under the future EPSAS	PwC	Sept. 2018
18	The notion of control and its implications for financial reporting requirements under the future EPSAS	PwC	Sept. 2018
19	Consolidation of financial statements with a view to financial reporting requirements under the future European Public Sector Accounting Standards (EPSAS)	PwC	Oct.2018
20	Accounting treatment of service concession arrangements with a view to financial reporting requirements under the future EPSAS	PwC	Oct. 2018

Table 13.1: EPSAS Issue papers

For example, Table 13.2 shows the table of contents of the EPSAS issue paper on the accounting treatment of infrastructure assets, prepared by EY.

> **Table of contents**
>
> 1. Objectives of the Issue Paper
> 2. Background
> 3. Description of accounting guidance available
>   3.1 IPSAS
>   3.2 European Union Accounting Rules
>   3.3 IFRS
>   3.4 National accounts/statistical reporting (ESA 2010 and GFS)
>   3.5 National public sector accounting frameworks
> 4. Discussion of matters relevant for a European harmonization
>   4.1 Taking stock of infrastructure assets
>   4.2 What are the problematic points/issues with regards to definition, recognition, measurement and disclosure of infrastructure assets?
>   4.3 Financing of infrastructure assets
>   4.4 Impairment of infrastructure assets
>   4.5 Service concession arrangements
>   4.6 What are the advantages and disadvantages of the existing approaches to recognition and measurement?
>   4.7 Need for supplementary guidance to what is currently foreseen under IPSAS and format of that guidance
>   4.8 What are the consequences for a possible convergence between IPSAS and GFS/ESA?
> 5. Develop an approach for organizing the future discussion on infrastructure assets with the EPSAS stakeholders
> Annex 1: Summary accounting treatment National public sector accounting frameworks versus the IPSAS 17 treatment.

Table 13.2: Table of Contents of an Issue Paper[32]

In this case, the issue paper took into consideration the materials of IPSASB and IPSAS, the EU Accounting Rules, IFRS and ESA 2010 and the accounting standards of France, Austria and the City of Essen (Germany).

The issue paper analyses the most important categories of infrastructure assets and problematic aspects about their definition, recognition and measurement as well as the different approaches of the existing standards. The last section of the issue paper contains some recommendations about how to organize future discussions on accounting for infrastructure assets with

---

[32] Source: EPSAS issue paper on the accounting treatment of infrastructure assets (European Commission, 2022b).

the EPSAS stakeholders. For example, in order to reduce the options offered by IPSAS 17 for the measurement of these assets, the issue paper recommends to explore the application of the revaluation model in order to evaluate if it can be removed from a practical point of view.

Finally, the appendix compares the accounting treatment of infrastructure assets in IPSAS 17 with the accounting standards applied in France, Austria and the City of Essen.

2.5 EPSAS screening reports on IPSAS

One of the issues that emerged during the EPSAS project was about the impact that EPSAS could have in MS. This led the Council and ECOFIN to ask the EC to work on the impact assessment of the EPSAS in November 2017 in order to provide a comprehensive account of both positive and negative impacts. With a view to analyze the impact considerations, Eurostat contracted two studies:

- In 2017 contracted with EY the report *Collection of additional and updated information related to the potential impacts of EPSAS.*
- *In 2018,* contracted with PwC the report *Collection of further and updated information related to the potential impact of implementing accrual accounting in the public sector*

With these two reports underlying the benefits of accrual accounting in general and EPSAS in particular, and the issue papers supporting the implementation of the EPSAS, the Commission started in 2019 to evaluate the suitability of the IPSAS for the European context. It was in the ninth EPSAS WG meeting (November 2019) that Eurostat announced a process reviewing individual IPSAS to assess their consistency with the draft EPSAS CF with a view to informing future EPSAS standard-setting.

In the tenth, eleventh and twelfth meeting of the EPSAS WG (November 2020, April 2021 and November 2021)[33], Eurostat presented a number of screening reports on IPSAS. The list of EPSAS screening reports published up to October 2022 is provided in Table 13.3. The screening reports are available at https://ec.europa.eu/eurostat/web/epsas/key-documents/technical-developments. Table 13.4 contains the EPSAS screening reports under preparation.

Screening report IPSAS 2 – Cash flow statements
Screening report IPSAS 4 – The effects of changes in foreign exchange rates
Screening report IPSAS 5 – Borrowing costs
Screening report IPSAS 12 – Inventories
Screening report IPSAS 13 - IFRS 16 – Leases
Screening report IPSAS 16 – Investment Property
Screening report IPSAS 17 – Property, plant and equipment
Screening report IPSAS 18 – Segment Reporting
Screening report IPSAS 19 – Provisions, contingent liabilities and contingent assets
Screening report IPSAS 21 – Impairment of non-cash-generating assets
Screening report IPSAS 22 – Disclosure of financial information about the General Government Sector
Screening report IPSAS 26 – Impairment of cash-generating assets
Screening report IPSAS 27 – Agriculture
Screening report IPSAS 28 – Financial instruments: presentation
Screening report IPSAS 30 – Financial instruments: disclosures
Screening report IPSAS 31 – Intangible assets
Screening report IPSAS 32 – Service Concession Arrangements: Grantor
Screening report IPSAS 35 – Consolidated financial statements
Screening report IPSAS 36 – Investment in associates and joint ventures
Screening report IPSAS 37 – Joint arrangements
Screening report IPSAS 38 – Disclosure of interests in other entities
Screening report IPSAS 39 – Employee benefits
Screening report IPSAS 41 – Financial instruments
Screening report IPSAS 42 – Social benefits

Table 13.3: EPSAS Screening reports published

---

[33] European Commission (2022a).

> Screening report IPSAS 1 – Presentation of Financial Statements
> Screening report IPSAS 3 – Accounting Policies, Changes in Accounting Estimates and Errors
> Screening report IPSAS 9 – Revenue from Exchange Transactions
> Screening report IPSAS 10 – Financial Reporting in Hyperinflationary Economies
> Screening report IPSAS 11 – Construction Contracts
> Screening report IPSAS 14 – Events after the Reporting Date
> Screening report IPSAS 20 – Related Party Disclosure
> Screening report IPSAS 23 – Revenue from Non-Exchange Transactions
> Screening report IPSAS 24 – Presentation of Budget Information in Financial Statements
> Screening report IPSAS 33 – First-time Adoption of Accrual Basis IPSAS
> Screening report IPSAS 34 – Separate Financial Statements
> Screening report IPSAS 40 – Public Sector Combinations

Table 13.4: EPSAS Screening reports under preparation (October 2022)

The purpose of the screening reports is to assess the consistency of individual IPSAS standards with the draft EPSAS CF and the principle of European Public Good, in order to inform future EPSAS standard setting. The analysis reflects whether the criteria of the draft EPSAS CF are met by taking into account the IPSAS authoritative text, together with non-authoritative guidance where this is necessary[34].

The screening reports assess individual IPSAS standards against the criteria listed in the draft EPSAS CF, in particular whether the IPSAS are [35]:

- conducive to the European Public Good,
- conducive to the objectives of the GPFRs, and
- conforming to the qualitative characteristics and the application principles; taking into consideration the constraints, and other concepts defined in the draft EPSAS CF.

---

[34] European Commission (2020).

[35] European Commission (2020).

In order to assess whether an IPSAS would be conducive to the European Public Good, the EPSAS screening reports analyze: a) whether the IPSAS standard would improve financial reporting; b) the costs and benefits associated with the implementation of the standard in the MS; and c) whether the standard could have an adverse effect to the European economy, including financial stability and economic growth. For example, the Screening report IPSAS 2 – Cash flow statements, prepared by PwC, uses the following procedure (Table 13.5):

> *First, the paper addresses whether IPSAS 2 would meet the qualitative characteristics of the EPSAS framework, i.e. whether it would provide relevant, reliable, complete, prudent, neutral, verifiable, economically substantive, understandable, timely and comparable information and would not be contrary to the true and fair view principle.*
> *This report then considers recognition, classification, measurement, presentation and disclosure requirements applicable to the cash flows each of the qualitative characteristics of the EPSAS framework.*
> *Further, this paper includes a high-level comparison between the requirements of IPSAS 2 and other international accounting and financial reporting frameworks applied by the public sector entities in various jurisdictions, such as IFRS, ESA 2010 and EU Accounting Rules (AR), bearing in mind the objective of alignment, reduction of cost of implementation and compliance cost.*

Table 13.5: Procedure followed in the Screening report IPSAS 2 – Cash flow statements[36]

The paper concludes that the IPSAS 2 is consistent with the EPSAS CF and that is conductive to the European Public Good (Table 13.6):

---

[36] Screening report IPSAS-2 (European Commission, 2022b).

> Assessing IPSAS 2 against the criteria formulated in the EPSAS CF
> The analysis has not revealed major conceptual issues with IPSAS 2 'Cash flow statements' and has not identified any inconsistency between IPSAS 2 and the EPSAS CF.
> - IPSAS 2 'Cash flow statements' provides relevant, reliable, complete, prudent, neutral, verifiable, economically substantive, understandable, timely and comparable information needed for making economic decisions and achieving the necessary level of financial transparency and comparability of financial reporting in the European Union;
> - the information resulting from the application of IPSAS 2 would not be contrary to the true and fair view principle
>
> Assessing whether IPSAS 2 is conducive to the European public good
> The analysis revealed no reasons why IPSAS 2 would not be conducive to the European public good:
> - Transparent presentation of cash flows generated by the public sector entities in the cash flow statement prepared in accordance with IPSAS 2 will provide useful information to the users of the GPFSs and will improve the overall quality of financial reporting in the public sector.
> - Implementation of the standard should result in moderate one-off costs and should be relatively cost-neutral on an ongoing basis for preparers. Any one-off costs are expected to be limited to updating internal processes and systems in order to generate the required cash flow information. The requirements of IPSAS 2 only deal with presentation and disclosure and as such do not change existing recognition or measurement requirements in other standards. Cash flow information can be useful to support better budgetary decisions and accountability of the public sector entities.
> - The standard will bring improved financial reporting when compared to the heterogeneous reporting requirements currently applied in the EU. As such, its endorsement is conducive to the European public good in that improved financial reporting improves transparency and assists in the assessment of management stewardship. The analysis has not identified any adverse effect of the standard to the European economy, including financial stability and economic growth, or any other factors that would mean the standard is not conducive to the European public good.

Table 13.6: Conclusions in the Screening report IPSAS 2 – Cash flow statements[37]

In the majority of the IPSAS analyzed in the screening reports, no major conceptual issues were revealed, and no inconsistencies were identified with the draft EPSAS CF, while the IPSAS were considered conductive to the European Public Good. However, in many cases, the analysis concluded that for the IPSAS to achieve consistent application within the EU context and better address the

---

[37] Screening report IPSAS-2 (European Commission, 2022b).

comparability objective of the EPSAS GPFS, additional guidance and improvements in certain areas might be desirable.

3. Challenging issues

EPSAS are expected to bring public sector entities and governments at different levels, all the benefits that are related to accrual accounting[38]. Apart from the benefits that relate to accrual accounting information for both internal and external users in terms of decision-making and accountability[39], EPSAS are expected to offer comparability and transparency in the EU that will, among others, facilitate the production of comparable data to ensure high-quality input for statistical purposes that are important for monitoring and following up the requirements of the EU policies and obligations. This is especially relevant considering the recent inflation in the Euro zone (relevant to the energy crisis and the war in Ukraine), problems of the Euro exchange rate (in relation to its parity with the dollar), and the deterioration of public finances in EU MS due to the COVID pandemic of 2020-2021 which has resulted in the introduction of changes in the fiscal rules.

However, the EPSAS project also faces some challenges. The most prevailing ones are: a) the cost related to EPSAS implementation; b) the closeness of EPSAS to IPSAS and c) the unclear competences of the EU to establish compulsory accounting standards for MS and the suitable legal approach to be used for EPSAS.

The cost of EPSAS implementation is a challenging issue. The cost of accrual accounting adoption (EPSAS included) is expected

---

[38] Brusca et al. (2015).
[39] World Bank (2022).

to be significant for several MS based on the analysis of PwC[40]. The EPSAS-related costs largely depend on the accounting maturity of the public sector accounting in the country, at the different government levels and types of public sector entities, the availability of IT systems, and the size of the public sector to be applied. However, the estimated cost of EPSAS implementation is expected to be spread over several years and therefore the total cost will burden several yearly government budgets. The cost of EPSAS, that in essence related to accrual accounting implementation, corresponds to the renewal or upgrading of IT systems, the training for existing and newly employed personnel, the fees for consulting and expert assistance, among others[41].

The difference between IPSAS and EPSAS is also another issue that deserves attention. The initial idea was that EPSAS would stay as close to IPSAS as possible. Hence, some IPSAS might be implemented with minor or no adaptation, while for some other adaptation or amendment would be necessary. Furthermore, it could be convenient to develop some additional standards for issues that the IPSAS do not deal with yet, such as standards govering differential reporting and simplified standards for less risky entities. The recent screening reports reveal that IPSAS standards are consistent with the EPSAS CF and the European Public Good. Since the EU initiated the idea for EPSAS development, several EU MS have moved on by adopting IPSAS or IPSAS-like public sector accounting standards, sometimes with financial support of the EU.[42] Changing the newly implemented standards to a new set

---

[40] PwC (2014; 2020).
[41] World Bank (2022).
[42] Brusca et al. (2021).

of standards especially if the differences are not material might cause resistance or reluctance.[43],[44]

The third challenge the EPSAS face and that can affect the progress of the project is the doubts about the competence of the EU to set compulsory accounting standards for MS, considering that public sector accounting forms part of the administrative organization of the MS and therefore sovereignty issues can emerge. The option of binding EPSAS could need the support of all EU MS[45] and for the moment there are some countries that show some resistance towards the development of a set of common standards for EU. In this context, uncertainty also appears about the legal approach to be used for developing the standards, being a Directive, a Regulation or any other option. In fact, at the moment the options considered at the beginning of the project about the binding versus voluntary character of the EPSAS and the conceptual framework are all still on the table.

4. Conclusions

The EPSAS project was initiated in 2013 and it is still in progress. The process has gone through different phases that included two public consultations, Task Forces, EPSAS Cells and the EPSAS WG. Several documents produced by Eurostat as a result of the work of these groups and several studies and papers commissioned to accounting firms (EY and PwC) will serve as a preparatory work for

---

[43] A similar case fostering this concen is analysed by Mann and Lorson (2021).

[44] Cohen et al. (2022).

[45] Helldorff and Christiaens (2021) analyzed what are the possibilities for the EU to regulate a common set of accounting standards for MS.

the EPSAS. The draft of the EPSAS CF already prepared is expected to support the standard setting process.

In parallel during these almost ten years, the EU MS move steadily towards adopting accrual accounting (and even IPSAS) at different levels of government, while waiting for the EPSAS project to conclude. Still, it has not been decided yet what is going to be the binding level of the EPSAS for the public sector in the EU and the legal form that will be used for this purpose. Whether the EPSAS CF or the EPSAS standards *per se* or both are going to be binging for the MS is something still to be decided. Whether the EU is able to enforce a set of European accounting standards has still to be clarified.

Moreover, the recent COVID-19 crisis has put additional strain on public sector finances and it has also affected public sector accounting. Maybe this could provide a good opportunity for the EU to start moving faster to develop EPSAS[46] and conclude with the harmonization process in public sector accounting in the MS. The crises that the governments face seem to be continuous (e.g. war in Ukraine, energy crisis) and it is for the benefit of the MS to fortify their public financial systems the soonest possible both for their own good at the micro-level and for being able to cooperate with transparency, comparability and solidarity with the other MS in the EU.

Bibliographical references

AGGESTAM, Caroline and BRUSCA, Isabel (2016) – The first steps towards harmonizing public sector accounting for European Union member states: strategies and perspectives. *Public Money & Management*, 36(3), 181-188.

---

[46] Cohen et al. (2021).

BASKERVILLE, Rachel and GROSSI, Giuseppe (2019) – Glocalization of accounting standards: Observations on neo-institutionalism of IPSAS. *Public Money & Management*, 39(2), 95-103.

BRUSCA, Isabel, CAPERCHIONE, Eugenio, COHEN, Sandra and MANES ROSSI, Francesca (Eds), (2015) – *Public Sector Accounting and Auditing in Europe. The Challenge of Harmonization*. Palgrave Macmillan.

BRUSCA, Isabel, GOMES Patrícia, FERNANDES, Maria José and MONTESINOS, Vicente (Eds.) (2021) – Challenges in the *Adoption of International Public Sector Accounting Standards. The Experience of the Iberian Peninsula as a Front Runner*. Palgrave Macmillan.

CARUANA, Josette, DABBICCO, Giovanna, JORGE, Susana and JESUS, Maria Antónia (2019) – The Development of EPSAS: Contributions from the Literature. *Accounting in Europe*, 16(2), 146-176.

COHEN, Sandra, MANES ROSSI, Francesca, CAPERCHIONE, Eugenio and BRUSCA, Iisabel (2021) – Debate: If not now, then when? Covid-19 as an accelerator for public sector accrual accounting in Europe, *Public Money and Management*, 41(1), 10-12.

COHEN, Sandra, MANES ROSSI, Francesca and BRUSCA, Isabel (2022) – Public Sector Accounting Harmonization in the European Union through the lens of the Garbage Can model, *Financial Accountability and Management*, https://doi.org/10.1111/faam.12348s.

DABBICCO, Giovanna and STECCOLINI, Ileana (2020) – Building legitimacy for European public sector accounting standards (EPSAS): A governance perspective. *International Journal of Public Sector Management*, 33(2-3), 229-245.

ERNST & YOUNG (2012) – Overview and comparison of public accounting and auditing practices in the EU Member Status. Eurostat.

EUROPEAN COMMISSION (2010) – Proposal for a Council directive on requirements for budgetary frameworks of the Member States.

EUROPEAN COMMISSION (2011) – Communication from the Commission to the European Parliament and the Council, *Towards robust quality management for European Statistics*. https://eur-lex.europa.eu/legal-content/EN/ALL/?uri=CELEX%3A52011DC0211

EUROPEAN COMMISSION (2012) – Assessment of the suitability of the International Public Sector Accounting Standards for the Member States – Sumary of Responses. Available at https://ec.europa.eu/eurostat/documents/10186/752720/D4_2012-EN.PDF

EUROPEAN COMMISSION (2013a) – Towards implementing harmonized public sector accounting standards in member states, the suitability of IPSAS for the member states. Report from the Commission to the Council and the European Parliament. https://eur-lex.europa.eu/legal-content/EN/TXT/?qid=1410447825715&uri=CELEX:52013DC0114

EUROPEAN COMMISSION (2013b) – Commission staff working document, accompanying the report from the commission to the council and the European parliament. Towards implementing harmonized public sector accounting standards in Member States, The suitability of IPSAS for the Member States. https://eur-lex.europa.eu/legal-content/EN/TXT/?qid=1410447910591&uri=CELEX:52013SC0057

EUROPEAN COMMISSION (2014) – "Public consultation on future EPSAS governance principles and structures: Draft Report". Paper presented for the Task Force "EPSAS

Governance". Luxemburg, March. https://circabc.europa.eu/ui/group/8b9f731d-4826-4708-9069-5f65a9edc9bf/library/f4eba8a3-9516-4132-bef1-d5ccd5fb29b9/details.

EUROPEAN COMMISSION (2017) – *EPSAS impact assessment considerations*. https://circabc.europa.eu/sd/a/c272e5c7-4478-4d10-9dd4-8f5adadb0d73/Agenda%20Item%204%20-%20EPSAS%20Impact%20assessment%20considerations.pdf

EUROPEAN COMMISSION (2018) – *European Public Sector Accounting Standards-Conceptual Framework. Reflection paper for discussion*. https://circabc.europa.eu/d/a/workspace/SpacesStore/f2d052e0-2821-4a25-96fc-6cbbc3ffcf07/Item%204%20-%20The%20EPSAS%20Conceptual%20Framework.pdf

EUROPEAN COMMISSION (2020) – Introduction and Overview to EPSAS Screening Reports. https://circabc.europa.eu/sd/a/dd5b0382-8304-4276-b9f7-19806af0db97/Introduction%20and%20Overview%20to%20EPSAS%20Screening%20Reports.docx.pdf

EUROPEAN COMMISSION (2022a) – Working Group on EPSAS and other Expert Groups. Material of the EPSAS project. In https://ec.europa.eu/eurostat/web/epsas/expert-groups.

EUROPEAN COMMISSION (2022b) – Technical developments: issue papers and screening reports. https://ec.europa.eu/eurostat/web/epsas/key-documents/technical-developments

EUROPEAN PARLIAMENT (2011) – Report on the proposal for a Council directive on requirements for budgetary frameworks of the Member States. 6-5-2011. https://www.europarl.europa.eu/doceo/document/A-7-2011-0184_EN.html

EUROSTAT (2013) – European System of National and Regional Accounts: ESA 2010 https://ec.europa.eu/eurostat/documents/3859598/5925693/KS-02-13-269-EN.PDF/44cd9d01-bc64-40e5-bd40-d17df0c69334 .

EUROSTAT (2017) – EPSAS Working Group Guidance for the first time implementation of accrual accounting. Available on https://circabc.europa.eu/sd/a/d1b2b587-c4b8-4fdf-a2e2-5735ae362b15/First%20time%20implementation%20guidence.pdf

HELLDORFF, Karoline and CHRISTIAENS, Johan (2021) – Harmonizing public sector accounting laws and regulations of the European Union member states: powers and competences. *International Review of Administrative Sciences*, online first, https://doi.org/10.1177/00208523211060

MANES-ROSSI, Francesca, COHEN, Sandra and BRUSCA, Isabel (2021) – The academic voice in the EPSAS project. *Public Money & Management*, 41(6), 447-455.

MANN, Bianca, LORSON, Peter C., OULASVIRTA, Lasse and HAUSTEIN, Ellen (2019) – The quest for a primary EPSAS purpose–insights from literature and conceptual frameworks. *Accounting in Europe*, 16(2), 195-218.

MANN, Bianca and LORSON, Peter C. (2021) – New development: The first-time adoption of uniform public sector accounting standards - A German case study. *Public Money & Management*, 41(2), pp. 176-180 (https://doi.org/10.1080/09540962.2019.1672931).

PRICEWATERHOUSECOOPERS, PwC (2014) – Collection of Information Related to the Potential Impact, Including Costs, of Implementing Accrual Accounting in the Public Sector and Technical Analysis of the Suitability of Individual IPSAS Standards. https://ec.europa.eu/eurostat/documents/1015035/4261806/EPSAS-study-final-PwC-report.pdf

PRICEWATERHOUSECOOPERS, PwC (2020) – Updated accounting maturities of EU governments and EPSAS implementation cost. June 2020. https://ec.europa.eu/eurostat/documents/9101903/9700113/Updated-accounting-maturities-and-EPSAS-implementation-cost-June+2020.pdf

WORLD BANK (2022) – Caperchione, Cohen, Manes Rossi, Brusca, Warzecha, PULSAR – Benefits of Accrual Accounting in the Public Sector. https://cfrr.worldbank.org/sites/default/files/2022-07/accrual_report.pdf

Additional reading

BRUSCA, Isabel, CAPERCHIONE, Eugenio, COHEN, Sandra and MANES-ROSSI, Francesca (2018) – IPSAS, EPSAS and other challenges in European public sector accounting and auditing. In Ongaro, E. & van Tiel, S. (Eds) *The Palgrave handbook of public administration and management in Europe* (pp. 165-185). Palgrave Macmillan, London.

MATTEI, Giorgia, JORGE, Susana and GRANDIS, Fabio Giulio (2020) – Comparability in IPSASs: Lessons to be Learned for the European Standards. *Accounting in Europe*, 1-25. DOI: 10.1080/17449480.2020.1742362

MUSSARI, Riccardo (2014) – EPSAS and the unification of public sector accounting across Europe. *Accounting, Economics & Law, 4*(3), 299–312.

OULASVIRTA, Lasse O. and BAILEY, Stephen J. (2016) – Evolution of EU public sector financial accounting standardization: critical events that opened the window for attempted policy change. *Journal of European Integration, 38*(6), 653-669.

POLZER, Tobias, GROSSI, Giuseppe and REICHARD, Christoph (2022, January) – Implementation of the international public sector accounting standards in Europe. Variations on a global theme. *Accounting Forum, 46*(1) 57-82.

POLZER, Tobias and REICHARD, Christoph (2020) – IPSAS for European Union Member States as Starting Points for EPSAS - Analysis of the Discourses among Countries and Stakeholders, *International Journal of Public Sector Management*, Vol. 33 No. 2/3, pp. 247-264. https://doi.org/10.1108/IJPSM-12-2018-0276

Discussion Topics

– What was the initial objective of developing EPSAS and why IPSAS were not considered suitable for the EU countries?

– What reasons can be argued for the process of EPSAS development taking so long?

- What options can be adopted for EPSAS implementation and what implications do they have on the accounting harmonization among the EU MS?
- What advantages and disadvantages could be pointed out in the impact assessment of the EPSAS options maintained so far?
- What is the difference between EPSAS issue papers and EPSAS screening reports?
- Which are the basic cost categories that are related to EPSAS implementation and what parameters influence EPSAS implementation cost?

Chapter 14
Alternative Reporting and Non-Financial Accounting Formats

Francesca Manes Rossi
University of Napoli Federico II, Italy
manes@unina.it
https://orcid.org/0000-0001-9617-4379

Isabel Brusca
University of Zaragoza, Spain
ibrusca@unizar.es
https://orcid.org/0000-0002-2897-1744

Sandra Cohen
Athens University of Economics and Business, Greece
scohen@aueb.gr
https://orcid.org/0000-0002-4795-0527

Peter C. Lorson
University of Rostock, Germany
peter.lorson@uni-rostock.de
https://orcid.org/0000-0002-2699-5451

Summary

Alternative and non-financial reporting has gained attention in public sector organizations in the last decades, as a result of the increasing need to provide stakeholders with understandable information on how public resources have been managed and public value has been created for the benefit of the whole community. This need springs not only from accountability duties, but also from the recognized role of citizens as co-producers in designing public services and, more broadly, in engaging in public decision-making. In this chapter, after an introduction on the scope of non-financial disclosure, some of the most widespread formats are discussed, including popular reporting, sustainability reporting, the most recent SDGs reporting and integrated reporting, which are finally compared in a synopsis. Some reflections on possible use of the different non-financial reports and technical reporting issues conclude the chapter.

Keywords

Non-financial disclosure, sustainability reporting, popular reporting, integrated reporting, SDGs reporting

1. Introduction

Public sector organizations are expected to engage with their stakeholders in order to actively involve them in the co-creation of public services, contributing in this way to create value for the benefit of the community (public value creation). Under this perspective, accountability is considered as a fundamental prerequisite, to allow all types of stakeholders to better understand strategies, plans, actions already in place, output and outcomes resulting from managing public resources available and, thus, consider how to cooperate in co-designing public services. In this perspective, the adoption of alternative reporting formats may help overcoming technical terms and language barriers generally surrounding financial accounting reports. At the same time, alternative reporting formats to annual General Purpose Financial Reports (GPFR) may be a suitable means to answer the request for more transparency raised by citizens, lenders or governments who wish to have access to a holistic view of the activities undertaken by each public entity. The chapter aims at discussing the scope and the content of the most common alternative reporting formats for public sector organizations (i.e., popular reporting, sustainability reporting, Sustainable Development Goals (SDGs) reporting and integrated reporting), including not only non-financial reporting but also alternative tools that can offer a more understandable access to financial information. The chapter also offers some reflections on possible evolutions in the development of reports especially designed to meet citizen information needs.

To this end, the chapter is structured as follows: In **Section 2**, the role of non-financial reporting is outlined. **Section 3** describes the aims and the content of the formats most commonly adopted by public sector organizations. **Section 4** provides some reflections on the benefits deriving from the adoption of alternative reporting formats both for managers and politicians, as well as for citizens and other external stakeholders. Finally, **Section 5** concludes the chapter.

2. The role of alternative and non-financial reporting

The quest for accountability and transparency is a never-ending theme while discussing about both the duty of public sector entities and governments in discharging accountability as well as when considering the role of citizens in public decision-making processes and the consequent need to provide information suitable to support a dialogue.[1] **Accountability** means for example that a government (as an agent) explains its actions to citizens (as its principal) inter alia touching on the use of resources and the achievement of objectives.[2]

---

[1] Manes-Rossi et al. (2020).

[2] Figure 9.3 highlights the relationship between transparency, accountability and financial information.

To this end, there is an ongoing global campaign for the implementation and use of accrual-based financial accounting regimes in the public sector, including International Public Sector Accounting Standards (IPSAS).

Although financial information – as provided by annual GPFR – has an important role for accountability purposes, it is not enough considering the type of activities developed by public sector organizations and the way they are financed. Beyond this, it is important that this type of information is communicated in a simplified and more easily understandable manner (e.g. by popular reports) and be complemented with non-financial information (e.g. as for example in sustainability, SDGs or integrated reports). For governments it is of utmost importance to explain how their activities are linked to public services and how they contribute to their objectives which are derived from their pursuit for the common good and public welfare.

> Example
>
> A local government could inform on its strategies in fostering and enlarging carbon neutral public transportation to limit climate change risks by touching upon timing and activities (e.g. technology, number and capacity of new buses) as well as the resources invested in the current period and the overall strategy and budget including future periods. Whereas corresponding GPFR provide information on the monetary dimension of fixed assets, which include buses, non-financial reports may usually mention the financial (economic) dimension, but they will focus on ecological and social aspects, too (e.g. expected short-term reduction of greenhouse gas emissions, reduced noise pollution and long-term health effects). [3]

---

[3] Also, the relevance of non-financial information is derived from their nature as early-warning indicators and thus called 'pre-financials', which is not always accurate (e.g. migration of companies may indicate a lower amount of taxes in the future; but their departure could also be due to the high local tax rates); see Böcking and Althoff (2017).

In contrast to an annual GPFR, a non-financial report in this sense can be categorised under the umbrella term 'sustainability report'. It offers not only "past, but also future-oriented information in the form of strategy reporting, and cover[s] how the entity interacts with its environment, society and governance ... aims at delivering an overview of an economic, environmental and social performance of an organisation"[4]. Thus, the content of non-financial reports can be characterised by the perspectives or dimensions of the goals depicted in them: 'ESG' (environmental, social, governance), 'social, ecologic, economic', '3 P's (PPP; people, planet, profit) or 5 P's (people, planet, prosperity, peace and partnership)[5]. Summarizing, the nature of non-financial information is mainly narrative, but complemented by qualitative and quantitative indicators (incorporating also financial information) explaining strategies, targets and achievements in a progress reporting style.

The way information is presented may affect the willingness of citizens and other stakeholders to read financial and non-financial information and make informed decisions or actively take part in the political life. Consequently, it is necessary not only to define the content and the focus of reporting, but also the format, the language, the use of visuals (e.g., infographics), the responsiveness to readers' needs and the technology tools they use (e.g. interactive, clickable reports), because all these elements may influence the engaging power of the report.

Public sector organization might liaise with their stakeholders to define the content, the focus, the definition of material issues to be reported, as well as to test the understandability of the drafted reports to ensure broader dissemination[6].

---

[4] Chapter 1, pp. 34f.

[5] The latter refers to a special non-financial report type focusing on the SDGs as released by the United Nations (UN) Department of Economic and Social Affairs: Transforming our world: the 2030 Agenda for Sustainable Development; https://sdgs.un.org/2030agenda

[6] Cohen et al. (2022).

Nowadays different types of reports may support public administrations in satisfying their stakeholders' information needs. The choice may depend on several factors including:

- political willingness to focus on specific issues (e.g. environment, social services, sustainable development, gender equality, financial condition, etc.);
- knowledge and ability of managers and civil servants that may contribute to the preparation of the report;
- the availability of information and the easiness in circulating data and creating indicators, based on the information systems in place;
- the perceived benefits (or shortcomings) of the reporting process on the internal processes and procedures by both politicians, managers and civil servants;
- the expected benefits in activating or nourishing stakeholders' dialogue and favoring citizens' engagement in the political life, triggering their participation as co-producers of public services.

To provide a better understanding of the most commonly adopted, or emerging types of reports (i.e. SDGs reporting), the next section offers an overview of popular, sustainability, SDGs and integrated reporting. However, some other types of reports may be preferred by public entities/governments, such as 'environmental reporting' (focusing mainly on the environmental perspective of sustainability and neglecting the (linkage to) the other two, social and economic), 'climate (action) reporting' (focusing on the most pressing environmental aspect) or 'gender reporting' (focusing mainly on strategies and action adopted to contrast or prevent gender inequality), depending on what the public entities consider material for their stakeholders, as well as on specific requirements imposed by overarching institutions, legislature or fund providers[7].

3. The main formats of alternative and non-financial reporting

The section presents some alternative reporting formats that public sector organizations around the world are adopting, even with a different degree of intensity. The selected formats serve not always as alternatives to traditional financial reporting. Especially, integrated reporting aims at complementing the GPFR by mixing and linking financial with non-financial information.

When a specific format is selected, some other choices have to be made with regards to how to make the report available to all stakeholders (i.e. reporting technology). Nowadays, each institution has its own website, and in some countries all official documents prepared by public entities have to be published in a specific section in this website to ensure transparency.

However, this form of communication might not be sufficient to get in contact with stakeholders, especially with citizens. Consequently, it is advisable to organize public presentations, events or use mass media to let citizens know about the availability of the reports and summarize the content available in a comprehensive manner. In some countries (e.g. UK) municipalities often send the reports directly by mail to citizens in order to overcome the technological gap still existing for elderly people. Each organization has to consider the most suited strategies to reach out the final recipients of

---

[7] For instance, Horizon Europe considers the possession of a Gender Equality Plan as an eligibility criterion for all higher education establishments, research organisations, as well as public bodies from Member States and Associated Countries applying to the programme. This requirement has pushed European universities and research centre to prepare the requested plan and report on gender equality.

the report, which is a prerequisite for an open dialogue. Also, this might lead to an interactive website design and selection criteria, by which a user can design its own report – encompassing only the information he or she is interested in[8].

3.1. Popular reporting

GPFR can be very extensive in terms of pages and therefore inevitably lead to information overload for 'normal' addressees who do not have the necessary expertise. It was against this background that the idea for **popular reports** arose. Born in Anglo-Saxon countries and later spread all over the world, popular reporting is a kind of tool adopted by governments to provide **citizens** with understandable and readable **financial information**, to restore trust and legitimation, but also as a first step to open a dialogue with and actively involve citizens in political life. Through the use of graphs, figures, tables and indicators, governments can create the condition to let citizens understand the financial position of the organization, the cost of public services as well as the value of assets and liabilities belonging to the community. Furthermore, the opportunity to incorporate in one document accessible, engaging and readable non-financial information – creating in this way a **popular integrated report** – is also gaining attention by public sector organizations[9]. To fully exploit the potential of popular financial or popular integrated reporting, citizens might be involved

---

[8] In private sector reporting, we can observe an increasing and also mandatory use of XBRL. For example, the European Union aims at implementing an ESAP (European Single Information Access Point) for mandatory financial and also non-financial reports and reporting contents; https://www.eesc.europa.eu/de/our-work/opinions-information-reports/opinions/european-single-access-point-esap.

[9] Cohen et al. (2017).

in designing the content of these reports including a glossary and connect it with other participation tools adopted by the same entity.

Information technology has increased the opportunity to develop and update a popular report that can convey financial information avoiding technical terms, in a comprehensible and understandable language, allowing the reader to have an overall view of the financial situation of a public entity.[10]

Several standard setters in the **USA and Canada**, starting in early 1990s, have developed guidelines and principles to guide public administration – especially local governments – in preparing popular (annual financial) reports (PAFR). Awards have been created to stimulate the adoption of the PAFR (also called citizen-centric reports) which are actually largely adopted, especially by big cities[11]. Variations in the content of these reports may also depend as well on the constituencies' awareness and sensitivity towards the information conveyed in this report and more generally by citizens' tendency in participating to the political life as on the local setting (due to different jurisdictions and political systems).

Example

The City or Woodstock (Ontario, Canada) discloses four financial reports on its website: Budgets, Capital Improvement Program, Comprehensive Annual Financial Reports and PAFR.[12] For the fiscal year 2020/2021 – ending at April 30, 2021, the latter consists of eight pages and eleven sections.[13] The following figure shows the expenditure section of the Government Funds section.

---

[10] Cohen et al. (2022).

[11] Biondi and Bracci (2018).

[12] https://www.woodstockil.gov/finance/page/popular-annual-financial-reports

[13] Letter from the Mayor (p. 1); Governmental Funds (p. 2); Business-Type Activities (p. 3); Component Unit Funds (p. 4); Sales Tax (p. 5); Capital Improvement (p. 5); Dividing Up The Dollar (p. 6); Property Taxes (p. 6); economic development (p. 7); Long-Term Debt Update (p. 8);. City Directory (p. 8).

EXPENDITURES

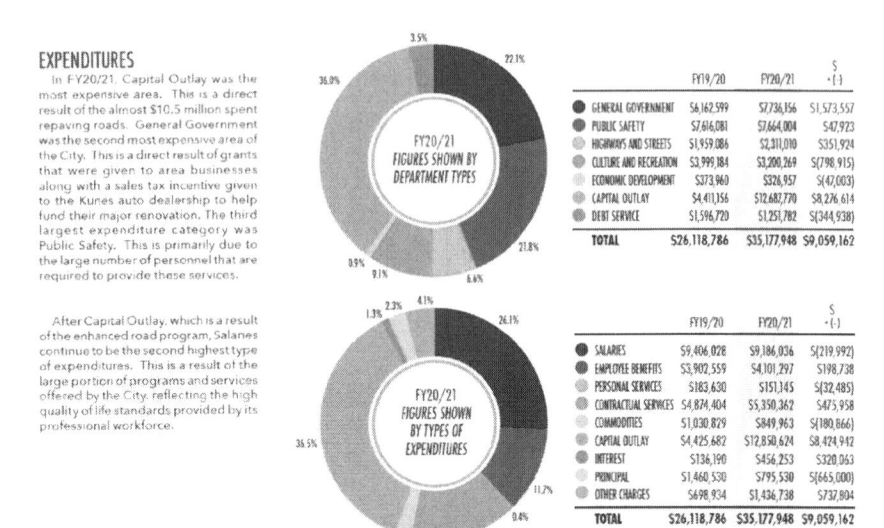

In FY20/21, Capital Outlay was the most expensive area. This is a direct result of the almost $10.5 million spent repaving roads. General Government was the second most expensive area of the City. This is a direct result of grants that were given to area businesses along with a sales tax incentive given to the Kunes auto dealership to help fund their major renovation. The third largest expenditure category was Public Safety. This is primarily due to the large number of personnel that are required to provide these services.

After Capital Outlay, which is a result of the enhanced road program, Salaries continue to be the second highest type of expenditures. This is a result of the large portion of programs and services offered by the City, reflecting the high quality of life standards provided by its professional workforce.

FY20/21 FIGURES SHOWN BY DEPARTMENT TYPES	FY19/20	FY20/21	$ (-)
GENERAL GOVERNMENT	$6,162,599	$7,736,156	$1,573,557
PUBLIC SAFETY	$7,616,081	$7,664,004	$47,923
HIGHWAYS AND STREETS	$1,959,086	$2,311,010	$351,924
CULTURE AND RECREATION	$3,999,184	$3,200,269	$(798,915)
ECONOMIC DEVELOPMENT	$373,960	$326,957	$(47,003)
CAPITAL OUTLAY	$4,411,156	$12,687,770	$8,276,614
DEBT SERVICE	$1,596,720	$1,251,782	$(344,938)
TOTAL	$26,118,786	$35,177,948	$9,059,162

FY20/21 FIGURES SHOWN BY TYPES OF EXPENDITURES	FY19/20	FY20/21	$ (-)
SALARIES	$9,406,028	$9,186,036	$(219,992)
EMPLOYEE BENEFITS	$3,902,559	$4,101,297	$198,738
PERSONAL SERVICES	$183,630	$151,145	$(32,485)
CONTRACTUAL SERVICES	$4,874,404	$5,350,362	$475,958
COMMODITIES	$1,030,829	$849,963	$(180,866)
CAPITAL OUTLAY	$4,425,682	$12,850,624	$8,424,942
INTEREST	$136,190	$456,253	$320,063
PRINCIPAL	$1,460,530	$795,530	$(665,000)
OTHER CHARGES	$698,934	$1,436,738	$737,804
TOTAL	$26,118,786	$35,177,948	$9,059,162

Figure 14.1: Example of expenditures included in a popular report

The example of Woodstock illustrates that PAFR are intended to open an informed discussion, but not to encompass all facets of information presented in annual GPFR. Therefore, the selection process is crucial for the informative value of such reports. As such, the Woodstock's PAFR is an example of an alternative reporting format for a GPFS, but not a non-financial reporting format.

3.2. Sustainability reporting

In the last decades, public sector entities started to be engaged in the preparation of sustainability reports, in order to address environmental, social and governance concerns. Despite its voluntary nature, there are rare cases where their preparation has been mandated or strongly recommended in some countries or for specific organizations. In any case, sustainability reporting is undoubtedly, the most adopted alternative reporting format to complement financial information provided through the annual GPFR.[14] The widespread adoption of sustainability reporting derives from the recognition that sustainability-related issues are at the core of public sector entities' mission and, consequently a broad disclosure should be provided to meet stakeholders' information needs.

Broadly speaking, a sustainability report should offer an overview of the organization, its history, mission and values, how the entity is organized (often including an organizational chart) and the main strategies pursued. Then the main financial data may be reported, generally summarized into broad areas to permit the reader to easily identify resources invested in service creation. A further section may disclose how the organization interacts with the main stakeholders, also providing direction on future plans and actions. In order to summarize the ability of the organizations to achieve the proposed targets, qualitative and quantitative indicators are included. Thus, a sustainability report should be designed as a progress report disclosing sustainability performance, progress and remaining gaps. To ensure trust, data disclosed in the report should be consistent with data provided in other financial or non-financial reports.

These ideas are common to all sustainability reports. Nevertheless, there is a broad diversity in practice with respect to the understanding of sustainability and its facets or focus to be included, the structure and the metrics (e.g. the set of qualitative and quantitative indicators) depending on the frameworks used for sustainability accounting and reporting. Explicit standard setting for sustainability reporting for public sector entities is rare (with the exception of SGDs). Often, governments and other public entities compile their reports based on at least one sustainability framework primarily designed for private sector entities.

In several countries, national standard setters have prepared guidelines in the aim of supporting organizations in the preparation

---

[14] Manes-Rossi et al. (2020).

of these reports, sometimes labeled 'Intellectual Capital Statement'[15]. An example of a public sector specific sustainability guideline can be found in Baden-Württemberg/Germany[16]: Such municipal sustainability reports shall disclose three municipal fields of action as follows:

A: Ecological sustainability
- Climate protection and energy transition
- Sustainable mobility
- Natural resources

B: Economy and Social Affairs: Good life in municipalities
- Sustainable economy and work
- Social, healthy and safe city/municipality
- Culture and education
- Family friendliness and a balanced population development
- Coexistence, integration and equality

C: Framework conditions for sustainable municipal development
- Framework for sustainable, future-oriented sustainable municipal development
- Municipal sustainability management
- Fiscal sustainability
- Citizen participation
- Citizen engagement
- Inter-municipal cooperation
- Global responsibility

Examples for corresponding key performance indicators in the field of action of C: Framework conditions for sustainable municipal development are:

Field of action: municipal sustainability management
C1 Good municipal energy management
- Energy consumption of municipal properties
- per square meter of used space in kilowatt hours

C2 Sustainable municipal procurement
- Proportion of recycled paper in paper consumption of municipal facilities in percent

Field of action: Fiscal sustainability
C3 Healthy structure of the public budget
- Municipal debt per inhabitant

Field of action: Citizen participation
C4 High level of democratic commitment
- Voter turnout in elections for municipal representation and mayoral elections in percent

C5 High level of civic participation
- Number of citizens' meetings according to municipal regulations

Field of action: Civic engagement
C6 High level of voluntary commitment
- Number of registered associations per 1,000 inhabitants and inhabitants

---

[15] E.g. Intellectual Capital Statement – Made in Europe (http://akwissensbilanz.org/en/incas-en/).

[16] LUBW-Leitfaden: N!-Berichte für Kommunen. Leitfaden zur Erstellung von kommunalen Nachhaltigkeitsberichten, 2. Ed., 2015 https://www.statistik-bw.de/Umwelt/Kommunale_Nachhaltigkeit/LUBW_Leitfaden.pdf.

At international level, the Global Reporting Initiative (GRI) is often considered a 'de facto standard setter' (in the private sector) because it seems to hold firmly the supremacy in defining principles and criteria to follow while preparing a sustainability report[17]. Former versions addressed the public sector, but not current standards and work-program[18]. Therefore, it is all but rare to see a fragmented application of GRI guidelines, with public sector entities cherry-pick elements of different standards to apply. The large variety of indicators provided by the GRI, for instance, can be a useful point of reference for organizations operating in different fields.

However, some other standards may coexist with GRI when drafting a sustainability report. For instance, and without attempting to be exhaustive, ISO 14001 standards are designed to support entities in implementing and control environmental management systems. Also, in 2021, GRI provided some guidelines in a joint effort with the Sustainability Accounting Standards Board (SASB) to link sustainability issues to long term financial performance.[19]

From a global perspective, sustainability reporting by public sector entities/governments could be facilitated in the future. In May 2022, the IPSASB launched a consultation paper aimed at establishing global sustainability guidelines specific to the public sector.[20]

---

[17] The GRI offers a reporting framework and 34 topic-specific standards. The modular structure allows organizations to compose their report in accordance with their features and their business model. Also, in future, GRI will develop standards for 40 sectors; https://www.globalreporting.org/standards/sector-program/ The public sector is not addressed in the revised list, but Non-profit organizations (Non-governmental organizations, foundations, professional and civic associations, charities) are; https://www.globalreporting.org/media/mqznr5mz/gri-sector-program-list-of-prioritized-sectors.pdf

[18] Dumay et al. (2010).

[19] https://www.globalreporting.org/media/mlkjpn1i/gri-sasb-joint-publication-april-2021.pdf. SASB's Industry Classification System is designed for companies and distinguishes 77 industries (across 11 sectors) without an explicit reference to the public sector.

[20] IPSASB (2022) proposes to "Serve as the standard setter for global public sector specific sustainability guidance, ... Develop initial guidance focused on general disclosure requirements for sustainability-related information and climate-

In the following section, we continue to discuss sustainability reporting, but with a focus on SDGs.

3.3. SDGs Reporting

Public sector organizations are institutionally inclined to public welfare, i.e. to work towards sustainable development, e.g. to promote social, environmental and economic development that meets the needs of the society without compromising the opportunities of next generations.

In 2015, the United Nations have released the Agenda 2030 and the related 17 goals, well known as (UN-)SDGs, that are also summarized as 5 P's (**people, planet, prosperity, peace and partnership**)[21] and disclosed in Figure 14.2.

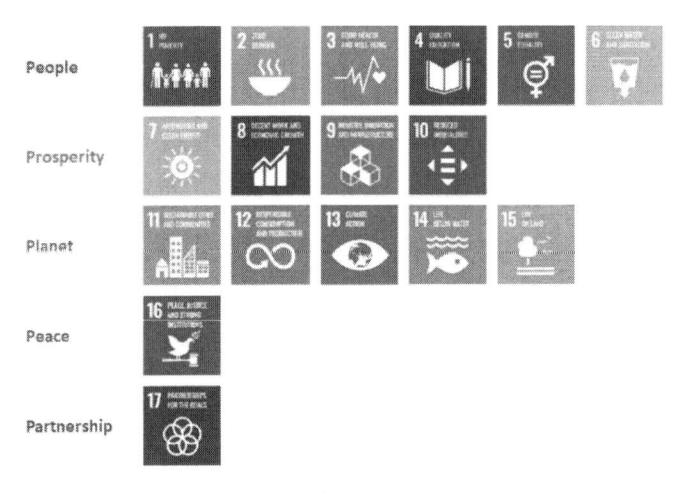

Figure 14.2: UN-SDGs

-related disclosures. Approach guidance development at an accelerated pace, with a potential for releasing initial guidance by the end of 2023"; https://www.ipsasb.org/publications/consultation-paper-advancing-public-sector-sustainability-reporting

[21] United Nations (UN) Department of Economic and Social Affairs: Transforming our world: the 2030 Agenda for Sustainable Development; https://sdgs.un.org/2030agenda

Addressees are international organizations, the business sector, other non-state actors, individuals and especially all levels of governments all over the world. Since the introduction of SDGs, the need to measure and report on efforts dedicated and results obtained for their achievement has emerged[22]. Sustainability strategies adopted by public sector organizations are progressively getting connected with the SDGs and the adoption of monetary and non-monetary measures can help in disclosing resources invested towards the goals sought as well as the output and the outcome achieved. Sometimes, entities publish information about SDGs in their websites, but do not prepare a specific report. In this respect, it has been already proposed to include SDG information and data in the **integrated report** (and maybe in a popular integrated report).

Furthermore, the option of creating a "live document", a kind of web reporting continuously updated when resources are directed towards the achievement of specific goals could be considered as a future reporting means.

In most of the cases, a set of indicators selected from those included in the Global Indicator framework for the Sustainable Development Goals and the targets for the 2030 Agenda for Sustainable Development stated by the United Nations is the solution to concisely represent results obtained.

Some examples of voluntary SDGs annual reports have been published on the UN's website. However, the limited number of reports available is possibly an indicator of the fact that public sector organizations prefer to include information about their action towards SDGs in other reports, such as sustainability reports or other alternative formats.

Also, the European Commission (EC) integrates the SDGs in its policies and strategies[23] as illustrated in Figure 14.3. The EC uses

---

[22] Sobkowiak et al. (2020).

[23] https://ec.europa.eu/info/strategy/international-strategies/sustainable-development-goals_en

its own EU SDGs indicator set – selected both for their EU policy relevance and their statistical quality. Eurostat reports on the SDGs progress in an EU context overall and per member state.[24]

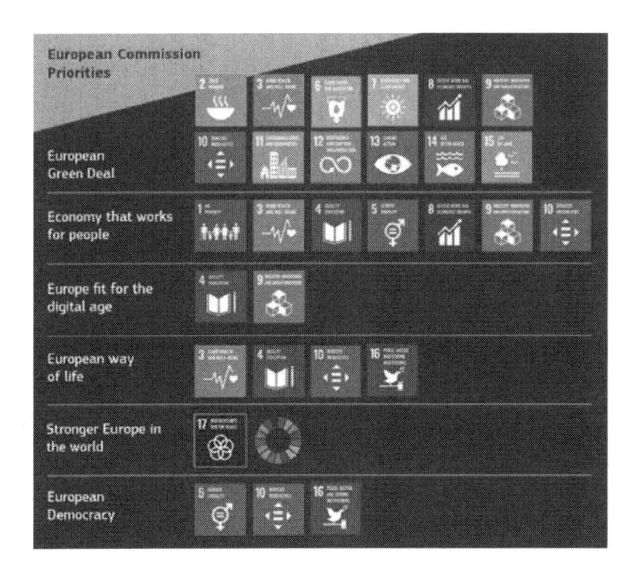

Figure 14.3: European Commissions SDGs priorities[25]

Furthermore, national governments and standard setters propose indicators that might better represent the national context. For instance, in 2018, a common SDG indicator set was selected for Federal Government (central level) and Länder (state level) in Germany (see Figure 14.4), whereas local authorities (municipal and county level) are supported in making their own choice due to diversity of local strategies, individual conditions and constraints. [26]

---

[24] https://ec.europa.eu/info/strategy/international-strategies/sustainable-development-goals/monitoring-and-reporting-sdgs-eu-context_en

[25] https://ec.europa.eu/info/strategy/international-strategies/sustainable-development-goals/eu-holistic-approach-sustainable-development_en

[26] German Sustainable Development Strategy 2021 (short form); https://www.bundesregierung.de/resource/blob/997534/1941044/81190075aa2808adaeb73fa08b6e9bea/2021-07-09-kurzpapier-n-englisch-data.pdf?download=1

No.	Indicator field *Sustainability postulate*	Indicators	Targets	Status
SDG 1. End poverty in all its forms everywhere				
1.1.a	Poverty *Limiting poverty*	Material deprivation	Keep the proportion of persons who are materially deprived considerably below the EU-28 level by 2030	
1.1.b		Severe material deprivation	Keep the proportion of persons who are severely materially deprived considerably below the EU-28 level by 2030	
SDG 2. End hunger, achieve food security and improved nutrition and promote sustainable agriculture				
2.1.a	Farming *Environmentally sound production in our cultivated landscapes*	Nitrogen surplus in agriculture	Reduction of the nitrogen surpluses of the overall balance for Germany to 70 kilograms per hectare of utilised agricultural area on an annual average between 2028 and 2032	
2.1.b		Organic farming	Increase the proportion of organically farmed agricultural land to 20% by 2030	
2.2	Food security *Realising the right to food world-wide*	Support for good governance in attaining appropriate nutrition worldwide	Funds disbursed for the application of the guidelines and recommendations of the UN Committee on World Food Security (CFS) to be increased appropriately as a percentage of total spending on food security by 2030	–

Figure 14.4: German SDG indicator set for Federal Government and Länder (excerpt)[27]

3.4. Integrated Reporting

As already mentioned, there can be at least two large separate reports (a financial (e.g. annual GPFR) and a non-financial (e.g. sustainability or SDGs report)), each of which draws a different picture of the reporting entity. This situation challenges the users in their effort to have a holistic view of the public sector entity. As in practice, the number of different reports is much higher, the need for **one**, concise and effective **report** able to convey to the readers all relevant perspectives by means of both financial and non-financial information, thus drawing a holistic picture, has been particularly intense in corporations. This is a common theme of academics promoting "One Report"[28], of FEE/ACE[29]

---

[27] Ibid.

[28] Eccles and Krzus (2010).

[29] Since 2016, FEE (Fédération des Experts Comptables Européens) has become ACE (Accountancy Europe).

pleading for "Core & More"[30] as well as the International Integrated Reporting Council's (IIRC) 'Integrated Reporting' (IR) concept to which we turn in the text that follows as IR in the narrow sense.

The IIRC, created in 2009 by actors with a strong regulatory power in the private sector accounting domain, issued in 2013 a framework primarily addressing private sector entities, which was revised in 2021.[31] Nonetheless, also public sector entities may be interested in creating a report through which they could demonstrate their value creation process by explaining their own 'business model' and making use of the **'integrated thinking'** (i.e. considering the interrelatedness of actors, processes and capitals). Value creation in this sense means enhancing the six resources (capitals) put in place in this 'production' (e.g. service delivery) process:

- financial (i.e. pool of funds),
- manufactured (i.e. physical objects as buildings for use e.g. for providing services),
- intellectual (i.e., knowledge-based intangibles as licenses or tacit knowledge),
- human (i.e. people's competencies and experience),
- social and relationship (i.e. ability to share information within and between communities to enhance individual or collective well-being including common values, reputation and social license to operate) and

---

[30] FEE (2015), The Future of Corporate Reporting – creating the dynamics for change, https://www.accountancyeurope.eu/wp-content/uploads/FEECogitoPaper_-_TheFutureofCorporateReporting.pdf; ACE (2017): Core &More. An opportunity for smarter corporate reporting; https://www.accountancyeurope.eu/wp-content/uploads/170918-Publication-Core-More-1.pdf

[31] https://www.integratedreporting.org/wp-content/uploads/2021/01/InternationalIntegratedReportingFramework.pdf

– natural capital (i.e. all environmental resources and processes supporting the past, current and future prosperity as air, water and bio-diversity) – see Figure 14.5.[32]

Consequently, in 2016, the IIRC and the Chartered Institute of Public Finance and Accountancy (CIPFA) published an introductory Guide to IR in the public sector. The main aim of this document is "to explain to public sector leaders and their teams how integrated thinking and reporting can help the sector consider how to make the most of resources, encourage the right behaviours and demonstrate to stakeholders how they are achieving the strategy and creating value over the short and longer term"[33] – "for the organization itself ... and others (e.g. shareholders and society at large"[34].

Example (continued from Section 2)

A local government prepares an integrated report to inform on its strategies in fostering and enlarging carbon neutral local public transportation (here acquisition of new buses). This relates to the following capitals: financial (decreases by the acquisition, training and infrastructure amendment cost), manufactured (increases by the acquisition cost), intellectual (may raise as new processes have to be designed), human (raises because bus drivers and maintenance personal gain new skills), social and relationship (may increase as new supplier relationships are to be established and – at least in the long run – positive outcomes on citizens' health are expected), natural (may increase due to a decrease in air pollution).

---

[32] Guthrie et al (2017).
[33] IIRC/CIPFA (2016).
[34] IIRC (2021), Rz. 2.4, p. 16.

As such, one of the distinctive features of the integrated report is that it provides to the reader not only information on results achieved, but also it has a **future orientation** (i.e., long-term effects). For the selection of the information to be conveyed, each organization/government has to engage with its stakeholders and identify what is material to be communicated. The disclosure should cover all capitals involved in the value creation process as well as the risks and opportunities, especially those known or potentially affecting financial, environmental, social or governance performance. Basically, the holistic content embedded in the integrated report may provide a deep understanding of processes and results, bringing together a multi-faceted ensemble of information.

Among the guiding principles (e.g. 'materiality'; 'conciseness', 'reliability and completeness', 'consistency and comparability') the 'strategic focus and future orientation' and especially '**connectivity** of information' (bold letters added) stand out: "An integrated report should show a holistic picture of the combination, interrelatedness and dependencies between the factors that affect the organization's ability to create value over time"[35]. The capacity to those combinations as well as the knowledge about interrelatedness and dependencies are the core of integrated thinking and the prerequisite and enabler to **integrated decision-making** in which all relevant perspectives are taken into account. Although the IIRC Framework explains principals and content elements, there is room left for including specific sets of standards for sustainability reporting (e.g. GRI).[36] Thus,

---

[35] IIRC (2021), Rz. 3.6, p. 26.

[36] GRI (2017): Forging a path to integrated reporting. Insights from the GRI corporate leadership group on integrated reporting; https://www.globalreporting.org/umbraco/Surface/ResourceCentre/PopupResource?id=8959

integrated reports are to be designed individually based on the (entity-specific) management approach taken.

State-owned enterprises (SOE) have experimented with IR mainly because they have to confront their peers in the market. Nonetheless, both universities and local governments seem interested in adopting this tool. One of the main advantages of IR is the adoption of integrated thinking in defining strategies and actions. Integrated thinking could be a catalyst in breaking down the traditional boarders between the different organization's units (e.g. departments) to achieve a common view on how to manage resources and develop future activities.[37] Furthermore, engaging stakeholders in identifying material issues to be included in the integrated report, may enhance their relation ties with the organization.

The IR Framework was recently revised, in January 2021, after a consultation process to update its content and principles on the basis of past experiences. In the same year, the IIRC merged with the Sustainability Accounting Standards Board (SASB) to create the Value Reporting Foundation. Later at the same year, it was announced that the new foundation together with the Climate Disclosure Standards Board (CDSB) are to be consolidated into the IFRS Foundation's International Sustainability Standards Board (ISSB). The consolidation process has been concluded in August 2022. This process testifies an increased attention in the private sector towards the publication of integrated reports and this process is expected to reverberate (or it has already reverberated) to public sector entities, starting with SOE. More generally, for example, the European Confederation of Institutes of Internal

---

[37] For the distinction between integrated and integrative thinking refer to McGuigan et al. (2020).

Auditing (ECIIA) engaged in promoting IR in the public sector.[38] Furthermore, International Accounting Standards Board (IASB) and International Sustainability Standards Board (ISSB)[39] announced to rely and to build in future on the principles of IR. As such, the IPSASB will most likely follow, when updating its standards based on International Accounting Standards (IAS)/International Financial Reporting Standards (IFRS).

However, despite conciseness is one of the principles governing the preparation of the integrated reports and the fact that IR reports are mainly narrative, in any cases IR is characterized by technical terms and specific jargon (as capitals) that might create some barriers for their understanding in full by ordinary citizens. Moreover, the management approach inherent in IR hampers the comparability of these reports.

Besides IR in the narrow sense (based on the IIRC framework), there are also other versions of IR and integrated reports. On the one hand, the IIRC concept could be used as a basis for creating an individual integrated report, e.g. by linking capitals to the SDGs (see Figure 14.5)[40] or for deriving a (simplified) **Integrated Popular Report** with a focus on the information needs and interests of citizens. On the other hand, IR could be understood as a generic term for reports in which non-financial information is presented on a voluntary basis together with mandatory General Purpose Financial Statements (GPFS) or GPFR.[41]

---

[38] ECIIA (2021). Integrated Reporting in the European Public Sector: It's time to act! https://www.eciia.eu/wp-content/uploads/2021/07/IR-in-the-PS-Final-version.pdf

[39] https://www.ifrs.org/news-and-events/news/2022/05/integrated-reporting--articulating-a-future-path/

[40] Adams (2017).

[41] In some legislations, an assurance topic arises from the voluntary integration of non-financial information in (e.g. management reports accompanying) GPFR. When reporting entities combine these two types of information, the reporting entity must make clear (by icons or use of different colors or similar), which information has been subject to assurance and which not. This may raise further understandability problems.

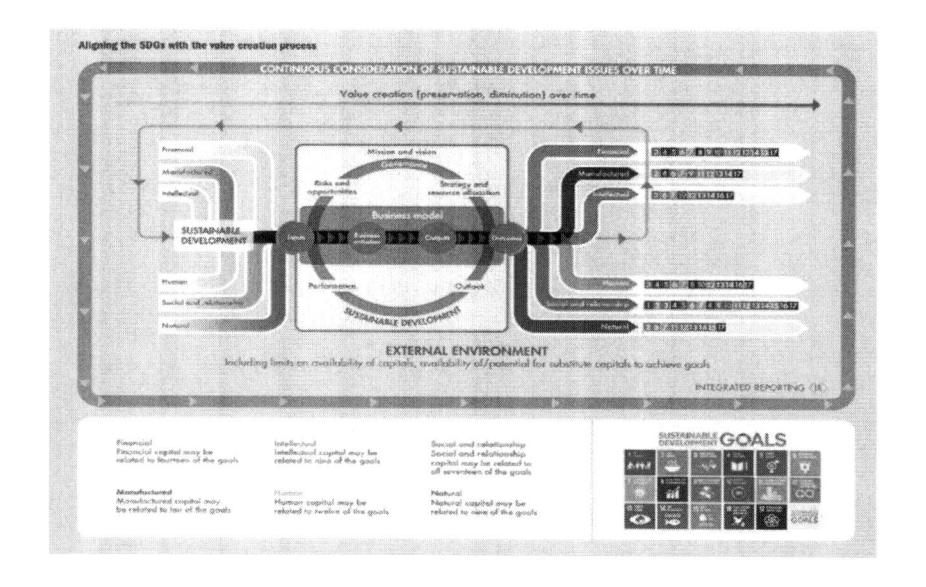

Figure 14.5: Integrated thinking, integrated reporting and SDGs.
Source: Adams (2017), p.14

4. Evaluation of alternative and non-financial reporting formats

The brief analysis conducted above about the content of the most widespread (and emerging) alternative and non-financial reporting formats adopted by public sector organizations allows us to gain a general understanding of the range of opportunities available to entities in their endeavor to present a specific or even a holistic view of their financial and non-financial (sustainability) results and, above all, of the related outcomes obtained.

Different stakeholders may have different benefits from the information disclosed – also in terms of expected impacts – depending on the focus areas that each organization decides to concentrate on while reporting its past, present and future performance. Table 14.1. shows the expected impact on stakeholders across all reporting formats.

Stakeholder Group	Expected impact
Preparers (Reporting entity)	Increase in qualifications and skills Use of language and communication tools attuned to increase understandability and readability Engage stakeholders in defining relevant information and open dialogue with citizens
Internal users	Better understanding of output and outcome produced by the different organization units Ability to manage information for decision-making and performance evaluation
External users	Transparent, understandable and comprehensive information on financial and non-financial performance Opportunity to better understand strategies, plans and actions (intended and/or already in place) Ability to make informed decisions and participate in public management life

Table 14.1: Summary of expected impact of alternative and non-financial reporting (Source: Own elaboration)

Table 14.2 summarises the differences among the alternative and non-financial reporting formats discussed in the chapter. However, it is important to underline that there is no one best solution. Rather, each organization has to identify the most convenient format to open a sincere dialogue with the citizens and other stakeholders. A reference to SDGs remains in this moment an obligation (until 2030), because of the role that public administrations have to play in the path towards a sustainable development. However, SDGs can be integrated in each of the previous formats discussed.

Generally speaking, a main difference between standardised GPFR and the at least less standardised alternative reporting formats is that the latter are mainly characterised by a management approach. Thus, reports are more or less entity specific which hampers inter-reporting-entity comparability. The management approach allows for reports to explain what is relevant and important to know from the perspective of the persons and institutions responsible for decision-making, but allows also for 'misleading' information or for the inclusion of 'distraction manoeuvres'.

In the previous text we argued inter alia for standard setters to engage in designing integrated popular reports together with users/addressees (e.g. citizens). Figure 14.6 illustrates this vision or proposal in relation to the IPSASB - as a global standard setter in the area of public sector reporting from a financial and, in the future, perhaps also from a non-financial perspective. From a bird's eye view, this can be seen as an application of the concept of hierarchical information communication, bridging from the most relevant (condensed) information to the underlying details. This approach will lead to offer a full overview of financial performance in the GPFS, but also to add further information (e.g. related to financial-sustainability, service performance, KPIs, etc.) through the management commentary. Popular Integrated Reporting can condense both financial and non-financial information considered of major interest for citizens and make it available in a simplified language and with the support of graphs and figures. "As such, Citizens could take a top-down approach, while the IPSASB and the preparing public bodies face the challenge of developing policies for selecting and condensing the information to be included in the popular (integrated) reports in a form with a drill down option.

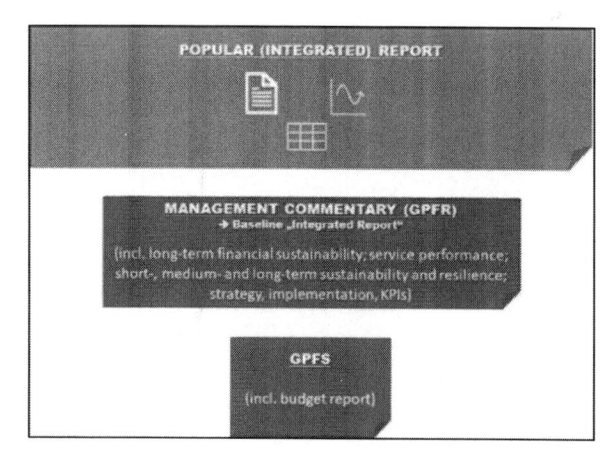

Figure 14.6: Proposed information transfer to addressees/users (e.g. citizens)[42]

---

[42] Lorson and Haustein (2022).

	Popular Reporting	Sustainability reporting	SDGs Reporting	Integrated Reporting (IR)
Most commonly name used	Popular Report, Popular Annual Financial Report (PAFR), Citizen-centric report, Value-for-money report	Sustainability report, ESG report, Environmental report, Social report	Voluntary national (or local) review; SDGs reporting	Integrated Report
Purpose of the report	To inform *citizens* on the financial performance of the (local) entity with a concise and easy-to-read report	To inform *all stakeholders* about environmental, social, economic and governance performance	To inform *all stakeholders* on progress made towards SDGs	To provide *all stakeholders* with integrated information on financial and non-financial performance, with an outlook on future trends
Content of the report	Features of the entity Basic financial information It can include also some non-financial information (e.g. Integrated Popular Reporting)	Overview of the entity Summary of financial information Stakeholders' relationships and indicators to show the non-financial performance	Narrative disclosure and quantitative indicators on each relevant SDG	Organizational overview and external environment Capitals Governance Business model Risks and opportunities Strategy Performance Outlook

Table 14.2: Comparison of selected alternative and non-financial reporting formats

5. Conclusion

Non-financial information and alternative reporting formats have consistently evolved in the last decades in an effort of public sector entities not only to discharge accountability duties but also to engage citizens and other stakeholders in decision-making and support their involvement as public services' co-producer.

The analysis conducted in this chapter regarding the most widespread reporting formats underlines that the situation is still evolving. It is possible that standard setters and governments will be involved in the near future in actions to set up a set of standards and guidelines specifically designed for public sector entities, to ensure understandable information that can provide all interested parties with a holistic picture of both financial and non-financial (sustainability) performance of public sector entities, creating the ground for conscious participation in designing their future strategies and actions.

We already acknowledge the efforts of several standard setters in this direction, especially the ones by the IPSASB within the project on Advancing Public Sector Sustainability Reporting[43].

We trust, however, that apart from the support that standards and guidelines can undoubtedly provide, institutional pressures could also give a necessary extra push. Institutional pressures could guide and facilitate public sector organizations to find their way in preparing their comprehensive reports by engaging citizens in the process. They could contribute in the design of the reports' content and outlay with multiple expected benefits in democratic governance.

It remains to be seen how citizens and other stakeholders will respond to a pervasive (if ever) adoption of these alternative reporting formats by public sector organizations, especially because is it difficult to foresee if and to what extent they intend to exercise

---

[43] IPSASB (2022a and b).

their role as co-producers and responsible receivers of services and consumers of resources.

Bibliographic references

ADAMS, Carol A. (2017) – The Sustainable Development Goals, integrated thinking and the integrated report, https://www.integratedreporting.org/wp-content/uploads/2017/09/SDGs-and-the-integrated-report_full17.pdf (accessed 1/07/2022)

BIONDI, Lucia & BRACCI, Enrico (2018) – Sustainability, popular and integrated reporting in the public sector: a fad and fashion perspective, Sustainability, 10(9), 1-16, 3112.

BÖCKING, Hans-Joachim and ALTHOFF, Carolin (2017) – Paradigmenwechsel in der (Konzern-) Lageberichterstattung über nicht-monetäre Erfolgsfaktoren – Pre-Financial Performance Indicators als Vorstufe, nicht als Gegensatz von Financial Performance Indicators –, in: Der Konzern, 15(5/2017), pp. 246-255.

COHEN, Sandra; MAMAKOU, Xenia J. and KARATZIMAS, Sotirios (2017) – IT-enhanced popular reports: analyzing citizen preferences, Government Information Quarterly, 34(2), 283-295.

COHEN, Sandra; MANES-ROSSI, Francesca; MAMAKOU, Xenia J. and BRUSCA, Isabel (2022) – Financial accounting information presented with infographics: Does it improve financial reporting understandability? Journal of Public Budgeting, Accounting & Financial Management, 34(6), pp. 263-295.

DUMAY, John; GUTHRIE, James; FARNETI, Federica (2010) – GRI Sustainability Reporting Guidelines For Public And Third Sector Organizations, Public Management Review, 12(4), 531-548.

GUTHRIE, James; MANES-ROSSI, Francesca; ORELLI, Rebecca L. (2017) – Integrated reporting and integrated thinking in Italian public sector organisations. Meditari Accountancy Research, 25(4), 553-573.IIRC/CIPFA (2016) Focusing on Value Creation in the Public Sector. https://www.integratedreporting.org/wp-content/uploads/2016/09/Focusing-on-value-creation-in-the-public-sector-_vFINAL.pdf (accessed 1/07/2022).

ECCLES, Robert G. & KRZUS, Michael P. (2010) – One Report: Integrated Reporting for a Sustainable Strategy, New York: John Wiley & Sons.

IPSASB (2022a) – Advancing Public Sector Sustainability Reporting, Consultation Paper https://www.ipsasb.org/publications/consultation-paper-advancing-public-sector-sustainability-reporting. (accessed 1/07/2022).

IPSASB (2022b) – Exposure Draft (Ed) 83, Reporting Sustainability Program Information IPSASB https://www.ipsasb.org/publications/exposure-draft-ed-83-reporting-sustainability-program-information

LORSON, Peter Christoph and HAUSTEIN, Ellen (2022) – The IPSASB and pressing primary, but not only financial, challenges. Critical reflections on IPSASB's statements and guidelines in the context of fundamental challenges such as sustainability, climate change and the COVID 19 pandemic. Presentation at the EGPA PSG Public

Sector Financial Management (PSFM) - Spring Workshop "Rethinking Public Sector Financial Management (PSFM): Public Value and Other Challenges for Accounting Studies (in the Aftermaths of COVID-19). LUMSA University/Rom on 27.05.2022

MANES-ROSSI, Francesca; NICOLÒ, Giuseppe; ARGENTO, Daniela. (2020) – Non-financial reporting formats in public sector organizations: a structured literature review. Journal of Public Budgeting, Accounting & Financial Management, 32(4), 639-669.

McGUIGAN, Nicholas; HAUSTEIN, Ellen; KERN, Thomas and LORSON, Peter Christoph (2021) – Thinking through the Integration of Corporate Reporting: Exploring the Interplay between Integrative and Integrated Thinking, in: Meditari Accountancy Research, 29(4), pp. 775-804 (https://doi.org/10.1108/MEDAR-04-2020-0872).

SOBKOWIAK, Madlen; CUCKSTON, Thomas and THOMSON, Ian (2020) – Framing sustainable development challenges: accounting for SDG-15 in the UK. Accounting, Auditing & Accountability Journal, 33(7), 1671-1703.

Additional readings

BRUSCA, Isabel; LABRADOR, Margarita; LARRAN, Manuel. (2018) – The challenge of sustainability and integrated reporting at universities: A case study. Journal of Cleaner Production, 188, 347-354.

MANES-ROSSI, Francesca. (2019) – New development: alternative reporting formats: a panacea for accountability dilemmas?. Public Money & Management, 39(7), 528-531.

RAIMO, Nicola; RUBINO, Michele; ESPOSITO, Paolo; VITOLLA, Filippo. (2022) Measuring quality of popular annual financial reports: Features of the rewarded US reporting municipalities. Corporate Social Responsibility and Environmental Management. First published https://doi.org/10.1002/csr.2336

UNITED NATIONS https://sdgs.un.org/topics/voluntary-local-reviews

Further public sector related EXAMPLES OF POPULAR AND ALTERNATIVE REPORTS can be found here,

- For a PFAR see https://apps.pittsburghpa.gov/redtail/images/18548_2021.PAFR_Report.6.29.22.Final_Single.Pages_with_Final.Edit.4.30pm.pdf (it is interesting also because it makes large use of infographics and the city has a long experience with popular report)

- For a SDGs Report see https://www.iges.or.jp/en/pub/shimokawa-town-sustainable-development-goals/en

- For an Integrated Report see https://arge.com/wp-content/uploads/2020/12/Kadikoy-Municipality-First-Integrated-Report.pdf

- The IPSASB and pressing primary, but not only financial, challenges. Critical reflections on IPSASB's statements and guidelines in the context of fundamental challenges such as sustainability, climate change and the COVID 19 pandemic

Discussion topics

- Does non-financial information disclosure enhance the dialogue between citizens and public sector organizations?
- Which is the main content of sustainability reporting in public sector organizations?
- How can the IIRC Framework be a point of reference for public sector organization in preparing their integrated reporting?
- How can overall value creation be measured when applying the IIRC Framework?
- How can a public sector organization identify the most suitable content to be disclosed in its popular report?
- Does SDG reporting stimulate citizens, companies and NGOs to create partnerships with public sector organizations?
- Critically discuss IPSASB's sustainability reporting policy (https://www.ipsasb.org/focus-areas/sustainability-reporting).

CONCLUSION

Peter C. Lorson, Ellen Haustein
both University of Rostock, Germany
peter.lorson@uni-rostock.de
https://orcid.org/0000-0002-2699-5451
ellen.haustein@uni-rostock.de
https://orcid.org/0000-0002-1218-1043

Susana Jorge
University of Coimbra, Portugal
susjor@uc.pt
https://orcid.org/0000-0003-4850-2387

This book presents a general overview about PSA in Europe. However, it was not intended to provide a full overview about the PSA systems in each member state in the EU. Instead, the objective was to provide insights into different views of PSA in Europe primarily focusing on the former DiEPSAm project partner countries (Austria, Germany, Finland, Portugal, and the UK). Therefore, this is not a book about (the future) EPSAS. Nevertheless, these final remarks open up the possibility of drawing conclusions for the EPSAS project.

The book demonstrates that PSA has a long history and did not only evolve since the 1980s together with the reforms of the 'New Public Management' movement. This also includes the evolution of different accounting systems (such as cash *versus* accrual accounting *versus* mixed approaches) and accounting techniques (such as single *versus* double entry bookkeeping). Each of the systems and techniques has its advantages and disadvantages. The idea of the book is to sensitise the reader to existing differences and (dis-)advantages.

In addition, each EU member state does have a specific accounting tradition (may it be, for example, rather neutral or prudent valuation of assets and liabilities) as well as its own accounting standards – meanwhile sometimes building on or including IPSAS – in place. All of these facts make harmonization of PSA in the EU member states a very challenging task. This book also discusses reasons for and against harmonization within the EU, in particular with respect to the EPSAS project.

Nevertheless, the aim was to show that the reference of PSA to private sector accounting standards is not naturally given, as there are indeed some specificities of the public sector to be considered. Therefore, according to the view of some of the chapters' authors, the adoption of IFRS or the IFRS-based IPSAS needs to be carefully evaluated.

A further issue to be considered is the high relevance of budgeting and budgetary accounting and reporting for PSA. Currently, the EPSAS project does not foresee to change any budgetary accounting rules of its EU member states – as such, the EU PSA harmonization project does not cover an essential part of the public sector financial reporting. In consequence, this could mean that EU member states would run their financial reporting systems with accrual-based EPSAS and their budgetary systems with their own systems, be they cash, modified cash, modified accrual, or accrual-based. This could possibly lead to frictions in the delivery of data for statistical purposes (possibly coming from whole of government budgetary reporting) and contradicts the starting point of the EPSAS project.

Presently (as of April 2023), regarding the future of EU PSA harmonization, one needs to wait for the further steps to be taken by the EPSAS project. Whilst the decision about a (mandatory) implementation of the EPSAS Conceptual Framework and/or standards has been postponed to the next EC (to be elected in 2024), it can be expected that the development of standards proceeds based on the IPSAS screening reports.

Meanwhile, the harmonization within the EU member states continues and the adoption of IPSAS increases. As such, it is questionable whether governments will be willing to adopt EPSAS once they have adopted IPSAS.[1] Still, the divergence between potential EPSAS and IPSAS is not expected too large. The most imminent change would occur for those countries that use cash-based accounting systems at least at some government levels. For those countries with very heterogeneous accounting systems in the public sector, such as Germany, the EPSAS project could offer a unique chance for a country-wide and all government levels encompassing harmonization, as there are different accounting systems in place, not only differing between government levels (central, state and local), but also differing at the same level of government, such as municipalities in different states ((*Bundes-*)*Länder*).

Against this backdrop, it will be interesting to see the future development of the EPSAS project and its consequences (for example, for Germany, the last eager opponent of accrual accounting among all EU member states at least at central level).

With regard to the content of Chapter 14, the EPSAS project needs a complement in the field of sustainability. While the EU is very active in promoting and requiring non-financial sustainability information (e.g. reporting on UN SDG implementation and progresses) from a dramatically increasing number of private sector entities, there is apparently no corresponding development for

---

[1] Conclusion of Cohen et al. (2022), as well as a result of Mann and Lorson (2019) analysis of the Hessian first time SsD adoption.

public sector entities on its way. This information and regulative gaps need to be closed as fast as possible.

As in the first edition, the second edition of this book tackles the aforementioned matters, attempting to support students and professionals to be better knowledgeable in PSA, while making them aware of the still considerable heterogeneity of PSA systems across Europe. As before, any feedback and suggestions for improvement are very welcome.

Bibliographic references

COHEN, Sandra; MANES ROSSI and Francesca, BRUSCA, Isabel (2022) – Public sector accounting harmonization in the European Union through the lens of the garbage can model. *Financial Accountability & Management*, 00, pp. 1-22. https://doi.org/10.1111/faam.12348

MANN, Bianca and LORSON, Peter (2019): New development: The first-time adoption of uniform public sector accounting standards – a German case study, *Public Money & Management*, 41(2), pp. 176-180.

ADDITIONAL MATERIAL

1. Questions

Chapter 1

Single-choice questions (always select the option that is *true*)

1. According to the European System of Accounts (ESA), the public sector consists of:
   a) All institutional units, resident in the economy that exercise non- market activities.
   b) Those public organisations, which provide utilities and services to the community.
   c) All institutional units, resident in the economy that are not private corporations.
   d) All institutional units, resident in one economy that are controlled by the government.

2. In the public sector, budgeting and budgetary accounting is seen as the most important source of accounting information because:
   a) It relies on single entry bookkeeping and is therefore easy to understand.

b) The approved budget is legally binding and serves as an authorization for any future expenditure.
   c) It contains the main information about the financial situation and resource consumption of a public entity.
   d) Budgetary norms are internationally equal and therefore budgets are comparable at an international level.

3. Conceptually, the difference between assets and liabilities is called:
   a) Net liabilities.
   b) Revaluation surplus.
   c) Net assets in the public sector and equity in the private sector.
   d) Surplus in the public sector and profit in the private sector.

Open questions

1. What are advantages and potential challenges of a harmonisation of public sector accounting in Europe?
2. Describe the difference between individual and consolidated financial statements and name reasons for setting up consolidated financial statements.

Chapter 2

Single-choice questions (always select the option that is *true*)

1. When is government deemed to be financially sustainable?
   a) When it has no debt.
   b) When it is capable to repay its debt at will.

c) When it can pursue its ongoing public benefit missions while fulfilling its financial obligations when they are due in time and amount.
   d) When its accrued (accrual-based) result is positive.

2. When the financial organisation of the modern state – based on taxation and borrowing – was definitely established?
   a) By the eighteenth century.
   b) By the beginning of the second millennium.
   c) By the feudal age.
   d) By the beginning of the third millennium.

3. In which aspect public sector entities are different from business sector entities?
   a) Public sector entities are different because they do not pay taxes.
   b) They are different because they enact a specific financial economic process based on taxation and public debt management.
   c) Public sector entities are not fundamentally different from business entities.
   d) Public sector entities are owned by citizens.

4. What shows the net result – difference between expenses and revenues of the period - of a public sector entity under an accrual basis of accounting?
   a) Profit generated by the public sector entity.
   b) The cash accumulated during the period by the public sector entity.
   c) The benefits delivered to the citizenship.
   d) The capacity of the public sector entity to cover the expenses of the period by matching revenues.

Open questions

1. Denote and explain the main public sector specificities.
2. Summarise the historical evolution of public sector accounting, its universal features and the specificities of the modern state.
3. Critically discuss the 'New Public Management / 'New Public Governance' movement from the viewpoint of public sector specificities.
4. Critically discuss the convergence between public sector and business sector accounting from the viewpoint of public sector specificities.

Chapter 3

Multiple-choice questions

1. Which of the following claims are *more wrong than right?*
   a) In public sector entities, the allocation principles of expenditure and income items to the budget (and budgetary accounting) and financial accounting are necessarily kept on different bases.
   b) Cash budgeting serves money usage control and accountability purposes well.
   c) Capital budgets as separate budget parts show investment cash flow effects but have no significant operative cost effects.
   d) Budget rules can, practically considered, consist of only financial budget rules and not of non-financial budget rules.

e) Accrual-based budgeting includes more reliable data than cash-based budgeting.

2. Which of the following claims are *right?*
   a) IPSAS standards do not require that actual amounts presented on a comparable basis to the budget shall, where the financial statements and the budget are not prepared on a comparable basis, be reconciled.
   b) Examples of items that usually are not included in budgetary appropriations include the following: Provisions and depreciations.
   c) Virement rules are a process of controlling the transfer of funds from one budget head to another.
   d) If net budgeted revenues are more than estimated in the budget, the entity may always by its own decision increase its expenditure.
   e) According to Schick, accrual budgeting is not ready for widespread application as a budget decision rule because of its complexities.

Open questions

1. What are the different functions of budgeting in the public sector and how are they different from private sector budgeting?
2. What is the role of financial and non-financial information in budgets and budget outturn reports? How have these two dimensions been merged in output-based budgets?

Chapter 4

Multiple-choice questions

1. Which of the following claims are *wrong*?
   a) Assets = Financial capital is the basic equation of the entity theory of accounting.
   b) Fair value cannot be lower than the historical transaction-based price.
   c) The realisation principle accepts revaluations, holding gains and holding losses in the income statement.
   d) Current value as the basis of the valuation of an asset is the amount which it would currently cost to obtain it.
   e) Matching in public sector accounting is not possible.

2. Which of the following claims are *right*?
   a) Depreciations are recognised in the private sector accrual accounting but not in the public sector accrual accounting.
   b) Neutrality principle in the public sector means care in estimating incomes so that they are not exaggerated and care in estimating expenditures so that they are not underestimated.
   c) The Initial measurement reflects the value at the transaction date.
   d) The IASB assumes that financial accounting information that satisfies the needs of shareholders and creditors also satisfies the information needs of other users of the financial statements.
   e) Holding gains are realised non-exchange transactions.

Open question

Local government X owns a school building in a rural village. It was built in 1955, and its book value after several renovations and depreciations in the 2018 financial statement is 500,000 €. **However, later it becomes probable that the usage will end.** If the old building is taken again into governmental service use, it requires a renovation costing 200,000 €. A small school building with capacity for the same number of pupils is now estimated to cost about 650,000 €.

Local government X tried to sell the building via an estate agent but received no offers. After the competitive bidding, a local artist suddenly made an offer to buy the schoolhouse for 50,000 €.

Think about what is the historical cost, fair value, replacement cost and settlement amount of the school.

Case study question

A local government has the following transactions, events and decisions during the one-year accounting period. Money units are in 1,000 units. In its accounting, the local government obeys precisely all the accounting rules valid in the country. The example is simplified from real life: for instance, value-added-taxes are not taken into consideration. However, all obligatory financial statements (the budget statement reports excluded) are presented in the Case Appendix.

1. The opening balance includes real estate, a school, a health care centre, bank money, own capital and long- and short-term debts.
2a. The local government collects own tax incomes in its bank account of 10,000.

2b. It received a state grant into its bank account of 10,000.
3. It pays the special health care hospital 1,000 as compensation for services consumed by its inhabitants.
4. It orders materials for use in street construction and recognises a liability of 1,000.
5. It buys medicines to its own health care centre inventory for 500. It uses 450 during the accounting period. The opening balance of the inventory was 0.
6. It receives a facility from a construction company, the acquisition cost was 4,000. The depreciation plan for the facility is 40 years. The straight-line depreciation per year (4000/40) is 100. The facility is taken to use 1.7., and the half year depreciation is 50.
7. The local government owns real estate (opening balance) bought for 2,000 during the previous accounting period. At the book closure date, it has an external reliable assessment that the selling price would probably be 3,000. The local government would like to recognise the increase in the value in the balance sheet, but because of carefulness it recognises an appreciation of 800.
8a. It pays short-term liabilities connected to wages of 1,000.
8b. Furthermore, it pays salaries to wage-earners of 10,000.
8c. The wage-earners have earned during the accounting period a certain amount of annual vacation days that they will use next year. The wage cost of this annual vacation will be 1,000.
9a. It has borrowed 10,000 from a bank.
9b. Instalments are not paid during the accounting period but at the book closing date interest has accrued of 50. This will be paid next year.
9c. The interest on the old loan of 100 is paid.
9d. Instalment of the old loan of 500 is paid as well.
10. It has placed surplus cash money in a stock portfolio held for active trading of a total of 1,000. At the time of book closure the value of the placement was 1,500.

11. It has an old waste water utility that has been totally depreciated but can still be used for 5 years. After 5 years it must be demolished because of new effluent regulations and a new sewage treatment plant must then be built. The estimation of the demolition works is 2,000.
12. It has taken a hedging derivative (no speculative traits) instrument for the 10,000 loan, which has a variable interest rate. It makes a Swap agreement with another bank than the bank that offered the loan. The Swap has no acquisition cost at the time of signing the agreement. The Swap changes the variable rate to a fixed rate. The bank that sold the Swap announces that the market value of the Swap agreement at the book closing date is 1,000.
13a. It pays 2,000 to a service company that installs equipment for leisure and play to local government parks.
13b. It grants 1,000 to several local non-governmental organisations in December. The organisations must show a plan and their latest annual reports in February next year to the local government in order to get the promised money.
14. The local government forbids the usage of two polluted beaches.
15. The local government school receives maintenance services from the local government facility management unit and makes an internal payment of 1,000.
16. The local government decides that it will close its industrial development office next year and buy the corresponding services of a regional joint venture. The estimated annual savings are estimated to be 500 per year.
17. Shortly before finalising the financial statement of the accounting period and closing the books in February of the next year, the local government receives a notice from the Tax Authority that it has to pay back tax revenues that it received in excess and has to return 2,000 in April (the year following the year of the accounting period).

18. It receives a financial statement of the fully municipality--owned company and decides that the CEO must be changed. The board of the company dismisses the CEO and nominates a new CEO.
19. The local government plans to sell its real estate next year and includes a selling revenue of 3,000 in the next year's budget.
20. The council decides to add 1,500 to the current budget's transferable appropriation of 5,000 for constructions. By the end of the current year, 6,300 has been consumed of this transferable appropriation, and 200 has been left over to the next year.
21. The depreciations of the school are 100 and of the health care centre 200.
22. The local government receives from an art collector a donation of valuable sculptures. The donation incorporates restrictions that the collection must be in the museum benefitting the public and that selling it is forbidden. The sculptures will inevitably increase the number of visitors and ticket revenues in the future. On the other hand, the collection causes some conservation and maintenance costs. The museum has collections of heritage assets and donated art items.

Assignments

a) The accounting entries and the financial statements are all shown in the Appendix. Check how the entries have been done to the T-accounts and also the financial statement calculations. There are two items that seems to be missing from the balance sheet. If you were a certified auditor, you should notice them.

b) Earlier we stated that we can discern two different accounting methods as reference frames that have an impact upon deter-mining the of elements of financial statements, recognition and measurement criteria. These are the revenue-expense-led approach and the asset and liability-led approach. What signs of these methods do you find in the example? In particular, what valuation methods have been used?

c) Point out places where you find signs (or lack of signs) of the following accounting conventions/principles/concepts:

1. Accounting entity	6. Consistency
2. Money measurement	7. Prudence
3. Going concern	8. Accruals principle
4. Cost concept	9. Matching
5. Realization principle	10. Periodicity

d) Think about the budgeting in the local government: what would the budget look like if it was made on a cash basis, a modified cash basis or an accrual basis. You do not have to write any answers, just return to Chapter 3 to review this.

APPENDIX TO CASE STUDY QUESTIONS

	Opening balance		
Bank money	1,000	6,000	Own capital
Real estate	2,000	3,000	Loan (long-term)
School	3,000	1,000	Short-term liabilities
Health care centre	4,000		
Total	**10,000**	**10,000**	**Total**

	Bank account		
Opening balance	1,000	1,000	3.
2a.	10,000	500	5.
2b.	10,000	4,000	6.
9a.	10,000	1,000	8a.
		10,000	8b.
		500	9d.
		100	9c.
		2,000	13a.
		6,300	20.
		1,000	10.
		4,600	Balance
Total	**31,000**	**31,000**	**Total**

	Income statement		
Health care exp.	1,000	8,000	Tax revenues
Material exp.	1,000	10,000	State grants
Medicine exp.	450		
Salaries	11,000		
Depreciations	350		
Interest	150		
Awarded grants	1,000		
Demolishing exp.	2,000		
Balance = **Surplus**	1,050		
Total	**18,000**	**18,000**	**Total**

	Balance sheet		
School	2,900	6,000	Own capital
Health care centre	3,800	800	Capital appreciation fund
Facilities	3,950	**1,050**	**Surplus**
Constructions	8,300	2,000	Reserves
Real estates	2,000	10,000	New loan
Asset appreciations	800	2,500	Old loan
Trading assets of stocks and bonds	1,000	5,050	Short term liabilities
Inventory	50		
Bank money	4,600		
Total	**27,400**	**27,400**	

Funds flow statement					
Operational activities		2a.		10,000	Tax revenues
		2b.		10,000	State grants
	Service	payments		1,000	3.
	Material	payments		500	5.
	Wage	payments		11,000	8.
	Interest	payments		100	9.
		net		7,400	
Investment activities		Facilities		4,000	6.
		Park		2,000	13.
	Other	constructions		6,300	20.
	Stocks &	bonds		1,000	10.
		net		-13,300	
Net cash flow after operations and investments					
				-5,900	
Financing activities		9.		10,000	New loan
				500	Instalments of old loan
Change in cash money				**3,600**	
Check:					
Cash money; opening balance				**1,000**	
Change in cash money				3,600	
Cash money; ending balance				**4,600**	

T-accounts

Tax revenues	
2a.	10,000
2,000	17.
	8,000

State grants	
	2b.
	10,000

Salaries	
10,000	8b.
1,000	8c.
11,000	

Construction materials	
1,000	4.

Medicine expenditure	
450	5b.

Medical inventory	
500	5.
5b.	450
50	

Health care service costs	
1,000	3.

Loan interest expenses	
50	9b.
100	9c.
150	

Facilities	
4,000	6.
6b.	50
3,950	

Depreciations	
50	
300	
350	

Real estates	
2,000	7., opening balance

Capital appreciation fund	
7b.	800

Trading assets of stocks and bonds	
1,000	10.

Awarded grants	
1,000	13b.

Reserves	
11.	2,000.

Demolishing service expenses	
2,000	11.

SWAP instruments	
0	12.

2,000	13a.
6,300	20.
8,300	

1,000	15.

4,000	Opening balance
21.	200

School	
3,000	Opening balance
21.	100

Internal maintenance revenues	
15.	1,000

Asset appreciations	
800	7b.

SWAP liabilities	
12.	0

Internal maintenance costs	

Health care center	

Contracting construction costs	

Short-term liabilities	
Opening balance	1,000
1,000	8a.
4.	1,000
8c.	1,000
9b.	50
13b.	1,000
17.	2,000
	5,050

Long-term liabilities (loan)	
Opening balance	3,000
9a.	10,000
500	9d.

Museum art collections, heritage assets	
0	22.

Chapter 5

Single-choice questions (always select the option that is *true*)

1. GFS stands for ...
   a) Government Finance Statistics.
   b) General Fiscal Standards.
   c) Gorgeous Fiscal Show.

2. The economic value of a harmonisation is....
   a) A higher level of infrastructure budgets.
   b) A higher level of social budgets.
   c) Less transactions costs.

3. The IPSAS are standards and interpretations published by the...
   a) International Public Sector Accounting Standards Board (IPSASB).
   b) International Public Sector Accruals Setting Board (IPSASB).
   c) International Public Sector Asset Speculation Board (IPSASB).

Open questions

1. What is the conceptual difference between accrual accounting and GFS?
2. What is the difference between the harmonisation paths of international private sector accounting and public sector accounting?

Chapter 6

Single-choice questions (always select the option that is *true*)

1. The IPSAS standards are derived from the…
   a) IFRS standards.
   b) IFCS standards.
   c) Conceptual basis of public sector accounting and no specific standards.
   d) IDW standards.

2. The IPSAS encompass …
   a) Only accrual-based standards.
   b) Only cash-based standards.
   c) Both accrual-based and cash-based standards.
   d) Only budgetary reporting standards.

3. Who is expected to use IPSAS?
   a) International companies only.
   b) Public sector entities at a global level.
   c) European countries only.
   d) Countries that are in financial distress.

Open questions

1. Why should a state apply IPSAS? And why not?
2. What are challenges in adapting the national accounting system to IPSAS?

Chapter 7

Single-choice questions

1. According to the IPSAS CF, which of the following *better reflects* the pre-requisites for an item to be recognised as an asset in a public sector entity:
   a) To be a resource presently controlled by the entity.
   b) The control of that item by the entity must result from a past event.
   c) The item must have service potential or the ability to generate future economic benefits.
   d) All of the above pre-requisites are required.
2. In the IPSAS CF, the Net Financial Position of a public sector entity results from:
   a) The difference between ownership contributions and ownership distributions.
   b) The difference between revenue and expense.
   c) The difference between assets and other resources and liabilities and other obligations.
   d) The difference between assets and legal obligations only.

3. From the sentences below regarding measurement criteria of assets and liabilities, please select the *false* one:
   d) The net selling price may be used for assets as an exit value.
   e) The value in use may be used for assets as an observable entry value.
   f) The assumption price may be used for liabilities as an entry value.
   g) The market price may be used for assets as an observable exit value.

Open questions

1. Referring to the IPSASB's CF, discuss who the users of GPFRs of a public sector entity might be, as well as their needs. Give examples of what type of information needs may be particularly proper to citizens at large.
2. Considering the financial information qualitative characteristics in the IPSASB's CF, what is the difference between relevance and faithful representation? Refer also to the main concepts associated with each of those attributes.

Chapter 8

Single-choice questions

1. Which of the following is *not correct* if an entity presents a statement of financial performance by function:
    a) Expenses are displayed considering their allocations, for example to health, housing, economic affairs, education and other programs the entity develops.
    b) Expenses are displayed considering their nature, i.e. origin, such as wages, consumables, depreciation, impairment losses, financial costs, among others the entity may have incurred.
    c) Revenues are displayed considering their nature, i.e., origin, such as taxes, transfers and grants, revenue from exchange transactions, among others.
    d) The surplus/deficit of the period is presented, highlighting the part belonging to non-controlling interest, if existent.

2. Transfers received by a local authority from the central government to cover current expenditure, according to the IPSAS 2 – Cash flow statements:
   a) Are classified as a cash flow from operating activities.
   b) Are classified as a cash flow from financing activities.
   c) Are classified as a cash flow from investing activities.
   d) Should not be included in the cash flow statement.

3. GPFR audits ensure fair presentation, financial regularity and legality of the public sector entities' accounts. Which of the following is *true*:
   a) Legality audits aim essentially at fighting exaggerating or underestimating figures in the reporting.
   b) Fair presentation audits aim essentially at assessing conformity with the law, namely the budget.
   c) Financial statements audits are generally carried out by Supreme Audit Institutions, such as Courts of Audit.
   d) Financial statement audits assess conformity with accounting and reporting standards and are based on professionals' pronouncements.

Open questions

1. Please identify the main components of the GPFR of a public sector entity using IPSAS, briefly describing the information each of those statements convey. In addition, please give examples of types of statements that are part of the annual accounts in some jurisdictions in the EU, namely those not adhering to IPSAS.
2. Please briefly explain the importance of disclosing audited GPFRs to improve public sector entities' transparency and political accountability.

Chapter 9

Single-choice questions (always select the option that is *true*)

1. Which can be the consequences of applying the revaluation model for subsequent measurement of PPE?
   a) An impairment test is not necessary any more.
   b) If the revaluation model is applied for one item of PPE, it needs to be used for all other PPE as well.
   c) Assets with a definite useful life do not need to be depreciated any more.
   d) The revalued amount of an item may exceed its initial carrying amount.

2. How is a non-exchange transaction, in which the transferred asset partly also holds a condition, to be accounted for?
   a) The asset is capitalized at its fair value minus the unfulfilled obligation and a revenue is recorded.
   b) The asset is capitalized at its fair value, a revenue is recorded for the fulfilled obligation and a liability for the unfulfilled obligation.
   c) The asset is capitalized at its fair value minus the fulfilled obligation, and a revenue is recorded.
   d) The asset is capitalized at its fair value minus the fulfilled obligation, and a liability is recorded.

3. How is a service concession asset to be initially measured?
   a) At the discounted value of the sum of unearned revenues.
   b) At its net cost minus the finance cost.
   c) At fair value at the point of recognition.
   d) It is not measured because it is not controlled by the public entity.

4. If a State Government provides basic healthcare services to all its citizens, and to other individuals who meet residency requirements, those services should be accounted for as:
   a) Transfer expenses
   b) Collective services
   c) Individual services
   d) Social benefits

Open questions

1. Why are inflows from non-exchange transactions recorded in surplus and deficit (i.e. as revenues)?
2. Which are the differences between the financial liability model and the grant of a right to the operator model according to IPSAS 32? Please provide examples and reasons why to choose one or the other model.
3. When should transfer expenses be recorded by the transfer provider if there are no performance obligations for the transfer recipient?

Chapter 10

Single-choice questions

1. A public entity uses the revaluation model for subsequent measurement of an asset of PPE (carrying amount 100 kEUR, 10 years useful life). For the first revaluation in the first year of use, a straight-line depreciation of 10 kEUR is accounted for. Then, its market value determined by appraisal is found to be 130 kEUR. What is the respective accounting record for the revaluation?

a) Revaluation reserve	40 kEUR	to PPE	40 kEUR
b) PPE	40 KEUR	to Reversal of impairment	10 kEUR
		Revaluation reserve	30 kEUR
c) PPE	40 kEUR	to Revaluation reserve	40 kEUR
d) PPE	40 kEUR	to Income from revaluation	40 kEUR

2. What needs to be considered when determining the value in use for a non-cash generating asset according to IPSAS 21?

   a) If the fair value less costs to sell is lower than the carrying amount of the asset, the value in use does not need to be determined.
   b) The age and wear of the asset needs to be taken into account by determining the value in use based on depreciated replacement costs.
   c) The non-cash generating assets are to be clustered into cash generating units.
   d) A sound interest rate based on public sector bonds for discounting the cash flows needs to be found.

3. What is the accounting record for a tax receipt through bank transfer by a public sector entity?

a) Tax income	to	Cash inflow
b) Tax liability	to	Bank account
c) Bank account	to	Tax authority
d) Bank account	to	Tax revenue

Open questions

1. Which types of non-exchange expenses are to be accounted for according to IPSAS 42?
2. Describe the methods for measuring value in use for impairment of non-cash generating assets according to IPSAS 21.

Chapter 11

Single-choice questions (always select the option that is *true*)

1. According to entity theory of consolidation:
   a) CFS are compiled as extended SFSs of the controlling entity by recognizing the proportionate share of the assets and liabilities of the controlled entity.
   b) CFS are compiled from the perspective of the economic entity assuming that the controlling and the controlled entities are dependent permanent operations of the economic entity.
   c) CFS are compiled from the perspective of the non-controlling interests recognizing the proportionate share of the assets and liabilities of the economic entity.
   d) CFS are compiled from the perspective of the controlling entity assuming that the controlling entity has the power to control the assets and liabilities of other entities to the full extent.

2. Whole of government financial reports present:
   a) The overall financial position of a single controlling public sector entity (e.g. a local government) and are prepared via the consolidation of the financial statements and transactions of all the entities controlled by this entity.

b) A comprehensive overview of financial and non-financial performance information of public sector programs and services.
c) A public entity's assets, liabilities and net assets at a specific point in time.
d) The overall financial position of the government of a particular jurisdiction via the consolidation of the financial statements and transactions of all the entities controlled by the jurisdiction's government.

3. Full consolidation means that:
a) The assets and liabilities as well as expenses and revenues of the controlled entities are included in the CFSs depending on the controlling entity's share in the net assets of the controlled entities.
b) The assets and liabilities as well as expenses and revenues of the controlled entities, the associated entities and the joint arrangements are included in full in the CFSs, irrespective of the controlling entity's share in the net assets of the controlled entities.
c) The owned share of the controlled entity's net asset and the share of the net operating income are included in full in the CFSs.
d) The assets and liabilities as well as expenses and revenues of the controlled entities are included by 100% in the CFSs, irrespective of the controlling entity's share in the net assets of the controlled entities.

Open questions

1. What are reasons for difficulties to adopt private sector consolidated accounting in the public sector?
2. Why FS II and III are prepared?

Chapter 12

Single-choice questions (always select the option that is *true*)

1. According to IPSAS 35, an entity has power over another entity when, for example:
   a) The entity has the right to direct the financial and operating policies of another entity.
   b) The entity owns 50% of the voting rights of another entity.
   c) The entity has potential rights that give it future ability to direct the relevant activities.
   d) The entity exercises regulatory over control another entity.

2. According to IPSAS 35, a controlling entity shall:
   a) Adjust its own accounting policies to its controlled entities accounting policies to ensure uniformity.
   b) Present non-controlling interests in the consolidated statement of financial position together with the net assets of the owners of the controlling entity.
   c) Prepare CFSs that consist of a statement of financial performance and a statement of financial position only.
   d) Present non-controlling interests in the consolidated statement of financial position within net assets separately from the net assets of the owners of the controlling entity.

3. According to IPSAS 36, the equity method is to be used for
   a) Joint ventures and associate entities.
   b) Joint arrangements.
   c) Joint ventures and controlled entities.
   d) Joint arrangements and associate entities.

Open questions

1. Which entities have to present CFSs according to IPSAS 35?
2. What are the differences between full consolidation, proportionate consolidation and the equity method?

Chapter 13

Single-choice questions (always select the option that is *true*)

1. What was the main reason for the EC to think about introducing harmonized accrual accounting standards in the public sector in the member states (MS)?
   a) To deal with the financial crisis of 2008.
   b) To facilitate the economic and fiscal surveillance of the MS.
   c) To use accounting data to calculate the GDP of the MS.
   d) To force the public sector to apply private sector accounting standards.

2. The first public consultation about the suitability of IPSAS to be adopted at the EU member states resulted into:
   a) The majority of responses considering IPSAS as unsuitable.
   b) The EU deciding into developing a new set of standards to be called EPSAS.
   c) Eurostat developing a set of issue papers.
   d) IPSAS making adjustments to account for EU specificities.

3. The EPSAS working Group substituted:
   a) The EPSAS Cell First Time Implementation.
   b) The EPSAS Cell on Governance Principles.

c) The EPSAS Cell on Principles related to the EPSAS Standards.
d) The TF on EPSAS Governance and the TF EPSAS standards.

4. Which of the following is not an option considered for the EPSAS impact assessment:
   a) Recommended EPSAS Conceptual Framework and binding IPSAS.
   b) Recommended both EPSAS Conceptual Framework and EPSAS.
   c) Binding Conceptual Framework and recommended EPSAS.
   d) Binding both Conceptual Framework and EPSAS.

5. Which of the following is **not part** of the structure and elements of the EPSAS CF:
   a) Objectives of the GPFR and GPFS.
   b) Users of the GPFR.
   c) A hierarchy in the qualitative characteristics of accounting information.
   d) Measurement bases.

6. In which report(s) IPSAS are assessed against the European Public Good?
   a) The issue papers drafted by EY.
   b) The EPSAS CF.
   c) The screening reports.
   d) The issue papers drafted by PwC.

Open questions

1. Why is the EPSAS process progressing with such a low pace?
2. What do the screening reports reveal about the suitability of IPSAS in relation to the EU public sector accounting requirements?

3. How do you assess the EPSAS governance process?
4. What are the most important barriers for EPSAS development and implementation?

Chapter 14

Single-choice questions (always select the option that is *true*)

1. Alternative and non-financial reporting in public sector entities are:
   a) Largely standardized at international level, as there is a clear and shared international strategy about content and format to be adopted.
   b) Mainly adopted voluntarily by public sector entities, also in accordance with strategic choice on dialogue with citizens and other stakeholders.
   c) Standardised at national level in all European countries, with IPSASB working on the preparation of a common format for sustainability reporting.

2. The most common alternative and non-financial reporting formats are:
   a) General purpose financial reporting, Popular reporting, Social reporting and General purpose financial statement.
   b) General purpose financial statement, Sustainability reporting, SDGs Reporting, General purpose financial reporting.
   c) Popular Reporting, Sustainability Reporting, SDGs Reporting, Integrated Reporting.

3. In accordance with the United Nations, public organizations:

a) Are obliged to include SDGs in their annual report and budget.
b) Are encouraged to include SDGs in their plans and action, cooperating with other entities.
c) Are obliged to include SDGs on their website.

Open questions

1. Does non-financial information disclosure enhance the dialogue between citizens and public sector organizations?
2. Does SDG reporting stimulate citizens, companies and NGOs to create partnerships with public sector organizations?

SOLUTIONS

Chapter 1	Chapter 2	Chapter 5
1) d	1) c	1) a
2) b	2) a	2) c
3) c	3) b	3) a
	4) d	

Chapter 3
1. The following claims are more wrong than right: a; c; d; e.
2. The following claims are right: b; c; e.

Chapter 4
1. The following claims are wrong: b; c; e.
2. The following claims are right: c; d.

Case study of Chapter 4

The local government is an accounting entity. Money measurement is present in most of the numbered descriptions, but not in all. It uses the accrual principle.

The local government is steadily good in a going concern, if not merged with another local government. But inside the budget entity, some units may be closed, as in description 16. Based on description 18, it is a parent for a subsidiary, but it does not make a consolidated financial statement (there is no such in the financial statement collection).

Regarding the cost concept, it seems that the historical cost concept is used with some exemptions, see description 7. Appreciations are not done in description 10, seemingly because the country probably mainly follows the realisation and prudence principles, and in current assets the historical cost or the lower value of the selling price.

The matching and periodicity principles are present in several points, for instance description 6. The prudence principle is also present in description 7.

Based on description 12, it seems that local governments are forbidden to take any speculative derivative instruments in the country in question. If the Swap is identical to the bank loan in all relevant aspects, it seems probable that the local government may show the market value that is not realised only in the notes to the disclosure.

At first glance, there seems to be a problem with consistency because it seems that in description 13a no depreciations are recorded regarding the park equipment. However, the explanation must be that the local government has received the park equipment at the end of the year, and depreciations are not recorded before the next year's accounting period.

According to the description number 18 the local government has a subsidiary. The local government owned shares are not shown in the balance sheet, which is an error. This omission may be significant and the auditor must probe deeper in to the accounting books.

It seems also that the local government does not recognise donated art items or heritage items to the balance sheet (description 22). It is probable that it keeps a record of all museum items in a way that will satisfy planning and control purposes. The museum makes budget plans containing all expenditures, incomes and investments. The management of the museum seems to think that recognising these items with an infinite life cycle and no initial transaction prices to the balance sheet as assets would not make sufficient sense.

However, a transparent control of donated assets requires that given items with restrictions must be recognised as commissioned assets and as commissioned capital on the liability side.

Chapter 6
1) a
2) c
3) b

Chapter 7
1) d
2) c
3) b

Chapter 8
1) b
2) a
3) d

Chapter 9
1) d
2) b
3) c

Chapter 10
1) c
2) b
3) d
4) d

Chapter 11
1) b
2) d
3) c

Chapter 12
1) a
2) d
3) a

Chapter 13
1) b 2) b
3) d 4) a
5) c 6) c

Chapter 14
1) c
2) c
3) a

GLOSSARY AND KEYWORD INDEX

Pages

Accountability: The means by which an agent provides explanations for its actions to its superior or controlling body. From the perspective of public sector entities, accountability covers the obligation for public officials to report on the usage of public resources and answerability of government to the public, to meet stated performance objectives. Also, accountability is one of the objectives of IPSAS GPFRs (Preface of IPSAS CF Par. 23). — 59, 79, 96 ff., 118, 218 ff., 379 f., 507

Accounting basis: A description of how financial activities are recognized and reported. For example accrual accounting, cash accounting or other basis of accounting. — 40 ff., 162, 173

Accounting entity: The purpose of the entity concept is to characterise the accounting boundary and make a clear distinction between the economic affairs of the accounting entity and those of other entities. — 53, 129 ff., 136 f., 146, 376 ff.

Accounting /reporting period: The period covered by the accounts or financial statements, the period over which all the transactions are summarised to form the accounts. — 111

Accounting policies: "Specific principles, bases, conventions, rules and practices applied by an entity in preparing and presenting financial statements" (IPSAS 3.7). — 260, 267, 278, 284

Accounting theories: Logical reasoning in the form of a set of broad principles that provide a general frame of reference by which accounting practice can be evaluated and guide the development of new practices and procedures. — 123 ff., 210, 396

Accounting standards: Detailed explanations of the accounting approaches by different bodies that should be adopted to ensure that comprehensive and comparable financial statements are produced. — 153 ff., 209 ff.

Accrual/accrual-based accounting: Resource-based accounting system in which revenues are recognized in the period earned and expenses in the period they are incurred. — 80 f., 163 ff, 222, 241

Acquisition: a public sector combination, in which a party (acquirer) obtains control of one or more operations and there is evidence that the combination is not an amalgamation (IPSAS 40.5). — 234, 279, 420

Acquisition method: Method of capital consolidation, which requires remeasurement of the controlled entities' assets and liabilities at their acquisition-date fair values, thus revealing hidden reserves and hidden burdens. — 399 ff., 423, 433 ff., 438

Amalgamation: A public sector combination in which: a) no party to the combination gains control of one or more operations; or b) one party to the combination gains control over one or more operations, and the economic substance of the combination is that of an amalgamation (IPSAS 40.5). — 419 ff.

Area of consolidation ('scope of consolidation'): Perimeter of a group, i.e. which entities belong to a group and should consequently be included in the group's consolidated financial report. — 384 ff., 426ff.

Asset: "A resource presently controlled by the entity as a result of a past event" (IPSAS CF (2022) 5.6). — 106 ff., 162 f., 225 ff.

Associate: Entity over which the investor has the power to exercise a significant influence (see IPSAS 38.8). — 385 ff., 417 ff.

Assurance: Confidence on financial statements, usually expressed by an auditor, that the financial statements have been compiled in line with the budget and financial regulations (including reporting standards). — 289 ff.

Auditor: An independent professional who provides assurance to stakeholders on the financial statements. — 215, 289 ff.

Balance sheet: A financial statement that provides information of (current and non-current) assets and liabilities, in order to show the net worth (called net assets or equity) of the entity at a reporting date, usually at the end of the reporting period. It is also referred to as statement of financial position (e.g., by the IPSASB). — 106, 109 ff., 162 f., 228 f.

Bargain purchase: A negative difference between the controlling entity's interest in the acquired entity (consideration paid) and the controlling entity's share of the acquired entity's remeasured net assets. It is to be recognised as a gain in surplus or deficit (IPSAS 40.88). Under IPSAS, the bargain purchase fiction also applies negative differences due to negative future (e.g. regulatory) prospects or unrecorded future obligations. — 401, 436

Bookkeeping: Recording of financial impacts of economic transactions or events of an entity. — 96 ff., 116 ff.

Budget ('budgetary perspective'): An estimation of expenditure/expenses to provide public goods and services, to satisfy public needs; as well as the estimated revenue to cover those expenditures/expenses. It is an annual statement by the government, approved by parliament, that lays down the government's financial plans for the coming year and authorises a certain level of payments from public funds on specified goods and services. — 95 ff.

- **Annual budget:** Approved budget for one year. It does not include published forward estimates or projections for periods beyond the budget period. — 98, 101, 113 f.

- **Approved budget:** The expenditure authorisation derived from laws, appropriation bills, government ordinances and other decisions related to the anticipated revenue or receipts for the budgetary period. 98, 104, 109, 113, 259, 262
- **Budget appropriation:** Authorisation granted by a legislative body to allocate funds for purposes specified by the legislature or similar authority. 96, 102, 119
- **Budget dependence:** Dependence of an entity on the budgetary allocations by another superordinate entity. A case of economic dependence. A concept used for defining the consolidation area (as an alternative to control). 386 f., 426
- **Budget out-turn report:** A report summarising all actual the receipts and payments in comparison with the budget approved by parliament. This may typically be quarterly or annual. 97
- **Final budget:** The original budget adjusted for all reserves, carryover amounts, transfers, allocations, supplementary appropriations and other authorised legislative or similar authoritative changes applicable to the budget period. 98

Budgetary:
- **Budgetary accounting and reporting:** Recording of transactions related to the actual documentation of the actual payments and receipts (or expenditures and revenues) in a budgetary period and comparison with the previously agreed budget for that period. 96 ff.
- **Budgetary basis:** The accrual, cash or other basis of accounting adopted in the budget that has been approved by the legislative body, or similar authority. 95 ff.
- **Budgetary control:** Procedures to ensure that payments are only made properly in line with the budget approved by parliament. Applies also to collection of receipts. 98
- **Comparable basis:** The actual amounts are presented on the same accounting basis, using the same classification basis, for the same entities and for the same period as the approved budget. 117

Budgeting: The process of developing, setting up and approving the budget. 40 ff., 95 ff.

Capital consolidation: See net assets/equity consolidation.

Cash accounting: Accounting basis where revenues and expenses are only recognized when the cash inflow or outflow occur. 80 f., 223, 241

Cash flow statement: A financial statement that explains changes in the amount of a funds of an entity consisting of cash and cash equivalents over a certain accounting period. Basically, changes occur as cash in- and out-flows. These cash flows might be organized in different ways and can be prepared using the direct or the indirect method. According to the IPSASB, cash in- and out-flows are to be allocated to operating, investment and financing activities (IPSAS 2). Under this setting, both methods might be applied to the cash flow from operating activities, while the latter two are to be presented using the direct method. 223, 259 ff., 278 ff.

Citizens: People who have the right to vote for a government and thus hold it to account for its actions. — 96, 135, 139, 219 ff.

Consistency: Continuity of accounting methods and rules (e.g. between accounting periods and for categories of transactions). — 129, 134 ff., 227, 247, 267

Consolidated accounts manual: Guideline for the controlling entity and the controlled entities which incorporates the accounting, disclosure and measurement methods for the economic entity. The manual may include structures in the economic entity, reporting structures and the accounting environment, and may also prescribe a chart of accounts to be used. The guidelines will vary between different groups (economic entities), as individual decisions must be made with regard to accounting options and management judgement inherent in certain accounting policies. — 255, 270, 285, 407, 423

Consolidated financial statements: Financial statements that combine the controlling entity and all entities under its control, joint control and significant influence, into one financial report as if the group of entities was one economic entity. — 377 ff., 418 ff.

Consolidation: The process of preparing consolidated financial statements. The procedure contains steps like: (1) combining items such as assets, liabilities, revenue, expenses and cash flows of the controlling entity with those of its controlled entities; (2) offsetting the carrying amount of the controlling entity's investment in each controlled entity and the controlling entity's portion of net assets of each controlled entity; and (3) eliminating in full intra-economic entity assets, liabilities, revenue, expenses and cash flows relating to transactions between entities of the economic entity (IPSAS 35.40). — 130, 137, 171, 284 ff., 376 ff., 416 ff.

Consolidation methods: Methods by which the assets, liabilities, revenues, expenses, and cash flows of the controlling entity and its controlled entities are included in the Consolidated Financial Statements. Alternative consolidation methods are: (1) full consolidation, (2) proportional consolidation, and (3) the equity method. — 392 ff.

Consolidation of revenue and expenses: Consolidation task that aims to eliminate intra-economic entity transactions in terms of revenue and expenses in the consolidated balance sheet. Elimination can be achieved by reclassification, adjustment or transferral. — 402 f., 452

Consolidation procedures (or consolidation steps): Set of procedures used in full consolidation: Consolidation of revenues and expenses, debt consolidation, elimination of unrealized gains or losses, and net assets/equity consolidation — 400 ff., 433 ff.

Continuity in Consolidated Financial Statements: Similar to financial statements, the consolidated financial statements for any given period are conceptually the result of the consolidated balance sheet for the previous period and the transactions of the current period. — 424 f.

Control:

- **Control with respect to resources:** Ability of an entity to use a resource so as to derive the benefit of the service potential or economic benefits embodied in the resource (IPSAS CF 5.11). — 220 ff., 304

- **Control with respect to entities:** An entity controls another entity when it is exposed, or has rights, to variable benefits from its involvement with the other entity and has the ability to affect the nature or amount of those benefits through its power over the entity (IPSAS 35.14). — 159, 383, 425 f.

- **Controlled entity:** An entity that is controlled by another entity (IPSAS 35.14). — 384, 427 f.

- **Controlling entity:** An entity that controls at least one other entity (IPSAS 35.14). — 269, 276 f., 384

- **Direct control:** Form of control where an entity exerts direct influence over another entity (e.g. by holding voting rights). — 383

- **Indirect control:** Form of control where the economic entity consists of a chain of controlling relationships. For example, a controlled entity controls another entity, i.e., it is itself a controlling entity. Also called 'pyramid control'. — 383

Currency conversion: Conversion of a currency into another currency by using exchange rates. With reference to consolidation, currency conversion is required if the entities to be consolidated do not all produce their reports using the same currency. — 424 ff., 431

Debt consolidation: Consolidation procedure that aims to eliminate intra-economic entity items of debts and receivables in the consolidated balance sheet. It includes the identification of intra-economic entity items in terms of debt, consolidation (by offsetting debts and (loan) receivables) and clearance of any differences. — 401 f., 449 ff.

Decision usefulness: Objective of IPSAS GPFRs (Preface of IPSAS CF Par. 23). For example, [...] the amount and sources of cost recovery and the resources available to support future activities [...] will also be useful for decision-making by users of GPFRs including decisions that donors and other financial supporters make about providing resources to the entity (IPSAS CF 2.1). — 138 f., 147, 218

Depreciation: Accounting technique of systematically allocating the depreciable amount of a tangible asset over its expected useful life. — 109 ff., 230, 240, 275, 309 ff.

Double entry bookkeeping: Coherent bookkeeping technique, in which for each transaction there are at least two related recordings, balancing between each other. — 47 ff., 238, 241 f., 288

Economic benefits: Cash inflows or a reduction in cash outflows, possibly generated by an asset (IPSAS CF 5.10). — 225, 229 ff., 244, 483

Economic dependence: "Economic dependence may occur when: (a) An entity has a single major client and the loss of that client could affect the existence of the entity's operations; or (b) An entity's activities are predominantly funded by grants and donations, and it receives the majority of its funding from a single entity" (IPSAS 35 AG41). — 426

Economic entity: A controlling entity and its controlled entities. Also called a 'group' in the private sector context. — 377 ff., 382

Elimination of unrealised gains or losses: Consolidation of intra-economic entity transactions, where goods and services of the sending entity are capitalised by the receiving entity based on transfer prices, that are not yet realised with external third parties. The items have to be measured at acquisition or conversion cost from an economic entity perspective. — 404, 452 ff.

Entity theory: Accounting theory of consolidation which takes the perspective that the economic entity as a whole, is separate from its controlling owners. The economic entity is viewed as having two classes of proprietary interests (controlling and non-controlling) which, however, are treated consistently for consolidation purposes, with no special treatment accorded to either. — 125 f., 396 ff.

EPSAS: European Public Sector Accounting Standards (EPSAS) are a set of accounting standards being developed to be issued by the European Commission for use by public sector entities (containing all government levels and social security funds) in the EU member states in the preparation of financial statements. — 164 ff., 184, 215, 463 ff.

Equity method: Method of accounting for an investment in an associate or a joint venture, whereby the investment is initially recognised at cost and adjusted thereafter for the post-acquisition change in the investor's share of the investee's net assets of the associate or joint venture (IPSAS 38.8). — 269, 273, 393, 397, 455 ff.

ESA 2010: The European System of Accounts is an internationally compatible accounting framework for a systematic and detailed description of a total economy (that is, a region, country or group of countries), its components and its relations with other total economies. — 44 f., 165 f., 170

External stakeholder: Stakeholders are persons, institutions, or organisations, for whom the behaviour of an entity matters because of their interests resulting from justified claims. Examples of stakeholders are citizens in their capacities as voters, taxpayers, users of public services, suppliers, other public administrations, and financial institutions. — 381

Fair value: This is the price that would be received to sell an asset or paid to transfer a liability in an orderly transaction between market participants at the measurement date. — 47 ff., 140 ff., 234 f.

Financial accounting: Recording of all economic transactions and presentation of an overview of the resources, i.e. assets, and sources of finance (liabilities and net assets), as well as an overview of the resource consumption and creation, i.e. expenses & revenues; cash in- and out-flows, during the reporting period. The accounting procedures are needed to produce the annual financial statements of an entity. — 163, 168 ff., 210 ff.

Financial (statements) auditing: A type of auditing of the financial statements, usually carried out by professional bodies (e.g., auditing firms). The audit process may be determined by law but based on professionals' pronouncements, aiming at assessing conformity with accounting and reporting standards (with fair presentation stated in the auditor's report accompanying the accounts). 292

Financial dependence: See budget dependence.

Financial liability model: Model of subsequent measurement of a service concession arrangement, which is prevalent if the grantor has an unconditional obligation to pay for the construction, development, acquisition or upgrade of the asset (IPSAS 32.18). 328 ff.

Financial regulations: A set of detailed rules covering all financial procedures that are to be followed by all officials in a public sector entity or across the whole of government. 34 ff., 98 ff.

Financial reporting: The process of producing and (perhaps) publishing documents containing financial statements or selected financial statement information, with the aim of enabling users to understand the financial affairs of the entity and to assess the relative success of its financial management. 40 ff., 153 ff., 210 ff.

Financial statements: Reports prepared by an entity's management to present the financial performance for a reporting period and financial position at a point in time. A set of financial statements usually includes a statement of financial position (balance sheet), a statement of financial performance (income statement), a statement of cash flows, a the statement of changes in the net assets/equityand supporting disclosure notes. In the public sector context, if the reporting entity makes its budget publicly available, then its financial statements have to include a statement of budget execution, that is, tables of amounts of receipts and payments made by an entity compared to the annual budget approved by parliament. 155 ff., 210 ff.

Financial sustainability: A governmental entity is deemed to be financially sustainable when it can pursue its ongoing public benefit missions, while fulfilling its financial obligations when they are due in time and amount. 75, 529

Fresh start method: Method for capital consolidation, which requires remeasurement of both the controlled and the controlling entities' assets and liabilities at fair value on acquisition-date, thus revealing hidden reserves and burdens. Not allowed in IPSAS Consolidated Financial Statements. 399 f.

Full consolidation: Method of consolidation in which the assets, liabilities, revenues, expenses, and cash flows of the controlling entity and its controlled entities are fully included in the Consolidated Financial Statements on a line-by-line basis, irrespective of the controlling entity's share in the equity of the controlled entities. As a matter of principle, full consolidation is performed by three consolidation steps (see **Consolidation**). 392, 398 ff., 433 ff.

Full goodwill method: Method which measures non-controlling interests according to their (estimated) fair value at the acquisition date (IPSAS 40.73). — 434 f., 446 f.

General government sector (GGS): A sector of the economy which includes "all institutional units which are non-market producers controlled by government, whose output is intended for individual and collective consumption, and are financed by compulsory payments made by units belonging to other sectors; it also includes institutional units principally engaged in the redistribution of national income and wealth, which is an activity mainly carried out by government" (ESA 2010). — 167 ff., 387 f.

General Purpose Financial Reporting / Reports – GPFR(s): Set of statements, including financial statements, as well as other statements demonstrating compliance with the approved budget, management performance and service delivery, and also descriptive narrative with non-financial information. The report is designated as 'general purpose' because it aims at satisfying information needs of diverse users who do not have the power to require a report for a specific purpose. — 45 ff., 147, 212 ff., 252 ff., 481 ff.

Going concern: Assumption that the entity shall continue operating at least in the near future, and not on the verge of cessation. — 213, 222 ff., 237, 263, 266, 290

Goodwill: An asset representing the future economic benefits arising from other assets acquired in an acquisition that are not individually identified and separately recognised (IPSAS 40.5). — 434 f., 439 ff., 459

Government-owned enterprises: Also state-owned businesses. Enterprises which are owned by a public entity. — 367

Government Finance Statistics (GFS): Detailed data on revenues, expenses, transactions involving assets and liabilities, and cash flows of the general government and its subsectors, prepared in accordance with statistical bases of financial reporting and used to (a) analyse fiscal policy options, make policy and evaluate the impact of fiscal policies, (b) determine the impact on the economy, and (c) compare fiscal outcomes nationally and internationally (IPSAS Preface, IPSAS 22.9). — 165 ff., 388, 464

Grant of a right to the operator model: Model of subsequent measurement of a service concession arrangement for which there is no unconditional obligation to pay by the grantor to the operator, but the operator is given the right to earn revenue from third-party users or another asset (IPSAS 32.24). — 330 ff.

Group: A controlling entity and its controlled, jointly controlled or significantly influenced entities. Also called "economic entity" in the public sector context. — 157, 167, 376 ff., 418 ff.

Heritage assets: Assets with a (1) cultural, environmental, educational or historical value, which are, in addition, characterised by (2) sale prohibitions or restrictions laid upon those assets, (3) the difficulty to estimate their useful lives, and (4) their irreplaceability (IPSAS 17.10). — 303

Historical cost concept: Historical cost is the price paid to acquire, or the resources consumed to produce, an asset; or the amount received pursuant to the incurrence of a liability in an exchange transaction. 132 f., 140 ff.

IFAC: International Federation of Accountants. The IFAC was established in 1977 and aims to promote international harmonisation of accounting. 182 ff.

IFRS: International Financial Reporting Standards (IFRSs) are a set of accounting standards issued by the International Accounting Standards Board (IASB) for global use by private sector entities in the preparation of separate or consolidated financial statements. IFRSs are the basis for the IPSAS development. 138 f., 153 ff., 184 ff.

Impairment: A loss in the future economic benefits or service potential of an asset. For depreciable assets, impairment exceeds the depreciation recognised in the reporting period (IPSAS 21.14). 240, 273 f., 314 ff.

Income statement: A financial statement that reports on the revenues obtained/generated and expenses incurred during a reporting period, evidencing the entity's deficit or surplus at the end of that reporting period. The bottom line is included in the net assets in the balance sheet. The income statement is prepared on an accrual basis.. Also designated as statement of financial performance (e.g., by the IPSASB). Excluded are (other comprehensive income transactions leading to) revenues or expenses that are directly recorded in equity/ net assets. 109, 111 ff., 265 ff.

Initial consolidation: Consolidation when setting up first-time Consolidated Financial Statements that takes place after a controlling entity has gained control over a controlled entity. 405 ff., 423 ff., 437 ff.

Institutional units and sectors: Institutional units are economic entities that are capable of owning goods and assets, of incurring liabilities and of engaging in economic activities and transactions with other units in their own right. For the purposes of the ESA 2010 system, the institutional units are grouped together into five mutually exclusive domestic institutional sectors: (a) non-financial corporations; (b) financial corporations; (c) general government; (d) households; (e) non-profit institutions serving households. 167

Integrated Reporting: Process of presenting clearly and concisely how a public entity creates and sustains value (e.g. public welfare) in an interconnected way, taking into account economic, social and environmental factors and the value creation in the short, medium and long term. May be based on the International Integrated Reporting Council (IIRC) Framework. 506 ff., 521 ff., 527 f.

Internal control: Procedures introduced and individually designed by a reporting entity to avoid loss of goods or money, to ensure that the financial regulations are followed and reliable financial statements and other accounts are prepared. 43, 219, 528

Internal users: Politicians, managers, employees and other internal stakeholders. 401 ff.

Intra-group transaction: Transaction that occurs between entities belonging to the same group (e.g. between controlling and controlled entities or associates or joint-ventures) and is thus inconsistent with the single entity concept. 449 ff.

IPSAS: International Public Sector Accounting Standards (IPSASs) are a set of financial reporting standards issued by the IPSASB for global use by public sector entities in the preparation of separate or consolidated financial statements. IPSASs are based on IFRSs. — 177 ff.

International Public Sector Accounting Standards Board (IPSASB): The IPSASB is the Board developing the IPSAS. — 181 ff.

Joint arrangement: Arrangement of which two or more parties have joint control (IPSAS 36.8). — 428

Joint control: Unanimous consent of at least two independent parties to decide about the relevant activities of an arrangement (IPSAS 36.8). — 385, 428

Joint operation: Joint arrangement in which the jointly controlling parties have rights to the assets, and obligations for the liabilities, relating to the arrangement (IPSAS 37.7). — 428

Joint venture: Joint arrangement whereby the parties that have joint control of the arrangement, have rights to the net assets of the arrangement (IPSAS 37.7). — 385 ff., 428 ff.

Liabilities: Debts and related amounts of money that are expected to be paid by an entity in a future financial year. A liability is " a present obligation of the entity for an outflow of resources that results from a past event"(IPSAS CF (2022) 5.14). — 230 ff., 269

Management accounting: A system that allows for the calculation of the resource consumption (costs) of organisational units or product/service units for control or pricing purposes. The objective of management accounting is to assist management in the planning, control and decision making required to achieve the entity's goals. — 106 f., 115 ff., 162 ff., 213 ff.

Matching: Accounting principle for the accrual and deferral of expenses and income, where expenses are recognized when the related income is realized or revenues are recognized as income when they are probable and the related expenses have been incurred. It is based on the premise that a reporting entity must incur expenses in order to generate revenue. The missing link to match a significant portion of revenues (for example, those from taxes) and incurred expenses is a characteristic of the public sector. — 81 ff., 129, 135 ff., 222, 276 f.

Measurement bases/criteria: Bases to determine monetary values for elements to be recognized in the financial statements, e.g., historical cost, replacement cost, market value, or value in use. — 153 ff., 214, 233, 236 ff., 243 ff.

Money measurement: The common accounting convention is to measure transactions with (constant) monetary terms. Conversely, only items and transactions that can be measured in monetary terms are recognised in accounting records. — 129 ff., 137

Multi-year budget: An approved budget for more than one year. It excludes published future estimates or projections for periods beyond the budget period. — 115

Net assets/equity consolidation: Consolidation task to offset (eliminate) the carrying amount of the controlling entity's investment in a controlled entity and the controlling entity's portion of the net assets/equity of the controlled entity. — 400 f., 433 f., 437 ff.

New Public Management: The approach to public sector management adopted by some governments in the 1980s' that emphasises efficiency, encourages privatisation and outsourcing and the adoption of private sector style management tools by public sector entities. — 379 f.

Non-controlling interest (NCI): Also referred to as minority interest. Specifically used in relation to controlled entities included in consolidated financial statements to specify the interest in net assets that is held by outside investors rather than the controlling entity preparing the consolidated financial statements. The external investors' share of ownership in net assets gives them no influence on how the company is run. The external investors' portion of the surplus or deficit and net assets/equity of a controlled entity has to be disclosed separately. — 269 ff., 392 ff., 428 ff.

Non-exchange transactions: Transactions in which a public entity receives resources and provides no or nominal consideration directly in return (IPSAS 23.9). — 317 ff.

Notes: Additional financial and non-financial information that complements the financial statements within GPFR, helping users to better understand, interpret and place in context the information reported in the various financial statements (e.g. statement of financial position or statement of cash flows). The notes should also include a summary of the main accounting policies. The majority of the notes are required by financial reporting standards (like IPSAS and IFRS). — 45, 259 ff., 506 f.

Original budget: The initial approved budget for the budget period. — 113

Partial goodwill method: Acquisition method which measures non-controlling interests according to their "share in the recognized amounts of the acquired operation's identifiable net assets" as remeasured at their fair value om the acquisition date (IPSAS 40.73). — 434 f., 446

Parent: An entity that controls at least one other entity (IPSAS 35.14). See controlling entity. — 376 ff., 420 ff.

Parent company theory: Accounting theory of consolidation which assumes that, even in the presence of a non-controlling interest (NCI), the controlling entity has control over the subsidiaries' assets and liabilities in full, rather than on a proportionate basis. — 395 f.

Participatory budgeting: A budgeting method, in which citizens are given a possibility to be directly involved in the process of planning public money allocation. Worldwide, there are different models of the process of participatory budgeting and the decision-making authority assigned to citizens. In European countries, citizens are predominantly given an advisory role; but citizens could also have a decision-making role in the detailed usage of a small budget appropriation fora local community within a local government. — 99

Periodicity: This means that the life of a reporting entity must be divided into constant periods for reporting purposes, usually into one-year periods. 129, 136 f.

Pooling of interest method: Method for capital consolidation, which requires measurement of both the controlled and the controlling entities' assets and liabilities at their book values, thus not revealing any hidden reserves and hidden burdens. Applicable in a modified way in IPSAS CFS for amalgamations (IPSAS 40.16 ff.). 399 f., 421 ff.

Popular reporting: A tool adopted by governments to provide citizens with understandable and readable financial and non-financial information, to restore trust and legitimation. Popular reporting is a first step to open a dialogue with and actively involve citizens in political life. 506 ff., 512

Power: Consists of existing rights that give the current ability to direct the relevant activities of another entity (IPSAS 35.14). 382 ff., 425 f.

Primary government: Public sector entity whose governing body is elected by the citizens in a general popular election. 376 ff.

Private sector accounting: The style of financial accounting adopted by for-profit organisations, which enables the preparation of external financial reports that include a profit and loss account (indicating the annual profit earned by the organisation) and a balance sheet (indicating the assets that the organisation owns and the amounts that it owes). The private sector might encompass charities and non-profit organisations. 153 ff., 159

Property, plant and equipment: Tangible (i.e. physical) assets for the purposes of production or supply of goods or services, administrative purposes or rental to others, which are expected to be used during more than one reporting period (i.e. as non-current assets) (IPSAS 17.13). 302 ff., 340 ff.

Proprietary theory: Proprietary theory is basically the opposite of the entity concept. In accounting, the entity concept makes a distinction between the entity and its owners. On the other hand, proprietary theory perceives the organisation as an extension of its owners. In consolidation, this theory views the group through the eyes of its ultimate owners, that is, the shareholders of the controlling entity. The group's assets and liabilities are considered to be those of the owners and the CFS is viewed as an extension of the controlling entity's FS. The share of NCI is disregarded. 125, 396

Proportional consolidation: Method of consolidation where the assets, liabilities, revenues, expenses, and cash flows of the controlled entities are included only to the extent of the controlling entity's direct and indirect portion in the equity of such controlled entities. Transactions between the group's entities are eliminated only to that same extent. NCI are not recognized. 393 ff.

Prudence principle: Two notions of prudence exist, namely cautious and asymmetric prudence. Cautious prudence means, for example, care in estimating budget revenues so that they are not overestimated; and care in estimating budget expenditures so that they are not underestimated. Asymmetric prudence means that, for example, unrealized losses are recognized, but not unrealized gains. Asymmetric prudence is one of the core principles underlying the preparation of financial statements in Germany, whereas the cautious prudence notion prevails in IPSAS financial statements, although some standards require – as *ad hoc* deviations from the Conceptual Framework setting – accounting procedures characteristic for asymmetric prudence. 100, 129, 134 ff., 146, 226 ff.

Public sector accounting (PSA): The means by which governments, ministries, departments and agencies record, analyse and report their economic transactions. It depends on the system of accounting and accounting technique used (e.g., cash *versus* accruals, double *versus* single entry). In some jurisdictions, it includes a comparison of cash receipts and payments actually undertaken in comparison with the annual budget approved by parliament. 40 ff., 96, 99, 153 ff., 212 ff.

Public sector combination (PSC): The bringing together of separate operations into one public entity. 418 ff.

Public sector: All institutional units, resident in the economy, that are controlled by government, including social security funds (ESA 1.35). 37 ff., 161 ff., 212 ff.

Public sector specificities: Denote the specific financial organisation of the modern state based upon taxation and borrowing. They include: absence of commercial revenues; public debt and monetary base management; public debt management for redistribution purpose; and assurance of social protection (social benefits) through non-debt commitments. 71, 73

Public-private partnership (PPP): Contractually regulated cooperation between the public sector and private sector companies, organised, for example, in a special purpose vehicle. Service concession arrangements are one form of a PPP. 100, 376

Qualitative characteristics: Attributes that financial information must have to satisfy the main objectives of financial reporting. In IPSAS financial statements, accounting, the qualitative characteristics should ensure the usefulness of the information provided in GPFRs for several users, namely for the purposes of accountability and decision making. Qualitative characteristics are criteria that may overlap, and should, therefore, be balanced against each other. Examples are relevance, faithful representation, understandability, verifiability, comparability and timeliness. 210 ff., 247, 480 ff.

Realisation: Refers to the initial recognition of revenue. Revenues can only be realised after they have been earned. In sales transactions, revenues are realised when the underlying goods associated with the revenues have been delivered or the services have been provided. 133, 137, 145 f.

Recognition criteria: Features that an item in a transaction must have, in order to be included in the financial statements. Recognition criteria relate to (a) the definition of an element in the financial statements, such as, asset, liability, revenue or expense; and (b) the ability to be measured in a way that achieves the qualitative characteristics (that is, include reliable measurement). — 229, 236 ff., 250, 301 f., 483

Regularity auditing: A type of auditing in a government or public sector entity, aiming at assessing conformity with legal form, assuring propriety and probity (explicit in the law) of records of transactions, and transactions themselves. Regularity audits also include assessing whether transactions conform with the budget or not. They are generally carried out by Supreme Audit Institutions (SAIs), following rules from the International Organization of SAI (INTOSAI). — 290 f.

Replacement cost: The price that would be paid to acquire an asset with equivalent ability to generate economic benefits or service potential, in an orderly market transaction at the measurement date. — 141 ff, 234 ff., 245 f., 315, 351 f.

Reporting date: the last day of the reporting period to which the financial statements relate. — 223, 226, 239, 261, 268 ff.

Reporting entity: A government or other public sector organization, program or identifiable area of activity of the public sector, that prepares GPFRs. A reporting entity need not have juridical/legal personality (IPSASB CF 4.1, 4.4). — 155, 167 f., 223, 255 ff., 268

Reporting unit: The entity, formally or informally existent, that produces reporting. — 37 ff., 53, 167

Requirements of uniformity: Financial statements of the individual entities to be consolidated must be adjusted to comply with the group's accounting policies, reporting date, and currency. — 402, 406 f., 430 ff.

SDG Reporting: SDG reporting aims at measuring and reporting on efforts dedicated and results obtained by each public sector organization for the achievement of United Nation's Sustainable Development Goals. This information can be also incorporated in other alternative and non-financial reports. — 506 ff., 514, 518

Separate financial statements (SFS): Financial statements presented in addition to consolidated financial statements or in addition to financial statements by an investor that does not have controlled entities but has investments in associates or joint ventures (IPSAS 34.7). — 417 f.

Service concession arrangement: Binding agreement between a grantor and an operator, whereby the operator uses an asset to provide a public service on behalf of the grantor for a specified period of time; and the operator is compensated over the service concession period (IPSAS 32.8). — 326 ff., 363 ff.

Service concession asset: An asset which is either (a) provided by an operator, who constructs, develops or acquires the asset for the grantor or an existing asset of the operator; or (b) provided by the grantor as an existing asset of the grantor or an upgrade to an existing asset of the grantor (IPSAS 32.8). 326 ff., 363 ff.

Service potential: An asset's capacity to provide services that contribute to an entity's objectives (without necessarily generating net cash inflows) (IPSAS CF 5.8). 255, 299 ff., 236, 244, 304

Service providing entity: An alternative term for economic entity. It is a public-sector specific term, since economic entity may be misleading because government entities do not strive for profits and have other purposes than private sector entities. 382, 418

Settlement amount: This is the amount at which an asset could be realised or a liability could be liquidated with the counterparty, other than in an active market. 141, 143, 239

Significant influence: Power to participate in the financial and operating policy decisions of another entity, but is not control or joint control of those policies (IPSAS 38.8). 385, 429

Single/individual entity: Presentation of the assets, liabilities, net assets/equity, revenues, expenses, and cash flows of the controlling entity and its controlled entities in the CFS as if they were a single entity. 257, 367 ff., 382, 398 f., 417 ff.

Single entry bookkeeping: Simple bookkeeping technique, in which each transaction is only recorded once, with no counterpart entry. The technique is generally associated with the cash-basis accounting regime. In single entry, only cash inflows and cash outflows are recorded. 47 ff., 127 ff., 241, 257

Special purpose entity: Legal entity that has been created to fulfil a specific purpose. For example, it can be a subsidiary created by a parent entity to isolate financial risk. 367

Stakeholders: The key groups of people to whom an entity (in the private sector or in the public sector) is accountable for the quality of its management. 221, 252 ff., 470 ff., 509 ff.

Subsequent consolidation: Consolidations that happen in the reporting periods after initial consolidation. 399 ff., 424 ff., 432 ff., 441 ff.

Subsidiary: See controlled entity.

Sustainability Reporting: Process of delivering an overview of the economic, environmental and social performance of an organisation; consisting of financial and non-financial information. The Global Reporting Initiative (GRI) is a global de facto standard setter for sustainability reports, at least in the private sector. Sustainability reports in a broader sense could also focus on ESG (environmental, social and governance issues) or SDGs (sustainable development goals). 43 f., 157, 184 f., 506 ff.

Taxation: The main source of public sector or government income; mandatory payments to be made on the receipt of income and other gains by a person or company. — 71 ff., 161, 319 ff., 355 f.

Taxes: Economic benefits or service potential compulsorily paid or payable to a public sector entity other than fines or other penalties (IPSAS 23.7). — 212 ff., 317

Theories of consolidated accounts: see (1) Entity theory, (2) Parent company theory, (3) Proprietary theory. See **accounting theories**. — 396

Transfers: Inflows from non-exchange transactions, other than taxes, such as, cash or non-cash assets, debt forgiveness, bequests, donations, and goods and services in-kind (IPSAS 23.7). — 232, 269, 275 ff., 317

Transparency: Unfettered access by the public to timely and reliable information on decisions and performance by a reporting entity. — 152 ff., 252 ff.

Treasury: The central department in the Ministry of Finance, which is responsible for the collection of receipts, making payments, recording these transactions, ensuring liquidity, and taking care of financial planning. — 65 ff., 194 ff., 258

Users of GPFR: Examples include citizens, Parliament, investors, national statistics institutes and the media. These users do not have the power to require (individually tailored) specific purpose reporting to satisfy their financial information needs. — 45 f., 138 ff., 182, 217 ff., 482 ff.

Variable benefits: Positive or negative, financial or non-financial benefits, which may vary as a result of the controlled entity's performance (IPSAS 35.30). — 425 ff.

Whole of government accounting /accounts (WGA), Whole of government financial reporting (WGFR): Consolidation of the financial statements and transactions of all the entities controlled by a jurisdiction's government with the aim to present the overall financial position and performance of a whole tier of government (e.g., the central government, all state / regional governments, or all local governments). — 167, 258, 389 ff.

AUTHORS' BIOGRAPHIES

CAROLINE AGGESTAM PONTOPPIDAN is associate professor at the Department of Accounting at the Copenhagen Business School (CBS), Denmark. She gained her PhD in accounting from CBS in 2005. Her key research interests engage with institutional interplay and the governance of global public sector accountancy practice as well as sustainability reporting. In 2016 she published the book 'Interpretation and Application of IPSAS' (Wiley) since then IPSAS has been a recurring theme in her research.

CHRISTOPHE VANHEE is senior scientific researcher at the department of Accounting, Corporate Finance and Taxation of Ghent University, Belgium. His research, consulting and teaching activities are within the field of expertise 'Accounting, Financial Management and Auditing in the public and non-profit sector'. He's also director of the FEB Academy, the Academy for Lifelong Learning of the Faculty of Economics and Business Administration.

ELLEN HAUSTEIN is a post-doctoral researcher and lecturer at the Chair of Financial Accounting, Auditing and Management Control at University of Rostock, Germany. She obtained her doctoral degree in management accounting at University of the West of England in Bristol. She was coordinator of the EU-funded projects 'Developing and implementing European Public Sector Accounting modules' (DiEPSAm) and 'Empowering Participatory Budgeting in the Baltic Sea Region'

(EmPaci). She currently serves as co-treasurer in the Board of Directors of People Powered – Global Hub for Participatory Democracy.

EUGENIO ANESSI-PESSINA is Full Professor of Public Management at Università Cattolica del Sacro Cuore, Milan, Italy. His work includes research, teaching, and expert support to public-sector institutions. He is also director of Cerismas (Centre for Research and Studies in Health-Care Management); coordinator of Università Cattolica's Doctoral Programme in Management and Innovation; senior fellow at the Wharton School of the University of Pennsylvania; and member of the Italian public-sector standard setter board. His research interests focus on public-sector accounting, both in general and with specific reference to public health-care organisations. Within this domain, specific interests include: international and national standard setting, financial statement analysis, earnings management, accounting change, internal and external auditing, budgeting, and asset management.

FRANCESCA MANES-ROSSI is Associate Professor of Accounting in the Department of Economics, Management and Institutions at the University of Naples, Federico II (Italy). She earned her PhD in International Accounting from the same university. She is an experienced educator and researcher in several accounting issues related to financial reporting and disclosure (including sustainability and integrated reporting), performance measurement and audit, particularly in public sector organizations. In the last few years, she has researched and published intensively and has been visiting professor in several universities in Europe, China, and United States. Francesca is Co-chair of XII PSG EGPA and Member of EGPA Steering Committee.

GIOVANNA DABBICCO is a senior researcher at the Italian National Statistical Office (ISTAT) and has been an Adjunct Assistant Professor of Planning and Control in Public administrations at University of

Roma Tre, Department of Business studies. She held previous positions as a statistical officer at the European Commission (Eurostat). She received her PhD from University of Naples 'Parthenope' and she is a Chartered Certified Accountant. She is a member of the CIGAR network, and of the Task Force representing three research networks on public sector accounting, namely, IRSPM A&A SIG, CIGAR and EGPA PSG XII, and she is an observer at EPSAS working group. Her research develops at the interface among public sector accounting, government finance statistics and financial management.

ISABEL BRUSCA is Professor in Accounting in the Department of Accounting and Finance at the University of Zaragoza. Her research and professional interest is focused mainly on public sector accounting and management. She has participated in numerous research projects in this field and in several consulting projects for both the private sector and the public sector entities. Her research work has been published in several ranked journals and is author of several international books and co-author in numerous chapters in international books. She is co-chair of the XII Permanent Study Group of EGPA (European Group of Public Administration).

JOHAN CHRISTIAENS is professor in the Department of Accounting, Corporate Finance and Taxation at Ghent University. Until 2020 he has been registered auditor specialized in public and not-for-profit sector within EY. This explains his continuing relationship with oversight bodies, governments, legislators and standard setting bodies in terms of reform projects, coaching, advisory boards. Accordingly, his research areas are accounting standard setting, accounting user need research, auditing in the public and not-for-profit sector.

JOSETTE CARUANA is a certified public accountant and associate professor at the Department of Accountancy of the University of

Malta. She coordinates and lectures on courses related to public sector accounting, which is her area of research interest. She is a member of the CIGAR (Comparative International Governmental Accounting Research) Network Advisory Board and co-chairs the Academic Task Force on Public Sector Financial Management and Reporting. She is an Associate Editor of the Public Money & Management — CIGAR Annual Issue and a member of the Editorial Board of the *Journal of Public Budgeting, Accounting and Financial Management*.

LASSE OULASVIRTA is professor at Tampere University, Faculty of Management and Business, and an expert in the field of public sector accounting. He holds a PhD in administrative sciences and a M.A. in business economics. His research focus has been broadly on public sector and local government financing, accounting and auditing. Some of his latest publications concern concern auditing and public sector financial accounting reporting and concolidation principles in the public sector. During 2003 and 2010 he was first vice-member and then member of the Finnish Government Accounting Board. He is also a member of the Scientific Council of the National Audit Office of Finland and of the Finnish EPSAS group in the Ministry of Finance.

PETER LORSON is Full Professor holding the Chair of Financial Accounting, Auditing and Management Control; Executive Director of the Center for Accounting and Auditing at University of Rostock, Germany, and member of the Working Group "Integrated Reporting" (Schmalenbach Association for Business Administration; Schmalenbach-Gesellschaft für Betriebswirtschaft e.V.). He was coordinator of the EU-funded projects 'Developing and implementing European Public Sector Accounting modules' (DiEPSAm) and 'Empowering Participatory Budgeting in the Baltic Sea Region' (EmPaci). His preferred research fields are Financial and Management Accounting and Reporting for Private and Public Sector Organizations as well as Convergence of

Accounting, Management and Reporting Systems (external – internal, national – international, private – public sector, financial – non-financial/sustainable).

SANDRA COHEN is a Professor of Accounting in the Department of Business Administration at Athens University of Economics and Business. Her research interests lie in the fields of "Public Sector Accounting", "Management accounting" and "Intellectual Capital". Her research work has been published in several ranked journals and has been presented in several international conferences. She is currently a Co-chair to the XII Permanent Study Group "Public Sector Financial Management" of the European Group of Public Administration and a Member of the Comparative International Governmental Accounting Research (CIGAR) Network Board. She is a co-author in several accounting books in Greek, she has co-authored several chapters in international books, she has been a guest editor in a plethora of Special Issues and she is the co-editor in the Public Sector Financial Management Book Series published by Palgrave. She has participated in numerous consulting projects for both the private sector and the public sector and she has been a member of the research team in projects funded by the Expertise France, the Word Bank, the Council of Europe and the EU. She is a member of the Editorial Board in four reputable academic journals.

SUSANA JORGE is associate professor with habilitation at the Faculty of Economics, University of Coimbra, Portugal, and lecturer in Business Financial Accounting and Public Sector Accounting. She is researcher in Public Sector Accounting and Financial Management, especially focusing financial reporting and the Local Government, affiliated researcher of CICP – *Centro de Investigação em Ciência Política* (Research Centre in Political Science), University of Minho, Portugal, and collaborator researcher at the CeBER – Centre for

Business and Economics Research, University of Coimbra, Portugal. She is chair of the Executive Board of the Comparative International Governmental Accounting Research (CIGAR) Network.

YURI BIONDI is a senior tenured research fellow of the CNRS (IRISSO – University Paris Dauphine PSL) in France. A graduate of the Bocconi University of Milan (DES), the University of Lyon (DEA, PhD), the University of Brescia (PhD) and the University of Paris I Pantheon-Sorbonne (HDR), he is a founding editor of the Journal "Accounting, Economics and Law: A Convivium" and convener of the SASE Research Network devoted to "Accounting Economics and Law". He was chair of the Financial Accounting Standards Committee (FASC) of the American Accounting Association (AAA) from August 2011 to August 2013 (member since August 2010). He is a member of the Task Force on Public Sector Financial Management and Reporting jointly established by the CIGAR network, the EGPA PSG XII, and the Accounting and Accountability SIG of the IRSPM (https://psaar.net/task-force).

Printed in Poland
by Amazon Fulfillment
Poland Sp. z o.o., Wrocław